Race Still Matters

SUNY series in African American Studies
John R. Howard and Robert C. Smith, editors

Race Still Matters

The Reality of African American Lives and the Myth of Postracial Society

Edited by Yuya Kiuchi

Published by State University of New York Press, Albany

Printed in the United States of America

For information, contact State University of New York Press, Albany, NY
www.sunypress.edu

Production, Ryan Morris
Marketing, Kate R. Seburyamo

Library of Congress Cataloging-in-Publication Data

Names: Kiuchi, Yuya, editor of compilation.
Title: Race still matters : the reality of African American lives and the myth of postracial society / edited by Yuya Kiuchi.
Other titles: Reality of African American lives and the myth of postracial society
Description: Albany : State University of New York Press, [2016] | Series: SUNY series in African American studies | Includes bibliographical references and index.
Identifiers: LCCN 2016007296 (print) | LCCN 2016028131 (ebook)
ISBN 9781438462738 (hardcover : alk. paper)
ISBN 9781438462721 (pbk : alk. paper)
ISBN 9781438462745 (e-book)
Subjects: LCSH: African Americans—Social conditions—21st century. | African Americans—Race identity. | Race discrimination—United States. | Racism—United States. | United States—Race relations—21st century.
Classification: LCC E185.86 .R245 2016 (print) | LCC E185.86 (ebook) | DDC 305.896/073—dc23
LC record available at https://lccn.loc.gov/2016007296

10 9 8 7 6 5 4 3 2 1

To Nicki

Contents

Part 3: African American Youth

Part 4: Popular Culture

Preface

Americans agree that slavery was racist. So were Jim Crow laws, residential segregation in the early to mid-twentieth century, and disenfranchisement of Blacks. Americans across the color line also agree that the civil rights movement in the 1950s and '60s dramatically changed racial politics in the United States. Supposedly, employers are not allowed to make hiring decisions based on race. Car dealers should treat white and Black customers equally. The police should not stop a driver just because he or she is Black. White students and Black students should have equal access to high-quality educational resources, including facilities, equipment, and teachers. The reality is far from what these promises seem to suggest.

In the nation of collective amnesia and color-blind idealism, many Americans choose to believe that their nation has finally become a City upon a Hill. Choosing to believe in this postracial idealism has pragmatic values. It legitimizes American dreams. Many Americans idolize the idea of the self-made person. If you work hard enough, you can attain anything. If race mattered and racism existed, such a promise is nothing but a mirage. But if one rejects the presence of racism and believes that postracialism has realized in the United States, one can truly claim that the United States is the land of opportunities where anyone regardless of his or her race can be the next Horatio Alger.

Believing in the postracial idealism also allows Americans to claim that the country has moved on from its past's wrongdoings, justifying their diplomatic efforts to bring freedom and equality to the rest of the world. It also offers a sense of superiority and fairness that Americans need as they believe in their assumed role to lead the world economically, politically, and also morally. Especially after the turbulent decade of the 2000s, starting with the terrorist attacks on September11, 2001 and ending with a major economic downturn, the color-blind idealism enabled the country to feel that it had a strong collective identity. To nurture proud citizens, many educational institutions have taught that racism is a thing of the past and postracialism is new reality. Consequently, majority of Americans are now convinced that the United States has truly become postracial and color-blind. Successes of some African American figures also seemed to justify such a belief. African American actors and singers are as successful as, if not more successful than, their white counterparts. Many high-performing and well-paid athletes are African Americans. They may see an African American couple sitting at the VIP table in a high-end casino in Las Vegas. Moreover, the White House has been occupied by a Black president.

All of these examples of so-called progress have led many to believe in the idea of "postracial society." It meant social progress. It also signified America's collective identity. But the idea of postracialism is not new to the 2010s. The phrase was sometimes used to recognize the achievements of the civil rights movement, but most often to overestimate the level of racial equality that the United States has achieved and to underestimate the existing racism in the nation. Oprah Winfrey's growing popularity in the 1990s, Tiger Wood's victory at the Masters in 1997, and most significantly, Barack Obama's election as president in 2008 and reelection in 2012 have all been used as evidence of postracial America. Even though Pew Research Center, the National Urban League, and other research groups show that African Americans state their life as better than it was in the past and that they believe it will continue to improve, there is strong evidence that African Americans continue to face racism and that the United States is far from attaining a postracial status.

All of these success stories are nothing but life experiences of the limited few. It is true that an African American can win the Oscars, sell millions of copies of music, and lead the nation. Marvin L. Oliver and Thomas M. Shapiro explain that "the large number of blacks on the top income list generates an optimistic view of how black Americans have progressed economically in American society."[1] But many African Americans continue to face realities of racism on a daily basis. Some are explicit and public. After Barack Obama won the presidential race in 2008, we saw signs and read blogs that stated "I would rather move to Canada than to live in the U.S. with a Black president." Oliver and Shapiro follow up by stating "the near absence of blacks in the *Forbes* listing, by contrast, presents a much more pessimistic outlook on black's economic progress."[2]

Some other instances of racism are less explicit and more codified. Erick Harris, Dylan Klebold, and Adam Lanza, all white perpetrators of the Columbine High School shooting case in 1999 and the Sandy Hook Elementary School shooting in 2012, were described as victims of psychological pathology. The Black perpetrator of the recent LAPD murder case in 2013, Christopher Jordan Dorner, on the other hand, was portrayed as a simple rampant Black murderer. As Ellis Cashmore argued, even Black celebrities are not exempt from racist treatments by the American public.[3] After Hurricane Katrina, whites "found" food from empty stores while Blacks "looted" the stores. We are surrounded by an endless list of lived racist examples.

With the rise of social media, examples of racism are widely shared. If traditional media outlets failed to report them first, citizen journalists will, eventually leading major media corporations to follow up. Even though we are exposed to such news feeds and stories, media fail to truly address the ill of American society. Trent Lott's comment in 2002, the Jena Six case in 2006, the arrest of Henry Louis Gates in 2009, and many other national and local race-based incidents are often characterized as misbehaviors by a very exceptional few. "It is incredible how some people are still racist" as a comment about these cases not only underestimates the prevalence of racism in the United States today, but also portrays the contemporary American society as nonracist. Reality is different. Residents of Akers Hall at Michigan State University in 2011 saw a sign on a dormitory room door that said, No Niggers Please. Three whites students at San Jose State University were charged with hate crimes against their African American roommate that lasted for months, in 2013. At Arizona State University in 2014, an "MLK Black Party" hosted by a fraternity had attendees drink from cups made out of watermelons. Making light of the national to local news is a way to avoid discussions on racism.

In some cases, it is structural, systemic, and implicit racism that cast a dark shadow in the United States today. Such racism is just one kind of racism that continues to affect African Americans every day. Therefore, the point of the discussion that should happen within and outside this book is not a simplistic view that the nature of America's racism has shifted to structural and systemic. Aforementioned examples from college campuses show that signs of racism are not always tacit. African Americans may not face a sign that says Whites Only every day. A bus driver will not tell them to sit in the back of a bus. They are admitted to selective private universities. African

Americans can vote. But racism is still real. This real racism is not de jure racism. However, the de facto racism is felt regularly and manifests both visibly and invisibly.

Leslie Houts Picca and Joe R. Feagin's work based on diaries by hundreds of college students refutes the belief that no American today is racist and it is just the society that is race-based. Picca and Feagin argue that whites live in two worlds—the frontstage and the backstage—and in between. The frontstage is a "public space, a multiracial place where there are interactions among whites and people of color."[4] In this arena, whites try to prove that they are not racists, to avoid minorities in general, or to use "it's just a joke" as an excuse for their racist ideas and comments. The backstage is safer for the whites. The authors argue that racist comments and jokes are "tolerated if not encouraged—and sometimes are even expected."[5] They conclude that "well-meaning whites agree that racism is a problem with others, but never take the difficult step to analyze how they themselves may be contributing to individual and systemic racism in the United States."[6]

When I had an opportunity to lead a group of young undergraduate students on a study abroad program, I happened to overhear a conversation of eight students from various parts of the United States. These students—all of whom were white—began to talk about geographical variances of different expressions. Some said "seat check" was a way to claim their seat when they step away from their seat for a few minutes. Others said "seat back" was what they were used to saying. Then a student said, "But you can say 'Rosa Parks,' to steal someone's seat." On the one hand, the concept of "saving" a seat for oneself is an arbitrary practice. Nothing would and should prevent anyone else from taking an empty seat available for public use. In a way, Rosa Parks's well-known bus ride was identical. Whites claimed empty seats to be theirs and Parks pointed out the obvious absurdity of the practice. However, on the other hand, the students framed the expression, "Rosa Parks," as a symbol of "stealing" a seat that rightfully belonged to someone else. The group of all white students laughed, and the conversation moved on. Would this conversation have happened if one of the three African American students from the same study abroad program was sitting around the table with them?

Furthermore, America's myopic view of its history and its inability to understand the negative consequence of pre-civil rights era racism over generations of African Americans make it difficult to materialize the postracial idealism. It was not long ago that we celebrated the fiftieth anniversary of the iconic speech by Martin Luther King Jr. In other words, it has only been half a century since the civil rights movement struggles began to pay off. Changes come slowly. From education to economics, Blacks in the United States lag behind white Americans. The unemployment rate, the incarceration rate, and the poverty rate are all higher for African Americans than any other racial groups. Many of these issues are intertwined with each other. There continue to be numerous examples of stereotypes and prejudices against African Americans as lazy, unintelligent, and reckless. Although class and gender also contribute to various prejudices and disadvantages in life, race continues to matter in the United States. This edited volume is a collection of such evidence to reveal the current state of racism and race relations in the United States. The book does not intend to call all white Americans racists or to emphasize negative African American experiences. It does not aim to attribute all social injustices to race alone. Rather, it is a project that reveals that institutional and individual racism does exist in the United States today, that postracial idealism is yet to be achieved, and that race continues to matter.

There is no question that progress has been made since the pre-civil rights period. But it does not mean that the problem has been solved. Malcolm X once said, "You don't stick a knife in man's back nine inches and then pull it out six inches and say you're making progress." If we continue with this analogy, where is the knife today? Has "progress" been really made? If the postracial hypothesis is true, then not only should the knife be out and have disappeared, but the scar on the body must have also been healed. The reality is that the knife is still in the body. In some instances, there still are attempts to push the knife in even deeper.

Notes

1. Marvin L. Oliver and Thomas M. Shapiro, *Black Wealth/White Wealth: A New Perspective on Racial Inequality* (New York: Routledge, 2006), 2.
2. Ibid.
3. Ellis Cashmore, *Beyond Black: Celebrity and Race in Obama's America* (New York: Bloomsbury, 2012).
4. Leslie Houts Picca, and Joe R. Feagin, *Two-faced Racism: Whites in the Backstage and Frontstage* (New York: Routledge, 2007), 43.
5. Ibid., 91.
6. Ibid., 274.

Bibliography

Cashmore, Ellis. *Beyond Black: Celebrity and Race in Obama's America.* New York: Bloomsbury, 2012.

Oliver, Marvin L., and Thomas M. Shapiro. *Black Wealth/White Wealth: A New Perspective on Racial Inequality.* New York: Routledge, 2006.

Picca, Leslie Houts, and Joe R. Feagin. *Two-faced Racism: Whites in the Backstage and Frontstage.* New York: Routledge, 2007.

Acknowledgments

This book would not have been possible without all the hard work by its contributors. Some of them have been my friends over ten years. We took graduate seminars and attended conferences together. We have established a strong friendship. Some others are now my new friends and colleagues whose work I have read and admired, and whom I personally contacted to ask if they would be interested in contributing a chapter to this volume. Either way, I cannot thank them enough for their commitment to this project. They all agreed on the need for and significance of the kind of a book I had in mind. It was a book that would be multidisciplinary and accessible, examining the status quo of the American society that was often characterized as postracial. All the contributors agreed that there was a need for a book that spelled out much of what we knew, what we talked about, and what we believed others should also know about the current status of African American lives. As the editor of this book, their belief in the project was extremely encouraging. It was not just me but many others that felt the need to show the truth of the so-called postracial American society which, in reality, has yet to come. However to discuss the myth of postracialism inevitably demands a wide array of topics. It was thanks to the contributors that what was originally my overly ambitious idea came to be realized and is now in your hands.

My undergraduate students at Michigan State University, especially the ones who have taken my freshman writing seminar titled, WRA125: American Racial and Ethnic Experiences, between 2012 and 2014, and my integrative social sciences course ISS335: National Diversity and Change in the U.S., in 2014 helped me frame this project. In class meetings, I tested out many of the hypotheses and ideas that I had for this book project. Many of these emerging adults wanted to believe that racism was a thing of the past. Some even were uncomfortable talking about race. They wanted to believe that the civil rights movement corrected all the racial injustices. Some indeed believed racism was a thing of the past. But interesting enough, when I asked them if race still mattered, they all agreed it did. But few had taken the time to question what it meant to live in a society where race still mattered but racism was supposed to be gone. As I edited this book, I kept in my mind these students, for whom its lessons may be most meaningful.

I would also like to thank Dr. Michael Rinella at the State University of New York Press. We initially worked together on my first monograph, *Struggles for Equal Voice: The History of African American Media Democracy*. Once I complete the book, I shared my interest in a project that discussed the reality of this so-called postracial society. He also agreed about the importance of such a project, and was helpful throughout the process. Mr. Rafael Chaiken helped me through the peer review process. I would also like to thank anonymous peer reviewers who had read the manuscript and offered precise and valuable recommendations. Dr. Pero Gaglo Dagbovie continues to inspire me. He opened my eyes to the reality of race and racism in the United States. Without his graduate seminars back in 2006 and 2007, this project would not have started. Without our regular discussions over coffee or sushi for the past few years, this would not have been a book-length project. Thank you, Dr. Dagbovie, for your guidance and encouragements.

Last but not least, I thank my family. As usual, my mother, Noriko Kiuchi, keeps me motivated with her daily e-mails from Japan, updating on me what is happening with the family and her dogs. My father, Tsuneo Kiuchi, has not been with us for over ten years, but his memories continue to stay with me, deep in my heart. My wife, Nichole, has been my best cheerleader and supporter. Despite the busy schedule of her own, she was willing to read some of the drafts and comment on them. She supported me throughout the process of editing. Our companion, Obie, was also there to make me smile even after a long day teaching, writing, or researching. I must also thank my in-laws who were willing to listen to me update them about the book every time they asked me how my day was going. Thank you.

Introduction

In 1903, W. E. B. Du Bois wrote in *The Souls of Black Folk* that "the problem of the twentieth century is the problem of the color-line." If he were alive today, over 110 years later, he would still write, "the problem of the twenty-first century is *still* the problem of the color-line." This book examines the realities of this continuing problem of the color line that the United States faces. Compared to the turn of the twentieth century, the United States is more diverse racially and ethnically. Controversies surrounding Asian Americans who claim to have been rejected admission to elite universities because of their race, Native American mascots that still appear at sporting events at various levels, and antagonism against Mexican immigrants all attest that the Black versus white dualism no longer does justice to explain the intricacy of American racial politics of the early twenty-first century. Nonetheless, the fault line between African Americans and Caucasian Americans continues to remain deep and distinct.

Furthermore, the nature of the gap has shifted. The shift has witnessed some signs of progress. African Americans are much better off today than they were when Du Bois wrote *The Souls of Black Folk*. But the shift has also complicated the racial dynamics in the United States. The United States has finally had its first African American president. Many of the wealthy popular culture icons are also African Americans. Simultaneously, African Americans are disproportionately incarcerated, attend schools with smaller budgets, and remain in poorer neighborhoods.

In this context, discussions on the current state of African Americans and postracial idealism have been a popular scholarly topic, especially in the last decade. Joe R. Feagin notes that "today, the costs of being black in the United States remain very high, costs that signal clearly the long-term impacts of white-on-black oppression."[1] To the cluster of existing scholarship on existing impacts, the chapters in this volume will add a more up-to-date and more in-depth view on racism in the United States. What is included in this book is not a series of consequences of past racism. It is about continuing racism. National Urban League's annual publication, *State of Black America*, is one of the well-researched and -read literatures. Similarly, Tavis Smiley's *The Covenant with Black America* is rich with both statistical and anecdotal evidence that race continues to matter. Tim Wise's *Color-Blind* and *Between Barack and a Hard Place* and H. Roy Kaplan's *The Myth of Post-Racial America* offer a general view on the myth of postracial society.[2] In the context of Obama's presidency and postracialism, Adia Harvey Wingfield and Joe R. Feagin accurately characterize the postracial theme as "still the white racial frame."[3]

Journalist, Farai Chideya, also examined myths about African Americans that portrayed them as welfare queens, poor academic achievers, fatherless individuals, and in many other different negative ways. She recognizes that Blacks and whites continue to live in two different spheres in the United States. But to simply picture whites as successful and Blacks as unsuccessful is just another way of imposing racist views.[4] These two spheres are difficult to integrate. Using a common statement among white students when challenged about their racial or racist views, namely "Some of my best friends are Black," as the powerful title of his book, Tanner Colby introduces multiple stories of racial separation that fuel racism today.[5]

Many other scholars have penned various books on racism against African Americans within different disciplines. In the area of African American incarceration, Michelle Alexander's *The New Jim Crow* argues that American prison system functions as a system of social control similar to Jim Crow and slavery. She writes, "Once you're labeled a felon, the old forms of discrimination—employment discrimination, housing discrimination, denial of the right to vote, denial of educational opportunity, denial of food stamps and other public benefits, and exclusion from jury service—are suddenly legal. She calls this "a racial caste system."[6] In education, Cecil Brown problematizes the disappearance of Black Studies departments and programs from campuses.[7] Karyn R. Lacy wrote that middle-class Blacks continue to face housing discrimination. She notes that predominantly Black suburbs and neighborhoods are on the rise.[8] The same story looked from a different angle is James W. Loewen's assessment on sundown towns.[9] As I noted elsewhere, one of the awakening moments about American racism when I first moved to the United States was when a school administrator told me to avoid a certain area of Boston after dark. Confining Blacks in certain areas and preserving other areas only for whites is still a common practice.

On popular culture, Ellis Cashmore's *Beyond Black*, and Jessie Daniels's *Cyber Racism* respectively refute the myth of postracialism. Examining various facets of American culture today, Cashmore questions, "if the postracial society is approaching, why is so much of America structured in a way that makes it deeply racially divided?" He shows that even celebrities cannot escape racism.[10] Daniels writes,

> When supremacist rhetoric existed in the print-only era, it was easier to dismiss their hardly ubiquitous publications the rants of a lunatic fringe. Now, however, with such racist vitriol easy to locate online, an important shift has occurred: anyone with an Internet connection—from a six-grader doing a report on Martin Luther King Jr. to a disaffected, potentially violent skinhead—can find white supremacy online.[11]

Daniels is correct that despite the utopian view about the Internet from the early 1990s, that it did not matter who you were as long as you were online, the reality has been that identity politics is very relevant in the digital era. "Miles White is both optimistic and cautious. He writes,

> Obama's victory is not the triumph of a post-racist society, but it may be the promise of one, embodied both in his person and in the fact that the hip-hop nation is more diverse and pluralistic than many would imagine only consuming much of what is made available through the popular culture industry.[12]

In order to shed light on this continuing problem of the United States and difficult conditions many African Americans continue to live in, this book focuses on continuing racism against African Americans since the last decade of the twentieth century until today within the context of so-called postracial America.

The title of this book, *Race Still Matters*, speaks to Cornel West's important work from 1993.[13] Over two decades after the end of the civil rights era, race continued to matter. Over two decades after that, it continues to matter. So-called postracial society has yet to arrive. Characterizing American society today as postracial, let alone postracist, is equal to ignoring how race continues to disadvantage a large group of population. For those who benefit from the disadvantaged conditions of others, it is an effective political tool to protect their vested interest. To make matters worse, it is a frequent occurrence that Martin Luther King Jr.'s famous remarks about a time when "people will not be judged by the color of their skin, but by the content of their character," is sound bite and distorted in order to justify the preservation of race-based inequality. In 2004, Barack Obama spoke at the Democratic National Convention and stated, "There's not a liberal American and a conservative America: there's the United States of America. There's not black American and white America and Latino America and Asia America; there's the United States America."[14] This statement of hope could also be a sound bite for some to justify the termination of the affirmative action. As Cornel West reminds us, it is important to remember that "Martin Luther King Jr. called for us to be lovestruck with each other, not colorblind toward each other."[15] The chapters that follow will reveal the reality of American racial politics as of the second decade of the twenty-first century to showcase that race continues to matter.

Chapter 1, "Reverse Racism: A Discursive History," brings the historiography of "reverse racism" using a corpus of instances from mainstream newspapers from the 1960s to the present. It traces out the complex history of this phrase, which is frequently used as a part of the argument that various race-based policies and concepts would create new problems. It is used to argue that the affirmative action, for example, is a form of "reverse racism," and a hindrance to a colorblind society. Tad Suiter helps readers understand why the phrase is so problematic. Phrases change meanings over time, and by looking at that history—especially with a term as fraught as *reverse racism*, we gain more perspective on what it means to use it now. Suiter reveals that in the early 1960s, *reverse racism* was a term that was primarily used within the Black community, during discussions of the merits of integration versus racial affinity groups: should Black folks vote as a bloc for Black candidates? Or should they vote their conscience no matter the race of the candidates? This also bled out into identity politics in general. A social psychologist spending time in West Africa made sure to clarify that the brotherhood and fellow feeling that he felt as a Black American with the more educated tribesmen around him was not "reverse racism," that whites would be welcomed too, but that this fellow feeling was an effect of a shared history. In the later 1960s, the term's meaning stays relatively similar—it's still about Black identity, affinity, and so on at odds with the desire for integration, but it's been made much more intense—people are talking about the Black Power Movement and the racial uprisings of the 1960s. In addition, white people start using the term, which can be problematic, as they do not always have the nuanced understanding of a racial insider. By the 1970s, whites are almost the only people talking about "reverse racism," and those discussions are centered around a rejection of affirmative action. Blacks, on the other hand, have stopped using the phrase, which he argues seems to have happened due to the mainstreaming of black power discourse, a shift in the common definition and understanding of the term *racism* to one that puts more emphasis on institutional racism, and the fact that the phrase is being used by whites as a condemnation of Black folks, rather than as something that comes up at times during in-group conversations. Finally, at the time between the 1980s and today, it is more or less a Republican dog-whistle word that helps their ongoing Southern Strategy. And white Democrats can fall into that trap too—though it's more dangerous due to the reliance of the Democrats on Black voters. Suiter argues that there is a nexus of history, of timing: these discussions spike in direct correlations to economic downturns. The chapter examines how the perception of the decline in white privilege might bring about resentment that leads people to feel that Blacks are coming out ahead and whites are coming out behind. Appropriate for the first chapter of this book, Suiter's work links his historiographical study to the dangers of color-blind racism, a major hindrance to improving the discussion—or the material reality—of race today.

In chapter 2, "'The Struggle Is Real out Here': The Contextual Reality of Being Black Couples and Families in America," Karlin J. Tichenor highlights the present struggle of Black families; drawing attention to evidence that requires a social response. Although the picture painted in the chapter may appear to characterize Black families in a negative way, he argues that Black families continue to survive in the face of insurmountable odds, showing significant resilience over the course of their existence in this country. As the chapter reveals, the resilience of African American families and communities is extremely strong. Nonetheless, Black families continue to face various challenges to family togetherness and cohesion. Tichenor identifies social factors that negatively impact the ability of Black couples to make long-term commitments and the indirect effect of commitment challenges on Black families.

Chapter 3, "Holy Smoke: Church Burnings, Journalism, and the Politics of Race, 1996–2006," reveals some key findings about arsons at Black churches. First, the fires seemed to mark a transition as white and Black Southerners alike formulated new racial identities in the generation following the civil rights movement and as the nation as a whole struggled toward a "postracial" ideal. Christopher Strain shows that this transition was neither clean nor orderly. Responses to the arsons by reporters, by government officials, by Black leaders, and by the general public reflected ongoing debates over the social and political status of African Americans—debates centering on such issues as the content and meaning of Black history, the state of Black leadership in the post–civil rights era, and inclusion in the body politic. Second, the fires revealed that, amid premature proclamations about the end of American racism at the close of the twentieth century, strife continued to define race relations just as race continued to define life in the United States; but, they also demonstrated that white supremacists of the sheet-wearing, Confederate flag–waving variety were much scarcer in the 1990s than they had been in previous decades. Third and most importantly, the fires provided a kind of referendum on American racism, happening as they did at a key moment of racial division. If they initially contributed to this division, providing stark reasons for mistrust across the black-white divide, then they also may have paradoxically provided an occasion for unification and reconciliation.

In chapter 4, "Fear of a Black President: Conspiracy Theory and Racial Paranoia in Obamerica," Travis L. Gosa and Danielle Porter Sanchez particularly examine the conspiracy theories surrounding Barack Obama. They argue that despite predictions that a Black president would signal the end of racism and prejudice, the Barack Obama elections have sparked a resurgence of racial paranoia and hate mongering in America. For many, Obama represents the conquering of white America by dark outsiders, while racialized conspiracy theories probing Obama's legitimacy have reverberated from the fringes to the mainstream of American society. The chapter evaluates the ideas about race-gender, American identity, and legitimacy found in popular Obama conspiracy theories, including the fake birth certificate, the reptilian-space-alien thesis, and the secret gay sex-club at Trinity United Church. It shows how the election of the first Black president has worked to further obscure and silence serious discussions of race. The chilling effect on race talk has led many Americans to resort to conspiracy theories as a way to discuss issues of race. It also demonstrates the continued currency of xenophobia and racism in American politics. Obama conspiracy theories are framed within the longer history of partisan politics of fear. Since the 1970s, Republicans have used think tanks and media propaganda to mobilize white voters based on the fear of communists, gays, Blacks, and the general "Other." The chapter explores how conservative news media and politicians have spread these theories in defense of white minority politics. Because Obama conspiracy theories thrive on the Internet, this exploration also contributes to the literature on the digital politics of paranoia. Internet technology is typically celebrated for flattening social relationships with user-generated, amateur knowledge. But in the age of Obama, technology has also been used to circulate hate and misinformation. While there is entertainment value in of some of these conspiracy theories, these fabrications obscure serious issues facing minority communities, and represent "new" ways to forward anti-Black/Muslim/gay ideology in a "color-blind" society.

In chapter 5, "From Orchards to Silicon Valley: African American Suburbanization in the U.S. West, the Black San Jose Model, 1945–2010," Herb Ruffin II addresses Black suburbanization in postwar San Jose as a model for the examination of African American community formation through their struggle against residential segregation. This happened in a place that had theoretically undergone legal desegregation in the 1890s, when most racially discriminatory codes were written out of California's Constitution. Unlike postwar suburbs in the East, where Blacks either were peppered in white communities, or were large and often extended from the central city, San Jose's African American population was small and has had to coexist within far more ethnically diverse communities with whites and larger groups of color such as Asian Americans and Mexican Americans. This has led to a different type of African American experience, which has been overlooked by scholars until now. For Ruffin, postwar housing was a critical barrier to freedom confronting Blacks in most U.S. urban communities outside of the South. In San Jose, its postwar African American community was forged during its fight to overcome housing discrimination and social isolation through civil rights and equal living activism and institutional building. Most importantly, they overcame redlining, unfair housing legislation, and subprime lending in a supposed color-blind era that coincided with twenty-first-century urban and information age industrial growth, since 1960. The end result was Silicon Valley Black relative meteoric population growth from 730 people in 1940 to over 56,000 in 1990.

In chapter 6, "African American Economic Experiences: Income, Occupations, Savings, Investments, and Social Security Trends since 2000," LaToya T. Brackett focuses on issues concerning economics. As she assesses, people enjoy hearing the stories of rags to riches, of humble beginnings and great success; no one wants to hear of the perpetual struggle of some groups. However, people sometimes forget that not everyone came to the United States willingly, with great expectations, and that without the Africans who were forced to build the new world, such stories of success may not have come to pass. The enslavement of Africans in the United States has greatly assisted whites, yet continually can be connected to the plight of some African Americans throughout American history, including today. A major variable in this plight revolves around the economic situation of African Americans. Even with more educational gains African Americans are still earning less on the dollar compared to whites, and they hold fewer assets; in actuality, single African American women aged thirty-six to forty-nine have an average net worth of $5, while single white women of the same age range have an average net worth of $42,600. Brackett shows that African Americans also receive fewer returns in investing due to a lack of risk-taking behavior; to this day they are still the last hired and the first fired; most have few to no assets and very little wealth, small savings, reduced access to retirement plans, and unfortunately they use their retirement plans for sudden current need more often than for future need; and they rely on Social Security much more than whites, despite their lower monetary returns from the program. Brackett examines jobs, income, wealth, savings, and investments and retirement options in regard to this group after the year 2000. It cannot be denied that the United States is not in a postracial society when, due to racial divisions and gaps, African Americans are still behind in economic stability and growth.

In chapter 7, "Confronting an Enduring Legacy: Health-Care Workforce Disparity," Costellia H. Talley and Henry C. Talley demonstrate that African Americans experience significant health disparities in major dimensions of health care, the health-care workforce, and population health. They argue that the health disparities experienced by African Americans occur within the context of a broader historical perspective, including social and economic inequality, racism, and ethnic discrimination. Health-care disparities are associated with increased morbidity and mortality, death at an earlier age, and decreased quality of life. Furthermore, health-care disparities have an impact on society that is realized through increased health-care cost, decreased productivity, and social inequities. Talley and Talley shed light on the persistent disparities in health-care experienced by African Americans (believed to be a major contributor to poor health status), including the historical underpinning of the problem, health-care access and quality health care, health-care workforce, contribution of the health-care system to the problem, and steps needed to improve the problem.

In chapter 8, "Sustained Inequality: African American Education in a 'Postracial' Nation," Daniel R. Davis focuses on the continued educational achievement gaps between African American—or Black—and white students in the allegedly "postracial" United States. In stark defiance of this postracial notion, this chapter examines the magnitude of the persisting educational inequalities confronting African American students in comparison to their white peers. These embarrassingly conspicuous deficits in educational achievement, access to quality teachers, academic resources, and socioeconomic status along racial lines cogently negate the assertion that race is no longer a significant American issue. Understandably, the entirety of this problem is far too vast and complex to respectfully examine within the confines of a single chapter, therefore, particular attention is given to the educational disparities in the northeast region of the United States. Additionally, Davis presents statistical illustrations of similar inequalities and fissures in educational achievement from the Midwestern, western, and southern United States.

In chapter 9, "'Nothing We Could Do or Say': African American Young Men's Lived Police Experiences," Rod K. Brunson and Amanda D'Souza focus on the relationship between African American youth and law enforcement officers. Commentators on various forms of media have chronicled the acrimonious relationship between African Americans and the police. Furthermore, numerous research projects in social science have consistently demonstrated that African Americans disproportionately report experiencing unwarranted stops, intrusive searches, and a wide range of additional harms at the hands of police. Brunson and D'Souza argue that the cumulative effect of these inimical encounters has reduced police legitimacy and severely threatened police-minority community relations. For African American youth, they have had the most frequent and negative involuntary interactions with the police. Negative experiences with the police naturally lead to the lack of perceived legitimacy of the law enforcement officers in the community. Justifying the police's discriminatory behaviors by stating that the Black youth are more likely to commit crime ignores the historical and institutional context within which the relationship between the two parties has negatively developed. The authors recommend that positive police-community partnership will increase police legitimacy and true crime prevention.

Chapter 10, "African American Youth and Postracial Societal Myth" by Carl S. Taylor and Pamela R. Smith, captures the current views about the world shared by the Black youth in Detroit. In this chapter, the authors expose us to the real voice of these young African Americans. The social ecology for the Black urban youth in Detroit has been difficult. The parents, families, and communities of the poorest big city with the largest black population in America have been the epicenter of racial polarization. The groups of young men and women, who are challenged by racial issues today, carry the burden of their families and ancestors. We hear the racial interactions, divide, and daily experiences that happen in the city once called the Arsenal of Democracy.

Chapter 11, "Leave the Prejudice, Take the Power: *Crash*, *Fruitvale Station,* and Race in Hollywood in the Twenty-First Century," explores the racial politics of the film, *Crash* (2005) in order to better understand not only Hollywood's assessment of racism in the twenty-first century, but also its contribution in framing racial discourse in the new millennium. Justin Gomer explains that with *Crash*, Haggis, a self-professed liberal, takes the perspective that everyone harbors racial prejudices. Yet, however progressive Haggis's views of race, as represented in *Crash*, may appear, in actuality they are ones in which racism is depoliticized and relegated strictly to interpersonal interaction. In acknowledging that race still matters, *Crash* eschews the power relationships and the structural forces behind the manner in which racism operates in favor of individuals who harbor prejudice attitudes. In this, the film replaces one racial fallacy—color blindness—with another, and leaves its audience at a dead-end without any perspective on the machinations of race in twenty-first-century America. Gomer argues that ultimately, *Crash* offers a neoliberal conception of racism in which, in Thatcheresque fashion, there are no groups in society, only individuals.

In chapter 12, "African American Female Athletic Image: What We Should Take Away from the London 2012 Olympic Games," Rachel L. Myers shows how structural racism and internalized racism still persist in U.S. society through the lens of sport. She focuses on the controversies surrounding gymnast Gabrielle Douglas's hair and the tension between hurdlers Lolo Jones and Olympic medalist teammates Dawn Harper and Kellie Wells. The chapter examines Gabrielle Douglas and internalized racism; hair matters; Jones, Harper, Wells, and structural racism. Myers uses Douglas's 2012 book, *Grace, Gold and Glory: My Leap of Faith*, to show how internalized racism has affected—and likely continues to affect—the Olympic champion. Through Douglas's experience, the chapter also offers an assessment on how significant the comments made about Gabby Douglas's hair were. Additionally, Myers delves into how media continue to be a site of structural racism. In her conclusion, the author showcases how controversies over hair and media are not isolated to the athletic realm. Analysis of more recent incidents at an Ohio school, a New York City art exhibit, and a national cereal commercial served to show a continued need for progress in eradicating structural and internalized racism within general society.

In chapter 13, "An Obama Effect?: African American Voting Behavior and the Political Symbolism of a Black President," David C. Wilson, Samantha S. Kelley, Emmanuel Balogun, Christian Soler, and Sahar Salehi examine an "Obama effect" on political participation among African Americans. They argue that Obama's presence as the first viable Black presidential candidate has such a strong symbolic meaning among African Americans that it provides informational cues and normative cues about how the group should behave politically. Ostensibly, Obama triggered a positive affective response throughout the Black community, activating value-laden predispositions related to pride and group loyalty; enthusiasm resulted among African Americans who shared his racial background, even if not all of his political values. This sense of shared identity and emotional connectedness likely contributed to dramatic increases in overall Black turnout, especially during presidential election years. Based on multiple years of survey data collected by the Census Bureau, the authors suggest that candidates and identity—including their message to voters—matter for turnout. Obama was likely able to tap into the symbolic predispositions of African American voters, leading to significant increases in African American voter turnout, further contributed to his winning the 2008 and 2012 elections, and to Black turnout now occurring at a rate higher than that of white voters. Race is still a significant psychological short-cut influencing African American political participation, but only to the extent that a candidate's presence has a positive symbolic meaning, enhancing group identity; an African American Republican, for example, might not offer such a message. The findings also suggest that Obama has potentially changed the political landscape of American politics in terms of both substance and sheer numbers, as African Americans are more engaged in the political process in the age of Obama. In a larger social context, increased rates of political participation by African Americans lead to implications signaling a new era that is witnessing political representation as less exclusionary and more pluralistic.

The United States has undoubtedly made much progress. Still, it has a long way to go. The lack of knowledge about African Americans among many non-Black counterparts is severe. After eight high school students were suspended when a picture appeared of them posing in a simulated lynching with a black doll wearing their rival school T-shirt, their lawyer explained, "[the students] did not intend to disparage anyone." According to the public statement, these wrestlers were unaware that their behavior "could be seen as insensitive."[16] Although their ignorance is inexcusable, it probably is a common problem of American society today. How many sociology classes in the United States talk about W. E. B. Du Bois, for example? How many high school students read Phillis Wheatley's work? Probably this is why during the second round of *Jeopardy!*'s 2014 College Championship Semifinal, contestants left the African American History category untouched. All three contestants, Laurie Beckoff from the University of Chicago, Tucker Pope from Texas A&M, and Whitney Thompson from the University of Oklahoma avoided this category. African American history is a part of American history. Many of those who teach at college may have had students ask why there are African American history classes but not white American history classes. The answer is simply because African American history has not been taught properly and sufficiently in American history classes. A significant part of American history continues to be under- and misrepresented in classrooms.

Of course, race is not the only problem that the country needs to address. Class, gender, sexual orientation, age, and many other facets in life are used to discriminate against others. This book focuses on just one of many areas of social justice. The thirteen chapters to follow will reveal the reality of the world we continue to live in. Racism is not a thing of the past. The death of Michael Brown in Ferguson, Missouri, in August, 2014 is often analyzed through the lens of racial tension. A month later, KKK newspaper, the *Crusader*, was delivered to the residents of Zeeland, a small town in Michigan. It is not just the high-profile cases including Walter Scott and Michael Slager, and Dylann Roof's shooting in Charleston that remind many African Americans of American reality. The endless list of names on T-shirts produced by the *And Counting Collection* is a powerful reminder of racism that exist in our world today. Many white undergraduate students are shocked when they read Peggy McIntosh's writing about the white privilege and realized how true it still is. This book will reveal the realities of African American lives today, demonstrate the inaccuracy of the postracial narratives, and suggest the areas in which further serious and dedicated work is imminently needed.

Notes

1. Joe R. Feagin, *Systemic Racism: A Theory of Oppression* (New York: Routledge, 2006), 20.

2. Tim Wise, *Color-Blind: The Rise of Post-Racial Politics and the Retreat from Racial Equity* (San Francisco, CA: City Lights Books, 2010); Tim Wise, *Between Barack and a Hard Place: Racism and White Denial in the Age of Obama* (San Francisco, CA: City Lights Books, 2009); H. Roy Kaplan, *The Myth of Post-Racial America: Searching for Equality in the Age of Materialism* (Lanham, MD: Rowman and Littlefield Education, 2011).

3. Adia Harvey Wingfield, and Joe R. Feagin, *Yes We Can?: White Racial Framing and the Obama Presidency* (New York: Routledge, 2013), 192.

4. Farai Chideya, *Don't Believe the Hype: Fighting Cultural Misinformation about African-Americans* (New York: Plume, 1995).

5. Tanner Colby, *Some of My Best Friends Are Black: The Strange Story of Integration in America* (New York: Viking, 2012).

6. Michelle Alexander, *The New Jim Crow: Mass Incarceration in the Age of Colorblindness* (New York: The New Press, 2012), 2.

7. Cacil Brown, *Dude, Where's My Black Studies Department?: The Disappearance of Black Americans from Our Universities* (Berkeley, CA: North Atlantic Books, 2007).

8. Karyn R. Lacy, *Blue-Chip Black: Race, Class, and Status in the New Black Middle Class* (Berkeley, CA: University of California Press, 2007), 44.

9. James W. Loewen, *Sundown Towns: A Hidden Dimension of American Racism* (New York: Touchstone, 2005).

10. Ellis Cashmore, *Beyond Black: Celebrity and Race in Obama's America* (New York: Bloomsbury, 2012), 10.

11. Jessie Daniels, *Cyber Racism: White Supremacy Online and the New Attack on Civil Rights* (Lanham, MD: Rowman and Littlefield Publishers, 2009), 5.

12. Miles White, *From Jim Crow to Jay-Z: Race, Rap, and the Performance of Masculinity* (Urbana, IL: University of Illinois Press, 2011), 133.

13. Cornel West, *Race Matters*. New York: Vintage Books, 1993.

14. "Transcript: Illinois Senate Candidate Barack Obama," *Washington Post*, accessed February 16, 2014, http://www.washingtonpost.com/wp-dyn/articles/A19751-2004Jul27.html

15. Cornel West, "Forward," in *The New Jim Crow*, Michelle Alexander (New York: The New Press, 2010, 2012), x.

16. "Members of High School Wrestling Team Suspended for Lynching Photo," *Black Youth Project*, accessed February 23, 2014, http:// www.black youth project.com/2014/02members-of-high-school-wrestling-team-suspended-for-lynching-photo/.

Bibliography

Alexander, Michelle. *The New Jim Crow: Mass Incarceration in the Age of Colorblindness*. New York: The New Press, 2012.

Brown, Cacil. *Dude, Where's My Black Studies Department?: The Disappearance of Black Americans from Our Universities*. Berkeley, CA: North Atlantic Books, 2007.

Cashmore, Ellis. *Beyond Black: Celebrity and Race in Obama's America*. New York: Bloomsbury, 2012.

Chideya, Farai. *Don't Believe the Hype: Fighting Cultural Misinformation about African-Americans*. New York: Plume, 1995.

Colby, Tanner. *Some of My Best Friends Are Black: The Strange Story of Integration in America*. New York: Viking, 2012.

Daniels, Jessie. *Cyber Racism: White Supremacy Online and the New Attack on Civil Rights*. Lanham, MD: Rowman and Littlefield Publishers, 2009.

Feagin, Joe. R. *Systemic Racism: A Theory of Oppression*. New York: Routledge, 2006.

Kaplan, H. Roy. *The Myth of Post-Racial America: Searching for Equality in the Age of Materialism*. Lanham, MD: Rowman and Littlefield Education, 2011.

Lacy, Karyn R. *Blue-Chip Black: Race, Class, and Status in the New Black Middle Class*. Berkeley, CA: University of California Press, 2007.

Loewen, James W. *Sundown Towns: A Hidden Dimension of American Racism*. New York: Touchstone, 2005.

"Members of High School Wrestling Team Suspended for Lynching Photo." *Black Youth Project*. Accessed February 23, 2014. http://www.blackyouthproject.com/2014/02/members-of-high-school-wrestling-team-suspended-for-lynching-photo/.

"Transcript: Illinois Senate Candidate Barack Obama." *Washington Post*. Accessed February 16, 2014, http://www.washingtonpost.com/wp-dyn/articles/A19751-2004Jul27.html.

West, Cornel. "Forward." In *The New Jim Crow*. Michelle Alexander. New York: The New Press, 2010, 2012.

———. *Race Matters*. New York: Vintage Books, 1993.

White, Miles. *From Jim Crow to Jay-Z: Race, Rap, and the Performance of Masculinity*. Urbana, IL: University of Illinois Press, 2011.

Wingfield, Adia Harvey, and Joe R. Feagin, *Yes We Can?: White Racial Framing and the Obama Presidency*. New York: Routledge, 2013.

Wise, Tim. *Between Barack and a Hard Place: Racism and White Denial in the Age of Obama*. San Francisco, CA: City Lights Books, 2009.

———. *Color-Blind: The Rise of Post-Racial Politics and the Retreat from Racial Equity*. San Francisco, CA: City Lights Books, 2010.

part 1
Race

1
Reverse Racism
A Discursive History

Tad Suiter

Introduction

In 1975, for the seventh episode of NBC's *Saturday Night Live*, the guest host was Richard Pryor. Pryor was the first Black host, the short list of prior hosts having included George Carlin, Lily Tomlin, and Candice Bergen. In perhaps the most memorable sketch of the night, Pryor is interviewed for a job as a janitor. On the other side of the table sat Chevy Chase. There was one last test in the interview, Chase told Pryor: a simple word association exercise. The exam begins simply enough—"Dog" elicits the response "Tree," to "Rain," Pryor responds "Snow," and so on. The interview quickly takes a turn, however:

Chase: Negro.
Pryor: Whitey.
Chase: Tarbaby.
Pryor: [Pryor looks dumbfounded. Surely he misheard.] . . . What'd you say?
Chase: Tarbaby.
Pryor: Ofay.
Chase: Colored.
Pryor: [Increasingly angry.] Redneck.
Chase: Junglebunny.
Pryor: Peckerwood!
Chase: Burrhead.
Pryor: *Cracker!*
Chase: Spearchucker.
Pryor: *White trash!*
Chase: *Jungle Bunny!*
Pryor: *Honky!*
Chase: *Spade.*
Pryor: *Honkey honkey!*

Chase: Nigger.
Pryor: [Immediately.] Dead *honky!*

By the end of this interaction, Pryor is visibly livid, his face twitching. Chase's character, on the other hand, quickly ends the word association. He attempts to dial back, offering Pryor a job, but Pryor is just too angry, shouting, "Your mama!" at the offer. Finally, Chase sputters out, "$15,000, Mr. Wilson. You'll be the highest-paid janitor in America. Just, don't . . . don't hurt me, please. . . . " Pryor, still angry, nods. "Okay."[1]

In some ways, this sketch gives lie to the very notion of "reverse racism." Chase's character represents a systemic impediment to Pryor's employment. Pryor's anger is reactive, his rage coming not necessarily from any prior prejudice, but to the racism of the word association test. One might imagine Chase's character's fear at the end of the sketch being attributed to Pryor's "reverse racism"—after all, he was just doing his job, administering the word-association test. Pryor is the one that took it badly, made it personal—Pryor is the one who had an emotional, negative reaction. But that argument would only hold water if we accepted the notion that he was completely oblivious to the (comically exaggerated) racism represented by the test. Moreover, such a reading would draw a false moral equivalence between the insults, one that is divorced from any historical reading. Pryor grows more and more angry as Chase slowly ups the level of racism. In perhaps the funniest moment of the sketch, Pryor simply runs out of words: the only response he has to "Spade" is "Honkey honkey!" There are only so many terms of contempt for white people, the sketch suggests, and these are fewer and far less loaded than the terms of contempt white people use for Blacks.

One might hope that the racial politics of America today are more advanced, more evolved than those of a late-night comedy show over thirty years ago. But unfortunately, there are signs that the opposite may be true. In 2013, during the murder trial of George Zimmerman for the shooting of the unarmed teenager Trayvon Martin, CNN aired a special on "The N-Word," where at one point, the chyron underneath the panel of discussants read "N-WORD VS 'CRACKER': WHICH IS WORSE?"[2] It should go without saying that it is a sad day when this question even needs to be asked.[3]

In the years since the late seventies, the dialogue on race in America has fallen victim to a pernicious myth of "reverse racism." It is often deployed as a term to silence or derail discussions of racism, or as a "dog-whistle" term, by which one can communicate discomfort with other races gaining any sort of advantage not likewise afforded to whites, under a veil of "color-blindness." This chapter aims to elucidate why this phrase is not productive, how it can do real damage to our discussions about race, and why people should stop using the phrase altogether.

This chapter is also strongly informed by the belief that words and phrases have histories, that their meanings shift over time. It is informed by Sam Wineburg's imperative in "Historical Thinking and Other Unnatural Acts" that we must see the concepts represented by a word or phrase "not as transcendent truths soaring above time and place, but as patterns of thought that take root in particular historical moments, develop and grow, and bear traces of their former selves but emerge as new forms with successive generations. . . ."[4] In other words, it is important to understand the *history* of the idea of "reverse racism," to look at how it is deployed in discourse over time, rather than to simply accept or reject the term out of hand.

While much history has been written that uses race and racism as integral to the narrative of history, relatively little has been written on the history of "racism"—which is to say, there is still much research to be conducted on how the *term* racism is deployed and understood over the years. Many readers may be surprised at how short the history of "racism" is; according to Robert Miles and Malcolm Brown, the phrase began to be widely used first in Europe, in French critiques of German nationalism in the twenties and thirties. The rise of Nazi racial systems, along with a mounting body of science that disproved that ideology, brought more people to speak out against it. Especially after the Second World War, when people were truly confronted with the horrors of Hitler's "final solution" to what he described as the "Jewish question," they needed a term to label, and thus distance themselves from, this racial ideology. The term they adopted was *racism*.[5]

Indeed, looking at Readex's database of Historical African American Newspapers, one sees *racism* gaining far greater currency right around 1938—and people are quick to recognize the similarities of European racism abroad and American racism at home: a column in the *Kansas City Plaindealer* from 1938 quotes the (white) Catholic priest, Father John LaFarge, as saying, "European Racism brings to its American congener a new and glittering apparatus—in reality much of it the same old machinery furbished up and nickled over—to place at our disposal. But American anti-Negro Racism is not just a poor relative. It offers its virulent European cousin an ideological, not just a pragmatic, foothold on this side of the Atlantic. . . ."[6] *Racism* may have been borrowed from the French *racisme* to describe a European ideology, but it quickly took hold in America to describe both European racism and its American analog—a phenomenon that had been described previously with terms such as *prejudice* and *race hatred*—because the phenomena were so inherently similar.

In order to look at the history of the phrase *reverse racism*, it is necessary to start with a representative corpus of text to be analyzed. I decided to focus on mainstream newspapers, as they tend to be a good indicator of public sentiment, as well as being neither too radical nor too reactionary—newspapers tend to court the center, even the ones with some ideological bias. To this end, I gathered articles from Proquest Historical Newspapers and LexisNexis Academic.[7] After eliminating duplicates, false positives generated by optical character recognition, and articles that do not substantively deal with "reverse racism," I was left with a corpus of over 270 articles—not enough to constitute a good statistical sampling, perhaps, but enough to track attitudes, issues, and themes over time. I then put them into DEVONthink Pro, a database program that allowed me to run optical character recognition to make the articles all searchable, as well as having a tagging feature that allowed me to code each article according to a somewhat idiosyncratic and subjective system, in order to be able to group articles by topic, rhetorical approach, and so on.

The first thing one notices, looking at this corpus, is the many different ways that the term *reverse racism* has been deployed throughout its short history. One quickly comes to recognize four distinct phases of how the term was used. Initially, in the early 1960s, *reverse racism* was used, almost exclusively by Blacks, in discussions of the problems of group Black identity and issues like bloc voting.[8] This meaning persisted, but by the mid- to late 1960s it had become inflicted with ideas of Black Power and racial uprisings. By the 1970s, the phrase had been co-opted by white discussions of affirmative action. Finally, in the 1980s, *reverse racism* settles into the contemporary meaning, serving increasingly as a "dog-whistle" term to interpolate white listener's frustrations at an imagined decline in white status.

Jackie Robinson and Pan-Africanism: Early Examples of "Reverse Racism"

One of the things that inspired this essay was the discovery that one of the earliest people to use the phrase *reverse racism* in the mainstream press—and certainly the first person to use the phrase who was a household name—was Jackie Robinson, best remembered as the player who broke the color barrier in modern professional baseball in 1947. It was shocking to see a phrase like *reverse racism* coming out of such a prominent Black figure—it led me to question what the term meant in the context in which Robinson used it, and how that meaning might be different from the meaning typically understood today.

By 1962, Robinson was retired, but was still viewed as an elder statesman of both his race and his sport by journalists. When the New York State Democratic Party nominated the Black Manhattan Borough President Edward Dudley for attorney general, it was the first time a Black candidate had been endorsed for a statewide office by either of the major parties. Likely because of his status as a fellow breaker of color lines, people were interested in Robinson's opinion on the matter, and perhaps also because of his Republican politics—he had supported Nixon two years earlier.[9]

Robinson came out in favor of white Republican Louis Lefkowitz over Dudley. Quoted in a brief piece in the October 18, 1962 *New York Times*, Robinson asserted that "To vote for a Negro only because he is a Negro would be reverse racism."[10] Two days later, this argument was expanded in an editorial in the *Chicago Defender*, where he made a fairly nuanced argument about bloc voting by the Black community:

> . . . Do you vote for a Negro for political office simply because he belongs to your race—or do you evaluate his candidacy in terms of his background, experience and qualifications compared with those of his opponent?
>
> . . . Do you turn your back on a white candidate for re-election who has built a reputation for being one of the most dedicated, militant public servants in the nation and who has steadily batted 1,000 per cent on the civil rights issue? Do you turn your back on him because he is a white man and you are a Negro who would like to see another Negro move up to a high office?
>
> . . . Our answer to the first question! To vote for a Negro only because he is a Negro would be reverse racism. It would give the lie to all we have believed in and stood for; that the Negro must have equal opportunities in our American society, but no special privilege based only on his color.
>
> Our answer to the second question! Personally, we could not turn our back on a crusading, sincere man like Louis Lefkowitz who has fought valiantly for human rights and social justice for many years; who has broken down barrier after barrier in business, sports, labor, and every other conceivable area. We could not say, in good conscience, that we must desert this man with his sterling

> record—because his opponent is a Negro. This would be unjust, racially bigoted—and in light of his proven and demonstrated conscientiousness and competence—impractical.[11]

While Robinson's language here might seem to mirror contemporary discourse around "reverse racism," especially the part about how "the Negro must have equal opportunities in our American society, but no special privilege based only on his color," he is actually looking to a deeper issue, about Black identity and the role of skin color in electoral politics. Robinson is discussing whether or not black skin is enough to warrant support of a candidate, while backing off from a condemnation of bloc voting in general. To Robinson, Lefkowitz represents an experienced candidate who, despite his race, has been an important supporter of civil rights and other causes important to the Black voters. He later expresses concern that Dudley might be too beholden to the New York Democratic machine, which had passed over fifteen opportunities to name a Black candidate to a judgeship in the last year.

Robinson questions which candidate the Black community should support but not the right of the Black community to vote as a bloc—which is perhaps best illustrated by the offense he takes at Dudley's use of class to try to detract from Robinson's endorsement of Lefkowitz:

> We think the Borough President is a fine man and a high class person. We were saddened to note that he is quoted in a recent newspaper interview as commenting that "all Negroes who make $50,000 a year and own homes in Connecticut with swimming pools, should vote Republican."
>
> Mr. Dudley has never been to our home, seen our paycheck nor taken a dip in a swimming pool which we do not own. Nevertheless, there is no question in our mind as to whether he was talking about us.
>
> To assume that we have no right to be interested in the election in New York because we live in Connecticut, is to assume we were wrong to accept Dr. Martin Luther King's invitation to come to Birmingham to address the SCLC Convention or to go to Albany, Ga., to help out with voter registration and then become involved in aiding in the rebuilding of bombed Negro churches.[12]

Dudley seems to have rejected the authority of Robinson's endorsement based on geography—Robinson does not live in New York—and on class—Robinson is wealthy, and more likely to support the Republicans on those grounds. He has framed the issues of the election in such a way that Robinson is excluded. Robinson rejects such exclusion, however, and presents his bona fides as a member of—and as an activist within—the Black community. Race trumps class, in other words, in Robinson's assessment. Suggesting otherwise, to Robinson, is a disingenuous distraction from the fact that some Black voters may not be sold on Dudley.

While some Blacks agreed with Jackie Robinson that bloc voting for Black candidates constituted "reverse racism," others disagreed. *Defender* columnist Lillian Calhoun rejected this description in a 1965 article:

> A friend chided us for implying Negroes should vote as Negroes in reporting that Republican Bill Robinson lost by almost 17,000 votes in the 2nd ward. Reverse racism, she called it. Maybe so, if Negroes were well represented in all councils of government, had a fair share of industry, top jobs, etc. But, as another friend said, politics is the Negro's only weapon. We have little money in a nation of great wealth; few positions of influence in the local or national power structure. All we have is that vote—and we ought to cast it with some intelligence. Does anybody think, leaving race aside, that Vince Garrity, a charming radio personality, will be a better sanitary trustee than Robinson would have been?[13]

Calhoun's belief that "Negroes should vote as Negroes" comes from a belief in a need for Black voices in politics. The election for the Sanitary Trust position in the Second Ward that year pitted a white Democrat with little experience—though he did have the advantages of minor celebrity and being part of a very efficient Democratic machine—against a Black Republican who had been executive secretary of the Second Ward Organization for twelve years. Robinson had also served as supervisor of precinct captains for the ward, and had run for Alderman in 1963.[14] Chicago's Second Ward at the time was shifting demographically: forces of gentrification and urban renewal were forcing out some of the poor and working-class Black families that had previously made up the majority of residents.[15] If it was important to have Black faces in government representing the Black community—and Calhoun clearly believed it was—and whites were voting as a bloc for white candidates, then it becomes an imperative for the Black community to vote as a bloc as well, rather than splitting the vote, which would mean a win for the white candidate every time.

In both of these examples, the key question of "reverse racism" is whether Blacks engaging in a politics that is in part driven by skin color affinity—for Blacks to vote *as* Blacks *for* Blacks—reproduces in some way an endemic white racism. Bloc voting for Black candidates was not the only issue that brought up the question of "reverse racism" within the Black community in the early 1960s, however. More broadly, the entire formation around the phrase at this time seems to be ultimately a question of racially defined coalitions in general—whether there was a place for Black identity within a civil rights movement that was struggling for increasing integration.

An instructive example of how this notion of "reverse racism" was produced around questions of Black solidarity and Black affinity can be found in a 1962 article by Joseph C. Kennedy in the *New York Times*. Kennedy, a social psychologist by training, spent a year in the West African nations of Ghana, Nigeria, and Liberia, studying attitudes and social mores. Kennedy, a Black American himself, noted that less -educated West Africans would describe him as "white" or "European." Not having been indoctrinated into the complexities of American racial politics, he was a racial Other, despite his skin color. While this "skin-color confusion," as Kennedy describes it, is fascinating in its implications for the social construction of race, Kennedy is more taken with how he is received by more educated Africans: as an "American Negro," he was a "brother":

> Within the secondary schools this bond of warmth was quite evident. On numerous occasions, after interviewing, I would address the student body. Often the headmaster would introduce me by saying, "He is an American Negro; do you know what that means?" The students would reply, "His parents came from Africa; he is one of us."[16]

Kennedy notes that these more educated Africans were often very excited to meet an "American Negro," and had many questions about the status of Blacks in America, as well as about why more Blacks did not come back to Africa to teach and engage in aid. Toward the end of the article, Kennedy brings up the question of "reverse racism" in order to reject it:

> . . . This relationship, as with all relationships among people, is learned—born of the knowledge of the common suffering of all black men who originated in Africa. It is this knowledge which creates the skin-color affinity and bond of warmth that draws the African and the American Negro together.
>
> That this skin-color affinity exists should not be confused with "reverse racism." It is not, for the white visitor is treated well in Africa

> also. Nor should it be thought that a special relationship based on skin-color identity is a desirable and final one. Someday the color of a man's skin will not matter.[17]

Kennedy's language here is telling. He is loath to naturalize or essentialize the relationship between the two groups, preferring to historicize it as between a common past of exploitation and suffering and a triumphalist future where race will not be a factor. Nonetheless, there is a link, a deep one, and acknowledging this link is not to admit to a "reverse racism"—Africans are not racist against whites, whites will receive good treatment in Africa as well. They will simply not have the special connection to African elites that an "American Negro" would. It is also worth noting that Kennedy's rhetoric is careful not to reject the notion of "reverse racism" wholesale. He is simply asserting that racial common-feeling between Blacks in Africa and America is not rooted in reverse racism. Affinity and coalition around skin color are based on historic factors, to Kennedy, and are therefore not problematic. Ultimately, the history of racism will be overcome—the movement will be successful—and in that future, such affinities will no longer be important. In 1962, however, Kennedy clearly felt this day was still quite distant.

Black Power and Racial Uprisings: The Shifting Meaning of "Reverse Racism"

In 1965 and 1966, the Student Nonviolent Coordinating Committee (SNCC) organized "Black Panther" tickets of all-Black candidates for the 1966 midterm elections in several majority-Black Alabama counties. This effort—in many ways the beginning of the mainstreaming of the Black Power Movement—would later be recounted by SNCC organizer Stokely Carmichael in a chapter of his 1967 classic *Black Power: The Politics of Liberation in America.*[18] To a modern reader, the core message of the Black Power according to SNCC might not seem quite as revolutionary or problematic as it once did: Carmichael described it as ". . . a call for black people in this country to unite, to recognize their heritage, to build a sense of community . . . black people must lead and run their own organizations. Only black people can convey the revolutionary idea . . . that black people are able to do things themselves."[19]

But this campaign was deeply controversial within the civil rights movement. A *Chicago Defender* article published on April 25, 1966, quoted Hosea Williams of the Southern Christian Leadership Conference

(SCLC), the civil rights organization headed by Martin Luther King Jr., speaking out against this approach in no uncertain terms:

> The move was called "reverse racism" by Hosea Williams, Southern program director for King's Southern Christian Leadership conference.
>
> He described the effort to exclude all whites from public office as being as bad as the ancient Dixie custom of doing the same thing to all Negroes. It isn't integration, he indicated and it isn't likely—in the long run—to help cure the nation's number one headache.
>
> Williams said Dr. King had tried to talk SNCC out of following its "all-Negro" campaign in the forthcoming May 3 primary election—but without success.[20]

While previous discussions or debates around the notion of "reverse racism" could take on an almost academic tone, Williams's evocation of the phrase seemed graver—it represented a perceived threat to the very heart of the movement. In July of that year, this concern was voiced by Dr. King himself, saying that he was concerned that the civil rights movement was "very, very close" to a split over the issue of Black Power:

> My problem with SNCC . . . is not their militancy—I think you can be militantly nonviolent. It's what I see as a pattern of violence emerging and their use of the cry, "black power," which, whether they mean it or not, falls on the ear as racism in reverse.
>
> But I try to understand . . . The Negro is in dire need of a sense of dignity and a sense of pride, and I think black power is an attempt to develop pride. And there's no doubt about the need for power—he can't get into the mainstream of society without it.
>
> But the use of the phrase black power gives the feeling that Negroes can go it alone and that he doesn't need anybody but himself. We have to keep remembering that we are only 10 or 11 per cent of the population.[21]

In one sense, the definition of *reverse racism* had not changed too much: it still was being used to discuss the appropriateness of building coalitions of racial affinity while the civil rights movement was seeking integration, equality, and to overcome racial difference. The pitch and timbre of the discussion, however, had shifted dramatically. Rather than a debate within the Black community about the relative merits of this or that decision, this was something with the potential to rend or even end the civil rights movement.

This is not to imply that King was necessarily overreacting or playing politics simply because SNCC was advocating for a different sort of change. There was a real worry that events like the Watts Uprising in August 1965 were directly related to rhetoric like that of Black Power advocate Malcolm X in February of the same year, stating that "We declare our right on this earth to be a man, to be a human being, to be respected as a human being, to be given the rights of a human being in this society, on this earth, in this day, which we intend to bring into existence by any means necessary."[22] And indeed, the Watts uprising was but the first in a long series of riots and uprisings within Black communities in the late 1960s. While it would be hyperbolic in the extreme to argue that the rhetoric of the Black Power Movement was directly responsible for the racial uprisings of the era, it is also undeniable that it was a step away from the practiced, disciplined nonviolence advocated by the SCLC, and it is understandable why such a move might be divisive or worrisome. King's interview, coincidentally, took place a matter of days before a week of rioting broke out in Cleveland's Hough neighborhood.[23]

The tone of discussions of "reverse racism" had shifted in 1966, as discussion evoking the phrase came to center around a nexus of race riots, Black Power, and antiwhite racial antipathy within the Black community, a pattern that lasted into the early 1970s. The NAACP's Clarence Mitchell gave speeches against "reverse racism" and divisiveness in the civil rights movement.[24] The Urban League's Whitney Young said that "The overwhelming majority of black people . . . welcome whites who want to work with the black community, and they aren't letting legitimate racial pride and militancy be perverted into a reverse racism."[25] Charles Evers, brother of Medgar Evers, counseled against reverse racism in a 1971 speech: "We've had enough of racism. We've had enough of hatred. We've had enough of fighting. We must get along together. I don't believe in destroying black people and I don't believe in destroying white people. . . . Black folk, with all they have done to us, let's not hate. . . . If we become the haters they have been we are just as wrong."[26]

Perhaps most importantly, whites started talking about "reverse racism." What had previously been an in-group conversation took on new weight coming from the outside. Senator Jacob Javits, a liberal Republican with a strong record on civil rights, addressed an audience in Harlem in 1966 where he urged the community to reject the "reverse racism and the iconoclastic demagoguery" of Black Power leaders. Javits claimed that the white community was "frightened" by growing militancy, and that this fear created a "white backlash" that led to the move against the Civil Rights Bill of 1966: "I think many of you would agree with me . . . that it was the sudden violence, the call to reverse racism and the iconoclastic demagoguery of a few which have threatened and frightened the white community almost to the point where right and reason became secondary to visions about self-preservation."[27]

From a white perspective, the line between the Black Power Movement and the pacifistic multiracial coalition of Martin Luther King could be hazy, and almost seem to disappear. Covering the debate over the above-mentioned Civil Rights Bill, the *Chicago Defender* reported on "an angry, shouting speech that drew applause, [where] Rep. John B Anderson, R-Ill., denounced all violence, including the 'reverse racism' of black power and Dr. King's 'horrible' call . . . for urban Negroes to take up civil disobedience on a massive scale."[28] This is a particularly good example of how the race of the speaker can inflect the use of a term, even when the issues at stake—"reverse racism," Black Power, racial uprisings—are the same. Over the late sixties and early seventies, there are more and more uses of "reverse racism" by white reporters as unsourced allegations against Black militants and those who subscribe to the ethos of Black Power. The term *reverse racism*, in other words, becomes part of the white lexicon of race at this time. And as we will see, the more widely adopted the term is by whites, the less frequently it comes to be used by Blacks.

Education and Jobs: "Reverse Racism" in the 1970s

From around 1972 onward there are almost no examples of Blacks using the term *reverse racism*, except to dispel claims made by others. There are exceptions, of course, such as the conservative political commentator Armstrong Williams or Supreme Court Justice Clarence Thomas,[29] and as I will discuss later, it is not irrelevant that these few Blacks who still do engage with the term are conservative Republicans. But if Black Americans were shying away from the phrase, more and more whites were using it. The period between 1971 and 1978 is the period of the highest use of the term yet, and the primary issues addressed were centered on affirmative action policies in hiring and education. It is reductive to assign a single specific reason for the movement of the majority of Black Americans from the phrase *reverse racism*. But I would suggest that three primary factors seem to be at work: the mainstreaming of Black Power discourse, a related shift toward a definition of racism centered on institutional and systemic racism, and finally, the fact that what had been a discussion from within the Black community had become an accusation leveled against Blacks by whites.

While it had been divisive in the late sixties, Black Power rhetoric had come to be more accepted, and many within the mainstream civil rights movement were incorporating elements of Black Power discourse. In the wake of Martin Luther King's assassination, leaders like Black Panther Huey Newton and "Black Power pluralist" Shirley Chisholm came to represent a new generation of Black leadership. Hosea Williams, the SCLC representative who in 1966 had described SNCC's endorsement of an all-Black ticket as "reverse racism" and "ridiculous," had come around to accepting the Black Power Movement by 1970, and inviting them into the SCLC fold. At a five-day "March against Repression" that year, Williams was quoted as saying:

> Black power has nothing to do with violence . . . Black power is when black people respect themselves. Black Power is when black men stop allowing themselves to be duped into filling the jailhouses while white men fill the colleges . . . Black power . . . is when we refuse to fight thousands of miles away from home for freedoms over there that we can't enjoy over here. How is America going to sell democracy abroad when she has never bought it herself?[30]

After a decade of successive civil rights legislation, much progress had been made in the way of eliminating the most onerous forms of de jure discrimination. However, America was still a nation with a strong racial hierarchy, and there were deep institutional problems that still needed to be addressed. Black Power rhetoric presented a powerful tool with which to theorize, explain, and attack these inequalities. In *Black Power*, Carmichael and Hamilton, drawing on the postcolonial theory of Franz Fanon and others, describe racism as "the predication of decisions and policies on considerations of race for the purpose of *subordinating* a racial group and maintaining control over that group," specifically—in America—the subordination by whites of Blacks and other minorities. They outline two kinds of racism: individual and institutional. Individual racism is understood as overt acts by individuals who are products of racial animus. Institutional racism, on the other hand, "relies on the active and pervasive operation of anti-Black attitudes and practices." While Civil Rights Legislation had done much to limit certain forms of overt, individual racism, it could do little against the institutional racism that still pervaded the United States.[31]

It is worth noting that this observation was not necessarily anything new. As far back as Du Bois's *The Philadelphia Negro*, which describes the "Negro problem" as a "complex" of different problems, Black intellectuals have wrestled with issues of the various forms that racism can take, and the complexities of institutional racism.[32] However, as many of the key issues facing the Black community by 1970 were these issues of institutional racism, the popular definition of racism within the Black community can be seen to shift at this time to a definition that brings institutional and systemic problems to the fore.

Finally, where discussion of "reverse racism" had started *within* the Black community, it had, by this time, become a charge leveled *at* the Black community, from a position of power: from white folks. And it was being used to make accusations of unfairness against Affirmative Action programs that were key to Black advancement toward parity in employment and education. A good illustration of this can be seen in the case of white aspiring medical student Allan Bakke.

In 1969, the University of California Medical School at Davis began a special admissions program for minority students. Before this program was put in place, less than 1 percent of UC-Davis Medical Students were racial minorities, despite California's minority population making up around a quarter of the population at the time. Sixteen out of a hundred admissions were, under this program, set aside for minority students. Under this program and others like it, Black representation in medical schools had risen from 2.7 percent in 1968 to 7.5 percent by 1974. This was considered especially important to the Black and minority population, as minority doctors were considered more likely to return to their communities and practice—more Black doctors meant a healthier Black community. In 1973 and 1974, Bakke applied to UC Davis and was rejected. He was also rejected from ten other schools. Nevertheless, when he learned that some "less-qualified" students had been admitted into those sixteen set-aside slots, he decided to sue the school. The school then countersued, requesting a finding on such race-based admissions programs.[33]

A similar case had come up recently, when Marco DeFunis sued the University of Washington Law School for discrimination when he was not admitted to that program. However, that case was eventually thrown out of court as moot, as DeFunis was actually admitted on appeal.[34] UC Davis, on the other hand, was looking for a test case. And while the court of law found that affirmative action programs of this sort were legal, in the court of white public opinion, many were incensed. A letter to the editor in the *Chicago Tribune* wrote, "In 30 short years the civil rights movement has come from opposing segregation and discrimination to supporting reverse racism. People who champion real equality will support Allan Bakke and his crusade against ever increasing reverse discrimination in this nation."[35] Republican commentator and former Nixon speechwriter Pat Buchanan warned that cases such as this and affirmative action programs in general would turn working-class white voters "To the only politician they ever felt really had their interest at heart. To George C. Wallace. His success was always the most precise measure of the failure of the major parties to heed the voice of the forgotten man."[36]

Buchanan's former position as a Nixon speechwriter was not coincidental, neither was his evocation of George Wallace, best known for his call for "segregation now, segregation tomorrow, segregation forever." Nixon ran on a "law and order" platform in 1968 that was designed, in part, to appeal to Southern white voters who would have earlier voted for a Democrat—by appealing to white fears around racial uprisings, Nixon could speak to these voters without being overt. In 1968, higher taxes and inflation caused by the war in Vietnam had caused the economy to begin to slow down—a prelude to the "stagflation" (little to no job growth combined with inflation) that would be endemic in the 1970s. The poor—especially the Black poor, who had most benefited from the wealth redistribution under Johnson's "Great Society" programs—were a natural scapegoat, and Nixon courted that anger. Nixon did this by conflating race and disorder.[37] With an eye to his reelection in 1972, Nixon had actually sent Postmaster General Winton Blount to meet with the segregationist Wallace, encouraging him to make an unsuccessful gubernatorial bid in 1970, and freeing up the segregationist South for himself in the 1972 presidential election.[38]

In this context, and in light of Buchanan's career generally, it becomes clear that by "the voice of the forgotten man," Buchanan was actually evoking a "forgotten" white privilege. And other press mentions of "reverse racism" seem to confirm this connection: reverse racism is used strategically in opposition to topics as disparate as desegregation busing programs,[39] to a hiring program for Black police officers in Virginia,[40] to hires of women and minorities at NASA.[41] In each case, the authors are defending white privilege. It may seem valid, superficially—ideally, nondiscrimination should mean that nobody, even whites, are discriminated against. But such an argument makes a false moral equivalency between very different historical situations. As Stanley Fish has argued:

> Only if racism is thought of as something that occurs principally in the mind, a falling-away from proper notions of universal equality,

> can the desire of a victimized and terrorized people to band together be declared morally identical to the actions of their would-be executioners. Only when the actions of the two groups are detached from the historical conditions of their emergence and given a purely abstract description can they be made interchangeable.[42]

That is, to claim that affirmative action represents "reverse racism," one must make a claim that the injustice of not getting a particular job or not getting into a particular school is somehow morally equivalent to the over 350 years of enslavement, brutality, Jim Crow, rape, and lynching, for which such policies are trying to serve as some sort of corrective. To claim equivalency shows a deep lack of empathy and compassion.

Nevertheless, the claim is made, and continues to be made.

"Reverse Racism" in an Era of Color-Blind Racism

The patterns around the use of the phrase *reverse racism* become much less clear looking during the last thirty-five years or so, even though it is deployed more than ever before. Rather than being fixed around a particular nexus of issues, like Black Power and racial uprisings in the late 1960s, or affirmative action in the 1970s, the term has taken on a sort of a catchall meaning. It is used at various times in regard to a host of different topics. This is because the term has been unmoored from any real fixed meaning, and instead has come to be deployed as a "dog whistle" used to interpolate a white audience dissatisfied with the changing relationship status quo.

Discussing how Ronald Reagan adopted and adapted Nixon's Southern Strategy in 1980, Lee Atwater, in a moment of what can only be described as audacious honesty, explained Reagan's approach thusly:

> Atwater: As to the whole Southern strategy that Harry S. Dent, Sr. and others put together in 1968, opposition to the Voting Rights Act would have been a central part of keeping the South. Now [the new Southern Strategy of Ronald Reagan] doesn't have to do that. All you have to do to keep the South is for Reagan to run in place on the issues he's campaigned on since 1964 and that's fiscal conservatism, balancing the budget, cut taxes, you know, the whole cluster.
>
> Questioner: But the fact is, isn't it, that Reagan does get to the Wallace voter and to the racist side of the Wallace voter by doing away with legal services, by cutting down on food stamps?

> Atwater: You start out in 1954 by saying, "Nigger, nigger, nigger." By 1968 you can't say "nigger"—that hurts you. Backfires. So you say stuff like forced busing, states' rights and all that stuff. You're getting so abstract now [that] you're talking about cutting taxes, and all these things you're talking about are totally economic things and a byproduct of them is [that] blacks get hurt worse than whites. And subconsciously maybe that is part of it. I'm not saying that. But I'm saying that if it is getting that abstract, and that coded, that we are doing away with the racial problem one way or the other. You follow me—because obviously sitting around saying, "We want to cut this," is much more abstract than even the busing thing, and a hell of a lot more abstract than "Nigger, nigger."[43]

The Republican Party, and the American right general, has come to count on the votes of a certain racist contingent that it cannot directly call out to for fear of retribution or perceived racism on the part of the party as a whole. For this reason, it has adopted a series of these "dog-whistle" terms that have become increasingly more and more abstract over the years—in Atwater's example, from "nigger" to "bussing" or "state's rights" to "fiscal conservatism." In so doing, they have found a way to continue to court a key demographic, especially in the South and among the rural working class, without being perceived as overtly racist. Reagan talked about cutting welfare or entitlement programs, and this audience understood that he was talking about Blacks, even though many whites benefit from such programs. This is not in any way to imply that all Republicans are racist. However, racism plays to a certain contingent within the Republican base, a somewhat tenuous coalition of moral conservatives, neoliberals, and rural, working-class whites. By interpolating racial feeling among a certain segment of the white population, without seeming so overtly racist as to alienate others within this coalition, they have managed to win five out of nine presidential elections since 1979, all but two presidencies in that time.

It is worth pointing out here that, while it is often deployed strategically by conservatives, the discourse of "reverse racism" is by no means limited to Republicans. The phrase is invoked by whites of every political affiliation, privately and publicly. Bill Clinton certainly evoked the spirit of the phrase, if not the exact wording, with what has come to be known as his "Sister Souljah moment." The hip-hop artist Sister Souljah, in response to the Los Angeles Uprisings, had been quoted as saying,

> I mean, if black people kill black people every day, why not have a week and kill white people? . . . White people, this Government and that Mayor were well aware of the fact that black people were dying every day in Los Angeles under gang violence. So if you're a gang member and you would normally be killing somebody, why not kill a white person?[44]

Sister Souljah spoke to Jesse Jackson's Rainbow Coalition, who then hosted Clinton the following night. Clinton spoke out against Souljah, angering Jackson and many others in the room. Roger Wilkins summed up the backlash quite well:

> I do not defend Sister Souljah's comments . . . It is wrong for anyone to justify violence. But Clinton didn't know what had gone on at that Rainbow meeting. And he didn't ask Jesse Jackson, didn't give him any warning of what he was going to do.
>
> At the panel the night before, Jackson stood up to Sister Souljah, insisting that you can and must work within the system. And she finally agreed with him . . .
>
> In that context Clinton's speech was arrogant, and it was cheap. He came there to show suburban whites that he can stand up to blacks. It was contrived.[45]

The myth of "reverse racism" is potent, and it can be quite an effective dog-whistle. But given the Democratic Party's reliance on the Black vote since the civil rights era, it is a dog whistle that is often best avoided by Democrats, where Republicans can use it with relative impunity. Despite this, it is deeply pervasive regardless of political affiliation.

While the phrase *reverse racism* has, in the years between 1980 and 2013, become unmoored from the sorts of topical threads that had previously defined different uses of the term, it is hardly random: the phrase comes into the national dialog at times of economic uncertainty. Just as the stagflation of the 1970s had encouraged whites to scapegoat poor minorities, hard times economically correlate strongly with incidences of the phrase in the press. The economic doldrums of the George Herbert Walker Bush administration—a period characterized by wildly fluctuating stock values, climbing unemployment, and expensive fuel prices, coincides with a strong spike in use of the phrase.[46] Likewise, the phrase has been used more than ever in the years after the global recession hit in 2008.

If one looks a bit more closely at the present-day situation, one quickly comes to see that the rise in interest in "reverse racism" correlates quite strongly with economic factors and a perceived decrease in the power of white privilege. A 2011 study showed that many white people believe "more progress has been made toward equality than do Blacks, but Whites also now believe that this progress is linked to a new inequality—at their expense"—that is, that racism is essentially a "zero-sum game," and that racism against whites is on the rise.[47] It seems likely that this is related to the falling of real income over the last thirty years. From 1973 to 2011, median hourly wages (adjusted for inflation) grew only 10 percent, while worker productivity increased by 80 percent. This has been especially hard on the working class, for whom union membership has declined by approximately 75 percent since the 1960s.[48] White workers have good reason to feel less stable, more exploited, and poorer in real terms. It makes sense to question what worth supposed white privilege has in such an environment.

But white privilege is still very much a factor: despite all this, a study of 1,700 households shows that the gap in median net worth between white and Black households has almost tripled: from $85,070 in 1984 to $236,000 in 2009.[49] Yet this is lost on many whites. De facto racial segregation, while it has declined in recent years, has done so quite slowly. Meanwhile, income segregation has increased. According to a 2013 report by the Russell Sage Foundation,

> . . . racial segregation coupled with income segregation means that low-income black and Hispanic families will tend to cluster in communities that are disadvantaged along a number of dimensions, such as average educational attainment, family structure, and unemployment. In contrast, low-income white families, although affected by income segregation as well, tend to live in neighborhoods with higher average incomes than even middle-class black and Hispanic families.[50]

Working-class and lower-middle-class white people are hurting financially, and are unlikely to think about their own privilege because they are inured by class and racial segregation from the segment of the population that is struggling far more. If they are in contact with Blacks or Latinos, they are likely to be in contact with only those who are in the same relative economic situation. Black and Latino families, on the other hand, are far more likely to be in contact with families within their own racial or ethnic group who are doing far worse. All of this creates a situation where working-class whites are distinctly unaware of their own racial privilege, and likely to be resentful of other groups they view as being in competition for scarce resources, even if the perceived scarcity of those resources is completely out of line with the lived reality for the racially Othered.

Many of those who invoke the notion of "reverse racism" would not even describe themselves as racist. Far from it. Rather, they often describe themselves as anything but—many evoke the memory of Martin Luther King, even while saying things that seem rather overtly racist. The irony of this evocation, made frequently in the articles I have analyzed from the 1990s and 2000s, should be clear to those who remember Dr. King being described as a reverse racist himself by John Anderson in the last year of his life for advocating for further civil disobedience.

Yet it makes sense in a certain context. The most popular quote brought up in these articles is from the March on Washington for Jobs and Freedom: "I have a dream that my four little children will one day live in a nation where they will not be judged by the color of their skin but by the content of their character."[51] This quote has become a rallying cry for people who are decrying the "reverse racism" of Blacks against whites because the discourse is extremely flexible: the same logic that Lee Atwater used in describing the Reagan approach to the Southern Strategy can also be applied here. This sort of neoliberal abstracted approach to race attempts to place the blame for issues within minority communities on issues of "content of character"—on moral failings within the community—rather than "color of skin." Thus, even while castigating or even demonizing the black community, they advocate for equality and a color-blind society.

Sociologist Eduardo Bonilla-Silva coined the term *color-blind racism* to describe the ideology by which "most whites maintain a color-blind sense of self and, at the same time . . . reinforce views that help reproduce the current racial order."[52] Color-blind racism rejects the argument of biological inferiority of the Jim Crow era for a new, liberal, market-driven morality:

> . . . instead of proclaiming God placed minorities in the world in a servile position, it suggests they are behind because they do not work hard enough; instead of viewing interracial marriage as wrong on a straight racial basis, it regards it as "problematic" because of concerns over the children, location, or the extra burden it places on couples.[53]

In this way, whites are able to distance themselves from being called (or having to view themselves as) a "racist"—a term that we have all learned to reject—without having to confront how their attitudes still support and buttress white privilege at the expense of Blacks and other racial and ethnic minorities. Indeed, it is a central tenant of color-blind racism that overt racism is aberrant, a thing of the past, or of minds stuck in the past. Yet one recent study that had students keep diaries of racial events for a semester found that, despite near universal agreement among the students that overt racism was no longer a major issue, their journals indicated that overtly racist incidents happened three times more often than "liberal" or color-blind examples.[54] While students were likely more able to identify (and more comfortable calling out) instances of overt racism, this is still quite telling. The idea that overt racism is in the past seems to be more a product of ideology than any sort of objective fact. In fact, the belief is often held despite ample factual evidence to the contrary. The notion of color blindness is at best still an aspirational one in America, and should be discussed as such, rather than as a part of an imagined new postracial order.

The myth of "reverse racism" is today very much a part of color-blind racism, and it points to what is perhaps the most dangerous thing about color-blind ideology—the facility with which this rhetoric can lead to sincere self-deception. In order to have a serious, real conversation about racial inequality in America, it is important that all parties, whatever their color, are able to come to the table in a spirit of honest self-appraisal. Race is but one of many factors, including class, gender, and sexuality that form a complex matrix of privilege and oppressions that we all have to live life negotiating. White people may be disenfranchised for many reasons—class, gender, sexual preference, disability—but they are not systemically disenfranchised because of their race. Racial animus toward whites may exist, but it can only be understood by an analysis that situates such antipathy within a context of systemic racism and white supremacy.

Color-blind racism and notions of "reverse racism" are problematic because one can honestly believe oneself to be color blind, or to be victimized by "reverse racism," even in the face of vast evidence to the contrary. White folks try to be color blind, many in complete sincerity, but in so doing, they obfuscate the reality of racial privilege. And by so doing, these well-meaning people are rendered incapable of having a discussion that takes into account white privilege, and the ways that the decisions and choices they make uphold institutional white supremacy. It is time to do away with the phrase *reverse racism*, as under the phrase's current formulation, it cannot have any positive or useful meaning. We must all commit ourselves to a notion of radical honesty about these issues if we want to do something about them. Until we can do that, without fear of occasionally having our own racism, or other prejudices, held up for us—there can be no real, meaningful change.

Notes

1. *Saturday Night Live*, "Richard Pryor/Gil Scott-Heron" (NBC, December 13, 1975).

2. Joe Coscarelli, "CNN Is Seriously Wondering Whether 'Cracker' Is Worse Than the N-Word," *Daily Intelligencer*, July 2, 2013, http://nymag.com/daily/intelligencer/2013/07/cnn-weighs-cracker-vs-n-word-trayvon-martin.html; "CNN Special Event, The N Word" (CNN, July 1, 2013), http://transcripts.cnn.com/TRANSCRIPTS/1307/01/se.01.html.

3. It should also be self-evident that, as many pointed out, if CNN felt free to use the word *cracker* but felt compelled to use the weak euphemism *the* n-*word*, the question should not have to be asked.

4. Sam Wineburg, "Historical Thinking and Other Unnatural Acts," *Phi Delta Kappan* 80, no. 7 (March 1, 1999): 495.

5. Robert Miles and Malcolm Brown, *Racism: Second Edition*, Key Ideas (London; New York: Routledge, 2004), 58–59.

6. Floyd J Calvin, "Calvin's Digest," *Plaindealer*, December 16, 1938.

7. Libraries' subscriptions may vary, so to be clear—my particular subscription to Proquest includes: *Atlanta Constitution* (1868–1945); *Baltimore Sun* (1837–1987); *Boston Globe* (1872–1927); *Chicago Tribune* (1849–1987); *Chicago Defender* (1910–1975); *Christian Science Monitor* (1908–1997); *Los Angeles Times* (1881–1987); *New York Times* (1851–2007); *Wall Street Journal* (1889–1993); *Washington Post* (1877–1994). Likewise, LexisNexis Academic includes mostly papers post-1980 from: *New York Times, St. Louis Post–Dispatch, Tampa Bay Times, Pittsburgh Post–Gazette, USA Today, Atlanta Journal–Constitution, Berkshire Eagle, New York Sun, Dayton Daily News, Tampa Tribune*, and the *Virginian-Pilot*.

8. I am deliberately putting aside two of the earliest uses, which seem to be anomalous, to try to get to a point where there begins to be a consensus of meaning around the term. In a February 5, 1950 article in the *Washington Post*, the term is used to describe the attitudes of a young wife of a U.S. District Court judge, who seems to be parodied or pilloried for asserting the cultural superiority of the North while living in the Jim Crow South. Essentially, this instance describes as "reverse racism" the defamation of whites living within and benefiting from a culture of racial apartheid—while there are some similarities to current deployments of the term, the fact that there are no other instances of the phrase being used for eight years suggests to me an individual use, rather than a widely adopted meaning. Likewise, a November 9, 1958 article in the *New York*

Times quotes Philippine Ambassador Carlos Romulo as using the term to describe Asian and Pacific Island countries' poor assessment of U.S. racial policies. Like the 1950 article, this meaning does not seem to be very widely adopted at the time.

9. "Jackie Robinson Tells Why He Favors Nixon: Former Baseball Player Says He Likes Republican for Stand on Civil Rights," *Los Angeles Times*, October 11, 1960.

10. "Jackie Robinson Favors Lefkowitz over Dudley," *New York Times*, October 18, 1962.

11. Jackie Robinson, "N.Y. Demo Choice Poses Race Queries," *Chicago Defender*, October 20, 1962.

12. Ibid.

13. Lillian S. Calhoun, "Confetti," *Chicago Daily Defender*, January 25, 1965.

14. "Challenges Robinson for 2nd Ward Post," *Chicago Daily Defender*, April 9, 1964.

15. Lloyd General, "Alderman Harvey Leader of New, Changed 2nd Ward," *The Chicago Defender*, February 23, 1963.

16. Joseph C. Kennedy, "The American Negro's Key Role in Africa: One Who Spent a Year There Reports on Some of the Special Associations He Discovered and Assays Their Potential," *New York Times*, February 4, 1962, sec. *New York Times Magazine*.

17. Ibid.

18. Stokely Carmichael and Charles V. Hamilton, *Black Power: The Politics of Liberation in America* (New York, Random House, 1967), 98–120.

19. Ibid., 44–46.

20. "Strife on Two Civil Rights Fronts: SNCC Is Scored By King Group," *Chicago Daily Defender*, April 25, 1966.

21. Gene Roberts, "Dr. King Declares Rights Movement Is 'Close' to a Split: Dr. King Fears Split in Rights Groups," *New York Times*, July 9, 1966.

22. Malcolm X, *By Any Means Necessary: Speeches, Interviews, and a Letter* (New York: Pathfinder Press, 1992), 84.

23. "Cleveland Gripped by Race Rioting: Woman Is Slain; 2 Men Shot," *Chicago Tribune*, July 19, 1966; "A Federal Inquiry of Hough Riot Asked," *New York Times*, August 13, 1966.

24. Harriet Douty, "Clarence Mitchell, Jr.—He Still Believes," *Washington Post and Times Herald*, January 12, 1969, sec. Potomac; Ethel L. Payne, "NAACP Head Warns Blacks to Reject Reverse Racism," *Chicago Daily Defender*, August 16, 1969.

25. Whitney Young, "To Be Equal: Myth of Black Anti-Semitism," *Chicago Daily Defender*, September 28, 1968, sec. Daily Defender's World of Features.

26. "Avoid Hate, Blacks Told by Evers," *Chicago Tribune*, January 29, 1971.

27. "Javits Urges Negro Calm: Appeals for Repudiation of Militance, 'Demagoguery,'" *Sun*, September 27, 1966; "Javits Bids Negroes Shun 'Black Power,'" *New York Times*, September 27, 1966.

28. "House Members Blast Dr. King's 'Disobedience' Bid," *Chicago Daily Defender*, August 17, 1967.

29. Armstrong Williams, "Blaming It on Race," *Washington Times*, September 17, 1999; Armstrong Williams, "Affirmative Action's Slippery Slope," *Washington Times*, April 7, 2001; Eric Lipton, "400 Activists Protest outside Justice's Home; Clarence Thomas's Record on Civil Rights Denounced," *Washington Post*, September 13, 1995.

30. Thomas A. Johnson, "5-Day March in Georgia Ends with Massive Rally," *New York Times*, May 24, 1970.

31. Stokely Carmichael and Charles V. Hamilton, *Black Power*, 3–5.

32. W. E. B. Du Bois, *The Philadelphia Negro: A Social Study* (Schocken Books, 1899), 385.

33. Robert L. Allen, "The Bakke Case and Affirmative Action," *Black Scholar* 9, no. 1 (September 1, 1977): 9–10.

34. Philip Hager, "Reverse Racism: Does It Exist?," *Los Angeles Times*, February 5, 1973, sec. Part I; Philip Hager and Los Angeles Times, "Suit Threatens Law Schools' Minority Admissions Plans," *Washington Post and Times Herald*, February 18, 1973, sec. National News; "The DeFunis Ruling," *Washington Post*, April 26, 1974.

35. John Allanson, "In 30 Short Years," *Chicago Tribune*, October 15, 1977.

36. Patrick Buchanan, "When Quotas Hurt Whites," *Chicago Tribune*, December 19, 1978.

37. Dan T. Carter, *From George Wallace to Newt Gingrich: Race in the Conservative Counterrevolution, 1963–1994* (Louisiana State University Press, 1999), 28–30.

38. Ibid., 46–47.

39. Mike LaVelle, "Blue-Collar Views: Busing Advocates Running out of Gas," *Chicago Tribune*, December 20, 1973.

40. John J. Pershing, "Letters to the Editor: Racism and Standards," *Washington Post*, December 19, 1974.

41. Richard Lapartin, "Reverse Racism?," *Chicago Tribune*, February 9, 1978.

42. Stanley Fish, "Reverse Racism or How the Pot Got to Call the Kettle Black," *Atlantic Monthly*, November 1993, 128.

43. Alexander P Lamis, *Southern Politics in the 1990s* (Baton Rouge: Louisiana State University Press, 1999), 7–8.

44. Anthony Lewis, "Abroad at Home; Black and White," *New York Times*, June 18, 1992, sec. Opinion.

45. Ibid.

46. Joe Weisenthal, "This Is What The Economy Did The Last Time A

President Didn't Win Re-Election," *Business Insider*, July 8, 2012, http://www.businessinsider.com/the-economy-under-george-hw-bush-2012-7.

47. Michael I. Norton, and Samuel R. Sommers, "Whites See Racism as a Zero-Sum Game That They Are Now Losing," *Perspectives on Psychological Science* 6, no. 3 (May 1, 2011): 217, doi:10.1177/1745691611406922.

48. Steven Greenhouse, "America's Productivity Climbs, but Wages Stagnate," *New York Times*, January 12, 2013, sec. Sunday Review, http://www.nytimes.com/2013/01/13/sunday-review/americas-productivity-climbs-but-wages-stagnate.html.

49. Thomas Shapiro, Tatjana Meschede, and Sam Osoro, "The Roots of the Widening Racial Wealth Gap: Explaining the Black-White Economic Divide" (Institute on Assets and Social Policy, February 2013), 2, http://iasp.brandeis.edu/pdfs/Author/shapiro-thomas-m/racialwealthgapbrief.pdf.

50. Kendra Bischoff, and Sean F. Reardon, "Residential Segregation by Income, 1970–2009" (Russell Sage Foundation: U.S. 2010, November 14, 2013), 16, http://www.s4.brown.edu/us2010/Data/Report/report10162013.pdf.

51. Martin Luther King, "I Have a Dream!," *Chicago Daily Defender (Daily Edition) (1960–1973)*, April 8, 1968.

52. Eduardo Bonilla-Silva, Amanda Lewis, and David G. Embrick, "'I Did Not Get That Job Because of a Black Man . . .': The Story Lines and Testimonies of Color-Blind Racism," *Sociological Forum* 19, no. 4 (December 1, 2004): 576.

53. Eduardo Bonilla-Silva, *Racism without Racists: Color-Blind Racism and the Persistence of Racial Inequality in the United States* (Lanham: Rowman and Littlefield Publishers, 2010), 3.

54. Margaret M. Zamudio and Francisco Rios, "From Traditional to Liberal Racism: Living Racism in the Everyday," *Sociological Perspectives* 49, no. 4 (December 1, 2006): 490.

Bibliography

"A Bore Is a Bore." *Wall Street Journal*, July 2, 1985.

"A Date to Keep; GOP Gripes about Sotomayor's Hearing Ring Hollow," *Pittsburgh Post–Gazette*, June 15, 2009.

"A Federal Inquiry of Hough Riot Asked." *New York Times*,August 13, 1966.

"A Man of Conviction." *Daily News*, October 7, 2008.

"A Tough Test for the Regents." *New York Times*, April 27, 1990.

Adams, Thelma. "Reel-Life Racism." *New York Post*, April 25, 1999.

Aizenman, Nurith C. "BSU Students, Neighbors Fight Waste Site; Transfer Station Would Be Built Near College." *Washington Post*, February 22, 2001.

———. "Trash Plan May Violate Federal Deal: Official Involved in

Desegregation Pact Questions Placement Near Bowie State." *Washington Post*, February 16, 2001.
Albom, Mitch. "A Man without Standards." *Buffalo News*, July 27, 2010.
Algar, Selim. "Race Mess on L.I.: Hamptons Cop Suit." *New York Post*, January 23, 2006.
Allanson, John. "In 30 Short Years." *Chicago Tribune*, October 15, 1977.
Allen, Robert L. "The Bakke Case and Affirmative Action." *Black Scholar* 9, no. 1 (September 1, 1977): 9–16.
Allison, Wes. "Sotomayor Has a New GOP Fan." *St. Petersburg Times*, June 10, 2009.
Andreatta, David. "School on Bias Alert: Upper E Side Fury." *New York Post*, April 25, 2005.
Ashmore, Harry S. "Americans Below the Bottom Line." *Chicago Tribune*, May 8, 1982.
Avery, Don. "'Ethnic Dilemmas' and 'Economics and Politics of Race.'" *Sun*, October 30, 1983.
"Avoid Hate, Blacks Told by Evers." *Chicago Tribune*. January 29, 1971.
Ayers Jr., B. Drummond. "With Richmond's Old Guard Watching, Blacks Take on Aging City's Problems." *New York Times*, July 30, 1977.
Baker, Ross K. "Bring Back the Panthers." *Washington Post*, August 24, 1975.
Barnes, Fred. "In Chicago, Race Touches Every Issue." *Sun*. April 10, 1983.
Barnes, Harper. "Hit the Road, You Other Nominees, Foxx Has Oscar Sewn Up." *St. Louis Post–Dispatch*, February 18, 2005.
Barnes, Robert. "Battle Lines Are Drawn on Sotomayor Nomination; Ideology, Abortion and Remarks on Ethnicity Come to Fore." *Washington Post*, May 28, 2009.
Barnes, Steven. "Be Aware of Tendency to Prefer One's Own Race." *Philadelphia Inquirer*, April 9, 2006.
Bates, Michael M. "'Backlash of Bigotry.'" *Chicago Tribune*, November 22, 1980.
Bell, Jr., Stanley M. "A Compliment." *Sun*. November 20, 1985.
"Bent Backwards." *Sun*. March 17, 1976.
Bentley, T. H. "Letters to the Times." *Los Angeles Times*, November 27, 1978.
Beyette, Beverly. "It's Kind of Made a Mess of My Life." *Los Angeles Times*, June 26, 1977.
Bischoff, Kendra, and Sean F. Reardon. "Residential Segregation by Income, 1970–2009." Russell Sage Foundation: U.S. 2010, November 14, 2013. http://www.s4.brown.edu/us2010/Data/Report/report10162013.pdf.
"'Black Studies' at SF State." *Los Angeles Times*, November 18, 1968.
"Blacks to Press Boycott of Law Course at Harvard." *New York Times*, September 15, 1982.
Blau, Eleanor. "Papp Starts a Shakespearean Repertory Troupe Made Up

Entirely of Black and Hispanic Actors." *New York Times*, January 21, 1979.

Blow, Charles. "Let's Rescue the Race Debate." *New York Times*, November 20, 2010.

Bonilla-Silva, Eduardo. *Racism without Racists: Color-Blind Racism and the Persistence of Racial Inequality in the United States*. Lanham: Rowman and Littlefield Publishers, 2010.

Bonilla-Silva, Eduardo, Amanda Lewis, and David G. Embrick. "'I Did Not Get That Job Because of a Black Man . . .': The Story Lines and Testimonies of Color-Blind Racism." *Sociological Forum* 19, no. 4 (December 1, 2004): 555–581.

Brown, DeNeen L. "Letter Arouses Tension at Fairfax School." *Washington Post*, May 13, 1993.

———. "Two Words with a Ring of Possibility." *Washington Post*, June 4, 2008.

Brown, Sylvester. "My Longtime Oracles Weigh in with a Split Decision on Mizzou Mess." *St. Louis Post–Dispatch*, December 28, 2003.

———. "Shift Shows Why Chief's Demotion Angers Blacks." *St. Louis Post–Dispatch*, October 7, 2007.

Bruckner, D. J. R. "Ticket Mate of Cleaver Still Fighting: Peggy Terry Sees Struggle Involving Classes, Not Races." *Los Angeles Times*, February 20, 1969.

Buchanan, Patrick. ". . . Must Now Be Reversed at Polls." *Chicago Tribune*, July 5, 1979.

———. "A Proposal to Spread Handicaps." *Chicago Tribune*, March 4, 1980.

———. "When Quotas Hurt Whites." *Chicago Tribune*, December 19, 1978.

Butcher, Tim. "White Extremists Face Treason Trial in South Africa." *New York Sun*, May 19, 2003.

Calhoun, Lillian S. "Confetti." *Chicago Daily Defender*. January 25, 1965.

Calvin, Floyd J. "Calvin's Digest." *Plaindealer*. December 16, 1938.

Canby, Vincent. "Screen: 'Penitentiary': Jailhouse Blues." *New York Times*, April 4, 1980.

Carmichael, Stokely, and Charles V. Hamilton. *Black Power: The Politics of Liberation in America*. New York: Random House, 1967.

Carroll, Maurice. "Badillo Will Back Beame for Mayor at Meeting Today." *New York Times*, October 2, 1973.

Carter, Bill. "Racial Humor—Some Good, Some Bad—Current Fad of Networks." *Sun*. September 15, 1977.

Carter, Hodding. "A Case of Bilboism in Reverse." *Washington Post*, February 5, 1950.

"Challenges Robinson for 2nd Ward Post." *Chicago Daily Defender*. April 9, 1964.

"Cleeland's Vision Still Blurry after Hazing Incident." *Atlanta Journal and Constitution*, August 25, 1998.

"Cleveland Gripped by Race Rioting: Woman Is Slain; 2 Men Shot." *Chicago Tribune*. July 19, 1966.

"CNN Special Event: The N Word." CNN, July 1, 2013. http://transcripts.cnn.com/TRANSCRIPTS/1307/01/se.01.html.

Coady, Elizabeth. "Living in Harmony." *Atlanta Journal and Constitution*, May 27, 1992.

Cohen, Richard. "Reverse Racism or Common Sense?" *Washington Post*, October 7, 1994.

Comaro, Murray. "'Common Sense' or 'Common Nonsense'?" *Washington Post*, October 18, 1994.

"Cooley Teacher Shifts Blame." *Chicago Daily Defender*, October 2, 1968.

Coscarelli, Joe. "CNN Is Seriously Wondering Whether 'Cracker' Is Worse Than the N-Word." *Daily Intelligencer*, July 2, 2013. http://nymag.com/daily/intelligencer/2013/07/cnn-weighs-cracker-vs-n-word-trayvon-martin.html.

Crouch, Stanley. "Obama Could Lose a Little of His Cool." *Daily News*. October 11, 2010.

Crowley, Kieran. "Reverse-Racism School Lawsuit." *New York Post*, September 15, 2008.

Dan T. Carter. *From George Wallace to Newt Gingrich: Race in the Conservative Counterrevolution, 1963–1994*. Louisiana State University Press, 1999.

Davis, Robert. "Byrne, McMullen Hit 'Abusive' Press." *Chicago Tribune*, January 19, 1980.

DeBose, Brian. "Detroit's Plan for 'African Town' Stirs Racial Tensions." *Washington Times*, October 8, 2004.

Deggans, Eric. "A Media Mess, Its Lessons." *St. Petersburg Times*, July 25, 2010.

———. "Our Great Diversity." *St. Petersburg Times*, February 7, 2010.

———. "We Need to Talk (Before This Happens Again)." *Tampa Bay Times*, April 1, 2012.

Del Olmo, Frank. "Chicano Group Seeks Control of South Texas." *Los Angeles Times*, August 23, 1970.

"Demotions Called Reverse Racism." *Christian Science Monitor*, June 10, 1971.

Dengler, Anna. "A White Woman's View." *New York Times*, September 10, 2006.

Dewan, Shaila. "Call for Justice Sets off a Debate." *New York Times*, July 19, 2010.

Dougherty, Michael H. "ABA: Leftward Ho." *Washington Post*, January 22, 1996.

Douty, Harriet. "Clarence Mitchell, Jr.—He Still Believes." *Washington Post and Times Herald*. January 12, 1969, sec. Potomac.

Dowd, Maureen. "Black, White & Gray." *New York Times*, March 19, 2008.

———. "Down from the Pedestal." *Pittsburgh Post–Gazette*, March 20, 2008.

———. "May We Mock, Barack?" *The New York Times*, July 16, 2008.

"Dr. Nkrumah's Ominous Prescription." *Los Angeles Times*, March 9, 1961.

Duckers, John. "White and Middle Class Sir? Sorry, Get to the Back of the Queue." *Birmingham Post*, March 28, 2006.

Egan, Timothy. "Indian Boys' Exile Turns Out to Be Hoax." *New York Times*, August 31, 1994.

Fank, Leah D. "'Hair' Helps Recall Love and Anarchy of the 60's." *New York Times*, September 2, 1990.

"Fence Post." *Chicago Daily Herald*, July 24, 2010.

Ferguson, Kristin. "Articles on Countryside Don't Help." *St. Petersburg Times*, April 17, 1994.

Fields, Carmen. "Growing, Effective NAACP Still Pulse of Rights Movement." *Boston Globe*, July 6, 1975.

Filipelli, Vera. "Herzog Backs Away from 'Reverse Racism' Comment." *St. Petersburg Times*, January 14, 2002.

"Finding Help on the Streets." *New York Times*, August 30, 1995.

Fish, Stanley. "Reverse Racism or How the Pot Got to Call the Kettle Black." *Atlantic Monthly*, November 1993.

———. "When Principles Get in the Way." *New York Times*, December 26, 1996.

Fitzgerald, Ray. "Black Sports: New Magazine in Town." *Boston Globe*, March 18, 1971.

Flint, Jerry M. "Detroit's Schools Woo Negro Aides." *New York Times*, April 21, 1968.

Former Teacher [pseud.]. "Racism at Malcolm X?" *Chicago Tribune*, November 12, 1971.

Frantz, Douglas, and Thom Shanker. "Racial Charges Fly as Epton Presses Attack." *Chicago Tribune*, March 11, 1983.

Freeman, Gregory. "Crying Wolf about Racism." *St. Louis Post–Dispatch*, November 24, 1992.

General, Lloyd. "Alderman Harvey Leader of New, Changed 2nd Ward." *Chicago Defender*. February 23, 1963.

Gibbs, Emily. "Racism Close to Home." *Pittsburgh Tribune Review*, October 20, 2010.

Gibson, Colley. "Letters: Blacks in Los Angeles Series." *Los Angeles Times*, September 11, 1982.

Givhan, Robin. "Essence's Hiring of a White Fashion Director Should Be a Symbol of Inclusiveness." *Washington Post*, August 22, 2010.

Gladwell, Malcolm. "Epidemiology: Public Health Experts Turn to Economic Ills; Sociological Research Suggests Class, Not Race, May Be Key Factor in Disease Rates." *Washington Post*, November 26, 1990.

Glazer, Nathan. "Leaning over Backwards: 'Reverse Racism.'" *New York Times*, March 12, 1972.
Golding, Bruce. "Second Try at Race Suit." *New York Post*, September 9, 2009.
Goldman, Ivan G. "Black Pupils Held Harassing Whites." *Washington Post*, November 17, 1972.
Goodwin, Michele Bratcher. "Reflections on Race." *Christian Science Monitor*, July 30, 2009.
Gosier, Elijah. "Maybe Racism Is Shortening All Our Lives." *St. Petersburg Times*, July 17, 1996.
Gosse, Van. *Rethinking the New Left: An Interpretative History.* 1st ed. Palgrave Macmillan, 2005.
Green, Mark J. "Letters to the Editor: Preferential Treatment." *New York Times*, April 4, 1969.
Green, Ronald M. "Reverse Racism." *New York Times*, August 16, 1983.
Greenhouse, Steven. "America's Productivity Climbs, but Wages Stagnate." *New York Times*, January 12, 2013, sec. Sunday Review. http://www.nytimes.com/2013/01/13/sunday-review/americas-productivity-climbs-but-wages-stagnate.html.
"Guard to Double Black Recruiting." *New York Times*, October 28, 1971.
Haga, Chuck. "A Long Year at Red Lake." *Star Tribune*, March 14, 2006.
Hager, Philip. "Reverse Racism: Does It Exist?" *Los Angeles Times*. February 5, 1973, sec. Part I.
Hager, Philip, and Los Angeles Times. "Suit Threatens Law Schools' Minority Admissions Plans." *Washington Post and Times Herald*. February 18, 1973, sec. NATIONAL News.
Haggerty, Sandra. "Special Consideration?" *Los Angeles Times*, October 21, 1974.
Hall, Christine B. "Needed: A Black State's Attorney." *Sun*. September 10, 1978.
Hammer, Robert. "Using Term 'Reverse Racism' Ignores Implications of Real Racism." *Salt Lake Tribune*, May 4, 2010.
Hand, George. "Role of Press in Inner-City Problems." *Boston Globe*, July 30, 1976.
Harbonski, Fred C. "Promoting Firemen." *Chicago Tribune*, March 2, 1978.
"Harvard Pickets Allege Bias—And Are Accused of It Themselves." *Sun*. January 6, 1983.
Herbeck, Dan. "$150,000 Awarded in Racial Suit: Black Boss Accused of Using Racist Slurs." *Buffalo News*, August 23, 2007.
Herbert, Ross. "Wildlife Poaching Rises amid Zimbabwe Chaos." *Washington Times*, September 9, 2000.
Herrity, John F. "Letters to the Editor: 'Reverse Racism' in Hiring Practices." *Washington Post*, December 14, 1974.
Hinson, Hal. "Spike Lee's Thin Skin Flick." *Washington Post*, June 7, 1991.

"Hiring Bill Called 'Reverse Racism.'" *New York Times*, February 4, 1972.
Hoagland, Jim. "Transition Pitfalls." *Washington Post*, November 29, 1988.
Hogan, Amy. "Acceptable Bias?" *Washington Post*, May 14, 2005.
Hollander, Daniel. "Black and White in Kenwood." *Chicago Tribune*, June 23, 1984.
Hollingsworth, Barbara. "Divide Colors School Board." *Topeka Capital-Journal*, April 19, 2008.
Horton, Lawanda R. "Letters: Obama Held to a Higher Standard." *Philadelphia Daily News*, February 15, 2010.
"House Members Blast Dr. King's 'Disobedience' Bid." *Chicago Daily Defender.* August 17, 1967.
Houston, Paul, and Kenneth Reich. "Cranston Irate over Junking of Judge Panel by Hayakawa." *Los Angeles Times*, January 17, 1981.
———. "Hayakawa Disbands Judicial Commission." *Los Angeles Times*, January 17, 1981.
Howe, Desson. "'Cry Freedom': Untimely Death." *Washington Post*, November 6, 1987.
Hummel, Rick. "Baker Reiterates His Controversial Comments." *St. Louis Post–Dispatch*, July 13, 2003.
Hurt, Charles. "Supremes Nix 'Soto' Ruling: Reverse-Racism Reversal." *New York Post*, June 30, 2009.
Hurwitt, Sam. "Theater Review: A Tense Ride-Along to Perdition in 'Steady Rain.'" *Marin Independent Journal*, February 9, 2012.
Ifill, Gwen. "The 1992 Campaign: Political Memo; Clinton Deftly Navigates Shoals of Racial Issues." *New York Times*, June 17, 1992.
"In the South: Main Emphasis Is Shifted from Demonstrations to Political Activity." *New York Times*, October 20, 1963.
"Jackie Robinson Favors Lefkowitz over Dudley." *New York Times*. October 18, 1962.
"Jackie Robinson Tells Why He Favors Nixon: Former Baseball Player Says He Likes Republican for Stand on Civil Rights." *Los Angeles Times*. October 11, 1960.
Jackson, Judy. "Bias Claimed in Public Art Project." *Boston Globe*, August 17, 1975.
"Jackson Perturbed By Rodino." *New York Times*, August 9, 1987.
Janich, Kathy. "Alliance Plays for 2000–2001 Season." *Atlanta Journal and Constitution*, April 4, 2000.
Jarrett, Vernon. "Black Medicine Facing Hurdles." *Chicago Tribune*, August 2, 1974.
———. "The Tax Revolt: Let Fit Survive." *Chicago Tribune*, June 18, 1978.
"Javits Bids Negroes Shun 'Black Power.'" *New York Times*. September 27, 1966.
"Javits Urges Negro Calm: Appeals for Repudiation of Militance, 'Demagoguery.'" *Sun*. September 27, 1966.

Jensen, Kris. "Newsstand Time Tackles Lessons in Reverse Racism." *Atlanta Journal and Constitution*, March 29, 1994.

Jhally, Sut, and Justin Lewis. *Enlightened Racism: The Cosby Show, Audiences, and the Myth of the American Dream*. Boulder: Westview Press, 1992.

Johnson, Alfred. "Reverse Racism." *Washington Times*, October 28, 2008.

Johnson, Thomas A. "5-Day March in Georgia Ends with Massive Rally." *New York Times*. May 24, 1970.

Jones, Arthur. "Revival of Boston Soul Patrol Sought." *Boston Globe*, December 29, 1976.

"Judge's Fete Cuts out Widow." *New York Post*, June 17, 2005.

Kalson, Sally. "Mixed Messages: A Good Week for the President Is Undercut by One of His Own." *Pittsburgh Post–Gazette*, July 25, 2010.

Kart, Larry. "Coarseness Takes Gold out of 2d 'Rainbow.'" *Chicago Tribune*, October 5, 1978.

Katz, Judy H. *White Awareness*, 1978.

Kelly, Kevin. "'Show Boat' Lost with All Hands." *Boston Globe*, December 5, 1980.

Kennedy, Helen. "Boss' 'Cracker' Crack Costs Him 150G." *Daily News*. August 24, 2007.

Kennedy, Joseph C. "The American Negro's Key Role in Africa: One Who Spent a Year There Reports on Some of the Special Associations He Discovered and Assays Their Potential." *New York Times*. February 4, 1962, sec. *New York Times Magazine*.

King, Brian. "Letters: So, JFK Should've Done More for the Irish?" *The Philadelphia Daily News*, June 2, 2011.

Kirsch, Robert R. "The Book Report: Writers Focus on Nat Turner." *Los Angeles Times*, September 26, 1968.

Krueger, Curtis. "NAACP Working for Equality, State Chief Says." *St. Petersburg Times*, December 21, 1995.

Lamis, Alexander P. *Southern Politics in the 1990s*. Baton Rouge: Louisiana State University Press, 1999.

Lapartin, Richard. "Reverse Racism?" *Chicago Tribune*, February 9, 1978.

LaVelle, Mike. "Blue-Collar Views: Busing Advocates Running Out of Gas." *Chicago Tribune*, December 20, 1973.

Ledbetter, Les. "Serpent of Reverse-Racism Case Bites Academic Eden." *Chicago Tribune*, October 16, 1977.

Lefever, Ernest. "Reverse Racism and White 'Guilt.'" *Washington Times*, May 12, 2002.

Lembke, Daryl. "Panthers Seek White Coalition to Gain Power." *Los Angeles Times*, July 22, 1969.

Lempert, Richard O., David L. Chambers, and Terry K. Adams. "Michigan's Minority Graduates in Practice: The River Runs through Law School." *Law & Social Inquiry* 25, no. 2 (April 1, 2000): 395–505.

"Let a Thousand Blums Bloom." *New York Post*, July 12, 1998.

Lewis, Anthony. "Abroad at Home; Black and White." *New York Times*, June 18, 1992, sec. Opinion.

Lingeman, Richard. "He Likes It Here, Mostly." *New York Times*, July 19, 1987.

Lipton, Eric. "400 Activists Protest outside Justice's Home; Clarence Thomas's Record on Civil Rights Denounced." *Washington Post*, September 13, 1995.

Littwin, Mike. "Morning Brew: It's the Birthers vs. The Blurters." *Denver Post*, July 28, 2010.

———. "MorningBrew Tancredo Barks up the Wrong Tree." *Denver Post*, May 29, 2009.

Lucadamo, Kathleen. "Race Card Tossed in AG Battle." *Daily News*. September 25, 2010.

Lyons, Richard L. "Rights Bill Is Delayed by House Southerners." *Washington Post*, August 16, 1967.

"Mag Moguls Freak over Fuhrman." *New York Post*, February 25, 1998.

Marler, Regina. "Clive James' 20th-Century Tutorial." *New York Observer*, March 19, 2007.

Martin, Louis. "Baraka Takes Sharp Turn to the Left." *Chicago Defender*, January 4, 1975.

Martinez, Michael L. "Court Case Stirs Debate on Affirmative Action." *USA Today*, October 11, 2012.

McClory, Robert. "Exorcist Swats Superfly." *Chicago Defender*, March 9, 1974.

McCurdy, Jack. "Trustees Reject Charge of Racism at S.F. State," September 22, 1967.

Means, Sean P. "Group Mobilizes to Fight Ban on Affirmative Action." *Salt Lake Tribune*, February 27, 2010.

Melone, Mary Jo. "A Little Sensitivity Wouldn't Have Hurt." *St. Petersburg Times*, February 29, 1992.

Meyer, Eugene L. "District Accused of Black Racism: Mayor and Dugas Are Targets." *Washington Post*, July 11, 1971.

Mfuasi, Len. "Letters: The Story of Racism Has Always Been about Whites." *Philadelphia Inquirer*, August 23, 2009.

Milbank, Dana. "Latina Woman, Tongue-Tied Man." *Washington Post*, May 28, 2009.

Miles, Robert, and Malcolm Brown. *Racism: Second Edition*. Key Ideas. London; New York: Routledge, 2004.

Milloy, Courtland. "Twisting Words in an Effort to Rewrite History." *Washington Post*, June 29, 2003.

Murlin, John F. "Did History Begin in the 1960s?" *Atlanta Journal and Constitution*, June 9, 1992.

Murray, Jim. "A Stump Grows Up." *Los Angeles Times*, March 2, 1972.

"Myths of Special Treatment for Black Students Fan Racial Fires." *New York Times*, March 26, 1993.

Naqvi, Shahid, and Nastasia Malatesta. "Expulsion Rate Prompts Calls for Black Schools." *Birmingham Post*, June 30, 2006.

Nation, Nancy Isles. "Appeals Court Says Novato Educators Violated Student's Rights." *Marin Independent Journal*, May 22, 2007.

———. "Court Rules Novato Schools Violated Student's Rights." *Marin Independent Journal*, May 23, 2007.

———. "Former Novato Student Wins Free-Speech Fight with School." *Marin Independent Journal*, September 13, 2007.

———. "Former Novato Student Wins Suit over Free Speech." *Marin Independent Journal*, February 20, 2008.

Newcomb, Horace M. "'Thicker Than Water' Offensive to Everyone." *Sun*. August 2, 1973.

"Newer Negro Marines Are Looking for Identity with Blackness." *New York Times*, December 21, 1969.

Norton, Michael I., and Samuel R. Sommers. "Whites See Racism as a Zero-Sum Game That They Are Now Losing." *Perspectives on Psychological Science* 6, no. 3 (May 1, 2011): 215–218. doi:10.1177/1745691611406922.

O'Keefe, Michael. "Gumbel-Gate's Nothing but a GOP Out." *Daily News*. February 26, 2006.

Odell, Malcolm. "The Real Reason to Back Mr. Obama." *Washington Post*, October 7, 2012.

"On Message: Pity the White Male." *New York Observer*, July 15, 2009.

Ordonez, Jennifer. "Police Role Probed in Burning Death." *Washington Post*, November 4, 1995.

Ordovensky, Pat. "SAT Under Assault as Admissions Tool." *USA TODAY*, September 11, 1989.

"Oregon's Harrington Injures His Right Knee." *St. Petersburg Times*, January 13, 2002.

Overbea, Louix. "De Mau Maus Try to Improve Their Image." *Christian Science Monitor*, December 9, 1972.

"Oyez! Oyez!" *New York Times*, October 7, 2002.

Page, Clarence. "How to Keep Hate Alive." *Buffalo News*, March 29, 2010.

Payne, Ethel L. "NAACP Head Warns Blacks to Reject Reverse Racism." *Chicago Daily Defender*. August 16, 1969.

Perlmutter, Nathan. "No Reverse Racism." *New York Times*, January 9, 1982.

Pershing, John J. "Letters to the Editor: Racism and Standards." *Washington Post*, December 19, 1974.

Peyser, Andrea. "Amen to the Gutsy Dolan—Now Fight Back vs. the Other Lib Bigots." *New York Post*, November 5, 2009.

———. "Ferrer Crying Racism Is Disgrace-Ism." *New York Post*, October 11, 2001.

———. "Good-Guy Knick Hero Linfectious." *New York Post*, February 20, 2012.

Pinksy, Mark I. "Centerpiece: The Embattled William Bennett." *Boston Globe*, December 11, 1981.

"Plan for New City Council Passes in Praise and Anger." *New York Times*, June 4, 1991.

"Policeman Claims He's Scapegoat in Slaying." *Chicago Tribune*, August 17, 1982.

"Pressure Is on Black Psychologists." *Chicago Daily Defender*, January 3, 1973.

Price, Joyce Howard. "Racism Considered Key in Shooting of 5 Whites." *Washington Times*, March 3, 2000.

Quindlan, Anna. "In the Racial Debate, Clinton Gave Us Heat Instead of Light." *St. Petersburg Times*, June 30, 1992.

R.K. "'Reverse Racism.'" *Chicago Tribune*, June 16, 1973.

"Racial Elections?" *Chicago Tribune*, March 14, 1972.

"Racial Expectations." *Richmond Times Dispatch*, June 1, 2011.

Raspberry, William. "Jackson: One Race Too Many . . ." *Washington Post*, July 13, 1988.

———. "They're Trying to Stop Jackson." *Washington Post*, April 8, 1988.

"Reverse Racism Keeps USA from Being Free." *USA Today*, September 7, 1989.

Roberts, Gene. "Dr. King Declares Rights Movement Is 'Close' to a Split: Dr. King Fears Split in Rights Groups." *New York Times*. July 9, 1966.

Roberts, Jeffery. "Truth, Sex and Advertising." *New York Times*, May 29, 1994.

Robinson, Jackie. "N.Y. Demo Choice Poses Race Queries." *Chicago Defender*. October 20, 1962.

Roundtree, Mildred W. "Letters to the Editor: 'Reverse Racism.'" *Washington Post*, August 10, 1974.

Roush, Matt. "'Blood Ties': Vampy Vampires." *USA Today*, May 24, 1991.

Rowan, Carl L. "Identifying the Real Underdog." *Los Angeles Times*, November 12, 1965.

Saraceno, Jon. "TV Ad Overload Buries Football." *USA Today*, January 15, 2002.

Sarris, Andrew. "Inside Man's Not So Lousy; Plus: Spike and Me on TV." *New York Observer*, April 10, 2006.

"Saturday Night Live." *Richard Pryor/Gil Scott-Heron*. NBC, December 13, 1975.

Schapiro, Jeff E. "A Mistake for Webb, or Strategy?" *Richmond Times Dispatch*, July 25, 2010.

Schwartz, Harry. "Resentment Complicates the Case: Sickle Cell." *New York Times*, November 5, 1972.
"Screen: A Fatal Flavor." *New York Times*, June 27, 1974.
Seghers, Frances. "Milloy's Reverse Racism." *Washington Post*, February 11, 1989.
Seper, Jerry. "Civil Rights Panel Faults Justice on Panthers: Report Questions Racial Neutrality." *Washington Times*, December 7, 2010.
Shankar, Rekha. "Your Essay." *Philadelphia Inquirer*, October 1, 2006.
Shapiro, Thomas, Tatjana Meschede, and Sam Osoro. "The Roots of the Widening Racial Wealth Gap: Explaining the Black-White Economic Divide." Institute on Assets and Social Policy, February 2013. http://iasp.brandeis.edu/pdfs/Author/shapiro-thomas-m/racialwealthgapbrief.pdf.
Sharkey, Patrick. *Stuck in Place: Urban Neighborhoods and the End of Progress Toward Racial Equality*. Chicago: University of Chicago Press, 2013.
Shaw, David. "Two Views of a Champion; Ali: Now a Socio-Political Symbol." *Los Angeles Times*, December 7, 1975.
"Shipley Racism Allusion Criticized by Burling." *Washington Post*, September 23, 1964.
Sisk, Richard. "She's Always Tried to Help the Poor, Celeb Pal Sez." *Daily News*. July 23, 2010.
Smith, J. Y. "Kwame Ture, Civil Rights Activist, Dies at Age 57." *Washington Post*, November 16, 1998.
Sparks, Joseph W. "From Our Readers: Excellence Only." *Chicago Defender*, August 31, 1974.
Sperer, Jerry. "GOP Lawmaker Acts to Shield Whistleblower." *Washington Times*, September 27, 2010.
Stelter, Brian. "When Race Is the Issue, Misleading Coverage Sets Off an Uproar." *New York Times*, July 26, 2010.
Stewart, Sally Ann. "'Raw Nerves': City Remains on Edge." *USA Today*, October 21, 1993.
Stingley, Jim. "Reverse Racism: Bahamas' New Rulers Caught in Own Web." *Los Angeles Times*, February 15, 1971.
"Strife on Two Civil Rights Fronts: SNCC Is Scored by King Group." *Chicago Daily Defender*, April 25, 1966.
Strong, James. "Union Curbs Are Urged by Chamber Head." *Chicago Tribune*, October 31, 1969.
Strout, Richard L. "Detroit Sifts through Riot Embers for Racial Lessons." *Christian Science Monitor*, September 11, 1967.
"The DeFunis Ruling." *Washington Post*, April 26, 1974.
"The 'Ethical Schizophrenia' of Mayor Barry." *The Washington Post*, January 17, 1989.

"The State: 'Reverse Racism' Charged in S.F. Demotions." *Los Angeles Times*, March 11, 1971.

Thompson, Jean. "My Turn: Reverse Racism Is a Con." *Taos News*, May 17, 2007.

Thompson, Krissah. "Sherrod Accepts Role She Never Wanted." *Washington Post*, June 16, 2011.

"Time for New Direction for Bias Debate." *Chicago Daily Herald*, June 6, 2011.

Tolchin, Martin. "Rage Permeates All Facets of Life in the South Bronx." *New York Times*, January 17, 1973.

Trombley, William. "The New, Black Harvard Man: Militant . . . Shuns 'Whitey's World.'" *Boston Globe*, December 17, 1968.

Trumbull, Robert. "That the Twain May Meet." *New York Times*, November 9, 1958.

Tucker, Cynthia. "Former Mayor Lines Pockets, Hurts Legacy." *Atlanta Journal–Constitution*, March 10, 2002.

———. "Post-Apartheid South Africa Needs Economic Justice." *Atlanta Journal and Constitution*, June 26, 1991.

Tucker, Neely. "A Contest in Step with the Times, Or One That Went a Step Too Far?" *Washington Post*, March 4, 2010.

Turner, Wallace. "4 Say Wrong SLA Members Were Convicted in Killing." *New York Times*, April 4, 1976.

Tyler, Richard. "Martinez Slanted on Magic Mountain." *Los Angeles Times*, April 29, 1988.

Vecsey, Peter. "Bird Shouldn't Have Bit; Playing Race Card Gray Matter." *New York Post*, June 11, 2004.

Virshup, Amy. "Newly Released." *New York Times*, June 19, 2008.

Von Hoffman, Nicholas. "Times Readers Need A New Decoder Ring." *New York Observer*, June 16, 2003.

W. E. B. Du Bois. *The Philadelphia Negro: A Social Study*. Schocken Books, 1899.

Walkowski, Paul J. "The Very Same . . ." *Boston Globe*, February 4, 1975.

Walters, Ronald. "Black Racism Is as Odious as Any Other." *Los Angeles Times*, July 12, 1985.

Watson, James H. "Reverse Racism?" *Chicago Tribune*, March 30, 1972.

Weisenthal, Joe. "This Is What the Economy Did the Last Time a President Didn't Win Re-Election." *Business Insider*, July 8, 2012. http://www.businessinsider.com/the-economy-under-george-hw-bush-2012-7.

White, Robert L. "'The Politics of Race.'" *Washington Post*, March 4, 1983.

White, William S. "Opposition to Coleman as U.S. Judge Called Ugly, Frightening." *Los Angeles Times*, July 6, 1965.

Whiteley, Paul L. "Do Breitbarts of the World Want Racial Harmony?" *USA Today*, July 27, 2010.

Whiteside, Larry. "To a Generation, Joe Meant Pride." *Boston Globe*, April 15, 1981.

Wicker, Tom. "No Retreat Needed." *New York Times*, January 14, 1975.

Wilkins, Roy. "Nothing Excuses Murder." *Los Angeles Times*, October 23, 1973.

Williams, Armstrong. "Affirmative Action's Slippery Slope." *Washington Times*, April 7, 2001.

———. "Blaming It on Race." *Washington Times*, September 17, 1999.

Wiltz, Teresa. "A Part Colored by History: Choice of White Actress for Mixed-Race Role Stirs Debate on Insensitivity." *Washington Post*, June 23, 2007.

Wineburg, Sam. "Historical Thinking and Other Unnatural Acts." *Phi Delta Kappan* 80, no. 7 (March 1, 1999): 488–499.

Winfield, Paul. "Equity Was Right the First Time." *New York Times*, August 18, 1990.

Wolf, Rabbi Arnold Jacob. "A Black Mayor." *Chicago Tribune*, February 27, 1989.

Wood, Daniel B. "'Machete' Has Immigration Subtheme. How Will It Play in Arizona?" *Christian Science Monitor*, September 4, 2010.

Wright, Katie. "Letters: One Reader's View; There's No Level Playing Field in Life." *Philadelphia Inquirer*, March 6, 2008.

X, Malcolm. *By Any Means Necessary: Speeches, Interviews, and a Letter*. New York: Pathfinder Press, 1992.

Young, A. S. Doc. "Good Morning, Sports!: More About Ali's Game . . ." *Chicago Defender*, September 30, 1975.

———. "Good Morning, Sports!: Winning and Racism . . ." *Chicago Defender*, May 16, 1974.

Young, Whitney. "To Be Equal: Myth of Black Anti-Semitism." *Chicago Daily Defender*. September 28, 1968, sec. The Daily Defender's World of Features.

"Yugoslavia Accepts Individuals-Only Plan." *St. Petersburg Times*, July 23, 1992.

Zamudio, Margaret M., and Francisco Rios. "From Traditional to Liberal Racism: Living Racism in the Everyday." *Sociological Perspectives* 49, no. 4 (December 1, 2006): 483–501.

Zelleke, Andy, and Phil Wang. "The Rhetoric of Racism Is Unfair to All US Citizens, Poisoning the Atmosphere for Democratic Debate." *Christian Science Monitor*, February 29, 1996.

2

"The Struggle Is Real out Here"

The Contextual Reality of Being Black Couples and Families in America

Karlin J. Tichenor

Introduction

During my childhood and adolescence, in the room of my parents, on my mother's office desk and nightstand rested a small, seemingly insignificant plaque with words written in cursive writing. The plaque was difficult to read from a distance. The only decipherable word was the concluding word, which read *Amen* in clear letters. As I approached the desk with youthful curiosity, the words became increasingly legible. The plaque read:

> God, give me the grace to accept with serenity the things that cannot be changed. Courage to change the things which should be changed, and the wisdom to distinguish the one from the other [to know the difference]. Living one day at a time. Enjoying one moment at a time. Accepting hardship as a pathway to peace. Taking, as Jesus did, this sinful world as it is, not as I would have it. Trusting that You will make all things right, if I surrender to Your will. So that I may be reasonably happy in this life and supremely happy with You in the next. Amen.

As a child, I often wondered about the meaning of such a text written so eloquently. I understood the term *grace* clearly, but was not too sure about the rest. What I did know, however, was that my parents often looked to this plaque as a daily reminder of the reality of the world from two specific perspectives—spirituality and Blackness. As I began my research trajectory in learning more about Black couples and families, I learned the significance of this text I read years ago very soon into my work. The text was as relevant in my youth to Blacks as it was during the enslavement of Black people and remains relevant to date. Still, it continues to be an important reminder of the present reality of being Black in America, and more specifically low-income Black—and of the need for acceptance, serenity, courage, and wisdom to endure surrounding impediments that linger outside of understanding. Through strong spirituality and connection to cultural history, Black people, in particular low-income Blacks, strive to survive the present reality before them, quite similarly to their ancestors.

There continues to be a dearth of knowledge on the complexities within romantic relationship development and the emotional processing of Black heterosexual couples, particularly the process of internal struggle and the potential illustration of this through relationship interactions, despite the perpetrated historical effects of slavery and current systemic inequities on low-income Black people and their relationships.[1] Contemporary research generalizes relationship development as similar across all couples regardless of ethnicity and race, assuming a more biological framework for development and ignoring the historically significant occurrences of slavery and other forms of racialization.[2] Likewise, current research depicts whites as the microcosm for relationship interactions, maintenance and survival. Although some parallels can be made between groups and within groups, group difference must be better accounted for through research studies.[3]

Empirical research shows a difficulty in transcending infancy attachment styles into adulthood for Black individuals in comparison to their white counterparts, illustrated in the differences between whites and Blacks on marital expectations and engagement in romantic relationships through dating during adolescence.[4] In a number of studies, white adolescents demonstrate a more pronounced predisposition to long-term romantic relationships than their counterparts, marrying earlier than Blacks. Studies also find Black adolescents are less inclined to develop romantic relationships, thus having a diminished number of prospects for long-term relationships (marriage) during adulthood. Causation of this divergence remains unclear. While this could paint a representation of perceived superiority for whites in comparison to Blacks in relationship functioning (researchers dispel this notion), [5] I draw particular attention to the findings indicating hindrances with relationship development for Black adolescents and the contributing variables outside of individual factors. Thus, it should most assuredly be noted that historical experiences and historical traumas do undermine and complicate the *simplicity* of romantic relationship development and maintenance for Blacks, both in adolescence and in adulthood; adding further confusion to an already difficult and complex process (coupling), and has direct implications for the development of Black families.[6]

Marriage in the Black Community

Currently, only 43.9 percent of adult Blacks are either married or in a coupled family. Of that percentage, 32 percent were married in 2010 and 46.8 percent were never married. Additionally, 10.9 percent of the Black population was divorced, and 4.1 percent were separated. These statistics equate to roughly 61 percent of the population as living nonmarried lives. Forty years prior, this same statistic was well over 60 percent in the other direction. Additionally, the 2010 Census found that the number of married households in the white community versus the Black community was 51 versus 28 percent, respectively. This drop in long-term, committed relationships illustrates a change in family life. This is not to say family life does not exist. However, the traditional makeup of families has transformed and adapted, thereby changing family roles and individual expectations of members within the family.[7]

It appears the idea of family for members of the Black community has drastically changed into a more fluid concept where roles are complex and dynamic. Marriage, a concept that was profoundly regarded as ideal for members of Black communities prior to and during enslavement (explicitly practiced in spite of the possibility of harm and intentional stripping of these cultural practices) has become *optional* and oftentimes, not a choice at all for contemporary low-income Blacks. Instead, research posits a growing tendency toward cohabitation and an increase in the age when individuals decide to marry (late 20s to early 30s), if at all.[8] Families, are becoming less and less cohesive and predictable—with the presence of both mother and father in the home; creating more flexible roles and fluid family expectations. If true, this reality would be more devastating for Blacks than for any other racial group, as statistics show a significant disparity for Blacks in comparison to their white counterparts in every statistically significant area measuring quality of life. The loss of family structure and consistency only confounds the preexisting hindrances.

Low-income Black families inequitably suffer from high rates of incarceration, death, crime, and school dropout. In 2008, the Department of Justice reported prison rate statistics for the overall population and provided a break down based on racial differences. In 2008, 2.3 million or 1 in every 131 U.S. residents was incarcerated. Among those inmates in custody, Black males were incarcerated at 6.6 times the rate of white males. One in every 21 Black males was incarcerated, compared to one in every 138 white males. This same disparity holds true for Black females. Black females were found to be over 3.5 times more likely to be or have been incarcerated than white females, and two times more likely than Hispanic females.[9] In 2010, the U.S. Department of Health and Human Services, after age-adjusting death rates per 100,000, found the number was 741.8 for whites, compared to 898.2 for Blacks and the average risk of death for the Black population was 21.1 percent higher than for the white population.[10] Statistical research in education finds similar disparities. According to a 2010 article written in the *New York Times*, the educational gap between Blacks continues to widen in comparison to white males, Latinos, and even low-income white males. Particularly, Black males are on the low end of the spectrum regarding academic achievement.[11]

For low-income Blacks, long-term relationships (i.e., marriage) are complicated by such social inequalities in the justice, health, and educational systems. In a nationally representative sample of low-income Black and white couples in their first marriage, being Black and less educated were significant longitudinal predictors of divorce after controlling for marital self-report variables, such as frequency of conflict and affectively affirming behaviors.[12] The implications of such stark inequitable realities for low-income and relatively low-educated Black couples and their prospects for marriage are significant considering already limited access to resources and constrained prospects for upward mobility.

The reasons for these statistical disparities continue to be investigated by researchers to ascertain causes and solutions for these extreme differences. Yet, one of the major concerns for these statistics is how they affect the development of long-term committed relationships for low-income Blacks, as strong commitment between parents is the foundation for family life and predictability for children. Without such commitments, Black families face potential dismantlement and incongruence in family togetherness and cohesion.

Various findings hypothesize reasons for the disparity between the marriage rates of white families in comparison to low-income Black families. Many scholars have posited theories and considerations to reduce the social difference. Some scholars have taken the perspective of blaming—placing blame on the Black mother, access to education, and cultural practices.[13] I argue this is not a case of individual differences, cultural superiority of whites, or a shift in values for Blacks, but rather a systemic impediment of historical and social factors interwoven into the fabric of this country that disrupts Black peoples' ability, in particular low-income Black couples, to establish cohesion and togetherness in the form of marital relationships, thereby influencing family development.

To understand the contributing factors for the circumstances of many low-income Black families, we must move beyond the interpersonal challenges *or* a *brief* acknowledgment of the social disparity, as if to note the unfortunate nature instead of systematically responding. As a culture, the United States and its policies must move toward a more critical view of the insidiously pervasive, systemic inequality embedded at the core of America; investigating the community and family factors that contribute to the obstacles low-income Black families face, the challenges these families endure to thrive in America, and the process of negotiating an existence in the dominant culture through resiliency.[14] Indeed, we must also interrogate the perpetual system that governs this community.

History of Black Families and Marriages in the United States

Research shows the dynamics of *being* American have an historical component that cannot be ignored for Blacks.[15] In the United States, Black couples and families face a culture that identifies Americanism as equivalent to being white, creating a standard that Blacks are genetically incapable of achieving.[16] "White Americans, who enjoy more power and higher status than other ethnic groups are seen as owning the nation, whereas ethnic minorities sit at the margin of American society."[17] To be American is, indeed, to be white, and minorities, Blacks particularly, are viewed as not *as American* as whites.[18] Therefore, low-income Black couples and families are devoid of the resources that whites are afforded by the privilege of being American (i.e., white). Blacks are lower on the social hierarchy and thus, lack the same privileges.[19]

Black couples and families have faced remarkable pressure within the American culture to strip their own practices and to submit to the dominant culture perceived to be more beneficial and more civilized.[20] Historically, through enslavement, the internal belief that to be American was to completely assimilate to the practices and beliefs of white Americans was systematically embedded into the psyche of Black individuals and families as a byproduct of being dehumanized.[21] This oppression consequently led to the loss of cultural beliefs from countries of origin through the imposition of American ideological beliefs that were not only intrusive, but in many ways contrary to existing cultural ideologies.[22] Black men were treated as commodities and Black women were treated as reproductive chattel. Fathers of slave children were sold and mothers continually and forcibly impregnated, and oftentimes raped, to produce offspring who would become productive workers in the slave plantations. This was also done to destroy the culture and will of this population systematically. Enslavement not only stripped away belief systems and cultural practices, but also produced internalized hatred and self-loathing.

As a form of resilience, for subsequent years Black families made efforts to circumvent inequality through such historical social moments as the Civil War (1861–65), the Harlem Renaissance (between 1918 and 1937), the Civil Rights Movement and the emergence of the Black Panther Party and Black nationalism (between 1954 and1968), and the Million Man March (1995). Much of these efforts have produced significant changes—opening doors that had been long-before closed for ethnic minorities.[23] Although resource allocation has minimally shifted to benefit this population to some degree, Black families, especially low-income ones, continue to face social inequality and resource depletion transgressed overtly and covertly through structural racism, inequity in education, prejudice, disenfranchisement, and disproportionality in access to resource and opportunity.[24]

Impact of Slavery

Slavery was the initial factor that sabotaged Black coupling, marriages, and the development of strong families. During slavery, Black men and women were forbidden to marry by law in some states and other states prevented the right to do so. Any beliefs about emotional bonds were challenged and undermined by the overarching belief that Blacks were inferior to whites. This was prescribed through ongoing messages regarding Black males as hypersexual and incapable of commitment, while the sale of slaves kept men and women separate, thereby disrupting relationships.[25] Many of the cultural practices that were deemed appropriate for this demographic were confronted by the status quo of Americanization. What was once practiced and understood by Africans became clouded by the societal expectations of relationship functioning, couched in the form of mandates during enslavement. These historical incidents worked together to disrupt the formation of Black families, while also negatively impacting the generational interactions between and within genders.

In addition to the historical trauma experienced and negotiated by this ethnic group, societal standards imposed a patriarchal belief-system regarding the *proper* structure of the family, arbitrarily establishing men above women on the social hierarchy. In the case of

Blacks, African men mimicked the familial hierarchy of white families, identifying men as superordinate to their Black female counterparts, contrasting that of the cultural egalitarian approach to relationships historically. This contrast fundamentally confused the culturally founded roles previously established, influencing the past and present coupling relationships of Blacks. Consequently, confusion of responsibilities, relationship expectations, and communication styles were confounded by Eurocentric relationship behaviors pervasively established as ideal. These adjustments to the family system, coupled with social inequities, systematically disrupted the long-term health of Black families.[26]

With the historical process of forced assimilation, we find Black families continuing to adapt to historical experiences with resiliency. However still, racial inequity and inequality plague this community, manifesting in structural policies in the criminal justice, education, and health systems (directly influencing coupling and family cohesion) and the absence of systemic accountability. Historically traumatic experiences coupled with contemporary marginalization, creates overwhelming barriers to the development of healthy couples and families for low-income Black people.

Systemic Postracialism: Ignoring through Color Blindness

In *Mis-education of the Negro*, Carter G. Woodson states,

> To handicap a student by teaching him that his Black face is a curse and that his struggle to change his condition is hopeless is the worst sort of lynching. It kills one's aspirations and dooms him to vagabondage and crime. It is strange, then, that the friends of truth and the promoters of freedom have not risen up against the present propaganda . . . and crushed it.[27]

Woodson makes this statement in reference to the structure of education and the standardized teaching pedagogy informing Black people. His statement describes a masked deception, disguised as purposive instruction, meant to build the minds of learners regardless of skin color, culture, or ethnicity. Yet, this same pedagogy that promises intellectual stimulation is a quiet lullaby that conditions Blacks to feel inferior.

Today, it seems a new lullaby emerges, buzzing across the podiums and chalkboards of this country. There is a wave of propaganda asserting a cultural shift away from historical marginalization and the prejudicial separation of minority groups by racism, toward a postracial, cosmopolitan society where individuals from diverse backgrounds (ethnic, racial, religious, and political) have equal access to the idealized American Dream. The concept driving this movement, *postracialism*, otherwise described by Black sociologists as color blindness, hinges on a notion of equity and equality racial inclusion and equal opportunity promotion. This idea rests on the premise that racism and prejudice are historical facts no longer practiced. Though there has been a change in the interpersonal expression of racism perpetrated by whites toward ethnic minority groups, racism has not yet dissipated. Instead, prejudice and racism have been ingrained into the very fabric of this country, manifested systemically and illustrated by existing social disparities, with low-income Blacks disproportionately at the margins of societal disenfranchisement.

A present stark reality for many low-income Black couples and families is they exist in environments that perpetuate a cycle which continues to limit the upward mobility of these families, while posing a postracial ideology. A lack of resources provided to these communities and systemic inequities enable this cycle. Restricted access to quality education and good jobs, and a perpetual low-income and high-poverty existence, and overaccess to unfavorable liabilities, including crime, drugs, and mortality are noteworthy causes of this racial imbalance.[28] Consequently, Black low-income families are highest among the unemployed, uneducated, and impoverished ethnic populations in the United States today.

The concept of postracialism in the United States chooses to ignore these realities by noting the progress made in contrast to a racial and ethnic inequality since enslavement, while discounting the ever-present conditions still in existence. These conditions are markedly distinguishable from historical conditions for Blacks, yet very similar in nature—stemming from a designation of ethnic inferiority as compared to whites.

Social Factors Effecting Marriage and Long-Term Commitment

Male-Female Relationships

In extant literature on this population, Black theorists have referenced the history of enslavement as the beginning of disconnection between Black men and women with regard to romantic relationship development and sustainability. Socioeconomic status further confounds the problem and increases interpersonal conflict.[29] Many of these issues add additional strain to historically oppressed male to female relationships. Black marriages represent one of the highest divorce rates in America. Researchers attribute this to the interrelationship between men and women. For instance, stereotypes of men play a major role in this negative interaction. Men have a response to being treated as invisible by society and women have a response to the expectation that they are responsible for compensating for these social injuries incurred by Black men. Additionally, social stereotypes about men as irresponsible and unreliable, abusive and exploitative, or women as domineering and suspicious permeate expectations of one another. [30]

Absent resilience, the many barriers that Black couples, particularly low-income ones, face in general to maintain functional romantic connections are tumultuous, at best. Below follows a few of these factors negatively impacting the rates of marriage or long-term relationships for Black heterosexuals.

Unequal Sex

Factors of so-called marriage-ability or commit-ability are of increasing concern for low-income Black families across the socioeconomic spectrum. Marriageable women significantly outnumber marriageable men, ten-to-one, respectively— a gender ratio that contributes to the struggle for marriage or committed relationships to occur or be maintained in the Black community at large.[31] A significant number of Black men are either in prison, deceased, existing with poor health-care, participants in violent crime or otherwise absent. A majority of these cases are made up of low-income Black men. Precursors to these social conditions pertain to socioeconomic status and the inequity of access to resources such as education, full employment, functional health-care facilities, and other social ills. Consequently, Black women have learned to cope with the stress of social challenges by becoming more independent, while men have become more *inconsequential*, struggling to reestablish a position in the family.

Socioeconomic Conditions

Socioeconomic conditions also produce alternative living lifestyles as a means of survival. Socioeconomic conditions include limited employment, unemployment, poverty, low education, and low-resourced living environments. According to the 2012 U.S. Census, 28.1 percent of Blacks are under the poverty line, compared to a national average of 15.9 percent of all U.S. citizens. For families, 11.8 percent represent the national average for families in poverty compared to 24 percent for Black families. Forty-eight percent of Blacks are either unemployed or not in the labor force. The unemployment rate of Blacks is nearly double the national average.[32] Poverty and unemployment impedes the ability of men to provide for their families—a traditional role Black men are socialized and drawn to perform, and Black women find desirable. Accordingly, men who are unable to provide for their families are less attractive to women, while these same men are less willing to marry due to the same financial constraints on their role as providers.[33] Thus, socioeconomic status is an enormous predictor of marriage and family cohesion.

This is not to say that families that are impoverished do not marry or desire to marry. Research shows low-income Blacks idealize marriage, yet it remains beyond their reach because of social disparities.[34] Accordingly, due to a cultural interest in togetherness, absent the means to "formally" (by way of marriage) create such cohesion, there is a growing trend of cohabitation, replacing marriage for low-income Black families.[35] Unfortunately, cohabitation is a status that has no long-term guarantees, thereby leaving Black families without long-term structural consistency and a need for a diffusion of roles for members therein. Thus, role diffusion has become a significant resiliency factor for this community to survive resource inequity.

Income and Education

Moreover, finances significantly predict relationship stability and interest in marriage for low-income Blacks. Couples with financial obstructions tend to have heightened cortisol and stress levels, more social problems, and relationship distress indicated by high frequency of arguments and relationship dissatisfaction. The financial issues are further exacerbated by an absence of *biological* kinship—shown to be associated with higher relationship stability for Black couples. Yet, being biological does not necessarily yield an escape from poverty and financial inequity.

In 2011, the two-income household average for Blacks was $33,000 compared to a $50,000 national average—a 40 percent difference. With the growing economy, $40,000 is required to survive with a small amount of comfort. Yet, most Black Americans have low incomes, grossing less than $35,000 yearly with two-incomes.[36] Families are thereby relegated to poverty requiring federal assistance, especially families with more than two children and only one provider. This reality makes it difficult for families to survive, forcing more flexible roles of individuals within the family, including extended and fictive kin.

Allen and Olson studied typologies of Black couples, identifying five types of married couples (from highest to lowest marital satisfaction): (1) vitalized, (2) harmonious, (3) traditional, (4) conflicted, and (5) devitalized.[37] Although the study was not from the perspective of socioeconomic positioning, there appears to be some parallel between the level of marital satisfaction and socioeconomic status as the majority of the couples involved in this study were relatively highly educated, and therefore higher paid in comparison to the general population of Blacks. For those who were highly educated, marital status was rated more positively.

Additionally, low-income Blacks tend to be less educated, which directly affects financial stability and increases financial strain. Hence, the likelihood to marry is largely diminished as education is found to be a predictor of marriage in Black couples.[38] This illustrates the importance of educational attainment as one primary source of upward mobility and relationship satisfaction for Black individuals and couples in this country. In theory, Black individuals could improve their personal and family income by investing in and pursuing an education. However, according to the U.S. Census American Community Survey in 2011, for Black men who are twenty-five years old or over, 16 percent had a bachelor's degree or higher compared to 20 percent of Black women. This statistic has increased since 2000, which is notable, but, access to education continues to be problematic for Black communities, particularly those from low-socioeconomic environments.[39]

Black Families: Family Instability, Parenting, and Child Rearing

The aforementioned contextual factors for low-income Black couples and families, in comparison to their white counterparts are increasingly important to understanding the significance of colorism and racialization in this country. Critical race theorists consider the magnitude of these structural embargos cascading through the very fabric of American culture, hypothesizing various reasons for the continuation of such occurrences. Teasing out the contextual intragroup differences for Blacks adds further understanding to this complex issue.

Difficulty in couple maintenance and family togetherness are further exacerbated by unemployment and a lack of access to education. Thus, the likelihood that low-income men and women will end up together is slim, diminishing the possibility that biological parents would raise children together.[40] So, for some low-income Black families, familial instability is common, given the high frequencies of divorce and couples who have never married. Co-parenting becomes the style of shared parenting for romantically uninvolved parents. This contributes to the emotional experience of the children as family instability is shown to have considerable negative effects on children.[41] This is considerable as children often become receptacles of the relational and environmental problems surrounding them, absorbing all messages and narratives. Black low-income youth, in particular, can experience many forms of relationship dysfunction through their parents, challenging their perceptions about relationships with others and also disrupting their self-regulation skills. Even parents who choose to divorce to spare the children these negative arguments and verbal exchanges scar the children—as children tend to blame themselves for the divorce and are affected by the transition and family instability.[42] Also, children internalize the negative messages about themselves prior to crossing the doors of educational systems bringing with them negative internal working models (socially and emotionally) that mitigate academic performance.[43]

Oftentimes coparenting becomes too challenging, leaving children to be raised in single-parent households. Studies have found that some children from single-parent households engage in the highest rates of problem behavior. Leventhal and Brooks-Gunn found a significant correlation between high socioeconomic status or SES for achievement and low SES and residential instability for behavior and emotional outcomes,[44] supporting the idea that residential instability can have negative effects on children who experience coparenting marital transition in the home.

What is more, unsupervised time and parentification for low-income children was associated with increased instances of smoking for girls, while strong parental monitoring was associated with less delinquency and fewer instances of drinking in boys. Eating family dinners together was associated with less aggression and delinquency in youth. Because of inflexible work schedules and long hours of work required to compensate for the lack of two incomes, single parents are often limited in their ability to provide adequate supervision and family meals together; this, in turn, can lead to increased asocial behaviors in children.[45]

Research also found differences in parenting styles for parents of low-income children. Youths from struggling families—those that consistently used poor parenting practices and had low levels of emotional cohesion—were more likely to be exposed to community violence. Whereas youth exposed to high levels of community violence but living in families that functioned well across multiple dimensions of parenting and family relationship characteristics perpetrated less violence than similarly exposed youth from less well-functioning families.[46]

Based on the research, there can be major negative differences for low-income Black children who are raised in single-parent homes, illustrating a possible negative trajectory for these youths. Yet, this is not an absolute truth. Some children do fare better with one strong and supportive parent, according to research and many social theorists. Nonetheless, the benefit of two strong parents who are romantically healthy and cohesive lends itself to significantly greater outcomes for children.

Black Couples in SES Context

According to Pinderhughes, Black men and women continually are working through issues resulting from historical and current racism.[47] The psychological effects of racism and prejudice commonly manifest themselves within relationships, particularly in the context of marriage and long-term commitments, regardless of environmental context for Blacks. In this case, it is important to investigate the differences between low-income and middle-class families in the United States. Compared to illustrations of middle-class Black men who are doing well for themselves and their families, Black men are often illustrated in hypersexual ways. These stereotypical depictions illustrate these men as incapable of maintaining commitments to the opposite sex with regard to committed relationships. Similarly, the stereotype that circulates around society is that this population is misogynistic and degrading toward women. Additionally, Black men have been labeled as aggressive and emotionless.[48] These labels have characterized these men as irresponsible and negligent.[49] Such identifying statements have made it difficult for Black men to be assumed as the opposite, and "This reality can easily give rise to perceptions of Black men as non-family-oriented or uncaring."[50] On entering relationships, Black men have to constantly overcome negative expectations to be less than desired by their partners. Conversely, Black women have begun to develop a reputation of becoming more independent and less interested in marriage, as they are described to prefer careers first and long-term relationships second.[51]

What is not highlighted in these communities is that middle-class Blacks, due to increased education in this community, are making the commitment to marry. In a study examining the predictors of relationship stability over five years among heterosexual cohabiting and married Black couples raising an elementary school–age child, Cutrona et al. found that men with higher education were more likely to be in couples where both partners were biological parents of the children.[52] Additionally, they found that higher levels of education were associated with higher income, lower financial strain, and more stable family structures. Unfortunately, the financial ability to purchase homes and contribute to society in a "functional" way allows the status and identification of being "American" to seep into the fabric of this community, creating pressures to assimilate to the practices and cultural strategies used by white Americans, such as individualism, capitalism, and independence, rather than interdependence.

For low-income Blacks, economic and racialized policies prevent families from moving away from particular environmental spaces—creating a high concentration of ethnic minorities in geographical low-income areas. Unfortunately, as a result of minimal financial resources provided by governmental policies, geographical low-income areas represent hotbeds for problematic behaviors, negatively influencing the development of healthy and functional families. Citizens of low-income environments are faced with the daily challenge of negotiating a reality of poverty, a lack of resources, poor educational systems, high rates of crime and drug abuse, increased death rates, and many other social disparities. In lieu of these facts, families continue to reproduce. Moreover, having to endure these daily challenges, the mental health of these families is in question.

For middle-class Blacks, efforts to become upwardly mobile produce challenges of stereotype threat, complete assimilation, and forfeiting of cultural practices. Although middle-class Blacks enjoy relative financial freedom, the racialized environment is significantly more apparent and insidious, as they have more interactions with whites, and, therefore, the experience of racialization is more frequent. Racialization for this economic locale is illustrated interpersonally and systemically within the workplace, community, and academic settings. Additionally, middle-class Blacks face pressure to prove themselves in both aspects of their identities—being either "Black enough" or "white enough," to fit both communities with whom they interact and represent.

Socioeconomic status yields certain types of access to resources for middle-class Black couples that eliminate the financial stressors of surviving in a racialized environment, unlike low-income Blacks who struggle daily with financial strain and efforts to identify resources and services. Access to resources creates better opportunities for education, job opportunities, and other forms of upward mobility. For middle-class Blacks, socioeconomic status is not perceived negatively given these factors. However, access to resources creates other contingencies.

Blacks in the middle-class context experience more subtle and covert forms of prejudice and racism given the racial/ethnic mixing in middle-class communities, educational settings, and places of employment. Micro-aggressions are more common in such spaces, forcing Black individuals to develop strategies to work through discriminatory micro-aggressions occurring daily and frequently. Such experiences generate stress individually, leading to relationship challenges while in the home. In addition to micro-aggression, these communities are coaxed to assimilate, whereas low-income communities may lack many interactions with the dominant group, and therefore are better able to maintain cultural norms and practices without assimilation. As a tradeoff to gaining resources, middleclass Black families learn to code-switch in efforts to maintain cultural practices, while utilizing the resources of more dominant communities, such as superior school systems, businesses, and so on. Middle-class Blacks have to walk tightropes to be consistently relevant depending on their context—Black enough for their families; white enough for their middle-class community.

On the other hand, low-income Blacks engage racism and prejudice systemically through legislation that prevents upward mobility, influxes in drugs and alcohol in the neighborhood community, and forceful introduction into the informal or illegal business trade in some cases. When low-income Blacks find themselves in the presence of dominant group members, they are often treated with disdain and marked as insignificant or hyperaggressive.

Roles and responsibilities are characterized differently for low-income individuals in comparison to middle-class Blacks. Within the low-income context, there are more cohabitating families than in middle-class communities. Within the cohabitation, the woman is oftentimes the bread winner for the household—working at least two jobs to support the family. Fathers are often working jobs that lack flexible schedules, have demanding workloads, and limited benefits, including insurance and paid vacations. There is often a blending of roles for low-income Black couples such that each person in the couple dyad contributes equally to the survival of the family, although roles might be drastically different, if both parents are in the home (which is rare). The limited resources and blended responsibilities further confound the ability of the couple to engage one another romantically.

For middle-class families there is more gender equity and a sharing of roles and responsibilities. As discussed before, these couples are oftentimes married as opposed to cohabitating, therefore increasing the financial benefits in the home. Fathers are usually the primary breadwinners, although mothers contribute significantly as these families have two household incomes. In effort to diminish financial strain, this couple forfeits opportunities to spend time with one another in avoidance of financial conflict, given the pressures to provide for the family.

Race as the Primary Impediment

Numerous research studies found that race and ethnicity, although social constructs, are the main contributors to the present and historical inequality experienced by Black couples, regardless of socioeconomic status.[53] Although experienced in many ways differently, Blacks face an insidious and pervasive system of inequality that marginalizes this community to the outskirts of social significance. Such concepts as stereotype threat, social positioning, Eugenics, and other forms of "othering" position Blacks as subpar. Racism and prejudice, according to family stress theory, plays a major role in compromised psychological functioning, which directly affects parent-child relationships and intimate partnerships, making them less supportive and more conflicting.[54] Murray and colleagues found that an accumulation of stressors, such as poverty, negative life events, racial discrimination, high crime rates, and influx of drugs and alcohol within the community, create high levels of distress in the families—potentially exacerbating existing strain or generating new strain.[55]

The effects of historical and contemporary racism have yet to be fully discovered or comprehended. Generations of Blacks have passed down the effects of historical trauma, while contemporary forms of racism and prejudice add further confounds to an already difficult process of survival. What remains clear, however, is that there is an indubitable effect. For Black couples, and consequently families, the precise effects must be studied to establish clear strategies for coping with the pervasiveness of structural racism.

The inequality of racism and prejudice and its effects on Black couples has more recently been studied more frequently. Murry hypothesized that stressor pileup would be associated with Black mothers' psychological distress. Additionally, they found that maternal distress was linked to the quality of both mother-child relationships and intimate partnerships. Finally, they found that when mothers reported experiencing higher levels of discrimination, there were stronger links between stressor pileup and psychological distress and the quality of relationship between mother and intimate partner.[56]

In spite of this, members of the Black community demonstrate significant resiliency and survival skills as established forms of resilience.[57] Spirituality, faith, and religion;[58] family connectedness (family, kin, and social support);[59] and ethnic identity[60] are several aspects that have protected African Americans and African American couples from complete social destruction and cultural eradication. Researchers posit that historical and systemic racism and prejudice against this population manifest themselves in diverse ways, including family life. In a qualitative dissertation study, Brooks engaged in a case study of eight couples using semi-structured interviews and follow-up interviews to understand the factors contributing to coupling success in this population in spite of contextual difficulties. In the study, commitment, trust, communication/conflict management skills, similarity, religion, love, doing things together, understanding, and willingness to forgive were significant factors of resilience for African American couples.[61] There are several studies that support these findings, illustrating an ability for Black individuals and families, and in particular, couples, to suffer through the effects of historical trauma and co-occurring social and contemporary marginalization to create healthy, enduring relationships.

Though clear examples of resiliency are evident in this population, we must not fall prey to only *acknowledging* the social ills, *highlighting* the resiliency shown, and *ignoring* the need for solutions. In spite of systemic unresponsiveness, illustrations of resilience are prevalent and notable within this community. It is apparent that Black communities have a strong capacity to overcome social inequality by adaptability and survival instincts. Through strong bonds to family, community, religion, and spirituality, Black families have continually thrived, despite being relegated to the margins of society. Thus, it is important to note that the survival of these families is based on a developed resiliency, cultivated by struggle and oppression, in spite of significant social change in the United States. For those families that are unable to respond in resilient prosocial ways, a more systemic resource that is culturally sensitive and relevant must be available. Also, mental health professionals who are familiar with the unique issues of this population must be adequately trained to provide services.

Implications for Working with Couples Therapeutically

Mental health services for Blacks are not only recommended, but a necessity given the contextual challenges and stressors inherent in being a person of color in the United States. Coupling for this population is becoming increasingly difficult, as men and women are less likely to marry and more likely to cohabitate, later leading to children without both parents in the home for low-income families. For middle-class families, the pressures of status maintenance and experienced racism take a toll on the intimate relationships. Each socioeconomic group experiences their own unique types of racism and prejudice, directly affecting the intimate relationship. Referring families to therapeutic services can diminish the negative effects of racism/prejudice, family dissolution and instability, and mental health issues such as depression, anxiety, and posttraumatic stress.

It remains unclear to what extent colonization has impacted and continues to impact social interactions, familial health, and cultural survival of Black couples and families. Yet, traditional treatment modalities alienate Blacks through the use of culturally irrelevant approaches. The metaphysical "dilemma" of being Black in this country brings with it several challenging realities.[62] Blacks are among the lowest attendees to psychotherapy, while being the highest in need of such services, given the historical and current traumas experienced by this ethnic group.

There remains a social stigma in attending psychotherapy for this community that stems from myths among low-income Blacks about psychological treatments as indicators of being "crazy," or past experiences with systems that have misdiagnosed and mislabeled this community throughout history. Blacks have developed a "healthy cultural paranoia" about systems that have, in the past and present, patronized and pejoratively prescribed treatments that are contextually irrelevant.[63] By attending therapy, individuals are either perceived to be ignoring the historical experience of their own group or offering themselves to ridicule and questioning from the community, diminishing social capital. Nevertheless, there remains an increasing need for Blacks who are also confounded by low-income and racism/prejudice, to receive mental health services to counteract the undiagnosed depression and posttraumatic stress that remains unaddressed in these communities, despite being high in frequency.

Services should address couples' spirituality, operating resilience, and work to identify strategies unique to the context of the family.

For example, low-income families would need support identifying community resources that can minimize the financial strain and stress pileup, whereas middle-class families would need strategies to facilitate more carved-out time to spend with one another. Each couple, regardless of context, would need to discuss racism and prejudice concerns that cascade throughout their lives. Transparency of clinician is paramount here given the constant experience of racism dealt with daily. An unwillingness to discuss such issues would further marginalize this population and support an existing paranoia in attending therapy. A clinician must know the contextual reality of this community, understanding that the struggle is quite real, the challenges are perpetual, and the need for continued response should be unwavering.

Conclusion

The current dilemma of low-income Black families is no longer battles against segregation and overt racism, but rather, systemic and implicit forms of "othering" that appeases the social agenda of the dominant group, castigating ethnic minorities. The evidence that proves the continued existence of racial formation and racialization is illustrated through the current reality of low-income Black families. The social disparities looming large within these communities show a very real social problem that continues to persist regardless of the described utopian society that American culture asserts as reality. Low-income Black families are continuing to dissolve , finding new ways to form family systems that are more flexible and fluid as a means to survive.

Low-income Black families are left with their resilience to overcome present obstacles. Though the current obstacles are different from historical experiences of racism and segregation, they still represent a far cry from the desire of racial/ethnic equality, equality, and access to resources for ethnic minorities, particularly low-income Black families. The plight of low-income Black families continues to be a reality of subordinance to the dominant group. Until a change comes, the fight to survive will continue and a prayer of serenity will be on the lips of members of the Black community. There remains a height yet to be climbed toward social justice in the United States, and a continued need for research that studies this population and the contextual response to the needs of this community. Cultures are fluid and precarious. What is learned today will be history tomorrow. Michelle Alexander, the author of *The New Jim Crow*, notes the following:

What is remarkable is that hardly anyone seems to imagine that similar political dynamics may have produced another caste system in the years following the collapse of Jim Crow—one that exists today. The story that is told during Black History Month is one of triumph; the system of racial caste is officially dead and buried. Suggestions to the contrary are frequently met with shocked disbelief. The standard reply is: "How can you say that a racial caste system exists today? Just look at Barack Obama? Just look at Oprah Winfrey!" The fact that some African Americans have experienced great success in recent years does not mean that something akin to a racial caste system no longer exists. No caste system in the United States has ever governed all Black people; there have always been "free Blacks" and Black success stories, even during slavery and Jim Crow. The superlative nature of individual Black achievement today in formerly White domains is a good indicator that the old Jim Crow is dead, but it does not necessarily mean the end of racial caste. If history is any guide, it may have simply taken a different form.[64]

Notes

1. Sarah R. Crissey, "Race/Ethnic Differences in the Marital Experiences of Adolescents: The Role of Romantic Relationships," *Journal of Marriage and Family* 67, no. 3 (2005): 697–709; Chalandra M. Bryant, Robert Joseph Taylor, Karen D. Lincoln, Linda M. Chatters, and James S. Jackson, "Marital Satisfaction among Black and Black Caribbeans: Findings from the National Survey of American Life," *Family Relations* 57, no. 2 (2008): 239–253.

2. Peggy G. Giordano, Wendy D. Manning, and Monica A. Longmore, "The Romantic Relationships of Black and White Adolescents," *Sociological Quarterly* 46, no. 3 (2005): 545–568.

3. Giordano, Manning, and Longmore.

4. Crissey.

5. Claudia Lawrence-Webb, Melissa Littlefield, and Joshua N. Okundaye, "African American Intergender Relationships a Theoretical Exploration of Roles, Patriarchy, and Love, *Journal of Black Studies* 34, no. 5 (2004): 623–639; Jay Lebow, *Research for the Psychotherapist: From Science to Practice* (New York: Routledge, 2013).

6. Joseph Veroff, Elizabeth Ann Malcolm Douvan, and Shirley Hatchett, *Marital Instability: A Social and Behavioral Study of the Early Years* (Westport, CT: Greenwood Publishing Group, 1995); Terri L. Orbuch, Joseph Veroff, Halimah Hassan, and Julie Horrocks, "Who Will Divorce: A 14-Year Longitudinal Study of Black Couples and White Couples," *Journal of Social and Personal Relationships* 19, no. 2 (2002): 179–202.

7. "Marriage in Black America," *BlackDemographics*, accessed February 5, 2014, http://blackdemographics.com/households/marriage-in-black-america.html.

8. Frank F. Furstenberg. "The Making of the Black Family: Race and Class in Qualitative Studies in the Twentieth Century," *Annual Review of Sociology*. 33 (2007): 429–448.

9. Bureau of Justice Statistics, "Prisoners in 2008," accessed Feb. 8, 2014, http://www.bjs.gov/index.cfm?ty=pbdetail&iid=1763.html.

10. United States Center for Disease Control and Prevention, "Healthy People 2010: General Data Issues," accessed February 15, 2014, http://www.cdc.gov/nchs/data/hpdata2010/hp2010_general_data_issues.pdf.html.

11. "Proficiency of Black Students Is Found to Be Far Lower Than Expected," *New York Times*, accessed March 5, 2014 http://www.nytimes.com/2010/11/09/education/09gap.html.

12. Veroff, Malcolm, and Hatchett.

13. Daniel Patrick Moynihan, Lee Rainwater, and William L. Yancey, *The Negro Family: The Case for National Action* (Cambridge, MA: MIT Press, 1967); Steven Selden, "Eugenics and the Social Construction of Merit, Race and Disability," *Journal of Curriculum Studies* 32, no. 2 (2000): 235–252; William Julius Wilson, *When Work Disappears: The World of the New Urban Poor* (New York: Random House, 2011); Carter G. Woodson, *The Mis-Education of the Negro* (New York: Book Tree, 2006).

14. John U. Ogbu, and John Wilson Jr., "Mentoring Minority Youth: A Framework" (1990).

15. Reginald G. Daniel, *More Than Black: Multiracial Identity & New Racial Order* (Philadelphia, PA: Temple University Press, 2010).

16. Selden; Daniel; Thierry Devos and Mahzarin R. Banaji, "American = White?" *Journal of Personality and Social Psychology* 88, no. 3 (2005): 447.

17. Devos and Banaji, 449.

18. Devos and Banaji, 447.

19. Patricia Hill Collins, "The Social Construction of Black Feminist Thought," *Signs* (1989): 745; Daniel; Thierry Devos and Mahzarin R. Banaji, "American = White?"773.

20. Selden.

21. Delgado and Stefancic.

22. Margaret L Hunter, *Race Gender and the Politics of Skin Tone* (New York: Routledge, 2013).

23. Delgado and Stefancic.

24. Burton, Bonilla-Silva, Ray, Buckelew, and Freeman.

25. Elaine B. Pinderhughes, "African American Marriage in the 20th Century," *Family Process* 41, no. 2 (2002): 269–282.

26. Boyd-Franklin, *Black Families in Therapy: A Multisystems Approach*; Boyd-Franklin, *Black Families in Therapy: Understanding the African American Experience*; Pinderhughes.

27. Woodson, 9.

28. Audrey Smedley, and Brian D. Smedley, "Race as Biology Is Fiction, Racism as a Social Problem Is Real: Anthropological and Historical Perspectives on the Social Construction of Race," *American Psychologist* 60, no. 1 (2005): 16.

29. Andrew Billingsley, *Black Families in America* (New York: Touchstone Books, 1988).

30. Pinderhughes.

31. Ibid.

32. U.S. Census Bureau, "Poverty: 2012," accessed on Mar. 15, 2014, https://www.census.gov/hhes/www/poverty/data.html.

33. Ibid.

34. Kathryn Edin and Timothy J. Nelson, *Doing the Best I Can: Fatherhood in the Inner City* (Berkeley, CA: University of California Press, 2013).

35. Frank F. Furstenberg, "The Making of the Black Family: Race and Class in Qualitative Studies in the Twentieth Century," *Annual Review of Sociology* 33 (2007): 429–448.

36. "African American Income," *Blackdemographics*, accessed February 10, 2014 http://blackdemographics.com/households/african-american-income.html.

37. William D. Allen, and David H. Olson, "Five Types of African-American Marriages," *Journal of Marital and Family Therapy* 27, no. 3 (2001): 301–314.

38. Carolyn E. Cutrona, Daniel W. Russell, Rebecca G. Burzette, Kristin A. Wesner, and Chalandra M. Bryant, "Predicting Relationship Stability among Midlife African American Couples," *Journal of Consulting and Clinical Psychology* 79, no. 6 (2011): 814.

39. U.S. Census Bureau, "Census Bureau Releases 2011 American Community Survey Estimates," accessed January 20, 2014, https://www.census.gov/newsroom/releases/archives/american_community_survey_acs/cb12-175.html.

40. Cutrona, Russell, Burzette, Wesner, and Bryant.

41. Cynthia Osborne, and Sara McLanahan, "Partnership Instability and Child Well-Being," *Journal of Marriage and Family* 69, no. 4 (2007): 1065–1083.

42. Paula Fomby, and Andrew J. Cherlin, "Family Instability and Child Well-Being," *American Sociological Review* 72, no. 2 (2007): 181–204.

43. Douglas S. Massey, *American Apartheid: Segregation and the Making of the Underclass* (Cambridge, MA: Harvard University Press, 1993); Lyndall Strazdins, Mark S. Clements, Rosemary J. Korda, Dorothy H. Broom, and Rennie M. D'Souza, "Unsociable Work? Nonstandard Work Schedules, Family Relationships, and Children's Well-Being," *Journal of Marriage and Family* 68, no. 2 (2006): 394–410.

44. Tama Leventhal and Jeanne Brooks-Gunn, "The Neighborhoods They Live in: The Effects of Neighborhood Residence on Child and Adolescent Outcomes," *Psychological Bulletin* 126, no. 2 (2000): 309.

45. Kenneth W Griffin, Gilbert J. Botvin, Lawrence M. Scheier, Tracy Diaz, and Nicole L. Miller, "Parenting Practices as Predictors of Substance Use, Delinquency, and Aggression among Urban Minority Youth: Moderating Effects of Family Structure and Gender," *Psychology of Addictive Behaviors* 14, no. 2 (2000): 174.

46. Deborah Gorman-Smith, David B. Henry, and Patrick H. Tolan, "Exposure to Community Violence and Violence Perpetration: The Protective Effects of Family Functioning," *Journal of Clinical Child and Adolescent Psychology* 33, no. 3 (2004): 439–449.

47. Pinderhughes.

48. Rod K. Brunson, and Jody Miller, "Young Black Men and Urban Policing in the United States," *British Journal of Criminology* 46, no. 4 (2006): 613–640.

49. Tom Burrell, *Brainwashed: Challenging the Myth of Black Inferiority* (Carlsbad, CA: Hay House, 2009).

50. Monica McGoldrick, Joe Giordano, and Nydia Garcia-Preto, *Ethnicity and Family Therapy* (New York: Guilford Press, 2005), 90.

51. Leonore Tiefer, "A New View of Women's Sexual Problems: Why New? Why Now?" (2001): 89–96.

52. Cutrona, Russell, Burzette, Wesner, and Bryant.

53. Burton, Bonilla-Silva, Ray, Buckelew, and Freeman.

54. Gene H. Brody, Xiaojia Ge, Su Yeong Kim, Velma McBride Murry, Ronald L. Simons, Frederick X. Gibbons, Meg Gerrard, and Rand D. Conger, "Neighborhood Disadvantage Moderates Associations of Parenting and Older Sibling Problem Attitudes and Behavior with Conduct Disorders in African American Children," *Journal of Consulting and Clinical Psychology* 71, no. 2 (2003): 211.

55. Murry, Velma M., Amanda W. Harrell, Gene H. Brody, Yi-Fu Chen, Ronald L. Simons, Angela R. Black, Carolyn E. Cutrona, and Frederick X. Gibbons, "Long-Term Effects of Stressors on Relationship Well-Being and Parenting Among Rural African American Women," *Family Relations* 57, no. 2 (2008): 117–127.

56. Ibid.

57. Cutrona

58. Marks, Loren D., Katrina Hopkins, Cassandra Chaney, Pamela A. Monroe, Olena Nesteruk, and Diane D. Sasser, "Together, We Are Strong": A Qualitative Study of Happy, Enduring African American Marriages," *Family Relations* 57, no. 2 (2008): 172–185.

59. Phillips, Tommy M., Joe D. Wilmoth, and Loren D. Marks, "Challenges and Conflicts . . . Strengths and Supports a Study of Enduring

African American Marriages," *Journal of Black Studies* 43, no. 8 (2012): 936–952.

60. Williams, Monnica Terwilliger, Lloyd Kevin Chapman, Judy Wong, and Eric Turkheimer, "The role of ethnic identity in symptoms of anxiety and depression in African Americans," *Psychiatry Research* 199, no. 1 (2012): 31–36.

61. Brooks, Pruedence, "A Qualitative Study of Factors that Contribute to Satisfaction and Resiliency in Long-Term African American Marriages." PhD diss., Our Lady of the Lake University, 2006.

62. Selden.

63. Grier, William H., and Price M. Cobbs, *Black Rage* (New York: Basic Books, 1992).

64. Michelle Alexander. *The New Jim Crow: Mass Incarceration in the Age of Colorblindness* (New York: The New Press, 2012), 21.

Bibliography

Alexander, Michelle. *The New Jim Crow: Mass Incarceration in the Age of Colorblindness*. New York: The New Press, 2012.

Allen, William D., and David H. Olson. "Five Types of African-American Marriages." *Journal of Marital and Family Therapy* 27, no. 3 (2001): 301–314.

Alvidrez, Jennifer, Lonnie R. Snowden, and Dawn M. Kaiser. "The Experience of Stigma among Black Mental Health Consumers." *Journal of Health Care for the Poor and Underserved* 19, no. 3 (2008): 874–893.

Amato, Paul R. "The Consequences of Divorce for Adults and Children." *Journal of Marriage and Family* 62, no. 4 (2000): 1269–1287.

Anyon, Jean. "Social Class and the Hidden Curriculum of Work." *The Sociology of Education* 162 (1980): 1250.

Banks, Ralph Richard. *Is Marriage for White People?: How the African American Marriage Decline Affects Everyone*. New York: Penguin, 2011.

Billingsley, Andrew. *Black Families in America*. New York: Touchstone Books, 1988.

Bonilla-Silva, Eduardo. *Racism without Racists: Color-Blind Racism and the Persistence of Racial Inequality in America*. Lanham, MD: Rowman and Littlefield Publishers, 2013.

———. "Rethinking Racism: Toward a Structural Interpretation." *American Sociological Review* (1997): 465–480.

Boss, Pauline, and Carol Mulligan. *Family Stress: Classic and Contemporary Readings*. New York: Sage, 2003.

Boyd-Franklin, Nancy. *Black Families in Therapy: A Multisystems Approach*. New York: Guilford Press, 1989.

———. *Black Families in Therapy: Understanding the African American Experience.* New York: Guilford Press, 2006.

Bradbury, Thomas N., Frank D. Fincham, and Steven RH Beach. "Research on the Nature and Determinants of Marital Satisfaction: A Decade in Review." *Journal of Marriage and Family* 62, no. 4 (2000): 964–980.

Brody, Gene H., Xiaojia Ge, Su Yeong Kim, Velma McBride Murry, Ronald L. Simons, Frederick X. Gibbons, Meg Gerrard, and Rand D. Conger. "Neighborhood Disadvantage Moderates Associations of Parenting and Older Sibling Problem Attitudes and Behavior with Conduct Disorders in African American Children." *Journal of Consulting and Clinical Psychology* 71, no. 2 (2003): 211–222.

Bryant, Chalandra M., Robert Joseph Taylor, Karen D. Lincoln, Linda M. Chatters, and James S. Jackson. "Marital Satisfaction among African Americans and Black Caribbeans: Findings from the National Survey of American Life." *Family Relations* 57, no. 2 (2008): 239–253.

Burrell, Tom. *Brainwashed: Challenging the Myth of Black Inferiority.* Carlsbad, CA: Hay House, Inc., 2009.

Burton, Linda M., Eduardo Bonilla-Silva, Victor Ray, Rose Buckelew, and Elizabeth Hordge Freeman. "Critical Race Theories, Colorism, and the Decade's Research on Families of Color." *Journal of Marriage and Family* 72, no. 3 (2010): 440–459.

Coatsworth, J. Douglas, Larissa G. Duncan, Hilda Pantin, and José Szapocznik. "Differential Predictors of African American and Hispanic Parent Retention in a Family-Focused Preventive Intervention." *Family Relations* 55, no. 2 (2006): 240–251.

Collins, Patricia Hill. "The Social Construction of Black Feminist Thought." *Signs* (1989): 745–773.

Crissey, Sarah R. "Race/Ethnic Differences in the Marital Expectations of Adolescents: The Role of Romantic Relationships." *Journal of Marriage and Family* 67, no. 3 (2005): 697–709.

Crohan, Susan E. "Marital Quality and Conflict across the Transition to Parenthood in African American and White Couples." *Journal of Marriage and the Family* 58, no. 4 (Nov. 1996): 933–944.

Cruz, Mario, Harold Alan Pincus, Jeffrey S. Harman, Charles F. Reynolds, and Edward P. Post. "Barriers to Care-seeking for Depressed African Americans." *The International Journal of Psychiatry in Medicine* 38, no. 1 (2008): 71–80.

Cutrona, Carolyn E., Daniel W. Russell, Rebecca G. Burzette, Kristin A. Wesner, and Chalandra M. Bryant. "Predicting Relationship Stability among Midlife African American Couples." *Journal of Consulting and Clinical Psychology* 79, no. 6 (2011): 814.

Daniel, G. Reginald. *More than Black: Multiracial Identity & New Racial Order.* Philadelphia, PA: Temple University Press, 2010.

DeMaria, Rita M. "Distressed Couples and Marriage Education." *Family Relations* 54, no. 2 (2005): 242–253.

Delgado, Richard, and Jean Stefancic. *Critical Race Theory: The Cutting Edge*. Philadelphia, PA: Temple University Press, 2000.

Devos, Thierry, and Mahzarin R. Banaji. "American = White?" *Journal of Personality and Social Psychology* 88, no. 3 (2005): 447–466.

Doherty, William J., and Jared R. Anderson. "Community Marriage Initiatives." *Family Relations* 53, no. 5 (2004): 425–432.

Duncan, Barry L., Scott D. Miller, Bruce E. Wampold, and Mark A. Hubble. *The Heart and Soul of Change: Delivering What Works in Therapy*. American Psychological Association, 2010.

Duncan, Barry L., and Scott D. Miller. "The Client's Theory of Change: Consulting the Client in the Integrative Process." *Journal of Psychotherapy Integration* 10, no. 2 (2000): 169–187.

Edin, Kathryn and Timothy J. Nelson. *Doing the Best I Can: Fatherhood in the Inner City*. Berkley, CA: University of California Press, 2013.

Evans, Gary W. "The Environment of Childhood Poverty." *American psychologist* 59, no. 2 (Feb./Mar. 2004): 77–92.

Farber, Barry A., Kathryn C. Berano, and Joseph A. Capobianco. "Clients' Perceptions of the Process and Consequences of Self-Disclosure in Psychotherapy." *Journal of Counseling Psychology* 51, no. 3 (2004): 340–346.

Fomby, Paula, and Andrew J. Cherlin. "Family Instability and Child Well-being." *American Sociological Review* 72, no. 2 (2007): 181–204.

Furman, Wyndol, and Elizabeth A. Wehner. "Adolescent Romantic Relationships: A Developmental Perspective." *New Directions for Child and Adolescent Development* no. 78 (1997): 21–36.

Furstenberg, Frank F. "The Making of the Black Family: Race and Class in Qualitative Studies in the Twentieth Century." *Annual Review of Sociology* 33 (2007): 429–448.

Garland, Diana R. "Training Married Couples in Listening Skills: Effects on Behavior, Perceptual Accuracy and Marital Adjustment." *Family Relations* (1981): 297–306.

Gaston, Louise, William Piper, Elie Debbane, Jean-Pierre Bienvenu, and Jacques Garant. "Alliance and Technique for Predicting Outcome in Short-and Long-Term Analytic Psychotherapy." *Psychotherapy Research* 4, no. 2 (1994): 121–135.

Giordano, Peggy C., Wendy D. Manning, and Monica A. Longmore. "The Romantic Relationships of Africa-American and White Adolescents." *Sociological Quarterly* 46, no. 3 (2005): 545–568.

Gold, Steven J. "From Jim Crow to Racial Hegemony: Evolving Explanations of Racial Hierarchy." *Ethnic and Racial Studies* 27, no. 6 (2004): 951–968.

Goodenow, Carol. "Classroom Belonging among Early Adolescent Students Relationships to Motivation and Achievement." *Journal of Early Adolescence*13, no. 1 (1993): 21–43.

Gorman-Smith, Deborah, David B. Henry, and Patrick H. Tolan. "Exposure to Community Violence and Violence Perpetration: The Protective Effects of Family Functioning." *Journal of Clinical Child and Adolescent Psychology* 33, no. 3 (2004): 439–449.

Gottman, John Mordechai. *The Marriage Clinic: A Scientifically Based Marital Therapy*. New York: W. W. Norton & Company, 1999.

Grier, William H., and Price M. Cobbs. *Black Rage*. New York: Basic Books, 1992.

Griffin, Kenneth W., Gilbert J. Botvin, Lawrence M. Scheier, Tracy Diaz, and Nicole L. Miller. "Parenting Practices as Predictors of Substance Use, Delinquency, and Aggression among Urban Minority Youth: Moderating Effects of Family Structure and Gender." *Psychology of Addictive Behaviors* 14, no. 2 (2000): 174–184.

Gurman, Alan S., and Neil S. Jacobson. *Clinical Handbook of Couple Therapy*. New York: Guilford Press, 2002.

Hall, Gordon C. Nagayama. "Psychotherapy Research with Ethnic Minorities: Empirical, Ethical, and Conceptual Issues." *Journal of Consulting and Clinical Psychology* 69, no. 3 (2001): 502–510.

Harding, David J. "Cultural Context, Sexual Behavior, and Romantic Relationships in Disadvantaged Neighborhoods." *American Sociological Review* 72, no. 3 (2007): 341–364.

Harper, Gary W., Christine Gannon, Susan E. Watson, Joseph A. Catania, and M. Margaret Dolcini. "The Role of Close Friends in African American Adolescents' Dating and Sexual Behavior." *Journal of Sex Research* 41, no. 4 (2004): 351–362.

hooks, bell. *Talking Back: Thinking Feminist, Thinking Black*. Cambridge, MA: South End Press, 1989.

hooks, bell, Michele Wallace, Andrew Hacker, Jared Taylor, Derrick Bell, Ishmael Reed, Nathan Hare et al. "The Crisis of African American Gender Relations." *Transition* (1995): 91–175.

Hunter, Margaret L. *Race Gender and the Politics of Skin Tone*. New York: Routledge , 2013.

Ladson-Billings, Gloria. "Critical Race Theory in Education." *The Routledge International Handbook of Critical Education* (2009): 110.

Leventhal, Tama, and Jeanne Brooks-Gunn. "The Neighborhoods They Live in: The Effects of Neighborhood Residence on Child and Adolescent Outcomes." *Psychological Bulletin* 126, no. 2 (2000): 309–337.

Lawrence-Webb, Claudia, Melissa Littlefield, and Joshua N. Okundaye. "African American Intergender Relationships a Theoretical Exploration of Roles, Patriarchy, and Love." *Journal of Black Studies* 34, no. 5 (2004): 623–639.

Lebow, Jay. *Research for the Psychotherapist: From Science to Practice*. New York: Routledge, 2013.

Massey, Douglas S. *American Apartheid: Segregation and the Making of the Underclass*. Cambridge, MA: Harvard University Press, 1993.

McCubbin, Hamilton I., and Marilyn A. McCubbin. "Typologies of Resilient Families: Emerging Roles of Social Class and Ethnicity." *Family Relations* (1988): 247–254.

McGoldrick, Monica, Joe Giordano, and Nydia Garcia-Preto. *Ethnicity and Family Therapy*. New York: Guilford Press, 2005.

Mistry, Rashmita S., Elizabeth A. Vandewater, Aletha C. Huston, and Vonnie C. McLoyd. "Economic Well-Being and Children's Social Adjustment: The Role of Family Process in an Ethnically Diverse Low-Income Sample." *Child Development* 73, no. 3 (2002): 935–951.

Mitrani, Victoria B., Guillermo Prado, Daniel J. Feaster, Carleen Robinson-Batista, and Jose Szapocznik. "Relational Factors and Family Treatment Engagement among Low-Income, HIV-Positive African American Mothers." *Family process* 42, no. 1 (2003): 31–45.

Moynihan, Daniel Patrick, Lee Rainwater, and William L. Yancey. *The Negro Family: The Case for National Action*. Cambridge, MA: MIT Press, 1967.

Nicholson, Heather Johnston, Christopher Collins, and Heidi Holmer. "Youth as People: The Protective Aspects of Youth Development in After-School Settings." *Annals of the American Academy of Political and Social Science* 591, no. 1 (2004): 55–71.

Ogbu, John U., and John Wilson Jr. "Mentoring Minority Youth: A Framework." (1990).

Orbuch, Terri L., Joseph Veroff, Halimah Hassan, and Julie Horrocks. "Who will Divorce: A 14-Year Longitudinal Study of Black Couples and White Couples." *Journal of Social and Personal Relationships* 19, no. 2 (2002): 179–202.

Orfield, Gary, and John T. Yun. "Resegregation in American Schools." (1999). Accessed February 16, 2014. http://civilrightsproject.ucla.edu/research/k-12-education/integration-and-diversity/resegregation-in-american-schools/orfiled-resegregation-in-american-schools-1999.pdf.

Orthner, Dennis K., Hinckley Jones-Sanpei, and Sabrina Williamson. "The Resilience and Strengths of Low-Income Families." *Family Relations* 53, no. 2 (2004): 159–167.

Osborne, Cynthia, and Sara McLanahan. "Partnership Instability and Child Well-Being." *Journal of Marriage and Family* 69, no. 4 (2007): 1065–1083.

Park, Nansook. "The Role of Subjective Well-being in Positive Youth Development." *Annals of the American Academy of Political and Social Science* 591, no. 1 (2004): 25–39.

Parra Cardona, Jose Ruben, Melanie Domenech-Rodriguez, Marion Forgatch, Cris Sullivan, Deborah Bybee, Kendal Holtrop, Ana Rocio

Escobar-Chew, Lisa Tams, Brian Dates, and Guillermo Bernal. "Culturally Adapting an Evidence-Based Parenting Intervention for Latino Immigrants: The Need to Integrate Fidelity and Cultural Relevance." *Family Process* 51, no. 1 (2012): 56–72.

Parra Cardona, José Parra, Kendal Holtrop, Ana Rocio Escobar-Chew, Sheena Horsford, Lisa Tams, Francisco A. Villarruel, Graciela Villalobos, Brian Dates, James C. Anthony, and Hiram E. Fitzgerald. "'Queremos Aprender': Latino Immigrants' Call to Integrate Cultural Adaptation with Best Practice Knowledge in a Parenting Intervention." *Family Process* 48, no. 2 (2009): 211–231.

Patterson, Joän M. "Integrating Family Resilience and Family Stress Theory." *Journal of Marriage and Family* 64, no. 2 (2002): 349–360.

Pinderhughes, Elaine B. "African American Marriage in the 20th Century." *Family Process* 41, no. 2 (2002): 269–282.

Pinsof, William M. "The Death of 'Till Death Us Do Part': The Transformation of Pair-Bonding in the 20th Century." *Family Process* 41, no. 2 (2004): 135–157.

Powell, Cecil L., and Kimberly R. Jacob Arriola. "Relationship between Psychosocial Factors and Academic Achievement among African American Students." *Journal of Educational Research* 96, no. 3 (2003): 175–181.

Reynolds, Arthur J. "Early Schooling of Children at Risk." *American Educational Research Journal* 28, no. 2 (1991): 392–422.

Seal, David Wyatt, and Anke A. Ehrhardt. "Masculinity and Urban Men: Perceived Scripts for Courtship, Romantic, and Sexual Interactions with Women." *Culture, Health & Sexuality* 5, no. 4 (2003): 295–319.

Selden, Steven. "Eugenics and the Social Construction of Merit, Race and Disability." *Journal of Curriculum Studies* 32, no. 2 (2000): 235–252.

Sellers, Robert M., Nikeea Copeland-Linder, Pamela P. Martin, and R. L'Heureux Lewis. "Racial Identity Matters: The Relationship between Racial Discrimination and Psychological Functioning in African American Adolescents." *Journal of Research on Adolescence* 16, no. 2 (2006): 187–216.

Sleeter, Christine. "An Invitation to Support Diverse Students through Teacher Education." *Journal of Teacher Education* 59, no. 3 (2008): 212–219.

Smedley, Audrey, and Brian D. Smedley. "Race as Biology is Fiction, Racism as a Social Problem is Real: Anthropological and Historical Perspectives on the Social Construction of Race." *American Psychologist* 60, no. 1 (2005): 16–26.

Strazdins, Lyndall, Mark S. Clements, Rosemary J. Korda, Dorothy H. Broom, and Rennie M. D'Souza. "Unsociable Work? Nonstandard

Work Schedules, Family Relationships, and Children's Well-Being." *Journal of Marriage and Family* 68, no. 2 (2006): 394–410.

Thompson, Vetta L. Sanders, Anita Bazile, and Maysa Akbar. "African Americans' Perceptions of Psychotherapy and Psychotherapists." *Professional Psychology: Research and Practice* 35, no. 1 (2004): 19–26.

Tiefer, Leonore. "A New View of Women's Sexual Problems: Why New? Why Now?" *The Journal of Sex Research* 38, no. 2 (May 2001): 89–96.

Veroff, Joseph, Elizabeth Ann Malcolm Douvan, and Shirley Hatchett. *Marital Instability: A Social and Behavioral Study of the Early Years.* Westport, CT: Greenwood Publishing Group, 1995.

Volling, Brenda L., Paul C. Notaro, and Joelle J. Larsen. "Adult Attachment Styles: Relations with Emotional Well-Being, Marriage, and Parenting." *Family Relations* (1998): 355–367.

Wehlage, Gary, and Robert Rutter. "Dropping out: How Much Do Schools Contribute to the Problem?" *The Teachers College Record* 87, no. 3 (1986): 374–392.

Wehlage, Gary, Robert A. Rutter, Gregory A. Smith, Nancy Lesko, and Ricardo R. Fernandez. *Reducing the Risk: Schools as Communities of Support*. New York: Falmer Press, 1989.

Whelan, Christine B. "Making Marriage Work: A History of Marriage and Divorce in the Twentieth-Century United States (review)." *Journal of Social History* 44, no. 3 (2011): 937–939.

Wilson, William Julius. *When Work Disappears: The World of the New Urban Poor.* New York: Random House, 2011.

Winant, Howard. "Racism Today: Continuity and Change in the Post-Civil Rights Era." *Ethnic and Racial Studies* 21, no. 4 (1998): 755–766.

Woodson, Carter G. *The Mis-Education of the Negro*. New York: Book Tree, 2006.

3

Holy Smoke

Church Burnings, Journalism, and the Politics of Race, 1996–2006

Christopher Strain

Introduction

The notion of living in a postracial America is alluring, appealing to a very real desire to shed this nation's torrid racial past. Few U.S. citizens would like nothing more than to disallow the enduring significance of race, in the hope of inventing a new society in which racial prejudice and discrimination do not exist, a society where people of different races and ethnicities are truly equal, and where skin color acts not as a negative delineation but as a positive demarcation only. The preponderance of what might be termed *racial relevancies*, however, belies this wish in undeniable ways. From the deaths of Michael Brown, Eric Garner, and other Black men at the hands of white police officers to the "passing" of Rachel Dolezal as African American to the savage attack on Emanuel AME Church in Charleston, race intrudes on the national conversation time and time again. No sooner do we declare race a nonentity than it reappears, manifesting like an obstinate poltergeist.

The most telling example of this phenomenon from recent U.S. history is the series of church burnings across the entire United States between 1996 and 2006. In June 1996, news of arsons at Black churches swept the national media, creating concerns of a racist conspiracy. The arsons captured public attention, particularly in the South where an alarming number of the fires occurred. As the number of fires increased, newspapers and television networks picked up the story, and soon it seemed as if white supremacists were launching a full-scale assault on African-American houses of worship. Media coverage diminished amid controversy over the scale and scope of these fires. The national news media was accused of exaggerating the problem, and when accusations of inflated statistics and misappropriation of rebuilding monies surfaced, the outpouring of support shown for victims of the arsons dried up. As quickly as the story appeared it faded from headlines.

Intrigue and controversy surrounded and continues to surround these fires, many of them unexplained and unsolved. Was there really an "epidemic" of Black church burnings? How many fires were attributable to racism? Even the number of churches involved has been indeterminate—not because hard evidence was lacking in individual cases, but rather because the larger news story became politicized quickly and a macroscopic view became blurry. Skeptics have questioned whether or not many of these fires were arsons, and whether the number of fires constituted a crisis; some have even questioned whether these fires occurred at all. However, a critical narrative of these chaotic events—of the context in which these events occurred, of how the press covered these crimes, of how the government responded, and of the obvious symbolisms, hidden meanings, and larger significances of these fires—shows that what one skeptic called "The Great Black Church Burning Hoax" was quite real, quite devastating to those affected, and quite significant in terms of understanding race in the United States at the beginning of the twenty-first century.

The fires marked a transition, as white and Black Southerners alike formulated new racial identities in the generation following the civil rights movement and as the nation as a whole struggled toward a "postracial" ideal. Analysis of the fires shows that this transition was neither clean nor orderly; in fact, postracialism in this instance actually may have inhibited clear understanding of the arsons as people groped for a handle on what was happening. Responses to the arsons by reporters, by government officials, by Black leaders, and by the general public reflected ongoing debates over the social and political status of African Americans—debates centering on such issues as the content and meaning of Black history, the state of Black leadership in the post–civil rights era, and inclusion in the body politick. Amid premature proclamations of the end of American racism, the fires revealed that strife continued to define race relations just as race continued to define life in the United States; however, they also demonstrated that white supremacists of the sheet-wearing, Confederate flag–waving variety were much scarcer in the 1990s than they had been in previous decades. Most importantly, the fires provided a kind of referendum on American racism, happening as they did at a key moment of racial division. If they initially contributed to this division, providing stark reasons for mistrust across the black-white divide, then the fires also may have paradoxically provided an occasion for unification and reconciliation.

Using as subheadings the language that arson investigators use to describe fire progression—ignition, growth, flashover (the hottest and most dangerous stage of a fire), smoldering, and decay—this chapter provides an overview of these incidents.

Ignition (1994–1995)

According to the National Fire Protection Association, arson is the leading cause of structure fires in the United States and the number-one cause of property damage. Each year, an estimated 267,000 fires are attributed to arson, which result in $1.4 billion in property loss and over 2,000 injuries and 475 deaths. Churches, which account for well under 1 percent of reported structure fires, are not a major part of America's arson problem; however, arson is the leading cause of fires in churches, accounting for more than one out of every four reported church fires and two-fifths of the reported property damage in those fires.[1]

Certain factors make houses of worship particularly susceptible to arson. As places of refuge, churches sometimes burn up in blazes unintentionally started by vagrants; as symbols of authority, they are sometimes targeted by angry teenagers, lashing out against their community, against their parents, or against God. Less often, a volunteer fireman with a hero complex will start a fire—only to put it out and bask in the glory of aiding his community. There have even been insinuations of pastors setting their own churches on fire to gain insurance money.[2]

Arsonists are drawn to inviting targets and churches, unfortunately, often make inviting targets. As Richard Gilman, executive director of the Insurance Committee for Arson Control in New York, has noted, "Churches are easy to burn." They are often unlit and uninhabited, empty at night or during weekdays. Often unlocked, without high-tech security systems, they are easy to enter. They are often remote or isolated, located along lonely country highways or at the end of windy roads. Many older churches fail to meet the fire-safety codes of other commercial buildings. They are often made of wood, with combustible pews and other furnishings inside; when torched, the high-vaulted ceilings and steeples of many churches provide the kind of dramatic conflagrations that thrill pyromaniacs.[3]

Perhaps for these reasons, news sources paid only nominal attention to a number of suspicious fires at churches across the nation in 1994 and 1995. Many of these fires occurred in the South, and an unusual number of them occurred at predominantly Black churches. For example, in

January 1994, a church burned in Fort Lauderdale, Florida. In February, three churches burned in Sumter County, Alabama: Bucks Chapel Church, Pine Top Baptist, and Oak Grove Missionary Church. That same month, two burned in Aiken County, South Carolina: Rock Hill Baptist Church and Old Rosemary Baptist Church. Five churches had burned in South Carolina in the previous two years; then, in June 1994, another church burned in Aiken County: Jerusalem Baptist Church. The following month, two churches burned in Georgia: Springfield Baptist Church in Madison and Elam Baptist Church in Jones County. In August, two houses of worship burned in Tennessee: Greater Missionary Baptist Church and Benevolent Lodge #210. The fires continued into the fall of 1994 when more churches burned in Tennessee, including New Wright's Chapel in Shelby County. Three more churches burned in South Carolina in September and October: Rice's Chapel in Buffalo, Shrub Branch Baptist Church in Blackville, and St. Paul AME Church in Cades. Winter snow flurries did not extinguish the fires as Salem Missionary Baptist Church burned in Fruitland, Tennessee, on December 30. Bluff Road United Methodist Church burned in Columbia, South Carolina, on New Year's Day. These fires were noted in local news outlets—in small-town newspapers and by local television affiliates.[4]

The U.S. Bureau of Alcohol, Tobacco, and Firearms (ATF) documented a number of fires in the Deep South in the coming months. Two churches burned in Tennessee on January 13, 1995: Johnson Grove Baptist in Bells and Macedonia Baptist in Denmark. On January 31, Mt. Calvary Baptist burned in Hardeman County, Tennessee. On February 20, authorities charged two white men and a white teen with attacking three Black churches with sledgehammers; prosecutors noted that nearby white churches were unharmed, suggesting the attacks were racially motivated. On May 15, someone broke into the Greater Mount Zion Tabernacle Church of God in Christ in Portsmouth, Virginia, and set the burgundy velvet curtains near the pulpit on fire. Police found a footprint in the middle of the church's backdoor, which someone kicked in before setting the fire.[5]

In most cases motives and suspects were few, but in a few instances arrests were made. For example, on June 20 and June 21, 1995, Timothy Welch and Christopher Cox burned two Black churches near Manning, South Carolina. The two young men, recent converts to the Ku Klux Klan, kicked in the doors of Macedonia Baptist Church and Mt. Zion AME Church, poured accelerants over the pews and pulpits, and lit fires. "It was something that needed to be done, and I did it," Welch confessed. "It was such devastation, people were crying that night just like it was a funeral," said Rev. Jonathan Mouzon of Macedonia Baptist. "When you lose a church, that's a major thing to Black folk. To Blacks the church is everything."[6]

Growth (January–May 1996)

It was not until early 1996 that the arsons attracted wider media attention. On January 8, in Knoxville, Tennessee, someone prepared and ignited a predawn fire at the Inner City Community Church—a multiracial but predominately African American church with four hundred members. The church burned to the ground. According to one investigator, the arsonist put a great deal of time and effort into the crime. "We found accelerants," said Dick Garner of the ATF. "We found numerous Molotov cocktails. We found gunpowder. We found gasoline cans and numerous other items of evidence at the scene." The smell of kerosene—a telltale sign of arson—still hung over the site when investigators arrived. The perpetrators left graffiti on an outside wall that read, "DIE NIGGER AND DIE NIGGER LOVERS." No person or group claimed responsibility for the fire, but a few days after the incident, a couple of local businesses received leaflets reading, "1996 shall be the year of white triumph and justice for the master supreme race." One church member noted, "It's the devil's job."[7]

What attracted attention to this fire was the fame of the church's associate pastor, a popular and successful pro athlete? Reggie White was not only a pastor at Inner City but also an All-Pro defensive end for the Green Bay Packers and the National Football League's career sack leader. He had maintained strong ties in Tennessee, where he had attended college and moonlighted as a preacher. White spoke out against the crimes. "When is America going to stop tolerating these groups?" he asked:

> It is time for us to come together and to fight it. One of the problems is that the people financing and providing the resources for this type of activity are popular people with money who are hiding under the rug. Some of them may be policemen, doctors, lawyers, prominent people who speak out of both sides of their mouths. That makes it difficult to stop but not impossible. Not when we come together as one force against hate.[8]

As he prepared for the biggest game of his eleven year career in the NFL—the NFC championship against the Dallas Cowboys, with the winner earning a trip to Super Bowl XXX—White found his attention divided between football and hate crime.

Despite their finding racist graffiti and flyers, federal investigators hesitated to label the incident a hate crime. "This was an arson, without doubt," said FBI agent Scott Nowinski. "But to say that this is definitely a bias or hate crime, we cannot say that." Others saw the incident differently. "This is an unmistakable act of terrorism," said Brian Levin of the Southern Poverty Law Center, a nonprofit agency that not only provides legal aid to disadvantaged persons but also monitors white supremacist organizations. "The fact that a church would be targeted is . . . a symbolic act," he stated. "Even if it was done without a racial motive, the fact of the matter is, it still sends shock waves throughout a community."[9]

Three days later, fire found more churches in Alabama. On January 11, Little Zion Baptist Church and Mount Zoar Baptist Church, both within six miles of each other in the tiny town of Boligee in Greene County, burned to the ground on the same night. Two weeks before that, another Black church in the area, Mount Zion Baptist Church, had burned to the ground, and neighboring Jerusalem Baptist Church was the target of an attempted arson in which the fire failed to ignite properly. "Given the locations of all of these fires, they could not have been started accidentally," said Barrown Langster, Greene County district attorney. "They may not be linked to any organized hate group, but we are concerned that it will continue if we don't have a thorough investigation." The Little Zion and Mount Zoar fires followed the January 4 sentencing of two white men convicted of vandalizing three Black churches in adjacent Sumter County in February 1995. At the sentencing, one defendant called the action "stupid" and explained how he and his friends got drunk, went to the churches, and smashed pews, windows, and kitchen equipment with a sledgehammer. A third man convicted in the case died of self-inflicted gunshot wounds days a few days before the sentencing. "I don't think any of this was accidental," said John Zippert, publisher of the weekly newspaper, the *Greene County Democrat*. "I think these particular churches were targeted. You have white churches in between all of them that were not touched." Meanwhile, three more churches burned in Zachary, Louisiana, on February 1. No one had yet to notice these fires as anything other than isolated events. Only the Inner City fire received significant news coverage; but, Reggie White's celebrity status and outspokenness drew attention not only to the plight of his own church but also to the plight of others.[10]

Federal agents began to look for links between the Inner City Church fire and four other unsolved arsons at Black churches in

Tennessee in 1995, and the ATF also looked at a series of suspicious fires at four Black churches in western Alabama that month to look for connections; however, it was two journalists working for *USA Today* who were the first to note a larger trend. "In scenes reminiscent of the 1960s' civil rights struggles, Black churches in the South are being set afire at an alarming rate," wrote Gary Fields and Tom Watson on February 8, 1996. In an article titled "Arson at Black Churches Echoes Bigotry of the Past," Fields and Watson laid out the facts. Arsonists had damaged at least seventeen churches in Alabama, Louisiana, South Carolina, Tennessee, and Texas since January 1995, according to the two journalists. Eleven fires were set in the previous two months. Following the lead of *USA Today*, national newspapers, television networks, and magazines began to consolidate and disseminate reports of at least thirty churches burned across the nation in the preceding eighteen months.[11]

As of March 19, fifteen arsons at Black churches in the South remained under investigation. The ATF had identified—but not arrested—suspects in arsons at six of the churches and had determined that none of the fires appeared to be racially motivated. Civil rights groups met the ATF's investigations with skepticism; Wade Henderson of the NAACP said he strongly questioned the findings. "We are going to demand a more detailed investigation," he said. Some feared that the ATF focused too quickly on members of the churches as possible arsonists; however, Donnie Carter, who headed the ATF's investigation into the crimes, staunchly defended the Bureau. As a Black Baptist deacon and a native of McComb, Mississippi, where fourteen churches were burned in the 1960s, Carter was particularly attuned to any indications of hate crime. "You can bet your bottom dollar as the guy heading this investigation [that] I'm looking for evidence of [race as a motivating factor]," he noted. "It just hasn't happened yet."[12]

St. Paul's Primitive Baptist Church in Meridian, Mississippi, burned on Easter Sunday. On April 29, fire gutted Effingham Baptist, a 114-year-old predominantly Black church in Florence County, South Carolina. Determining that a flammable liquid was thrown through a window, authorities ruled the fire arson. A week after the incident the prevailing mood in and around Effingham seemed to be one of incredulity. One man expressed anger: "Whoever did this needs punishment," declared David Johnson, a seventy-four-year-old retired farmer who said he would "put him behind a truck and drag him until his tongue hangs out." But most residents, Black and white alike, shrugged and expressed bewilderment. Curtis Boswell, a principal, said he had seen no signs of racial tension at the local high school, where Black and white students mixed easily on campus. "This surprised all of us," he said. "We just don't have trouble of that sort." Florence County prided itself on a progressive image that lured industries such as Hoffman-LaRoche, which was building a $500 million pharmaceuticals-manufacturing facility in the area. Any suggestion of racial intolerance was painful for a community eager to shed any remaining vestiges of the region's stereotypical bigotry, and most residents seemed willing to interpret any hint of the possibility of racism as a lone anachronism. "It's just one of those things . . . It don't mean nothing," said eighteen-year-old Christopher Allen at Effingham Feed and Seed, the local general store. "There's no need in getting mad," said sixty-five-year-old Willie McKever, a church deacon most concerned with getting an adjustment from the insurance company in order to begin the rebuilding process.[13]

The Justice Department disclosed no evidence of a regionwide conspiracy fomented by hate groups; yet, Deval Patrick, assistant attorney general for Civil Rights Division, characterized the fires as "an epidemic of terror." African American leaders complained bitterly that no one was paying attention or taking the fires seriously. Civil rights leaders began to blame what Reverend Jesse Jackson called "a cultural conspiracy"; that is, while there may have been no single organization plotting the arsons, the fires reflected racial tensions in the South exacerbated by political assaults on affirmative action and the neopopulist oratory of Republican politicians like Pat Buchanan. Jackson saw connections between the church burnings and other signs of deteriorating race relations, including the murders of a Black couple by white soldiers near Fort Bragg, North Carolina earlier that year. "There's a clear pattern and practice now," he said, "and there's not the vigorous pursuit of these arsonist terrorists that we deserve." The fires were unequivocal and unmistakable in their meaning. "They're not burning down Black barbecue joints, they're not burning down Black pool halls," said Randolph Scott-McLaughlin, vice president of the Center for Constitutional Rights, a New York–based civil liberties group. "They're burning down Black churches. It's like they're burning a cross in my front yard. They're burning symbols of resistance and community and hope and refuge."[14]

Fires continued across the region—indeed, across the entire nation. Media coverage intensified, and national concern of a possible conspiracy grew. The U.S. House Judiciary Committee held hearings on May 22 to find facts about the church burnings. The day after the hearing, U.S. Representative John Conyers Jr., D-Michigan, and House

Judiciary Chairman Henry Hyde, R-Illinois, penned and cosponsored the Church Arson Prevention Act of 1996. "The tragedy of the church burnings needs a national response," explained Conyers. "This legislation will increase the number of prosecutions and make the job easier for investigators so that terrorists involved can be brought to justice."[15]

On May 29, ATF agents began to investigate another fire, this time at the fellowship hall of Mt. Tabor Baptist Church in Cerro Gordo, North Carolina. The agents were following several leads in connection with threats phoned to the NAACP office in Durham. The caller, claiming he was "tired of you Blacks," warned that three more Black churches would burn by June. Special agent Mark Logan said, "We are aggressively pursuing the threats." Authorities continued to try to determine if the fires were either racially motivated or related or both.[16]

Mac Charles Jones, Associate for Racial Justice for the National Council of Churches and a pastor in Kansas City, Missouri, described the state of U.S. race relations as a "tinderbox." If Black churches were put in a position where they alone must address the arsons, then the problem would undoubtedly spread from rural areas to urban ones. "This country will explode," Jones said. "It is that serious." He suggested that federal authorities use any measure necessary, up to and including use of the National Guard, or declaring a state of emergency, to combat the problem. Reverend Joseph Lowery of the Southern Christian Leadership Conference also warned of turmoil if the fires did not cease. Lowery suggested that "unarmed vigils of Blacks and whites working together" should patrol Black churches to deter arsonists. Uniformly, national denominations issued denunciations of the arsonists and pledged their support to victimized congregations.[17]

A Black church burned near Greensboro in rural Hale County, Alabama on June 3, 1996, but it was unclear if the fire was racially motivated or even if it was deliberately set. The Rising Star Baptist Church was engulfed in flames when firemen were summoned at about 2:30 a.m. It was the fifth fire at a Black church in west Alabama since late 1995.[18]

Flashover (June 1996)

Then, on June 8, as President Bill Clinton and Republican candidate Bob Dole intensified their televised advertising campaigns for the upcoming presidential election, fire consumed the ninety-three-year-old sanctuary of the Matthews Murkland Presbyterian Church in Charlotte, North Carolina. Investigators said the fire had been set but they did not say how or by whom. That morning, President Clinton changed the text of his weekly radio address to discuss the arsons, which he called depraved. "We must rise up as a national community and safeguard the right of every citizen to worship in safety," he said. "As president, I am determined to do everything in my power to get to the bottom of these church burnings as quickly as possible. And no matter how long it takes, no matter where the leads take us, we will devote whatever resources are necessary to solve these crimes." The president announced the creation of a task force consisting of, among others, Assistant Attorney General Deval Patrick, Assistant Secretary of the Treasury for Enforcement James Johnson, FBI Director Louis Freeh, and ATF Director John Magaw. He asked the task force to report directly to him, instructed the ATF to inform churches of steps they might take to protect their properties, announced his support of Conyers and Hyde's bill, and announced the creation of a toll-free, twenty-four-hour hotline to report information related to church arsons. "Every family has a right to expect that when they walk into a church or synagogue or mosque each week, they will find a house of worship, not the charred remains of a hateful act done by cowards in the night," he said. President Clinton's creation of the National Church Arson Task Force (NCATF) was a decisive and significant move, one that symbolized the federal government's full commitment to the plight of the endangered churches. The task force concentrated the resources of the FBI, ATF, Department of Justice's Civil Rights Division, and U.S. Attorneys Offices; it also coordinated the efforts of local prosecutors, local law enforcement officers, victim and witness coordinators, and others to investigate fires, bombings, and attempted arsons on, at, or near houses of worship. The attorney general also directed all U.S. attorneys to form local church arson task forces within their respective districts.[19]

The fires reminded President Clinton and many other Americans of the 1960s, when white supremacists routinely attacked Black churches. The numbers were alarming. Records kept by the Congress of Racial Equality (CORE) indicate that no less than two hundred Black churches were burned and destroyed in the South during the civil rights era. In the twelve-week period surrounding the signing of the Civil Rights Act of 1964 by President Lyndon Baines Johnson, thirty-four Black churches were burned in Mississippi alone. For those bent on disrupting Black political participation in the 1960s, churches were obvious targets: by destroying the core ingredient in the lives of many African Americans, white supremacists sought to weaken the collective activism of the civil rights movement. The spiritual dimension of the civil rights struggle in the 1960s is well documented, as is the central importance of churches that served as command centers for political activism and as conduits of information in the civil rights movement.[20] These churches were not only symbolic centers of Black life but also high-functioning clearinghouses for organization and assistance. If there was a kind of twisted logic to this brand of hate crime, then it is hardly surprising that churches were firebombed.[21]

It was difficult, however, for many Americans to comprehend how church burnings could occur in 1996. Had the United States not solved most of its racial problems? Was this kind of overt bigotry not behind us? Indeed, it was impossible to understand these fires without understanding the context in which they occurred and without acknowledging the ways in which concepts of race continued to shape and structure civil society. The early 1990s were years of intense racial strife in the United States, as exemplified by obvious signifiers such as the Rodney King incident in 1991, the Los Angeles Riots in 1992, and the O. J. Simpson trial in 1995, and by less obvious signifiers, too. The rise of militias in the early 1990s, for example, signaled a union of neopopulist politics with a readiness to employ violence; some militias anticipated an eminent race war between whites and Blacks, or what their pamphlets and literature called "RaHoWa" (for "racial holy war"). So too did the Susan Smith case in 1994, and the 1995 Oklahoma City bombing carry ominous racial overtones. In the Smith case, investigators in South Carolina unquestioningly accepted the racially charged accusations of a woman who accused Black assailants of taking her children—when, in fact, she had drowned them herself. In Oklahoma City, law enforcement personnel scoured the area for Muslim terrorists after erroneous speculations by journalists that Islamic fundamentalists were the prime suspects in blowing up the Alfred P. Murrah Federal Building. Coming when they did—*before* the postracialism ascendant in the Obama moment, and amid new framings of race extant in the Clinton administration, which posited centrism on social policy as the "new normal"—such incidents highlighted the continuing divisiveness of race in the 1990s.

Other issues may have helped to create a climate in which hate crime might once again flourish. A July 6 piece by Dorothy Gilliam in the *Washington Post* described a sociopolitical environment conducive to such incidents, or what she called the "political tinder for church arsons." The article pointed to a host of interrelated factors, including Supreme Court rulings against affirmative action, other court rulings that reversed redistricting intended to improve minority voting power, "hate talk radio," negative media portrayals of young Black men as social predators and young Black women as welfare queens, and conservative politicking that minimized the impact of discrimination. "When people in power refuse to defend principles of fairness and use racial code words, they lay the groundwork that contributes to deep racial animosity," said Elaine Jones, director of the NAACP Legal Defense and Education Fund. The article also described the role of economic fears resulting from the shift from manufacturing to an information- and service-based economy. "When jobs in plants have gone offshore to Thailand and Cambodia, the employment problem it creates prompts people to look for scapegoats," said Mary Frances Berry, chairperson of the U.S. Commission on Civil Rights.[22]

Considering the church arsons in relation to these incidents and issues—a dystopian tangle of social mistrust, racial animosity, and economic uncertainty beneath a problem-free veneer of prosperity—allows a deeper understanding of hate crime as a function of political and social unrest. The arsons were examples of such troubles even as they were products of them. As Mary Frances Berry noted, "The church bombings are really a wake-up call to deal with the larger social context in which these fires are taking place." Clearly the fires acted as a way to measure popular attitudes about race and politics not only across the rural South but also across the entire nation: as racial and ethnic tension increased in the 1990s, so too did reported incidents of arson at Black churches.[23]

Questions about whether or not the fires constituted an epidemic began in July 1996. A review of six years of federal, state, and local records by the Associated Press (AP) found that arsons were up at both Black and white churches but that the arsons had only random links to racism. The AP report stated: "There is no evidence that most of the seventy-three Black church fires recorded since 1995 can be blamed on a conspiracy or a general climate of racial hatred. . . . In fewer than twenty cases racism is the clear motivation." The news bureau reported that insurance-industry officials said that the 1996 toll of church fires was within the range of what they would normally expect. A review of Black church fires in eleven southern states indicated racially motivated arsons in from twelve to eighteen cases; no overt racism in fifteen cases (including nine cases in which Black suspects were named and six cases involving sprees at both Black and white churches); and unclear motivation in the remaining dozen or so cases.[24]

Some critics questioned the severity of the crimes. Michael Fumento, in a July 8 piece for the *Wall Street Journal*, accused *USA Today* of overreporting the arsons and blowing them out of proportion. The number of actual arsons, he claimed, was actually far less than originally reported. Fumento's article had the effect of a yellow flag at an auto race—that is, the media frenzy slowed and journalists began to report the stories with greater caution—but it had other effects too. While his article did not specifically address President Clinton's public stand against the arsons, Fumento helped to foment cynicism about the Clinton administration's efforts to combat the problem. He and other skeptics cast doubt on the motivations of organizations such as the Center for Democratic Renewal (CDR), founded in 1979 as the Anti-Klan Network, and the National Council of Churches (NCC) that publicized the arsons as a crisis. In doing so they helped to politicize the issue of church burning.[25]

For instance, in an August 10 press release, Diane Knippers, president of the Washington-based Institute on Religion and Democracy (IRD), accused the National Council of Churches of creating the church arson story and manufacturing evidence that Black churches burn more frequently than white churches "to raise money for its leftist political agenda." The IRD spokeswoman cited three major media outlets that showed that arsons at Black churches represented a fraction of the 600 churches torched every year in the United States, and noted that church arson had declined dramatically from a figure of over 1,400 in 1980. Rev. Joan Brown Campbell of the NCC maintained that fires at Black churches had "increased dramatically and persistently over the past eighteen to thirty months"—a trend "all the more startling" because church burnings overall had declined in recent years. She noted that the rate of arson at white churches had remained constant in the past eighteen months, while the rate of arson at Black churches "is more than double" the rate in previous years. She noted that more than 60 churches had burned between January 1, 1995 and June 30, 1996—"more than in the previous five years combined." Most significantly, Campbell noted that while the same approximate number of Black and white churches had burned since 1995, Black churches were burning in proportion to their number at four times the rate of white churches; she estimated a total of 63,000 African American churches in the United States compared to approximately 235,000 white churches.[26]

The numbers involved were muddy at best, with conflicting reports and confusing statistics. The Center for Democratic Renewal (CDR) claimed that there had been ninety arsons against Black churches in nine southern states between 1990 and 1996, with numbers rising each year, to the peak of thirty-five by June 18, 1996; it also claimed that every suspect arrested or detained was white. However, the National Center for Policy Analysis (NCPA) claimed that the Center for Democratic Renewal was "fanning the church-burning issue out of proportion" by initiating more than 2,200 articles on the subject. The NCPA suggested that the CDR regularly ignored fires set by Blacks, and that it labeled fires as arsons that were clearly not; also, the CDR allegedly misrepresented the crisis by highlighting more recent cases and by ignoring fires that occurred earlier in the decade.[27]

Smoldering (July 1996–1999)

Like the *Wall Street Journal* article, a July 15 article in *The New Yorker* may also have helped to slow the avalanche of reporting; like Fumento's article, this article by Michael Kelly found the national news media overeager and undercautious in reporting the incidents. The increase in the number of fires in the Southeast during the previous eighteen months was much too dramatic to be explained away by a mere increase in reporting, noted the author. The article quoted ATF director John Magaw, who observed, "There are too many predominantly African-American churches being burned in too concentrated an area. This clearly indicates an underlying vindictiveness toward Black churches." Clusters of fires at Black churches accounted for the spike in otherwise normal levels of arson reports, and racist graffiti was left behind at some sites. However, the article also noted that the fire at Matthews Murkland Presbyterian Church, which President Clinton had highlighted in his June 8 address, was set by an emotionally troubled thirteen-year-old girl who seemingly harbored no racial animus. "The solitary act of pubescent madness seemed to have nothing to do with issues of race or politics," wrote Kelly, who also noted how Democrats and Republicans alike might benefit from public stands against the arsons. For Clinton, the fires offered an opportunity to play the role of "national father"; for the Republicans, whose Contract with America had led to accusations of callousness toward the needs of Black Americans, the issue offered "a chance for compassion on the cheap." Kelly suggested caution in reporting the arsons when he noted, "in a case of overreaction that seems to have been inspired in roughly equal measure by genuine concern, guilt, and self-interest, they [journalists and politicians] leaped on the bandwagon with a near hysteria as misplaced as their previous indifference." The recent fires did not warrant comparisons with those of the 1960s. "The acts of a relatively few misfits and miscreants in the night cannot be equated with the vast and purposeful campaign of terror directed against Black citizens in the South during the civil rights struggle," he concluded.[28]

Amid such controversy, the federal government continued to investigate the crimes diligently. According to the FBI, 790 investigations were initiated between 1996 and 1999 under the supervision of the new National Church Arson Task Force. During this time, 343 individuals were arrested in connection with 259 church arsons; of those 343, 68 were charged with federal violations and 275 were charged with state violations. Of the 790 church arsons investigations by the NCATF, 258 occurred at Black churches.[29]

The large number of investigations by the NCATF was overshadowed by its inability to correlate them or link them together. The federal government ultimately found no evidence of a wider racist conspiracy. According to the first NCATF report, released in the summer of 1997, the Ku Klux Klan was *not* mobilizing to orchestrate a campaign of terror across the United States.[30]

The NCATF report, coupled with allegations by skeptics, had a threefold effect. First, press coverage of the arsons plummeted. Most newspapers did not retract earlier reports of church arsons: they simply stopped reporting the incidents as they happened. On June 9, 1997, when the *Washington Post*, *Miami Herald*, *Philadelphia Inquirer*, and other major American newspapers publicized that the National Church Arson Task Force had found no evidence of a racial conspiracy in the fires, press coverage dropped off considerably. Other papers continued to cover fires at individual churches but failed to discuss these arsons as part of a larger trend.[31]

Second, the American public began to lose interest in the arsons. If the KKK was not involved, so went the reasoning, then there was little to fear. The public seemed to agree with the new message being reported: *No conspiracy, no problem*. The fires could be written off as the work of a few drunken teenagers or disgruntled rednecks. Third, and finally, contributions to rebuilding campaigns dried up. "Now we're having to dig deeply to find donors and actually have not met with a great deal of success," said Donna Derr, who oversaw the rebuilding effort for the National Council of Churches, in 1999. Even in-kind donations dropped, "be it choir robes or lumber or hymnals," Derr said.[32] The *New York Times* reported, "Clearly some of the sweeping descriptions of the church burnings by people trying to capture the public's attention have come back to haunt the [rebuilding] campaign." These developments happened even as churches worked to rebuild in the late 1990s, even as national news stories about the crimes lessened in number.[33]

If the public lost interest, then the fires certainly did not cease. Robert Press, a *Christian Science Monitor* correspondent and PhD candidate at the University of Florida, reported low public concern as fires continued through 1998 into 1999. Using statistics gathered by the NCATF, Press noted that church arsons continued in 1999 at the stunning rate of three to four per week, compared to six per week in 1996. The number of burned Black churches had declined from 40 percent in 1996 to 25 percent in 1997 and 1998; however, Press noted, even if only 25 percent of the churches burned during these years were Black, that number still indicated a much larger percentage than African Americans represented in the general population. Yes, the National Church Arson Task Force had speeded up federal response to suspected arsons, and yes, there was better coordination among federal agencies investigating church burnings; at 34 percent, the arrest rate was even double the 16 percent rate of arrests in arson cases nationwide. But Press worried that it was harder for groups to marshal funds and volunteers to help congregations rebuild because public attention had shifted elsewhere—even as the fires continued.[34] Reverend Terrance Mackey, executive director of the National Coalition for Burned Churches, said in April 1999, "We get fires every week that are reported to our office." [35]

Decay? (2006)

In early 2006, ten years after the initial scare, church arson again dominated national headlines. A series of fires scorched six rural churches in a single night in central Alabama. All but one occurred in Bibb County, south of Birmingham. Governor Bob Riley visited the sites of the arsons the following weekend to see the damage firsthand. Riley met with pastors and congregation members at each church. "I am outraged that anyone would deliberately set fire to churches," he said. "I want the people of the affected congregations to know that the state will do all that's possible to find those responsible and bring them to justice." Jim Walker, Alabama director of Homeland Security, said, "What strikes us the most is the senseless, needless act of burning down churches . . . It's hard to imagine a world that is starved for faith, love, and hope and the institutions that nurture those qualities would be the ones that these perpetrators chose to damage."[36]

Four days after the Bibb County fires, four more fires were reported at Black Baptist churches in western Alabama, in sparsely populated areas spread out over three counties, about sixty miles west of the earlier fires. The arsons in central and western Alabama were markedly similar. In each case, the arsonists deliberately made their way to the sanctuary to start multiple fires. Investigators found similar burn patterns at the churches. Fires were started in the area of the pulpit and/or church organ; the arsonists also burned flags (U.S. and religious) in the front of the church, as well as any floral arrangements. All of the fires occurred at Baptist churches. All of the churches were isolated, often tucked deep in the woods at the end of dirt roads. Because the churches were so remote, investigators suspected that the arsonists were local residents. National newspapers covered the fires; editorials decried the crimes. The investigation quickly turned into the biggest domestic manhunt since 9/11. Over two hundred investigators—ATF agents, FBI agents, state fire marshals, Justice Department officials, and local law enforcement personnel—sifted through seven hundred leads as they searched for the arsonists.[37]

On March 8, authorities arrested three suspects, all college students from Birmingham, for burning nine churches in central and western Alabama. Two of the suspects were identified as Benjamin Nathan Moseley and Russell Lee DeBusk Jr., both nineteen-year-old students at Birmingham-Southern College. Matthew Lee Cloyd, a twenty-year-old junior at the University of Alabama at Birmingham, also was arrested. The three were not only jailed on federal charges of conspiracy and arson but also faced state charges. Confronted by authorities, the young men claimed that the arson spree was a "joke" that "got out of hand." The boys plea-bargained federal charges in December 2006. On April 9, 2007, Matthew Lee Cloyd, and Benjamin Nathan Moseley were sentenced to eight years in prison for conspiracy and arson. The judge also ordered both to pay $3.1 million in restitution. Russell Lee DeBusk Jr. was sentenced to serve seven years in prison for conspiracy and arson at five of the churches. He was ordered to pay $1.8 million in restitution.[38]

Investigators, authorities, and concerned citizens wondered what had changed between this latest round of arsons and those of the previous decade. In the intervening period, a few observers recognized that the fires seemed to represent something above and beyond immediate circumstance, transcending localized instances of hate. Broader meanings came into focus in the months and years after the initial story crested in 1996. For example, the way the church fires were reported came to symbolize the growing problem of media bias and less-than-objective news reporting. "The church burning story is a classic example of media framing so strong that it can ward off even a sturdy set of actual facts," John Leo noted in *U.S. News & World Report* in May 1997. "Once the story was seen as a startling new epidemic of classic racial hatred, it was very difficult for the media to drop this powerful narrative line, even though evidence piled up very quickly that it was exaggerated to the point of being a hoax." As critics scoffed, some newspapers backpedaled. For instance, in June 1997 the *Seattle Times* congratulated itself for demonstrating restraint in an editorial titled "When Church-Fire Stories Swept Nation, *Times* Let Caution Be the Guide."[39]

While some skeptics questioned the numbers involved, others cynically suggested that African Americans were exploiting news of the church burnings in order to draw attention to themselves. Some suggested that there was profit to be made from what seemed to be a succession of tragedies. Mark Tooley, a research associate at the Institute on Religion and Democracy in Washington, DC, looked back in 2001 on the events of 1996. "We now know there never was any firm evidence of a church-arson epidemic and evidence of a racist conspiracy aimed at Black churches," he confidently asserted. "We also know that a significant chunk of the millions of dollars raised for church reconstruction never actually went for bricks and mortar." In a *Chronicles* magazine article, Tooley provided a detailed analysis of the financial dimensions of the 1996 fires. He charged that the entire story was "a fundraising tool" intended to "forestall the NCC [National Council of Churches]'s impending financial collapse."[40]

Unquestionably, the debate over the scope and significance of the arsons seemed to reveal as much about the super-heated political climate of the Clinton era as it did the intensity and frequency of hate crime in 1996. Amidst efforts to roll back affirmative action, those on the right sought to downplay the arsons and minimize the ongoing significance of race in American life. Those on the left saw right-wing complicity in the arsons themselves. A March 1996 editorial in *Time* magazine observed:

> [A]ll the conservative Republicans, from Newt Gingrich to Pete Wilson, who have sought political advantage by exploiting white resentment should come and stand in the charred ruins of the New Liberty Baptist Church in Tyler, a tiny hamlet ten miles east of Selma, and wonder if their coded phrases encouraged the arsonists . . . [T]o the Blacks who live here, the motive is transparent: intimidation. And they believe the politicians who have stoked the fires of hatred should be held accountable for whipping up a climate in which such terrorism is thinkable.[41]

"They [the politicians] may not start the fires," the author concluded, "but they fan the flames."[42]

Raking the Ashes

Today, many of the fires of the 1990s remain unsolved and unresolved, and on the whole it remains difficult to make sense of these crimes. Many of them seem to have been totally senseless, devoid of any larger significance or meaning. The poet Nikki Giovanni, in thinking about the church arsons, wrote, "There is no reason to ask 'why' since to ask 'why' is to enter some dark and crazy spot where one presumes there is reason."[43]

It is even difficult to know definitively the scope of the crimes. Statistics on the fires remain inconsistent; different data sets reveal different numbers. The known facts were few and the media tended to report widely varying numbers of churches involved. For example in his second article with Tom Watson, Gary Fields reported that twenty-three Black churches had been torched by arsonists since April 4, 1993, when white teenagers burned two Mississippi churches to celebrate the twenty-fifth anniversary of Martin Luther King Jr.'s assassination. Fields and Richard Price reported in *USA Today* that thirty fires at Black churches were being or had been investigated in the South between January 13, 1995 and June 4, 1996. CNN printed a record of fire investigations at Black churches on June 8, 1996 that listed thirty-seven total fires since January 1995 (twenty-nine of them in the South); seven fires certified as accidental; five cases closed by arrest; and twenty-five investigations still open. The presiding bishop's office of Trinity Episcopal Church in Houston named *eighty* Black churches that had burned during between January 5, 1990 and June 17, 1996 in Alabama, Arkansas, Florida, Georgia, Kentucky, Louisiana, Mississippi, North Carolina, Oklahoma, South Carolina, Tennessee, Texas, and Virginia.[44]

The media's problem in accurately reporting the number of church burnings reflected a larger problem in determining and recording the crime of arson. It would have been difficult for even the most diligent journalist to research and report definitive arson statistics before 1996, in the days before the federal government began to record the crimes in a systematic way; even after 1996, people could not agree on the figures involved. For example, in November 2002, the *Washington Post* reported that legal efforts did not halt the church arsons of the 1990s. The most recent NCATF report said that arsons, bombings, and attempts of both at houses of worship had decreased from 297 in 1996 to 140 in 1999—a drop from 25 per month to 12. In 2001 and 2002, the number of incidents averaged about 10 per month, according to Harold Scott Jr.

of the Bureau of Alcohol, Tobacco, and Firearms. The National Coalition for Burned Churches, which kept its own national registry of incidents culled from government statistics and reports solicited from state fire marshals' offices, published very different findings. "The numbers have come down, but not too much," said Rose Johnson-Mackey, NCBC research director. The NCBC found that the incidents are occurring at a much higher rate of 40 to 80 per month. Unlike the NCATF, the NCBC's figures include fires of undetermined cause, and attacks ranging from total to partial destruction of a building, as well as attacks causing no damage; however, Johnson-Mackey feels that the NCBC's own registry of incidents is incomplete due to underreporting by local fire departments. "The information . . . is based on available data reflecting less than 20 percent of all church burning and bombing activity nationwide," she said.[45]

Even if people had been able to agree what had burned and where and when—and they could not—different groups contemplating the same set of facts were seeing widely disparate scenarios. Attempts to verify claims of arson met difficulty in part because, prior to the creation of the NCATF, there was no central repository of information on arsons. State insurance agencies kept accurate records of alleged arsons but different newspapers posted different statistics on the events in question, and it was unclear which fires were accidental and which were set deliberately. It was even unclear which burned churches had predominantly Black congregations and which did not. The National Fire Protection Association (NFPA) reported in July 1996 that it could not comment on the racial dimension of the fires because it had never differentiated between arsons at Black and white churches. Said Julie Reynolds, NFPA spokesperson, "We kept records on churches, not the race of the congregation."[46]

If the number of churches affected remains unclear, then the political and social impacts of the arsons remain incontrovertible; and, if scrutinizing these arsons raises more questions than it answers, then doing so also provides some truths and lessons, however fleeting and unsatisfying. First, these incidents *did* have the intended effect of terrorizing and traumatizing Black churchgoers, but they also had the unintended effect of galvanizing communities, empowering congregations, and unifying Americans across racial lines. Apart from the resilience of the congregations affected by the fires, one of the most heartening aspects of the arsons was the response of tens of thousands of people from all over the nation—including white people in those southern communities where the arsons had occurred—who contributed time, money, resources, and support to those affected.

Second, if there existed a danger in rushing to judgment due to hyperbole, then there also existed a danger in waiting to sound an alarm or to intervene. Surely the eagerness of some critics to treat the arsons with skepticism blinded them to a larger truth: *someone* was burning churches across the nation, and many of them—a disproportionate number of them, in fact—were African American churches. As one journalist phrased it, "emotion and intuition can cloud analysis, but they can also rescue it from abstraction and sterility."[47]

Third, whether or not the number of arsons constituted a crisis or not remains fairly subjective. To some, the numbers suggested slipshod journalism in which rumor replaced fact-checking, and the way the story was reported created a sense of crisis where none existed. To others, *any* church burned out of malice indicated a grave problem that warranted concern.

Fourth, the fires laid bare a certain meanness that manifested itself in American society in the 1990s. The fires were happening organically, flaring across the country from Oregon to Florida without benefit of an organized, white-supremacist plot. As the Deval Patrick, assistant U.S. attorney general for the Civil Rights Division, noted in 1996, the prospect of a conspiracy was a chilling thing but the prospect that these were separate acts of racism was even worse. They seem to have been part of a larger social pathology that speaks as much to the disintegration of community in contemporary American society, the meaningless violence, and the fragmentation of social order as it does to open racial hatred.

Fifth and finally, however, they also revealed much about the ongoing significance of race in America on the eve of the twenty-first century. Regardless of whether they indicated a racist conspiracy, regardless of whether all of them were racially inspired hate crimes, and even regardless of the actual number of arsons, the fires illustrated that race still affected human relations in profound ways. The fires showed that—as much as Americans wanted it to no longer be relevant—*race still mattered.*

Liberals and conservatives, Northerners and Southerners, Democrats and Republicans, and Blacks and whites all spoke out against what they perceived to be overt examples of bigotry, and such a unified front against racism would have been hard to imagine fifty, forty, or even thirty years ago. This condemnation of race-based hate crime was loud and unequivocal, and the nationwide reaction to the fires showed just how far Americans had progressed in their commitment to race relations. The perception of racist intent forced a reaffirmation of unity at a time of great political and social divisiveness. Indeed, the fires ultimately helped to unite Americans across racial and class divides against overt racism and bigotry—even if bigotry was not ultimately the cause of all of the fires.

The arsons exposed the thorniest aspects of dealing with race in the post–civil rights era. How to confront racism—indeed, how to address issues of race in general—has always vexed a nation in which race has played enormous historical, cultural, and social significance. From one perspective, talking about racism and confronting it is the only way to excise its hold on American history and culture. From another perspective, to discuss racism is to somehow perpetuate it; therefore it is best to downplay it or if possible not discuss it at all. This latter perspective lost some credence in the fires of the 1990s, as the arsons necessitated a new dialogue about race at a time when many Americans were patting themselves on the back for having overcome racism. Race mattered during those fires and it continues to matter when we hear news of other possible bias crimes, from clear-cut ones such as the murder of James Byrd Jr., chained to a pickup truck and dragged to his death in 1998, to the problematic case of seventeen-year-old Trayvon Martin, shot and killed by a neighborhood watchman in Sanford, Florida, in 2012.

Perhaps it is still too soon to tell the full story of what happened. While a few attempts have been made to describe incidents at individual churches, more analysis is clearly necessary.[48] Like the figures and statistics involved, the meanings of these fires are open to interpretation, yet at least one additional generalization can be made about these events: good often comes out of tragedy. While the devastation of the fires cannot be underestimated, biracial unity, communal revitalization, renewed faith, opposition to intolerance, and a host of other positives may be counted among their outcomes. As Andrew Cuomo, then Secretary of the U.S. Department of Housing and Urban Development (HUD) said in 1997: "[T]he story of church burning in America over the past few years is a story with two bookends, one a bookend of discrimination and anger, the other a bookend of hope and renewal. In between is a story of national faith, devotion and humanity—the best chapters of which are still being written today."[49]

Notes

1. "Arson in the United States," *U.S Fire Administration Topical Fire Research Series* 1, no. 8 (January 2001): 1; "Fact Sheet on Arson and Church Fires in the USA," *National Fire Protection Association*, http://www.dps.la.us/sfm/arson/churchfires.htm.

2. For more information, see Christopher B. Strain, *Burning Faith: Church Arson in the American South* (Gainesville: University Press of Florida, 2008).

3. James K. Glassman, "Hiding Behind the Smoke," *Washington Post*, June 18, 1996: A13.

4. Information on these fires was later collected and consolidated by the Center for Democratic Renewal. See Center for Democratic Renewal, "Black Church Burnings in the South," *Statistical Data (June 1996)*, accessed February 14, 2014, http://www.hartford-hwp.com/archives/45a/121.html.

5. "List of Black Church Fire Investigations," *CNN Interactive*, last modified June 8, 1996, http://www.cnn.com/US/ 9606/08/arson.timeline/index.html; "Across the USA, News from Every State," *USA Today*, Feb. 20, 1995: A7; "Crime Report—Portsmouth," *Virginian-Pilot*, June 2, 1995: Portsmouth Currents Section, Final Edition, 12.

6. *Forgotten Fires*, produced and directed by Michael Chandler (1999: California Newsreel, 1999), VHS.

7. Brian Cabell, "Arson at Black Churches Revives Old Fears," *CNN Interactive*, last modified January 19, 1996, http://www.cnn.com/US/9601/church_arson/.

8. Thomas George, "For Reggie White, Racism Is Hardest Foe," *New York Times*, January 11, 1996: B9; see also Bob Ford, "Reggie Just Wants to Play through Terrible Distraction of Church Fire," *Philadelphia Inquirer*, January 12, 1996: D1.

9. Linda Kanamine, "'Unmistakable' Terrorism in Arson at Tenn. Church," *USA Today*, January 12, 1996: A3.

10. Ronald Smothers, "Black Church Fires Are Under U.S. Review," *New York Times*, Jan. 20, 1996: 7; Cabell, "Arson at Black Churches Revives Old Fears"; Kanamine, "'Unmistakable' Terrorism in Arson at Tenn. Church."

11. Gary Fields and Tom Watson, "Arson at Black Churches Echoes Bigotry of the Past," *USA Today*, February 8, 1996: A3.

12. Gary Fields, "Church Fires May Have No Racial Link," *USA Today*, March 19, 1996: A1.

13. "Black Ministers Ask for Arson Inquiry," *New York Times*, April 23, 1996: A19; "Arson Fire Guts a Church," *New York Times*, April 29, 1996: A20; Gary Fields and Richard Price, "Church's Faith Withstands the Fire," *USA Today*, May 6, 1996: A3.

14. Kevin Sack, "Links Sough in 'Epidemic of Terror,'" *New York Times*, May 21, 1996: A12.

15. U.S. Congress, House, Committee on the Judiciary, *Church Fires in the Southeast: Hearing before the Committee of the Judiciary*, 104th Congress, 2nd sess., May 21, 1996, 2–8.

16. Gary Fields, "Another Church in South Falls Victim to Fire," *USA Today*, May 29, 1996: A7.

17. "Rallying Against Church Fires," *The Christian Century* 113 (June 19–26, 1996): 648–649.

18. "Fire Destroys a Black Church in Alabama," *New York Times*, June 4, 1996: A12.

19. "Arson Strikes Black Church, 30th in 18 Months," *New York Times*, June 8, 1996: 6; Radio Address by the President to the Nation, Oval Office, June 8, 1996; Jill Dougherty, "Clinton Sounds Call to Stop Church Burnings," *CNN Interactive*, last modified June 8, 1996, http://www.cnn.com/US/9606/08/clinton.radio.cnn/.

20. For example, see Taylor Branch, *Parting the Waters: America in the King Years, 1954–63* (New York: Simon & Schuster, 1988).

21. Michael and Judy Newton, *The Ku Klux Klan: An Encyclopedia* (New York: Garland Science, 1990); Reginold Bundy, "Trail of Ashes," *Tri-State Defender*, January 24, 1996.

22. Dorothy Gilliam, "The Political Tinder for Church Arsons," *Washington Post*, July 6, 1996: B1.

23. Ibid.

24. "Racism Behind Few Fires," *Post and Courier* (Charleston, S.C.), July 7, 1996: A16.

25. Michael Fumento, "A Church Arson Epidemic? It's Smoke and Mirrors," *Wall Street Journal*, July 8, 1996: A8.

26. United Methodist News Service, "National Council of Churches Responds to Conservative Think Tank's Charges," last modified August 14, 1996, http://gbgm.umc.org/advance/Church-Burnings/firenccc.html.

27. National Center for Policy Analysis Month in Review, "Black Church Arson No Sudden Recent Epidemic" (July 1996), http://www.ncpa.org/pd/monthly/pd796d.html. The NCPA based its assessment on a single article in the *Wall Street Journal*; see Michael Fumento, "A Church Arson Epidemic? It's Smoke and Mirrors," *Wall Street Journal*, July 8, 1996.

28. Michael Kelly, "Playing With Fire," *The New Yorker*, July 15, 1996: 28–35.

29. Federal Bureau of Investigation, "Hate Crimes," *FBI Civil Rights Program*, accessed February 14, 2014, http://www.fbi.gov/hq/cid/civilrights/hate.htm.

30. National Church Arson Task Force, *Interim Report for the President*, January 1997.

31. George Lardner, Jr., "Varied Motives Are Found for Church Blazes," *Washington Post*, June 9, 1997: A1; "No Racial Plot Seen in Fires," *Miami Herald*, June 9, 1997: A1; Peter Selvin and Angie Cannon, "Church Arsons Were Not a Racist Conspiracy," *Philadelphia Inquirer*, June 9, 1997: A3.

32. Angie Cannon and Chitra Ragavan, "Another Look at the Church Fire Epidemic," *U.S. News & World Report*, November 22, 1999: 26.

33. Peter Steinfels, "Beliefs," *New York Times*, October 19, 1996. For more, see Strain, *Burning Faith*.

34. Robert Press, "Church Arsons Continue—Concern Oddly Low," *Christian Science Monitor* Online, last modified January 26, 1999, http://www.csmweb2.emcweb.com/durable/1999/01/26/p11s1.htm. Press is now Associate Professor of Political Science at the University of Southern Mississippi.

35. "Church Arson Cases Continue in 'High Numbers,'" *United Methodist News Service*, April 5, 1999, http://gbgm-umc.org/advance/Church-Burnings/arsonhigh.html; Lisa Greene, "St. John Church Rises Again," *The State*, August 16, 1999: B1, Avery Research Center Vertical File, Charleston, S.C.

36. Hollie Huey, "Arsonists Torch Five Baptist Churches," *Centreville Press* (Centreville, AL), February 8, 2006.

37. "Tenth Alabama Church Fire Ruled Arson," *CNN Online*, last modified February 12, 2006, http://cnn.worldnews.

38. "Church Arsonists Sentenced," WAFF 48 News, Birmingham, Alabama, April 9, 2007; Jay Reeves, "More Guilty Pleas in Alabama Church Fires," *Houston Chronicle*, April 12, 2007.

39. John Leo, "Why Ruin a Good Story?" *U.S. News & World Report*, May 5, 1997; Michael R. Fancher, "When Church-Fire Stories Swept Nation, *Times* Let Caution Be the Guide," *Seattle Times*, June 22, 1997.

40. Mark Tooley, "Church Arsons: The Real Story?" *Chronicles* (May 2001), http://www.chroniclesmagazine.org/Chronicles/May2001/0501Tooley.htm.

41. Jack E. White, "Playing With Fire," *Time*, March 18, 1996.

42. Ibid.

43. Nikki Giovanni, "Don't Worry, There's No Racial Hatred Here," *New York Times*, July 11, 1996.

44. Gary Fields and Tom Watson, "In 3 Years, 23 Churches Burned, Rate of Fires Higher Than First Thought," *USA Today*, February. 16, 1996: 3A; Gary Fields and Richard Price, "Black Church Fires at 30," *USA Today*, June 4, 1996: A1; "List of Black Church Fire Investigations," *CNN Interactive*, last modified June 8, 1996, http://www.cnn.com/US/9606/08/arson.timeline/index.html/; "Southern States' Black Church Burnings," *Church Burnings Information Page*, http://www.ghgcorp.com/trinity11/chlist.htm.

45. Bill Broadway, "Arson at Churches an Ongoing Problem," *Washington Post*, November 9, 2002: B9.

46. Robert Marquand, "Church Fire Phenomenon Goes Beyond Racial Lines," *Christian Science Monitor*, July 10, 1996: 1.

47. Steinfels, "Beliefs."

48. For book-length treatments, see Paul Hemphill, *The Ballad of Little River: A Tale of Race and Restless Youth in the Rural South* (New York: The Free Press, 2000); and Sandra E. Johnson, *Standing on Holy Ground: A Triumph over Hate Crime in the Deep South* (New York: St. Martin's Press, 2002). See also Norman A. Hjelm, *Out of the Ashes: Burned Churches and the Community of Faith* (Nashville: Thomas Nelson, 1997); and Strain, *Burning Faith*. For scholarly articles, see S. A. Soule and N. Van Dyke, "Black Church Arson in the United States, 1989–1996," *Ethnic and Racial Studies* 22, no. 4 (1999): 724–742; John P. Bartkowski, Frank M. Howell, and Shu-Chuan Lai, "Spatial Variations in Church Burnings: The Social Ecology of Victimized Communities in the South," *Rural Sociology* 67,

no. 4 (2002): 578–602; Carolyn S. Carter, "Church Burning: Using a Contemporary Issue to Teach Community Organization," *Journal of Social Work Education* 36 (2000):79–88; Carolyn S. Carter, "Church Burning in African American Communities: Implications for Empowerment Practice," *Social Work* 44 (1999): 62–68; Holly E. Ventura , Chris L. Gibson, and J. Mitchell Miller, "The Southern Church Burning Epidemic: An Examination of the South Carolina Experience," *Journal of Crime and Justice* 29, no. 2 (2006): 95–115; and Nicholas Adam, "Churches on Fire," *Journal of the Society of Architectural Historians* 55, no. 3 (September 1996): 236–237.

49. Prepared Testimony of Andrew Cuomo, Senate Banking, Housing, and Urban Affairs Committee, Subcommittee on Financial Institutions and Regulatory Relief, Oversight Hearing on the Federal Loan Guaranty Program, July 17, 1997.

Bibliography

Adam, Nicholas. "Churches on Fire." *Journal of the Society of Architectural Historians* 5, no. 3 (September 1996): 236–237.

"Arson Fire Guts a Church." *New York Times*, April 29, 1996, A20.

"Arson in the United States." *U.S Fire Administration Topical Fire Research Series 1*, no. 8 (January 2001): 1.

"Arson Strikes Black Church, 30th in 18 Months." *New York Times*, June 8, 1996, 6.

Bartkowski, John P., Frank M. Howell, and Shu-Chuan Lai. "Spatial Variations in Church Burnings: The Social Ecology of Victimized Communities in the South." *Rural Sociology* 67, no. 4 (2002): 578–602.

"Black Church Arson No Sudden Recent Epidemic." National Center for Policy Analysis Month in Review (July 1996), http://www.ncpa.org/pd/monthly/pd796d.html.

"Black Ministers Ask for Arson Inquiry." *New York Times*, April 23, 1996, A19.

Branch, Taylor. *Parting the Waters: America in the King Years, 1954–63.* New York: Simon & Schuster, 1988.

Broadway, Bill. "Arson at Churches an Ongoing Problem." *Washington Post*, November 9, 2002, B9.

Bundy, Reginold. "Trail of Ashes." *Tri-State Defender*, January 24, 1996.

Cabell, Brian. "Arson at Black Churches Revives Old Fears." *CNN Interactive*. Last modified January19, 1996, http://www.cnn.com/US/9601/church_arson/.

Canno, Angie, and Chitra Ragavan. "Another Look at the Church Fire Epidemic." *U.S. News & World Report*, November 22, 1999, 26.

Carter, Carolyn S. "Church Burning in African American Communities: Implications for Empowerment Practice." *Social Work* 44 (1999): 62–68.

———. "Church Burning: Using a Contemporary Issue to Teach Community Organization." *Journal of Social Work Education* 36 (2000):79–88.

"Church Arson Cases Continue in 'High Numbers.'" *United Methodist News Service*, April 5, 1999, http://gbgm-umc.org/advance/Church-Burnings/arsonhigh.html.

"Church Arsonists Sentenced." WAFF 48 News, Birmingham, Alabama, April 9, 2007.

Dougherty, Jill. "Clinton Sounds Call to Stop Church Burnings." *CNN Interactive*, June 8, 1996, http://www.cnn.com/US/9606/08/clinton.radio.cnn/.

Fact Sheet on Arson and Church Fires in the USA. *National Fire Protection Association*, http://www.dps.la.us/sfm/arson/churchfires.htm.

Fancher, Michael R. "When Church-Fire Stories Swept Nation, *Times* Let Caution Be the Guide." *Seattle Times*, June 22, 1997.

Federal Bureau of Investigation. "Hate Crimes," *FBI Civil Rights Program*, http://www.fbi.gov/hq/cid/civilrights/hate.htm.

Fields, Gary. "Another Church in South Falls Victim to Fire." *USA Today*, May 29, 1996, A7.

———. "Church Fires May Have No Racial Link." *USA Today*, March 19, 1996, A1.

Fields, Gary, and Richard Price. "Black Church Fires at 30." *USA Today*, June 4, 1996, A1.

———. "Church's Faith Withstands the Fire." *USA Today*, May 6, 1996, A3.

Fields, Gary, and Tom Watson. "Arson at Black Churches Echoes Bigotry of the Past." *USA Today*, February 8, 1996, A3.

———. "In 3 Years, 23 Churches Burned, Rate of Fires Higher Than First Thought." *USA Today*, February 16, 1996, 3A.

"Fire Destroys a Black Church in Alabama." *New York Times*, June 4, 1996, A12.

Ford, Bob. "Reggie Just Wants to Play through Terrible Distraction of Church Fire." *Philadelphia Inquirer*, January 12, 1996, D1.

Forgotten Fires. Produced and directed by Michael Chandler. 57 min. California Newsreel, 1999. Videocassette.

Fumento, Michael. "A Church Arson Epidemic? It's Smoke and Mirrors." *Wall Street Journal*, July 8, 1996, A8.

George, Thomas. "For Reggie White, Racism Is Hardest Foe." *New York Times*, January 11, 1996, B9.

Gilliam, Dorothy Gilliam. "The Political Tinder for Church Arsons." *Washington Post*, July 6, 1996, B1.

Giovanni, Nikki. "Don't Worry, There's No Racial Hatred Here." *New York Times*, July 11, 1996.

Glassman, James K. "Hiding Behind the Smoke." *Washington Post*, June 18, 1996, A13.

Greene, Lisa. "St. John Church Rises Again." *State*, August 16, 1999, B1.

Hemphill, Paul. *The Ballad of Little River: A Tale of Race and Restless Youth in the Rural South*. New York: The Free Press, 2000.

Huey, Hollie. "Arsonists Torch Five Baptist Churches." *Centreville Press* (Centreville, AL), February 8, 2006.

Hjelm, Norman A. *Out of the Ashes: Burned Churches and the Community of Faith*. Nashville: Thomas Nelson, 1997.

Johnson, Sandra E. *Standing on Holy Ground: A Triumph over Hate Crime in the Deep South*. New York: St. Martin's Press, 2002.

Kanamine, Linda. "'Unmistakable' Terrorism in Arson at Tenn. Church." *USA Today*, January 12, 1996, A3.

Kelly, Michael. "Playing with Fire." *The New Yorker*, July 15, 1996: 28–35.

Lardner, Jr., George. "Varied Motives Are Found for Church Blazes." *Washington Post*, June 9, 1997, A1.

Leo, John. "Why Ruin a Good Story?" *U.S. News & World Report*, May 5, 1997.

"List of Black Church Fire Investigations." *CNN Interactive*. Last modified June 8, 1996, http://www.cnn.com/US/ 9606/08/arson.timeline/index.html.

Marquand, Robert. "Church Fire Phenomenon Goes Beyond Racial Lines." *Christian Science Monitor*, July 10, 1996, 1.

National Church Arson Task Force. *Interim Report for the President*, January 1997.

"National Council of Churches Responds to Conservative Think Tank's Charges." *United Methodist News Service*. August 14, 1996, http://gbgm.umc.org/advance/Church-Burnings/firenccc.html.

Newton, Michael and Judy. *The Ku Klux Klan: An Encyclopedia*. New York: Garland Science, 1990.

"No Racial Plot Seen in Fires." *Miami Herald*, June 9, 1997. A1.

Prepared Testimony of Andrew Cuomo. U.S. Senate Banking, Housing, and Urban Affairs Committee. Subcommittee on Financial Institutions and Regulatory Relief. Oversight Hearing on the Federal Loan Guaranty Program, July 17, 1997.

Press, Robert. "Church Arsons Continue—Concern Oddly Low." *Christian Science Monitor* Online. January 26, 1999, http://www.csmweb2.emcweb.com/durable/1999/01/26/p11s1.htm.

"Racism Behind Few Fires." *Charleston Post and Courier* (Charleston, SC), July 7, 1996, A16.

Radio Address by the President to the Nation, Oval Office, June 8, 1996.

"Rallying Against Church Fires." *Christian Century* 113 (June 19–26, 1996): 648–649.

Reeves, Jay. "More Guilty Pleas in Alabama Church Fires." *Houston Chronicle*, April 12, 2007.

Sack, Kevin. "Links Sough in 'Epidemic of Terror.'" *New York Times*, May 21, 1996: A12.

Selvin, Peter, and Angie Cannon. "Church Arsons Were Not a Racist Conspiracy." *Philadelphia Inquirer*, June 9, 1997, A3.

Smothers, Ronald. "Black Church Fires Are Under U.S. Review." *New York Times*, January 20, 1996, 7.

Soule, S.A., and N. Van Dyke. "Black Church Arson in the United States, 1989–1996." *Ethnic and Racial Studies* 22, no. 4 (1999): 724–742.

"Southern States' Black Church Burnings." *Church Burnings Information Page*. http://www.ghgcorp.com/trinity11/chlist.htm.

Steinfels, Peter. "Beliefs." *New York Times*, October 19, 1996.

Strain, Christopher B. *Burning Faith: Church Arson in the American South*. Gainesville: University Press of Florida, 2008.

"Tenth Alabama Church Fire Ruled Arson." *CNN Online*. Last modified February 12, 2006, http://cnn.worldnews.

Tooley, Mark. "Church Arsons: The Real Story?" *Chronicles* (May 2001), http://www.chroniclesmagazine.org/Chronicles/May2001/0501Tooley.htm.

U.S. Congress, House of Representatives. Committee on the Judiciary. *Church Fires in the Southeast: Hearing before the Committee of the Judiciary*. 104th Congress, 2nd sess., May 21, 1996, 2–8.

Ventura, Holly E., Chris L. Gibson, and J. Mitchell Miller. "The Southern Church Burning Epidemic: An Examination of the South Carolina Experience." *Journal of Crime and Justice* 29, no. 2 (2006): 95–115.

White, Jack E. "Playing with Fire." *Time*, March 18, 1996.

4

Fear of a Black President

Conspiracy Theory and Racial Paranoia in Obamerica

Travis L. Gosa and Danielle Porter Sanchez

> White America died last night. Obama's reelection killed it. Our 200 plus year history as a Western nation is over. We're a Socialist Latin American country now. Venezuela without the oil. . . . I cried for hours. It's over for all of us. The great White nation will never survive another four years of Obama's leadership. . . . He's half White, [but] that's not the half I'm worried about.
>
> —The Fake Pat Buchanan[1]

> You can't go a day without hearing how Obama's a radical cactus sympathizer who wants to sap America of all its drinking water, or how he was actually born in the Kalahari Desert.
>
> —*The Onion*[2]

Since 2007, popular race-talk in *Obamerica* has been saturated with postracial optimism,[3] as many predicted that the Barack Obama presidency would remedy the pathology of racism and end anti-Black prejudice.[4] Unfortunately, a Black family in the White House has sparked a resurgence of racial paranoia and hate-mongering. For neoconservatives like Pat Buchanan and Tea Party "patriots," Obama represents the conquering of white America by dark outsiders, while racialized conspiracy theories probing Obama's legitimacy have reverberated from the fringes to the mainstream of American society.

This essay interrogates the madness of racial discourse in Obamerica. Instead of signaling the beginning of postracial America, Obama is further proof that America suffers from racial schizophrenia, a disorder defined by, "auditory hallucinations, paranoid or bizarre delusions, [and] disorganized speech and thinking about race."[5] In the madness of Obama-mania, the United States prematurely declared victory over racism, even when the demography of poverty, wealth, education, and incarceration denotes the continuation of a racialized caste system.[6] Worsening material conditions for Black and poor people in Obamerica has coincided with state-sanctioned racial profiling via New York City's "Stop-and-Frisk" policies, while the killings of Trayvon Martin, Oscar Grant, Michael Brown, Kimani Gray, Tamir Rice, and Aiyana Stanley-Jones have reignited concerns that it is open season on young, Black boys and girls.[7]

The saddening failure of postracial hope can be found in everyday and political discourse. Building on previous studies on contemporary race-talk,[8] we focus on racial framing during the Obama presidency. Specifically, this chapter looks at the discursive strategies, symbolisms, and linguistic manners found in popular Obama conspiracy theories. In 2010, the satirical website *The Onion* reported that "one in five Americans" believe Obama has "questionable links to the Cactaceae family."[9] According to real opinion polls during Obama's first term, about one-third of America wondered if Obama was secretly a Kenyan-born, Muslim, socialist.[10] More alarmingly, these rumors have persisted throughout Obama's presidency. A 2013 study concluded that one in four Americans believe that President Obama may be the anti-Christ.[11]

One goal of this essay is to evaluate the conspiratorial claims made against Obama, including the fake birth certificate, the reptilian-space-alien thesis, and the secret gay sex-club at Trinity United Church. What ideas about race, American identity, and legitimacy can be found in these conspiracy theories? Why might these outlandish stories be given currency by otherwise rational people? By exploring Obama conspiracy theories, we contribute to a growing social science literature on conspiracy theory culture.[12] Because Obama conspiracy theories thrive on the Internet, this exploration also contributes to the literature on the digital politics of paranoia.[13]

The chapter begins with a framing of Obama conspiracy theories within the context of color-blind, postracial discourse and the Right's politics of fear. After providing an overview of the numerous theories surrounding Obama, discursive analyses of the birther theories, New World Order reptile conspiracies, and homosexuality rumors is conducted. In-depth readings of these three Obama conspiracy theories are used to explore contemporary race-talk.

Postrace Talk in Obamerica

Centuries of capitalism established America's racial hierarchy,[14] but racism is also maintained by symbolic meaning systems embedded in language.[15] Discursive framing involves reducing complex situations into easy to grasp definitions, social actors, and stories that re-create the status quo.[16] The "white racial frame," as Joe Feagin calls racist discourse, operates in the hidden assumptions of language that normalize whiteness and deem blackness as a social problem.[17] As Patricia Hill-Collins observes, "Hegemonic ideologies concerning race, class, gender, sexuality, and nation" determine the ways in which we speak, making it "difficult to conceptualize alternatives to them, let alone ways of resisting the social practices that they justify."[18] This dynamic process can be conceptualized as *race talk*.

Postracialism has emerged as the newest paradigm of *color-blind* race talk. Color-blind or color-mute discourse avoids the specificity of race by talking in abstract terms like "hard work" or "educational values."[19] The veil of color-blind logic makes individual deficiencies the starting point of conversations about social problems, ensuring that talk about unearned white privilege and historical racial oppression is minimized. Postracialism is not a rebranding of antiracist philosophical idealism, or an attempt to privilege achieved characteristics over ascribed entitlements.[20] Rather, it silences sincere race-talk by claiming that we are "beyond" race, or are quickly moving toward an idealized postracial future.

Postracial talk attempts to depoliticize race by imagining racism as a coincidence. "Accidental racism," as the maligned Brad Paisley and LL Cool J duet celebrates,[21] denies both aspects of what Omi and Winant call "American racial formation": "the process by which social, economic and political forces determined the content and importance of racial categories, and by which they are in turn shaped by racial meanings."[22] In addition to refusing to acknowledge race, postrace assumes that minorities desire to achieve a common American identity, and are actively seeking full-inclusion into the existing American polity. This eventual assimilation from initial hardship to the mainstream occurs by adopting the cultural repertoires of white America, not through racial redress, agitation, or Nationalism. Third, postracial framing contains the ideology of meritocracy, the belief that the winners and losers of society are determined by individual effort. As Obama writes in his *Audacity of Hope* narrative, "America's original sin of slavery" and modern "petty slights" of prejudice have not destroyed the American Dream for anyone who wants to work hard.[23]

Of course, race still structures most aspects of American society, but postracial mythology works to define what conversations are "logical" or "crazy." The postracial frame, just like color-blind racism and its many tropes, works to preserve the existing status hierarchy while obscuring the historic and contemporary mechanisms of that power. "Having a black man 'in charge,'" according to Eduardo Bonilla-Silva, "allows whites to tell those who research, write, talk, and organize against racial inequality that they must be crazy."[24] It also allows individual whites to reclaim white privilege and to dismantle affirmative action programs under the guise of fairness. As the plaintiff in *Abigail Fisher v. The University of Texas* innocently stated about the exclusion of race as one factor in college admissions, "I was taught from the time I was a little girl that any kind of discrimination was wrong. And for an institution of higher learning to act this way makes no sense to me. What kind of example does it set for others?"[25]

How the Obama administration has forwarded postracial logic, and how Obama has maintained his claim to Black authenticity while espousing a post-Black political platform has already received much academic coverage.[26] Indeed, Fredrick Harris's warning that the symbolism of Obama's election has become a barrier to addressing racial inequality is an important point.[27] To this ongoing debate, this essay adds that the election of the first Black president has worked to further obscure and silence serious discussions of race.

Racial Paranoia and Conspiracy Theory

Obama was elected into an America in which public conversations about segregated housing and schooling, unemployment, and mass incarceration are framed by the loss of "traditional black values" and "personal responsibility."[28] Those invoking racism as a possible cause of these social problems are accused of practicing "victimology" or "playing the race card." To recall, Kanye West's suggestion that race influenced President George W. Bush's handling of the Hurricane Katrina disaster was called "racial bluffing" and a "rant."[29] The arrest of Harvard Professor Henry "Skip" Gates in his own home was treated as an overreaction by Gates—not a case of systemic racial profiling. Obama resolved the "misunderstanding" by apologizing to the Cambridge police and staging a beer summit on the White House lawn.[30]

The chilling effect on race talk has led many Americans to resort to conspiracy theories as a way to discuss issues of race. *Racial paranoia*, according to John Jackson, invokes "alarmist and conspiratorial attitudes and assumptions" to explain "race-based maliciousness and the benign neglect of racial indifference."[31] Racially paranoid speech counters postracialism by using conspiracy theory to reject explanations that involve accidents, while dramatizing social issues with easily definable villains.

For example, to disrupt the silence of race, the Hurricane Katrina disaster was retold with stories of the government blowing up the levees in order to purposely kill Black residents. Color blindness prevented discussions of how government neglect allowed Black/poor residents in the Gulf Region to suffer for decades in concentrated poverty, crime, and dysfunctional schools—all before the storm. Instead, the racialized conspiracy theory of controlled denotations was used to rerace/reclass the disaster. What if President Bush ordered FEMA to round up Black residents into modern-day concentration camp disguised as "emergency trailers" for Katrina evacuees?[32]

Conspiratorial thinking is often associated with white people, specifically, bearded recluses in the hills of Montana, babbling about government plots to hide space aliens or secret One World governments. However, conspiracy theories have become entrenched in mainstream American political discourse and entertainment.[33] In the aftermath of 9/11, upward of 70 percent of Americans bought into imaginary threats of al-Qaeda and Saddam Hussein detonating nuclear bombs in the United States,[34] while about 40 percent of Americans suspected that Bush ordered the destruction of the World Trade Center towers.[35] In 2013, about 37 percent of Americans thought that global warming was a "hoax," while 28 percent accepted New World Order conspiracies.[36] African Americans are especially apt to use conspiracy theories to discuss real issues of racial inequality. A plurality of Blacks, regardless of social class, believes that the government uses HIV/AIDS, needle exchanges, and transracial adoption to commit genocide against Blacks.[37]

Rapper Mos Def's 2007 interview with Bill Maher confirms that conspiracy theories are not reserved for those on the fringes of society. Explaining his belief that George W. Bush was behind the 9/11 attacks, Mos Def said, "Highly-educated people in all areas of science have spoken on the fishiness around the whole 9/11 theory. It's like the magic-bullet and all that shit [the JFK assassination]. . . . I don't believe these mother-fuckers have been to the moon either, but that's just me."[38]

Important is that conspiracy theories are often used as a conduit for expressing racial beliefs. In the case of 9/11, both Islamophobia and anti-Semitism could be found in rumors that Arab cab drivers and Jewish businessmen fled the towers right before the attacks.[39] Before the FBI released official information and photographs of the Tsarnaev brothers, Facebook users raced to identify Middle Eastern men as the 2013 Boston Marathon bombers. The absence of long-bearded jihadists led conspiracy theorists to propose that the bombing was a "false flag operation" or distraction engineered by Obama administration.[40]

Right-Wing Politics of Fear

Obama arrived on the national political stage with a promise to heal racial wounds and divisions in America. The young senator offered an inspiring message of undemarcated unity in uncertain times: "No red states . . . no blue states . . . no Black America . . . no White America . . . there's only the United States of America!"[41] Obama's dream of audacious, postracial harmony offered a solution to the paranoia and race baiting of American politics. In 2008, the message became the basis of the "Obama Youth" movement to elect the first Black president, with the highest Black and youth (18 to 29 years of age) voter turnout since 1972. However, most whites failed to ratify postracial America by actually voting for Obama. Obama lost to John McCain (the Republican candidate) by large margins among the majority of whites voters, and within the white men and women subgroups.[42]

The "Obama backlash" has involved "right-wing radicals" and "high-def hucksters" hell-bent on fanning the flame of white anger and old-school racism. [43] Obama conspiracy theories are part of the Right's partisan politics of fear. Republicans have used think tanks and media propaganda to win elections since 1970s.[44] The fear of communists, gays, Blacks, and the general "Other" is a proven tactic for mobilizing white voters. To undermine Obama's legitimacy and to neutralize his impact on public policy, the Right has spread rumors that Obama is really a shape-shifting-bloodsucking-reptilian-space-alien- Islamo-facist-Muslim-Kenyan-homosexual-terrorist-socialist- antichrist.

Some of the most popular Obama theories appeared in *Mother Jones's* "The Obama Conspiracy-o-rama." Apparently, Obama has been working for the Central Intelligence Agency (CIA) all along. Or is it the terrorists? Perhaps, he is a member of the "Illuminati," a secret Freemason organization hell-bent on enslaving the masses in preparation for the New World Order. Instead of signaling a rebirth of American leadership on the world stage, Obama has been labeled the return of the antichrist who plans to launch an apocalyptical race war predicted by Adolf Hitler.

Fox News, Bill O'Reilly, Sean Hannity, and the neoconservative talk-radio circuit have spread these theories in defense of white minority politics. "Grassroots patriots," known as the "Tea Party," use these stories to dramatize their message that a Black man has "stolen" America.[45] The illegitimate ruler, they warn, will first establish Obamacare "death panels," and socialist doctors will deny aging grandmas lifesaving medicine. Then the federal government, using Gestapo-style sweeps through middle-American neighborhoods, will take away the guns.[46] Shockingly, these stories worked insofar as gun sales skyrocketed after Obama took office and consumer demand continues to break records for background checks.[47]

The politics of fear can be seen in the language used by former Fox News host Glen Beck. Dana Milbank provides a rough quantitative assessment of Glen Beck's use of the Obama-Hitler conspiracy theory on his television show between 2008 and 2009. "Beck, it would seem," Milbank writes, "has a Nazi fetish. In his first fourteen months on Fox News, he and his guests invoked Hitler 115 times. Nazis, another 134 times. Fascism, 172 times."[48] After the election, Beck regularly compared Obama to Hitler, Joseph Stalin, and Vladimir Lenin—reinforcing the belief that Obama was a power-mad dictator leading America toward an Islamofascist-Socialist-Communist state.

However, the story is not as simple as "right wing wingnuts and a lunatic fringe hijacking America," as John Avlon puts it.[49] Adherence to Obama conspiracy theory stretches across traditional partisan lines and socioeconomics. Opinion polls suggest that many Americans lend credence to the outlandish stories circulating about Obama, yet there are clear partisan differences. For example, a 2010 Harris Poll found that Republicans are more likely to believe that Obama may be a socialist (40 percent of all Americans versus 67 percent of Republicans), a Muslim (32 percent vs. 57 percent), foreign born (25 percent vs. 45 percent), that he "resents America" (27 percent vs. 47 percent), resembles Hitler (20 percent vs. 38 percent), and may even be the anti-Christ (14 percent vs. 24 percent). Again, this pattern has remained stable into 2013.[50]

What do these numbers mean, exactly? It is our sense that many Americans do not really "believe" in the factuality of these claims about Obama. Rather, these conspiracy theories represent a way for Americans to express racial anxieties. In the following sections, we provide in-depth analyses of race talk found in three Obama conspiracy theories: Obama as Kenyan-born, Muslim terrorist; Obama as reptilian, space-alien, Illuminati operative; and Obama as closeted ("down-low") homosexual.

The Fake Birth Certificate and Muslim Jihad

For decades, *xenophobia*—the fear of others and (im)migrants—has been inspired by waves of not-yet-white Europeans, Mexican workers, and southern Blacks in search of better opportunities.[51] The election of a Black president has generated a similar crisis in Americanity. Vice presidential candidate Sarah Palin (former Alaska governor, reality television star, and self-claimed "maverick") attempted to exploit a white-only definition of American identity with the euphemism "real America." In stark contrast to Obama's campaign of progressive change and youth, the Palin-McCain campaign harkened back to yesterday's Americana of the 1950s. Real America symbolizes both iconic serenity and global dominance: middle-American small farmers, rugged Northern rural Moose hunters, hockey moms, Joe the Plumber, and chaste, abstinence-only daughters.

When the grand old party (GOP) threatened to "go rogue" and start kicking some Muslim terrorist butt, they created a social movement around Obama conspiracy theories known as *birtherism*. Under the auspices of the "Birther Movement," the right launched a media blitzkrieg casting doubt on Obama's citizenship and allegiance to American ideals. Skeptics have called for concrete proof (a long-form birth certificate) that Obama was really born in Honolulu's Kapiolani Maternity and Gynecological Hospital. The paranoid politics held that Obama was a Muslim born in Kenya, and had attended terrorist training schools as a child in Jakarta, Indonesia. In this framing of national identity, white Americans are assumed to be American, while all others must verify their allegiance.

E-mail chain letters circulated on the Internet claiming that Obama's family background made him an alien interloper, a former "foreign student" named Barry Soetoro, and an outsider intent on destroying Christian America. There are two common themes found in most claims that Obama is secretly a Muslim terrorist. The first premise plays on American fears of Black-white sexual coupling. Take for example, the opening lines of an e-mail circulating in July of 2007:

> *Subject: Who is Barack Obama?*
>
> Probable Democrat presidential candidate, Barack Hussein Obama was born in Honolulu, Hawaii, to Barack Hussein Obama, Sr., a black MUSLIM from Nyangoma-Kogel, Kenya and Ann Dunham, a white ATHIEST from Wichita, Kansas.[52]

The e-mail casts Obama's mother as an atheist, and describes how she was corrupted through a series of romantic relationships with nonwhite, non-Christian men. Second, the e-mail describes Obama's alleged Muslim upbringing as preparation for the destruction of America. Through an elaborate plot, Muslim extremists (or the CIA) planted fake birth announcements in a Hawaiian newspaper on August 13, 1961. The conspiracy, forty-eight years in the making, imagines Obama as a sleeper agent of terror, waiting to launch jihad from within. The same chain letter continues:

> Let us all remain alert concerning Obama's expected presidential candidacy. The Muslims have said they plan on destroying the U.S. from the inside out, what better way to start than at the highest level—through the President of the United States, one of their own!!!! ALSO, keep in mind that when he was sworn into office—he DID NOT use the Holy Bible, but instead the Kuran [*sic*] (Their equevelancy [*sic*] to our Bible, but very different beliefs) Please forward to everyone you know. Would you want this man leading our country? . . . NOT ME!!!

Many Americans are still wondering if the first Black president was really the first non-American president. The holy grail of birtherism, the "real" Kenyan birth certificate, continues to appear on conspiracy websites. The validity of these documents has been mired by poor Photoshop skills, and an even worse grasp of geography and history. Bunch provides a succinct description of the amateurish quality of the birth certificates: "Some documents that purported to disprove Obama's U.S. citizenship were about as valid as a $3 bill. . . . Never mind that it purported to be from the 'Republic of Kenya' when the African land was still under British rule, or that its city of issue, Mombasa, was actually part of Zanzibar at the time."[53]

"Baby towel head Obama," the most popular "real" birth certificate on the Internet, contains several of the ideas about racial and ethnic identity found in the birther conspiracies.[54] The image features Obama's head superimposed on a baby's body. He is adorned in a kaffiyeh scarf, bone necklace, and is playing with a zebra atop a haystack. The crude symbolism is that of savage Africanity mixed with the garb of Arab terrorism. The baby image in a haystack plays on the antichrist image, while also imposing a racist and emasculating view of an adult black male as a "boy" without adult facilities. The text reinforces the same messages about Obama's heritage, and his plans for corrupting America. The top-left titling suggests that the certificate is from the "Ministry of

Health Planning," a play on the belief that Obama will replace private health care with a socialist regime of death panel doctors. "Kenya, Africa" is listed as his birthplace, as the creator seems to believe that Kenya is a city or state in the country of Africa. The redrafted Obama campaign button reads, "Forget the Law," an assertion that Obama's ultimate goal is to replace American democracy with an Islamic Theocracy.

Birther conspiracy theories represent the destruction of serious public discourse, reason, and intellectualism in the post-9/11 era. Like Al Gore and Charles Pierce describe, supermarket tabloid sensationalism, conspiracy theories, and outlandish claims are now part of the mainstream conversation.[55] Internet technology is typically celebrated for flattening social relationships with user-generated, amateur knowledge. The Internet can be used for empowerment and challenging notions of expertise, authority, and centralized control. This is especially evident when one considers the Snowden controversy of 2013. But technology also can be used to circulate hate and misinformation.[56]

Obama's fake Kenyan birth certificate is not the only forged document seeking to challenge his legitimacy as president. An e-mail chain letter circulated in early 2012 sought to reignite the birther controversy by presenting an ID card from Columbia University that allegedly belonged to a Barry Soetoro. The ID card featured both a photograph of Barack Obama and the designation of "foreign student."[57] The image was quickly debunked due to the fact that the card featured a digital barcode. The university did not institute that form of ID technology until 1996, long after Obama completed his stint at Columbia.

Read in the logic of colorblind racism and the politics of fear, the birther conspiracies are really about protecting white, American identity. If American equals white, then Obama cannot be meaningfully American or legitimately the icon of America on the world stage. Because of his skin color, heritage, and funny-sounding name, he represents a direct threat to Sarah Palin's or Glen Beck's "Real America." When Fox News pundits mispronounce *Obama* as *Osama*, as in Bin Laden, the Freudian slip encompasses deep-seated racial, religious, and cultural anxieties that have not been resolved by the elections. In 2015, former New York Mayor Rudy Giuliani continued to question Obama's patriotism by declaring that Obama does not love America.

Deep into Obama's presidency, arguments now assert his loyalty to the "Muslim Brotherhood." In fact, there are a string of conspiracy theories that attempt to connect Obama's efforts in immigration reform to a desire for a mass influx of jihadi soldiers seeking to enforce sharia law in America. According to the website, Pray for US, "Barack Obama's private army is coming:

> Americans must rise up now to defend America from the onslaught of Muslim immigrants that will be brought in for this plan . . . We see how our fellow Christians are beheaded, strangled, beaten and burned in Muslim-controlled countries. We can't let an Islamic army to flood into America due to the cowardly efforts of our politicians. We have to stop them.[58]

The site urges readers to contact their Senators to address these concerns and even offers a faxable template. Amazingly, seven states—including North Carolina, Oklahoma, Arizona, Kansas, Louisiana, South Dakota, and Tennessee—have passed bills to ban Islamic laws, while similar measures have been introduced in twenty-two states.[59] These attempts to ban Sharia law demonstrate the continued currency of xenophobia and racism in American politics.

Obama's Reptilian-Alien, Illuminati Mind Control Plot

When Obama took the stage at the Democratic National Convention in 2004, it seemed as if he had appeared out of thin air. Few people outside of Illinois knew anything about the young senator, and he did not fit the mold of civil rights Black politicians like Jesse Jackson, Shirley Chisholm, Carol Moseley Braun, or Al Sharpton.[60] As Senator Joe Biden remarked about his running mate, he was "articulate, bright, clean, nice-looking," *and* Black. According to conspiracy theorists, in the trusting fog of Obama-mania, America did not elect a Black man, or even a Muslim terrorist, but an alien from outer space.

The conspiracy theory holds that Obama is really a shape-shifting reptilian humanoid from a faraway galaxy in the Alpha Draconis solar system. Supposedly, all world leaders come from a line of reptile aliens. Or, in another variation of the conspiracy, Obama is portrayed as a human servant of the Illuminati, which is in turn controlled by the reptile overlords. This claim was illustrated in the cover *of Los Angeles CityBeat* magazine in March 2009.

Why, exactly, have aliens traveled light years to Earth to become public officials? The answer varies in the storytelling, though it usually involves using humans for food. In one version of the theory, the reptiles control humanity through fear and mind control. Negative emotions from human slaves serve as a food source for the aliens. In a more violent light, the reptiles like to drink human blood. The latter motive, of course, contains undertones of anti-Semitism, as blood-sucking alludes to Jewish involvement.

New-Age conspiracy theorist David Icke has been one of the leading proponents of the Obama-space-alien thesis. In his *Los Angeles CityBeat* article, the author seeks to expose the mind control strategies of the Obama administration. According to Icke, the campaign slogan of "Change" can be decoded as a secret message used by reptilian dictators across the globe that America has elected another shape-shifter to office. Juxtaposing Obama's images with that of Adolf Hitler, Jewish billionaires, and Oprah Winfrey, his website suggest that Obama-mania will lead to mass enslavement of American citizens in a fascist, New World Order government.[61]

According to the conspiracy theories, one of Obama's Secret Service guards is also a Zionist shape-shifter.[62] A YouTube video that uncovered the reptilian humanoid guard received hundreds of thousands of views and created a flurry of commentary on conspiracy theorist boards across the Internet. Given the popularity of the video, a spokesperson for the National Security Council released the following statement: "I can't confirm the claims made in this video, but any alleged program to guard the president with aliens or robots would likely have to be scaled back or eliminated in the sequester [budget cuts]. . . . I'd refer you to the Secret Service or Area 51 for more details."[63]

Distrust about Obama's true identity, whether reptile or operative of aliens, is difficult to disentangle from more established theories about secret government plots involving the Illuminati. For example, On August 9, 2010, President Barack Obama made a speech at the University of Texas. When he entered the crowded gymnasium, he threw up the "Hook 'em, Horns!" hand sign, which was immediately followed by emphatic cheers from the Longhorn audience.[64] While every person in the gym immediately recognized the familiar symbol of university pride, Internet conspiracy theorists took this symbolic gesture out of context and argued that Obama was using a Satanic hand gesture to show his allegiance to a New World Order. Michelle Obama's appearance on the cover of *Vogue* also stirred rumors of her involvement in the Illuminati or a Satanic New World Order due to the position of her hand.[65]

Fear of Obama's New World Order agenda also stems from his 2010 speech at West Point Military Academy, in which he stated,

> The international order we seek is one that can resolve the challenges of our times. . . . Countering violent extremism and insurgency;

> stopping the spread of nuclear weapons and securing nuclear materials; combating a changing climate and sustaining global growth; helping countries feed themselves and care for their sick; preventing conflict and healing its wounds.[66]

Despite the seemingly good natured tone of the remarks, conspiracy theorists immediately asserted that the form of government that Obama advocated was secretly one that would promote the interests of "global finance oligarchs to construct a new world government."[67]

While allegations of a New World Order are nothing new among conspiracy theorists, it now seems that these concerns are no longer limited to the fringes of American society. According to Alex Jones, "almost one third of Americans believe that a secretive power elite is conspiring to rule the world via an authoritarian global government."[68]

Stevie Tee, a minister from the Church of Truth and Spirit in Tallahassee, Florida recently gained traction through a podcast (Internet radio show) seeking to bring down the Illuminati. *BeforeItsNews.com* posted an article emphasizing the importance of this podcast, especially because "Many don't know but under the health bill passed by Obama the government can inject citizens with anything without them knowing or doing anything about it (Read on the net) this includes the RFID chip which the government will use for ID's [*sic*] and to follow you as a citizen. It's all about control and preventing you from attacking back this is why Christians are at the front of their Illuminati attack and these laws were passed for the NWO preparation."[69]

Framing Obama as an alien, Illuminati operative in a larger New World Order scheme undermines the symbolic significance of a Black president, and works to discount the very real grassroots political mobilization by Blacks and a multiethnic coalition of youth voters. Yet, by delving deeper, it is evident that there are some serious race issues involved in these bogus extraterrestrial accusations. First and foremost, these nefarious arguments deny Black agency by attempting to strip away his achievements as part of larger ploy that began before he "was born in an Illuminati bunker far beneath the ground in Finland."[70] As an alien, he fulfills the xenophobic and racist tropes of being an "other," outside of the control of white interests, without explicitly stating the obvious sentiments of that constituency: that Barack Obama does not share white American interests or values. The continuation of this thinly veiled rhetoric of an Illuminati president sends the message that Obama's loyalty lies with a global elite seeking to squash the sacred American value of freedom.

As a result, these fabrications attempt to overshadow serious issues facing minority communities throughout the United States. Minority voters who elected Barack Obama were interested in a variety of issues that affect Americans on a daily basis, including health care, gun control, women's rights, and education. Yet, these voices demanding changes are often eclipsed by claims that Obama's agenda is manipulated by shadowy organizations. As a result, in the wake of Obama's (unsuccessful) efforts to address gun control following the horrific incidents in Newtown or Aurora, New World Order conspiracy theories encourage white militia groups to cling to their guns despite calls for stricter regulations from American citizens throughout the United States. "Obamacare" stories about government doctors injecting microchips to control the masses distract attention away from racial, gender, and social class inequality in access to quality, affordable health care.

Obama as Closeted ("Down-Low") Homosexual

Mother Jones published a chart detailing the prevalence of Obama conspiracy theories.[71] Beyond offering a succinct overview of the flurry of conspiracy theories that have become commonplace in an allegedly postracial Obamerica, the piece covers the framing of Obama as a "Sham/Weirdo/Pervert." An explicitly gendered set of conspiracy theories focuses on Obama's sexuality. Allegedly, President Barack Obama is a closeted homosexual on "the down-low."

In October 2012, *WND* reported on Obama's alleged involvement in gay sex through a matchmaking service at Rev. Wright's Trinity United Church in Chicago. According to an anonymous informant, Rev. Wright "connected Obama in the [down-low] community" and helped him "hide his homosexuality."[72] Kevin DuJan, a former gossip columnist in Chicago, was not afraid to speak openly about such allegations. According to DuJan, Obama was a regular at Chicago gay bars, and is "not heterosexual and he's not bisexual. He's homosexual."[73] In the article, DuJan hopes that Man's Country, a gay bathhouse that Obama allegedly visited often, "will eventually get a plaque of sometime commemorating that place as a gay hangout for the future leader of the free world."[74]

According to John Drew, Obama's homosexual behaviors began in college. Drew asserts that Mohammed Hasan Chandoo, Obama's Pakistani roommate from Occidental College, was Obama's "boy toy."[75] Despite the fact that Chandoo had a girlfriend, Margo Miffin, Drew was still convinced of a secret relationship going on between Chandoo and Obama. In an exclusive with *WND*, Drew recounts, "In fact, they looked so gay that my girlfriend, Caroline Boss, whispered to me, 'They're not gay.' So, that confirmed to me I wasn't the only one who thought Barack Obama and Hassan Chandoo looked like they were in a very close, intimate relationship."[76] Michelle Obama functions as Barack's "beard" in the down-low conspiracy theory, leading DuJan to give her the nickname Michelle Antoinette Obama, a reference to the extreme lifestyle and loveless marriage of Marie Antoinette and King Louis XVI of France. [77] In another publication, an investigator argues that the president's homosexuality may explain his choice of a "mannish wife with big, muscular arms."[78]

The discourse surrounding Obama's sexuality contains a fascinating set of ideas about larger issues of Black masculinity and gender politics. Rumors about Obama's alleged sexual appetites play to long-held stereotypes about violent, uncontrollable, deviant Black male sexuality. Surveillance of the Black body, especially as it relates to sexuality are not new in the American imagination. After all, the fear of and desire to control Black sexuality was the motivation for widespread racial violence across the American South. Black male hyper-sexualization has been used as a scapegoat to prevent desegregation (or even emancipation), due to the threat of putting white female virtue at risk.

In considering the issue of Black masculinity, Byron Hurt's documentary, *Barack & Curtis: Manhood, Power and Respect* highlights the narrow ways in which Black manhood is accepted in America.[79] According to Hurt, within the Black community, masculinity is associated with one's relationship to women, prison, and money. As such, gangster rapper 50 Cent is the ideal representative of "hood" and masculinity, especially due to his ability to control others by fear. On the other hand, Obama's Harvard educated image acts as an effeminizing force, which is in contrast to the work of white patriarchal racism that seeks to paint Black men as lawless and dangerous. As a result, it may be easier to read Obama as gay rather than redefine Black masculinity to include a wide range of emotions, including vulnerability and a desire for family life.

Despite the seemingly Spartan image that Obama presents to the world at large, it seems to not be enough to assuage critics on both sides of the aisle. Democrats and leftist political pundits like Bill Maher desire more than Obama's level-headed politicking; they want the "Angry Black Man" to emerge. As Ta-Nehisi Coates notes in his eloquent essay, calls for stereotypical racial performances reveal the limitations placed on Black Americans: "This need to talk in dulcet tones, to never be angry regardless of the offense, bespeaks a strange and compromised integration indeed, revealing a country so infantile that it can countenance white acceptance of blacks only when they meet an Al Roker standard."[80] Obama's performance in the first 2012 presidential debate reflected his characteristically subdued (white voter) conscious style, as he was hesitant to respond to harsh critiques from Romney. As a result, many critiqued Obama and demanded an appearance of the "Angry Black Man" that must reside in him somewhere.

Immediately following the 2012 election, Maher urged Obama to finally become an "Angry Black Man" to push a liberal agenda on issues like "civil liberties, the drug war, gun control, clean coal, the defense budget, Afghanistan and the Patriot Act."[81] No longer in fear of alienating white voters, Maher called for Obama start acting Black. By constantly painting Obama as a man unwilling or unable to tap into his "Angry Black Man" persona, the media reinforces stereotypes of ghetto Black masculinity. As such, the critiques that surround Obama's presented image and unwillingness to "keep it real" with republicans on issues like health care allude to a feminizing factor in the larger scope of discussions on masculine hegemony inside and outside of the Black community.

Allegations of homosexuality feed into a politics of fear on the religious right by violating the meme of "wholesome" American family values, while affronting public anxiety over shifting family structures in the Black community. For many African Americans, in particular, the candid displays of marital affection and commitment between Barack and Michelle, and their sound upbringing for Sasha and Malia while holding public office, is a source of racial pride. Their apparent commitment to making their marriage work and keeping the romance alive provides a counternarrative to the image of absentee Black fathers and baby-mamas living off welfare. Yet, despite the beautiful displays of love between the president and the first lady, the down-low rumors work to shatter the symbolism of the First Black Family.

The ideas of hegemonic masculinity contain an edge of sexism toward Black women. By presenting Michelle as a man in drag with muscular arms, she is labeled a deviant (alongside her husband) with radical Black extremism in her past and a threat to the foundation of the American people through a jihad on family values.[82] Michelle as the puppet wife discounts the labor power of Black women in general, and renders invisible her public service work in health and fitness as FLOTUS.

The current era of American politics captures tensions between progress and uneasiness with gay rights. While the Supreme Court made two landmark decisions regarding gay rights in the summer of 2013, and in 2015, struck down state bans on same-sex marriage, homosexuality is still seen as abnormal by some Americans. Rumors of Obama's homosexuality offer a way of demasculinizing Obama and to voice concerns that gay rights is eroding "American values." Homosexual conspiracy theories may appeal to those who believe that Obama is too soft with international policy and incapable of protecting America's interests. While being Black was clearly not enough to cost him the presidency, perhaps conspiracy theorists believe that questioning his masculinity and family values is enough to turn "real America" against him, especially religious members of the Black community.

Conclusion

While presidential conspiracy theories are not a new phenomenon—after all, John F. Kennedy, Ronald Reagan, George W. Bush, and Bill Clinton (among many others) have also been the center of antichrist conspiracy theories—this essay demonstrates the unusual number of conspiratorial claims surrounding Barack Obama. Considering the prevalence of these theories, it is unsurprising that the Obama administration has taken a tongue-and-cheek approach to rumors. In perhaps one of the most perplexing conspiracy theories, Obama was said to have engineered a hidden CIA intergalactic program on Mars. While it is unlikely that this theory could do much harm to the Obama's credibility due to its farfetched nature, the White House responded to the theory in a statement that asserted that the President's only encounters with the planet Mars were through watching the cartoon Marvin the Martian.[83] The entertainment value of some of these conspiracy theories is difficult to deny, though, as shown in this essay, Obama conspiracy theories often contain problematic ideas about race and gender. In our supposed, postracial world, these allegations of reptilian roots, gay affairs, and allegiance to a New World Order, have been used to "Other" Obama and deny blackness as a valid expression of Americanity and humanity. Despite hopeful dreams of a postracial America, these theories represent "new" ways to forward anti-Black/Muslim/gay ideology in a colorblind society. All joking aside, plots involving aliens and secret societies work to obscure the very real oppression caused by continued institutional racism.

Notes

1. "Buchanan: "'White America' Died Last Night,'" *Daily Currant*, last modified November 7, 2012, http://dailycurrant.com/2012/11/07/buchanan-white-america-dead/. The *Daily Currant*, like the *Onion*, is a satirical news outlet. Their impersonation mirrors Pat Buchanan's claims that President Obama is a "drug dealer of welfare" and that his reelection represented the

"demographic winter of White America." This kind of race-baiting exploits the legitimate concerns held by white people, and other Americans, who are becoming the casualties of widening inequality and the crippling costs of college education and health care.

2. The Onion, "Poll: 1 in 5 Americans Believe Obama Is a Cactus," the *Onion: America's Finest News Source*, last modified September 22, 2010, http://www.theonion.com/articles/poll-1-in-5-americans-believe-obama-is-a-cactus,18127/.

3. The term *Obamerica* situates this discussion within the time period since the 2007 candidacy, 2008 election, and 2012 reelection of Obama, with an emphasis on popular North American perceptions. Our use of Obamerica is meant to avoid the widespread use of the phrase "in the age of Obama," which relies on the postracial assumption that Obama represents a meaningful break with the past. The Obamerica label should signal the same caution exercised by Ama Mazama and David Roediger when they use the phrase "Obama phenomenon." Ama Mazama, "The Barack Obama Phenomenon," *Journal of Black Studies* 38, no. 1 (2007): 3–6; David R. Roediger, *How Race Survived US History: From Settlement and Slavery to the Obama Phenomenon* (London; New York: Verso, 2008).

4. Michael Crowley, "Post-Racial," *New Republic*, last modified March 12, 2008, http://www.newrepublic.com/article/post-racial; Orlando Patterson, "The New Mainstream," *Newsweek*, last modified October 31, 2008, http://www.newsweek.com/id/166827.

5. "Schizophrenia Clinical Trial," *CRILifetree*, accessed February 14, 2014, http://www.crilifetree.com/clinical-trials/schizophrenia-research-study.

6. David Roediger, 'Race Will Survive the Obama Phenomenon," *Chronicle of Education Review*, October 10, 2008, http://chronicle.com/article/Race-Will-Survive-the-Obama/21983; Adia Harvey Wingfield and Joe R. Feagin, *Yes, We Can?: White Racial Framing and the 2008 Presidential Campaign* (London: Routledge, 2009).

7. Gary Younge, "Open Season on Black Boys after a Verdict Like This," *Guardian*, July 14, 2013, http://www.guardian.co.uk/commentisfree/2013/jul/14/open-season-black-boys-verdict.

8. Eduardo Bonilla-Silva, *Racism without Racists: Color-Blind Racism and the Persistence of Racial Inequality in the United States* (Lanham: Rowman and Littlefield Publishers, 2009); Joe R. Feagin, *The White Racial Frame Centuries of Racial Framing and Counter-Framing* (New York: Routledge, 2009).

9. *Onion*.

10. Harris Interactive Poll, "'Wingnuts' and President Obama: A Socialist? A Muslim? Anti-American? The Anti-Christ? Large Minorities of Americans Hold Some Remarkable Opinions," *Harris Interactive*, last modified on March 24, 2010, http://www.harrisinteractive.com/NewsRoom/HarrisPolls/tabid/447/ctl/ReadCustom%20Default/mid/1508/ArticleId/223/Default.aspx.

11. Paul Harris, "One in Four Americans Think Obama May Be the Antichrist,

Survey Says," *Guardian*, April 2, 2013, http://www.theguardian.com/world/2013/apr 02/americans-obama -anti-christ-conspiracy-theories.

12. Mark Fenster, *Conspiracy Theories: Secrecy and Power in American Culture* (Minneapolis, MN: University of Minnesota Press, 2008); Timothy Melley, *Empire of Conspiracy: The Culture of Paranoia in Postwar America* (Ithaca: Cornell University Press, 1999); Jane Parish and Martin Parker, *The Age of Anxiety: Conspiracy Theory and the Human Science* (Oxford, UK: Wiley-Blackwell/Sociological Review Monographs, 2001).

13. Albert Gore, *The Assault on Reason* (London: Bloomsbury, 2007); Andrew Keen, *The Cult of the Amateur: How Today's Internet Is Killing Our Culture* (New York: Doubleday/Currency, 2007).

14. Robin D. G. Kelley, "How the West Was One: On the Uses and Limitations of Diaspora." *Black Scholar* 30 (2000): 31–35.

15. Bonilla-Silva.

16. Ronald J. Berger and Richard Quinney, *Storytelling Sociology: Narrative as Social Inquiry* (Boulder, CO: Lynne Rienner, 2005).

17. Feagin.

18. Patricia Hill Collins, *Black Feminist Thought: Knowledge, Consciousness, and the Politics of Empowerment* (New York: Routledge, 2000), 284.

19. Mica Pollock, *Colormute: Race Talk Dilemmas in an American School* (Princeton, NJ: Princeton University Press, 2004).

20. The Obama-inspired wave of postracial talk is different from David Hollinger's call for a "post-ethnic America." Hollinger's classic treatise against 1990s "multiculturalism" and "cultural diversity" attacked the notion of "racialized cultures" (i.e., that all Blacks must prescribe to a particular culture) and the ideology of race (i.e., that humans could be separated into five distinct racial categories). David A. Hollinger, *Postethnic America: Beyond Multiculturalism* (New York: Basic Books, 2000).

21. Brad Paisley, and LL Cool J, "Accidental Racist," *Wheelhouse*, CD (Arista Nashville, 2013).

22. Michael Omi, and Howard Winant, *Racial Formation in the United States: From the 1960s to the 1980s* (New York; London: Routledge, 1989), 61–62.

23. The subtext of Obama's *Audacity of Hope* narrative adds the new immigrant optimism to this story, but the point is the same. Barack Obama, *The Audacity of Hope: Thoughts on Reclaiming the American Dream* (New York: Crown Publishers, 2006), 231–233.

24. Bonilla-Silva, 233.

25. Nikole Hannah-Jones, "A Colorblind Constitution: What Abigail Fisher's Affirmative Action Case Is Really About," *ProPublica: Journalism in the Public Interest*, March 18, 2013, http://www.propublica.org/article/a-colorblind-constitution-what-abigail-fishers-affirmative- action-case-is-r.

26. Michael P. Jeffries, *Paint the White House Black: Barack Obama and the Meaning of Race in America* (Stanford: Stanford University Press, 2013);

Manning Marable, "Racializing Obama: The Enigma of Post-Black Politics and Leadership," *Souls* 11, no. 1 (2009): 1–15; Jabari Asim, *What Obama Means: For Our Culture, Our Politics, Our Future* (New York: William Morrow, 2009).

27. Fredrick C. Harris, *The Price of the Ticket: Barack Obama and the Rise and Decline of Black Politics* (New York: Oxford University Press, 2012).

28. Bill Cosby and Alvin F. Poussaint, *Come on, People: On the Path from Victims to Victors*. (Nashville: Thomas Nelson, 2007).

29. Claims by rapper Kanye West that perhaps Bush did not "care about black people" was dismissed as rants. See Richard T. Ford, *The Race Card: How Bluffing About Bias Makes Race Relations Worse* (New York: Farrar, Straus and Giroux, 2008); Larry Elder, *Stupid Black Men: How to Play the Race Card—and Lose* (New York: St. Martin's Press, 2008).

30. CNN, "Obama: I Didn't Mean to Slight Cambridge Police," July 24, 2009, http://www.cnn.com/2009/US/07/24/officer.gates.arrest/.

31. John L. Jackson, Jr., *Racial Paranoia: The Unintended Consequences of Political Correctness: The New Reality of Race in America* (New York: Basic Civitas, 2008), 2–3.

32. Likewise, David Neiwert provides a brief history of how White "patriot" militia groups have used FEMA concentration camp conspiracies to support White separatist politics. See David Neiwert, "Fema Concentration Camps? The Militia Good Times Are Rollin' Again," *Crooks and Liars*, last modified March 17, 2009, http://crooksandliars.com/david-neiwert/fema-concentration-camps-militia-goo.

33. Travis L. Gosa, "Counterknowledge, Racial Paranoia, and the Cultic Milieu: Decoding Hip Hop Conspiracy Theory," *Poetics* 39, no. 3 (2011): 187–204; Fenster; Melley.

34. Gore.

35. Kathryn S. Olmsted, *Real Enemies: Conspiracy Theories and American Democracy, World War I to 9/11* (New York: Oxford University Press, 2009).

36. Public Policy Polling, "Conspiracy Theory Poll Results," last modified on April 2, 2013, http://www.publicpolicypolling.com/main/2013/04/conspiracy-theory-poll-results-.html.

37. William Paul Simmons, and Sharon Parsons, "Beliefs in Conspiracy Theories among African Americans: A Comparison of Elites and Masses," *Social Science Quarterly* 86, no. 3 (2005): 582–598.

38. Mos Def, and Bill Maher, *Real Time with Bill Maher*, HBO, 2007. Television show.

39. Treading the line between hard political rhetoric and anti-Semitism, "raptivist" KRS-One declared that Blacks should applaud the government sponsored attacks, because they killed white and Jewish record executives at RCA and Universal Records who have been exploiting Black musicians. Alyssa Rashbaum, "KRS-One Denounced for Controversial Statements About 9-11," MTV News, October 15, 2004, http://www.mtv.com/news/

articles/1492288/krs-one-denounced-statements-about-9-11.jhtml. In a series of follow-ups interviews, the artist backtracked on his statements, apologized, and claimed his comments had been taken out of context.

40. Robert Beckhusen, "White House Can't Afford Its Shapeshifting Alien Reptile Guards," *Wired*, March 3, 2013, http://www.wired.com/danger-room/2013/03/secret-service-reptile-aliens/.

41. Barack Obama, "Democratic National Convention Keynote Address, Fleet Center, Boston," July 27, 2004, http://www.americanrhetoric.com/speeches/convention2004/barackobama2004dnc.htm.

42. David Paul Kuhn, "Exit Polls: How Obama Won," *Politico*, November 5, 2008, http://www.politico.com/news/stories/1108/15297.html.

43. As Pulitzer Prize–winning author Will Bunch puts it. William Bunch, *The Backlash: Right-Wing Radicals, Hi-Def Hucksters, and Paranoid Politics in the Age of Obama* (New York: Harper, 2010).

44. Manuel G. Gonzales, and Richard Delgado, *The Politics of Fear: How Republicans Use Money, Race, and the Media to Win* (Boulder, CO: Paradigm, 2006).

45. The Tea Party, of course, is comprised mostly of rich, white, neoconservatives that have little in common with the average white American, idealized as Joe Six-Pack, or more recently, Joe The Plumber.

46. John Amato, and David A. Neiwert, *Over the Cliff: How Obama's Election Drove the American Right Insane* (Sausalito, CA: PoliPointPress: Distributed by Ingram Publisher Services, 2010); Jill Lepore, *The Whites of Their Eyes: The Tea Party's Revolution and the Battle over American History* (Princeton, NJ: Princeton University Press, 2010); Kate Zernike, *Boiling Mad: Inside Tea Party America* (New York: Times Books/Henry Holt and Co., 2010).

47. Michael Cooper, "Sales of Guns Soar in the U.S. as Nation Weighs Tougher Limits," *New York Times*, January 11, 2013, http://www.nytimes.com/2013/01/12/us/as-us-weighs-new-rules-sales-of-guns-and-ammunition-surge.html.

48. Dana Milbank, *Tears of a Clown: Glenn Beck and the Tea Bagging of America* (New York: Doubleday, 2010), Kindle.

49. John P. Avlon, *Wingnuts: How the Lunatic Fringe Is Hijacking America* (New York: Beast Books, 2010).

50. Harris Interactive Poll, "Wingnuts" and President Obama." Paul Harris, One in four Americans. Public Policy Polling, Conspiracy Theory Poll Results.

51. Generations of North African Muslims, living in the countries of Western Europe, have inspired similar hysteria over the meaning of national identity.

52. Snopes, "Who Is Barack Obama?" last modified January 2009, http://www.snopes.com/politics/obama/muslim.asp. Interestingly, some claims of Obama's non-American status accept that he may have been born on U.S. soil, instead of Kenya. However, land-birth and a white, American mother are not enough to make him truly American.

53. Bunch, 17.

54. As of August 15, 2013, a Google search for "towel head Obama" garners about a 750,000 websites that declare Obama an "illegal alien," "Muslim terrorist," who still refuses to "honor the flag" by wearing a flag lapel pin. As many websites speculate that Obama is building a mosque on the rubble of the Twin Towers destroyed in the 9/11 attacks.

55. Gore; Charles P. Pierce, *Idiot America: How Stupidity Became a Virtue in the Land of the Free* (New York: Doubleday, 2009).

56. Keen; Damian Thompson, *Counterknowledge: How We Surrendered to Conspiracy Theories, Quack Medicine, Bogus Science and Fake History* (New York: W. W. Norton, 2008).

57. David Emery, "Obama's 'Foreign Student' ID Found," last modified February 2012, http://urbanlegends.about.com/od/barackobama/ss/Obama-Student-Id.htm.

58. Pray for the United States Pray for Us, "Help America Defeat Muslim Brotherhood-Sponsored Amnesty Plan!!" https://prayfor.us/muslim_bhood_immigration/.

59. Kimberly Railey, "More States Move to Ban Foreign Laws in Courts," *USA Today*, August 4, 2013, http://www.usatoday.com/story/news/nation/2013/08/04/states-ban-foreign-law/2602511/.

60. William Jelani Cobb, *The Substance of Hope: Barack Obama and the Paradox of Progress* (New York: Walker & Co., 2010).

61. David Icke, "The Reptilians—the Schism—Obama and the New World Order," July 24, 2013, http://www.davidicke.com/headlines/64856-david-icke-the-reptilians-the-schism-obama-and-the-new-world-order.

62. A YouTube clip debuted in early 2013 that allegedly showed one of Obama's security guards in the middle of a shape-shifting episode at the American Israel Affairs Committee meeting. The narrator manages to pair this farfetched conspiracy theory with anti-Semitism throughout the clip, most notably when he states the guard "could be a shapeshifter alien humanoid working for the powers that be, caught in a high-definition video during an event of the Zionist cabal." See Beckhusen.

63. Ibid.

64. *President Obama: "Put Education First,"* University of Texas at Austin Know, August 9, 2010, http://www.utexas.edu/know/2010/08/09/obama_speech_gregory/.

65. "Michelle Obama Flashes 'El Diablo' Sign on the Cover of Vogue," *Infowars.com*, last modified Feb. 13, 2009, http://www.infowars.com/michelle-obama-flashes-%E2%80%98el-diablo%E2%80%99-hand-signal-on-cover-of-vogue/.

66. Michael D. Shear, "At West Point, Obama Offers New Security Strategy," *Washington Post*, May 23, 2010, http://www.washingtonpost.com/wpdyn/content/article/2010/05/22/AR2010052201586.html.

67. Lucas Bowser, "Obama Doctrine: The New International Order," *Before*

It's News, April 23, 2013, http://beforeitsnews.com/alternative/2013/04/obama-doctrine-the-new-international-order-2628352.html.

68. Alex Jones, and InfoWars, "Special Report: The New World Order Is No 'Conspiracy Theory,'" *Infowars.com*, last modified April 4, 2013, http://www.infowars.com/special- report- the-new-world-order-is-no-conspiracy-theory/.

69. "Obama & Illuminati to Destroy US Constitution—Minister Stevie Tee Fights Back," *Before It's News*, May 12, 2013, http://beforeitsnews.com/obama/2013/05/obama-illuminati-to-destroy-us-constitution-minister-stevie-tee-fights-back-2450748.html.

70. Stephanie, "Ex Member Reveals," The Watchman's Cry, January 1, 2011, http://www.watchmanscry.com/forum/showthread.php?t=15124.

71. Asawin Suebsaeng, and Dave Gilson, "Chart: Almost Every Obama Conspiracy Theory Ever," *MotherJones*, October 2012, http:// www.motherjones.com/politics/2012/10/chart-obama-conspiracy-theories.

72. Jerome R. Corsi, "Trinity Church Members Reveal Obama Shocker," *WND*, October 2, 2012, http://www.wnd.com/2012/10/trinity-church-members-reveal-obama-shocker/.

73. Jerome R. Corsi, "Claim: Obama Hid 'Gay Life' to Become President," *WND*, September 11, 2012, http://www.wnd.com/2012/09/claim-obama-hid-gay-life-to-become-president/.

74. Ibid.

75. Jerome R. Corsi, "Occidential Activist: I Thought Obama Was Gay," *WND*, August 15, 2012, http://www.wnd.com/2012/08/occidental-activist-i-thought-obama-was-gay/.

76. Ibid.

77. Kevin DuJan, and The Hill Buzz, "Is Barack Obama Gay?" http://hillbuzz.org/is-barack-obama-gay.

78. Neal Gabler, "What's Behind the Right's 'Obama Is Gay' Conspiracy," *Nation*, October 23, 2012, http://www.thenation.com/article/170787/whats-behind-rights-obama-gay-conspiracy#.

79. Byron Hurt, "Barack & Curtis: Manhood, Power & Respect" October 9, 2008, http://www.youtube.com/watch?v=H5YoS3bqk5g.

80. Ta-Nehisi Coates, "Fear of a Black President," *Atlantic*, August 22, 2012, http://www.theatlantic.com/magazine/archive/2012/09/fear-of-a-black-president/309064/?single_page=true.

81. Jeff Poor, "Maher Lobbies Obama to 'Throw Caution to the Wind' and Become 'an Angry Black Man," *Daily Caller*, November 17, 2012, http://dailycaller.com/2012/11/17/maher-lobbies-obama-to-throw-caution-to-the-wind-and-become-an-angry-black-man-video/.

82. The cover of the *New Yorker* from mid-July 2008 plays into racialized conspiracy theories surrounding Barack and Michelle Obama through an illustration titled "The Politics of Fear." On the cover, Barack is dressed in

a turban and robes while fist bumping a militant Michelle with natural hair and an assault rifle slung on her back.

83. Spencer Ackerman, "White House Denies CIA Teleported Obama to Mars," *Wired*, January 3, 2012, http://www.wired.com/dangerroom/2012/01/obama-mars/.

Bibliography

Ackerman, Spencer. "White House Denies CIA Teleported Obama to Mars." *Wired*. January 3, 2012. http://www.wired.com/dangerroom/2012/01/obama-mars/.

Amato, John, and David A. Neiwert. *Over the Cliff: How Obama's Election Drove the American Right Insane*. Sausalito, CA: PoliPointPress: Distributed by Ingram Publisher Services, 2010.

Asim, Jabari. *What Obama Means: For Our Culture, Our Politics, Our Future*. New York: William Morrow, 2009.

Avlon, John P. *Wingnuts: How the Lunatic Fringe Is Hijacking America*. New York: Beast Books, 2010.

Beckhusen, Robert. "White House Can't Afford Its Shapeshifting Alien Reptile Guards." *Wired*. March 3, 2013. http://www.wired.com/dangerroom/2013/03/secret-service-reptile-aliens/.

Berger, Ronald J., and Richard Quinney. *Storytelling Sociology: Narrative as Social Inquiry*. Boulder, CO: Lynne Rienner, 2005.

Bonilla-Silva, Eduardo. *Racism without Racists: Color-Blind Racism and the Persistence of Racial Inequality in the United States*. Lanham, MD: Rowman and Littlefield Publishers, 2009.

Bowser, Lucas. "Obama Doctrine: The New International Order." *Before It's News*, April 23, 2013. http://beforeitsnews.com/alternative/2013/04/obama-doctrine-the-new-international- order-2628352.html.

Buchanan, Pat. "Buchanan: 'White America' Died Last Night." *Daily Currant*, November 7, 2012. http://dailycurrant.com/2012/11/07/buchanan-white-america-dead/.

Bunch, William. *The Backlash: Right-Wing Radicals, Hi-Def Hucksters, and Paranoid Politics in the Age of Obama*. New York: Harper, 2010.

Churcher, Sharon. "Obama Is Hit by 'Affair' Smears Following Claims That Attractive Aide Was Banned by His Wife." *MailOnline*. October 11, 2008. http://www.dailymail.co.uk/news/article-1076695/Obama-hit-affair-smears-following-claims-attractive-aide-banned-wife.html.

CNN. "Obama: I Didn't Mean to Slight Cambridge Police." July 24, 2009. http://www.cnn.com/2009/US/07/24/officer.gates.arrest/.

Coates, Ta-Nehisi. "Fear of a Black President." *Atlantic*. August 22, 2012. http://www.theatlantic.com/magazine/archive/2012/09/fear-of-a-black-president/309064/?single_page=true.

Cobb, William Jelani. *The Substance of Hope: Barack Obama and the Paradox of Progress*. New York: Walker & Co., 2010.

Collins, Patricia Hill. *Black Feminist Thought: Knowledge, Consciousness, and the Politics of Empowerment*. New York: Routledge, 2000.

Cooper, Michael. "Sales of Guns Soar in the U.S. as Nation Weighs Tougher Limits." *New York Times*. January 11, 2013. http://www.nytimes.com/2013/01/12/us/as-us-weighs-new-rules-sales-of-guns-and-ammunition-surge.html.

Corsi, Jerome R. "Occidential Activist: I Thought Obama Was Gay." *WND*. August 15, 2012. http://www.wnd.com/2012/08/occidental-activist-i-thought-obama-was-gay/.

———. "Trinity Church Members Reveal Obama Shocker." *WND*. October 2, 2012. http://www.wnd.com/2012/10/trinity-church-members-reveal-obama-shocker/.

———. "Claim: Obama Hid 'Gay Life' to Become President." *WND*. September 11, 2012. http://www.wnd.com/2012/09/claim-obama-hid-gay-life-to-become-president/.

Cosby, Bill, and Alvin F. Poussaint. *Come on, People: On the Path from Victims to Victors*. Nashville: Thomas Nelson, 2007.

Crowley, Michael. "Post-Racial." *New Republic: A Journal of Politics and the Arts*. March 12, 2008. http://www.newrepublic.com/article/post-racial.

DuJan, Kevin. "Why Won't the Agenda-Driven Media Report on Barack Obama Being Gay, Sexually Harassing Male Actor Kal Penn, and Frequenting Chicago Bathhouse Man's Country . . . You Know, the Way They Leaped to Trash Herman Cain with Unsubstantiated Sexual Innuendo?" *HillBuzz*. November 7, 2011. http://hillbuzz.org/why-wont-the-agenda-driven-media-report-on-barack-obama-being-gay-dating-actor-kal-penn-and-frequenting-chicago-bathhouse-mans-country-you-know-the-way-they-leaped-to-trash-herman-cain-with-u.

———."Is Barack Obama Gay?" *HillBuzz*. http://hillbuzz.org/is-barack-obama-gay.

Elder, Larry. *Stupid Black Men: How to Play the Race Card—and Lose*. New York: St. Martin's Press, 2008.

Emery, David. "Obama's 'Foreign Student' ID Found." *About.Com Urban Legends*. February 2012. http://urbanlegends.about.com/od/barackobama/ss/Obama-Student-Id.htm.

Feagin, Joe R. *The White Racial Frame Centuries of Racial Framing and Counter-Framing*. New York: Routledge, 2009.

Fenster, Mark. *Conspiracy Theories: Secrecy and Power in American Culture*. Minneapolis, MN: University of Minnesota Press, 2008.

Ford, Richard T. *The Race Card: How Bluffing about Bias Makes Race Relations Worse*. New York: Farrar, Straus and Giroux, 2008.

Gabler, Neal. "What's Behind the Right's 'Obama Is Gay' Conspiracy." *Nation*. October 23, 2012. http://www.thenation.com/article/170787/whats-behind-rights-obama-gay-conspiracy#.

Gonzales, Manuel G., and Richard Delgado. *The Politics of Fear: How Republicans Use Money, Race, and the Media to Win*. Boulder, CO: Paradigm, 2006.

Gore, Albert. *The Assault on Reason*. London: Bloomsbury, 2007.

Gosa, Travis L. "Counterknowledge, Racial Paranoia, and the Cultic Milieu: Decoding Hip Hop Conspiracy Theory." *Poetics* 39, no. 3 (2011): 187–204.

Hannah-Jones, Nikole. "A Colorblind Constitution: What Abigail Fisher's Affirmative Action Case Is Really About." *ProPublica: Journalism in the Public Interest*. March 18, 2013. http://www.propublica.org/ article/a-colorblind-constitution-what-abigail-fishers-affirmative- action-case-is-r.

Harris, Fredrick C. *The Price of the Ticket: Barack Obama and the Rise and Decline of Black Politics*. New York: Oxford University Press, 2012.

Harris Interactive Poll. "'Wingnuts' and President Obama: A Socialist? A Muslim? Anti-American? The Anti-Christ? Large Minorities of Americans Hold Some Remarkable Opinions." *Harris Interactive*. Last modified March 24, 2010. http://www.harrisinteractive.com/NewsRoom/HarrisPolls/tabid/447/ctl/ReadCustom%20Default/mid/1508/ ArticleId/223/Default.aspx.

Harris, Paul. "One in Four Americans Think Obama May Be the Antichrist, Survey Says." *Guardian*. April 2, 2013. http://www.theguardian.com/world/2013/apr/02/americans-obama-anti-christ-conspiracy-theories.

Hollinger, David A. *Postethnic America: Beyond Multiculturalism*. New York: Basic Books, 2000.

Hurt, Byron. "Barack & Curtis: Manhood, Power & Respect." Last modified October 9, 2008. http://www.youtube.com/watch?v=H5YoS3bqk5g.

Icke, David. "The Reptilians—the Schism—Obama and the New World Order." *David Icke Blog*. Accessed August 12, 2013. http://www. davidicke.com/headlines/64856-david-icke-the-reptilians-the-schism-obama-and-the-new-world-order.

Jackson, John L., Jr. *Racial Paranoia: The Unintended Consequences of Political Correctness: The New Reality of Race in America*. New York: Basic Civitas, 2008.

Jeffries, Michael P. *Paint the White House Black: Barack Obama and the Meaning of Race in America*. Stanford: Stanford University Press, 2013.

Jones, Alex, and InfoWars. "Special Report: The New World Order Is No 'Conspiracy Theory.'" *Infowars*, April 4, 2013. http://www.infowars.com/special-report-the-new-world-order-is-no-conspiracy-theory/.

Keen, Andrew. *The Cult of the Amateur: How Today's Internet Is Killing Our Culture*. New York: Doubleday/Currency, 2007.

Kelley, Robin D. G. "How the West Was One: On the Uses and Limitations of Diaspora." *The Black Scholar* 30 (2000): 31–35.

Kuhn, David Paul. "Exit Polls: How Obama Won." *Politico*. November 5, 2008. http://www.politico.com/news/stories/1108/15297.html.

Lepore, Jill. *The Whites of Their Eyes: The Tea Party's Revolution and the Battle over American History*. The Public Square Book Series. Princeton, NJ: Princeton University Press, 2010.

Marable, Manning. "Racializing Obama: The Enigma of Post-Black Politics and Leadership." *Souls: A Critical Journal of Black Politics, Culture, and Society* 11, no. 1 (2009): 1–15.

Mazama, Ama. "The Barack Obama Phenomenon." *Journal of Black Studies* 38, no. 1 (2007): 3–6.

Melley, Timothy. *Empire of Conspiracy: The Culture of Paranoia in Postwar America*. Ithaca, NY: Cornell University Press, 1999.

"Michelle Obama Flashes 'El Diablo' Sign on the Cover of Vogue." *InfoWars.com*. Last modified February 13, 2009, http://www.infowars.com/michelle-obama-flashes-%E2%80%98el-diablo%E2%80%99-hand-signal-on-cover-of-vogue/.

Milbank, Dana. *Tears of a Clown: Glenn Beck and the Tea Bagging of America*. New York: Doubleday, 2010.

Mohammadi, Saman. "Barack Obama's Allegiance Is Not to America and God, but to the New World Order and Satan." *InfoWars.com*, Last modified October 29, 2011. http://www.infowars.com/barack-obama%E2%80%99s-allegiance-is-not-to-america-and-god-but-to-the-new-world-order-and-satan/.

Mos Def, and Bill Maher. *Real Time with Bill Maher, HBO*. September 7, 2007.

Neiwert, David. "Fema Concentration Camps? The Militia Good Times Are Rollin' Again." *Crooks and Liars*. Last modified March 17, 2009. http://crooksandliars.com/david-neiwert/fema-concentration-camps-militia-goo.

Obama, Barack. *The Audacity of Hope: Thoughts on Reclaiming the American Dream*. New York: Crown Publishers, 2006.

———. "Democratic National Convention Keynote Address, Fleet Center, Boston." http://www.americanrhetoric.com/speeches/convention2004/barackobama2004dnc.htm.

"Obama & Illuminati to Destroy US Constitution —Minister Stevie Tee Fights Back." *Before It's News*, May 12, 2013. http://beforeitsnews.com/obama/2013/05/obama-illuminati-to-destroy-us-constitution-minister-stevie-tee-fights-back-2450748.html.

Olmsted, Kathryn S. *Real Enemies: Conspiracy Theories and American Democracy, World War I to 9/11*. New York: Oxford University Press, 2009.

Omi, Michael, and Howard Winant. *Racial Formation in the United States: From the 1960s to the 1980s*. New York; London: Routledge, 1989.

Onion. "Poll: 1 in 5 Americans Believe Obama Is a Cactus." *Onion: America's*

Finest News Source. September 22, 2010. http://www.theonion.com/articles/poll-1-in-5-americans-believe-obama-is-a-cactus,18127/.

Paisley, Brad. *"Accidental Racist" Featuring LL Cool J. Wheelhouse. Arista Nashville*, 2013.

Parish, Jane, and Martin Parker. *The Age of Anxiety: Conspiracy Theory and the Human Science*. Oxford, UK: Wiley-Blackwell/Sociological Review Monographs, 2001.

Patterson, Orlando. "The New Mainstream." *Newsweek*. October 31, 2008. http://www.newsweek.com/id/166827.

Pierce, Charles P. *Idiot America: How Stupidity Became a Virtue in the Land of the Free*. New York: Doubleday, 2009.

Pollock, Mica. *Colormute: Race Talk Dilemmas in an American School*. Princeton, NJ: Princeton University Press, 2004.

Poor, Jeff. "Maher Lobbies Obama to 'Throw Caution to the Wind' and Become 'an Angry Black Man." *Daily Caller*. November 17, 2012. http://dailycaller.com/2012/11/17/maher-lobbies-obama-to-throw-caution-to-the-wind-and-become-an-angry-black-man-video/.

Pray for Us, Pray for the United States. "Help America Defeat Muslim Brotherhood-Sponsored Amnesty Plan!!" Accessed August 9, 2013. https://prayfor.us/muslim_bhood_immigration/.

Public Policy Polling. "Conspiracy Theory Poll Results." *Public Policy Polling*. April 2, 2013. http://www.publicpolicypolling.com/main/2013/04/conspiracy-theory-poll-results-.html.

President Obama: "Put Education First." UT Austin Know, August 9, 2010. http://www.utexas.edu/know/2010/08/09/obama_speech_gregory/.

Railey, Kimberly. "More States Move to Ban Foreign Laws in Courts." *USA Today*. August 4, 2013. http://www.usatoday.com/story/news/nation/2013/08/04/states-ban-foreign-law/2602511/.

Rashbaum, Alyssa. "KRS-One Denounced for Controversial Statements About 9-11." *MTV News*. October 15, 2004. http://www.mtv.com/news/articles/1492288/krs-one-denounced-statements-about-9-11.jhtml.

Roediger, David. "Race Will Survive the Obama Phenomenon." *Chronicle of Education Review*. October 10, 2008. http://chronicle.com/article/Race-Will-Survive-the-Obama/21983.

———. *How Race Survived US History: From Settlement and Slavery to the Obama Phenomenon*. London; New York: Verso, 2008b.

"Schizophrenia Clinical Trial." *CRILifetree*. Accessed February 14, 2014. http://www.crilifetree.com/clinical-trials/schizophrenia-research-study.

Shear, Michael D. "At West Point, Obama Offers New Security Strategy." *Washington Post*. May 23, 2010. http://www.washingtonpost.com/wp-dyn/content/article/2010/05/22/AR2010052201586.html.

Simmons, William Paul, and Sharon Parsons. "Beliefs in Conspiracy Theories among African Americans: A Comparison of Elites and Masses." *Social Science Quarterly* 86, no. 3 (2005): 582–598.

Snopes. "Who Is Barack Obama?" *Snopes*. January 2009. http://www.snopes.com/politics/obama/muslim.asp.

Stephanie. "Ex Member Reveals." *The Watchman's Cry*. Last modified January 1, 2011. http://www.watchmanscry.com/forum/showthread.php?t=15124.

Suebsaeng, Asawin, and Dave Gilson. "Chart: Almost Every Obama Conspiracy Theory Ever." *MotherJones*. Oct. 2012. http://www.motherjones.com/politics/2012/10/chart-obama-conspiracy-theories.

Thompson, Damian. *Counterknowledge: How We Surrendered to Conspiracy Theories, Quack Medicine, Bogus Science and Fake History*. New York: W. W. Norton & Company, 2008.

Traynor, Ian. "Barack Obama Seeks to Limit EU Fallout over US Spying Claims." *Guardian*. July 1, 2013. http://www.theguardian.com/world/2013/jul/01/barack-obama-eu-fallout-us-spying-claims.

Wingfield, Adia Harvey, and Joe R. Feagin. *Yes, We Can?: White Racial Framing and the 2008 Presidential Campaign*. London: Routledge, 2009.

Younge, Gary. "Open Season on Black Boys after a Verdict Like This." *Guardian*. July 14, 2013. http://www.guardian.co.uk/commentisfree/2013/jul/14/open-season-black-boys-verdict.

Zernike, Kate. *Boiling Mad: Inside Tea Party America*. New York: Times Books/Henry Holt and Co., 2010.

part 2
Structural Inequality

5

From Orchards to Silicon Valley

African American Suburbanization in the U.S. West, the Black San Jose Model, 1945–2010

Herb Ruffin II

Introduction

The percentage of African Americans in San Jose is small compared to most U.S. metropolises. This has made for a very different story about Black suburbanization than is told in well-known places in the Eastern U.S., such as Prince George's County, Maryland, and East Cleveland, Ohio (in East Cuyahoga County), which have large Black populations ranging from 10 percent to 93 percent, and are often categorized as spillover suburbs extending from the central city where most African Americans reside.[1] This pattern has afforded African Americans in large urban areas the option of living in either suburban Black belt communities such as Ferguson, Missouri, or in white and affluent suburban communities like Fairfax County, Virginia, and Lakewood, Ohio (in West Cuyahoga County) where, similar to San Jose, their populations in the post–civil rights era are small—ranging from 1 percent to 9 percent—as well as scattered and socially isolated.[2] San Jose's model of Black suburbanization differs from the latter model in that Blacks are dispersed among multicultural communities with large Asian American and Mexican American populations that can range as high as 60 percent. Within this "postracial society" in which white privilege and race prejudice was widely believed to be nonexistent, de facto racial discrimination in housing has led to social isolation and has added to the difficultly Blacks have in developing a strong sense of community. Greater San Jose's pattern of Black suburbanization has been replicated, arguably, in other western metropolises whose suburban cities grew phenomenally after 1960, such as Dallas–Fort Worth (Texas), Las Vegas (Nevada), and Phoenix (Arizona), with Black populations ranging from 3 percent to21 percent. (See table 1.)[3] Arguably the best way to gauge how suburban metropolises of this type have developed during the postwar and "postracial" eras is to examine community formation through housing freedoms and constraints, opportunities and obstacles, fairness and unfairness. This chapter will address all those issues as a model for understanding the Black suburban experience in postwar-era San Jose. It will be informed by literature on Black migration and community formation in postwar urban and suburban America, in particular the works of Albert S. Broussard, Sheryl Cashin, Lawrence De Graaf, Karyn Lacy, Thomas Sugrue, Quintard Taylor, Joe William Trotter, and Andrew Wiese.[4]

Urban Sustainability and Race, 1945–1968

In the post-World War II era, perhaps the most urgent civil rights issues confronting African Americans in most U.S. urban communities outside of the South were residential segregation and the struggle for affordable quality housing.[5] In metropolitan San Jose, this struggle was critical, because most communities achieved their high standards of living by shutting out people of color from their housing markets, primarily because of race prejudice rather than to prevent a decline in property values. During the postwar period, suburban metropolises in the Southwest, such as Greater San Jose, rapidly urbanized and industrialized, and most residents lived in affordable, newly built homes. By 1960, these developments led to San Jose for the first time landing at number 57 on the U.S. Census Bureau's "Population of the 100 Largest Cities" list, and becoming designated an All-American City.[6] By 2005, the city surpassed Detroit as the tenth most populated U.S. city—patterns that have been replicated in cities such as Austin (Texas), Dallas, Fort Worth, Phoenix, and San Diego (California), to name a few. (See table 2.)[7]

For African Americans, the ambition to move to Greater San Jose and purchase housing during its first period of substantial suburban growth (ca. 1950–1970) was halted by racial prejudice, state and federal policies, affordability, and de facto segregation in the housing and employment markets.[8] In Metropolitan San Jose, the African American population rose from 1,718 in 1950 to 18,090 in 1970; or from 1 percent of the South Bay population to 2 percent. (See table 3.)[9] They were restricted to living in Northside San Jose (in downtown San Jose), East San Jose, downtown Palo Alto, Barron Park (Palo Alto), East Palo Alto (on the outskirts of metropolitan San Jose), and Sunnyhills (Milpitas).[10]

From 1946 to 1968, San Jose Blacks along with their Asian American, European American, and Mexican American allies fought residential

Table 1. Western Metropolises Patterned on San Jose's Model of Urbanization, 1950–2010

Community	State	Metro Area	Year Started	Starting Population	2000	Change (Percent)
Chandler	AZ	Phoenix	1950	3,799	176,581	4,548
Gilbert	AZ	Phoenix	1980	5,717	109,697	1,819
Glendale	AZ	Phoenix	1950	8,179	218,812	2,575
Mesa	AZ	Phoenix	1950	16,790	396,375	2,261
Peoria	AZ	Phoenix	1960	2,593	108,364	4,079
Scottsdale	AZ	Phoenix	1960	10,026	202,705	1,922
Tempe	AZ	Phoenix	1950	7,684	158,625	1,964
Anaheim	CA	Los Angeles	1950	14,556	328,014	2,153
Corona City	CA	Los Angeles	1950	10,223	124,966	1,122
Costa mesa	CA	Los Angeles	1960	37,550	108,724	190
Fontana	CA	Los Angeles	1960	14,659	128,929	780
Fullerton City	CA	Los Angeles	1950	13,958	126,003	803
Irvine	CA	Los Angeles	1980	62,134	143,072	130
Lancaster	CA	Los Angeles	1950	3,594	118,718	3,203
Moreno Valley	CA	Los Angeles	1990	118,779	142,381	20
Ontario	CA	Los Angeles	1950	22,872	158,007	591
Orange	CA	Los Angeles	1950	10,027	128,821	1,185
Oxnard	CA	Los Angeles	1950	21,567	170,358	690
Rancho Cucamonga	CA	Los Angeles	1980	55,250	127,743	131
Riverside	CA	Los Angeles	1950	46,764	255,166	446
San Bernardino	CA	Los Angeles	1950	63,058	185,401	194
Santa Ana	CA	Los Angeles	1950	45,533	337,977	642
Santa Clarita	CA	Los Angeles	1990	110,642	151,088	37
Simi Valley	CA	Los Angeles	1970	56,676	111,351	96
Thousand Oaks	CA	Los Angeles	1960	2,934	117,005	3,888
Chula Vista	CA	San Diego	1950	15,927	173,556	990
Escondido	CA	San Diego	1950	6,544	133,559	1,941
Oceanside	CA	San Diego	1950	12,881	161,029	1,150
Daly City	CA	San Francisco	1950	15,191	103,621	582
Fremont	CA	San Francisco	1960	43,790	203,413	365
Santa Rosa	CA	San Francisco	1950	17,902	147,595	724
Sunnyvale	CA	San Francisco	1950	9,829	131,760	1,241
Aurora	CO	Denver	1950	11,421	276,393	2,320
Lakewood	CO	Denver	1960	19,338	144,126	645
Westminster	CO	Denver	1960	13,850	100,940	629
Henderson	NV	Las Vegas	1950	3,643	175,381	4,714
North Las Vegas	NV	Las Vegas	1950	3,875	115,488	2,880
Salem	OR	Portland	1950	43,140	136,924	217
Arlington	TX	Dallas	1950	7,692	332,969	4,229
Carrolton	TX	Dallas	1960	4,242	109,576	2,483
Garland	TX	Dallas	1950	10,571	215,768	1,941
Grand Prairie	TX	Dallas	1950	14,594	127,427	773
Irving	TX	Dallas	1950	2,621	191,615	7,211
Mesquite	TX	Dallas	1960	27,526	124,523	352
Plano	TX	Dallas	1960	3,695	222,030	5,909
West Valley City	UT	Salt Lake City	1980	72,378	108,896	50
Bellevue	WA	Seattle	1960	12,809	109,569	755

Source: Robert E. Lang and Patrick A Simmons, "'Boomburbs': Fast-Growing Suburban Cities," in Bruce Katz, and Robert E. Lang (eds.), *Redefining Urban and Suburban America: Evidence from Census 2000* (Washington, DC: Brookings Institution Press, 2003), 106.

Table 2. San Jose's Black Population, 1970–2010

	1970	1980	1990	2000	2010
Metropolitan San Jose					
Total Black Population	18,090	43,716	56,211	47,182	46,428
Total Population	1,064,714	1,295,071	1,497,577	1,682,585	1,781,642
Black Population Percentage	1.6	3.3	3.8	2.8	2.6
Within San Jose					
Total Black Population	10,955	28,792	36,397	31,349	30,242
Total Population	445,779	629,442	782,225	894,943	945,942
Black Population Percentage	2.5	4.6	4.7	3.5	3.2

Sources: (Metropolitan San Jose) U.S. Bureau of the Census, 1970 *Census of Housing*, 7–10, 14–15, 453; U.S. Bureau of the Census, *U.S. Census of Population and Housing*, 215; and Social Explorer Dataset (SE), *Census 1990, Social Explorer; U.S. Census Bureau* (http://old.socialexplorer.com/pub/reportdata/htmlresults.aspx?ReportId=R10536377); *Census 2000* (http://old.socialexplorer.com/pub/reportdata/htmlresults.aspx?ReportId=R10536370); *Census 2010* (http://old.socialexplorer.com/pub/reportdata/htmlresults.aspx?ReportId=R10536341); (for San Jose city) Metropolitan Transportation Commission (MTA), and the Association of Bay Area Governments of Bay Area Governments (ABAG), *Bay Area Census—City of San Jose: 1890–2010 (URL: http://www.bayareacensus.ca.gov/cities/SanJose50.htm);* U.S. Bureau of the Census, *Census Reports, Volume I: Twelfth Census of the United States, 1900; Population Part I* (Washington, DC: U.S. Government Printing Office [GPO], 1901), 610; U.S. Bureau of the Census, *Thirteenth Census of the United States, 1910: Volume I; Population 1910* (Washington, DC: GPO, 1913), 179; U.S. Bureau of the Census, *Negroes in the United States, 1920–32* (New York: Kraus Reprint Co., 1969), 56; U.S. Bureau of the Census, *Sixteenth Census of the United States, 1940: Population, Vol. II; Volume I, Characteristics of the Population* (Washington, DC: GPO, 1943), 602.

segregation in loosely connected state and local fair housing movements. The local fair housing movement began in 1949, with the San Jose Council for Civic Unity (CCU). Three years later (1952), San Jose's newly formed NAACP "joined with the Council of Churches, the Catholic Interracial Council, The American Friends Service Committee [(Quakers)], and the Brotherhood [of Sleeping Car Porters], along with many White friends to counter the prevailing discrimination in housing."[11] By 1959, the local fair housing effort made considerable headway as approximately 2,000 San Jose homeowners signed an "open housing covenant," declaring "that I am ready to welcome into my neighborhood residents of whatever race, creed or national origin." As this was occurring, within real estate circles, Eichler Homes,

Table 3. Black Population in Metropolitan San Jose, 1940–1970

	1940	1950	1960	1970
Total Black Population	730	1,718	4,187	18,090
Total Population	174,949	290,547	642,315	1,064,714
Black Population Percentage	0.4	0.6	0.7	1.6

Sources: U.S. Bureau of the Census, *1950 Census of Population: Volume 11, Characteristics of the Population*, Part 5, *California* (Washington, DC: U.S. Government Printing Office, 1952), 5–21; U.S. Bureau of the Census, *1970 Census of Housing*, 7–10, 14–15, 453; and University of Virginia Library, *Historical Census Browser: County-Level Results for 1850–1960* (University of Virginia Library: Geospatial and Statistical Data Center, 2005).

J. S. Williams, and African American realtors Mary Anne Smith and Berthina Nelson were in the vanguard in desegregating exclusively European American neighborhoods throughout the Greater San Jose to qualified buyers of color.[12] Three years later, in 1962, fair housing activists pressured San Jose into becoming the second city in Santa Clara County to go through serious motions to resolve residential apartheid with a fair housing ordinance—the first city was nearby Milpitas, which had a fair housing ordinance built into its municipal codes before it incorporated in 1954.[13]

On the state level, the passage of the California Fair Housing Act of 1963 (aka the Rumford Act) made California central to the success of the fair housing and civil rights movements. On February 16, 1964, at the Negro Consolidated Realty Board of Los Angeles installation banquet, Dr. Martin Luther King Jr. acknowledged California's importance to the civil rights movement. At that time the movement was fighting the repeal of the Rumford Act through the initiative Proposition 14, which, following its passage in 1965, outlawed fair housing in California.[14] Metropolitan San Jose passed the initiative 162,029 to 143,689, which at the time arguably made most people of color feel like unwelcome neighbors.[15] In the example of Black professionals, who became San Jose's first beneficiaries of affirmative action (after 1965), persons such as Ocie Tinsley were recruited into the region to work at high-tech firms like Lockheed and IBM.[16] Most of these professionals initially failed to find housing where white recruits lived, such as in the San Jose suburbs of Campbell, Santa Clara, Saratoga, Sunnyvale, and West San Jose.

As Black professionals like Tinsley were adjusting to San Jose's color line, in 1966, Proposition 14 was overturned by the California Supreme Court, once more making fair housing the law, following the activist efforts of groups like San Jose's NAACP and the trial of six cases involving Blacks who were evicted or refused rentals because of their race. The most notable of these cases was *Mulkey v. Reitman* (1966), which declared that Proposition 14 was unconstitutional because it violated the Equal Protection Clause in the Fourteenth Amendment to the U.S. Constitution. In June of the following year (1967), the U.S. Supreme Court continued to outlaw Proposition 14 for violating the Fourteenth Amendment and the Civil Rights Act of 1866, which "prohibits all racial discrimination in the sale or rental of property."[17] Moreover, the Court said that Proposition 14 went well beyond Rumford and was applied to public assisted housing and housing financed with federal funds, making it a federal offense.[18] Attacking fair housing legislation did not end until the Fair Housing Act of 1968 was enacted.[19] According to historian Lawrence de Graaf the passage of this law,

> made [FHA] . . . insurance more accessible to African American home buyers and lower-income families, and Congress subsidized home purchases and renting by low- and moderate-income families under sections 235 and 236 programs of the 1968 Housing Act. The culminating measure was Title VIII of the 1968 Civil Rights Act, which prohibited most forms of discrimination based on race, color, religion, or national origin in the sale, rental, or financing of housing.[20]

The immediate result of the 1968 Fair Housing Act was a spike in metropolitan San Jose's Black population in 1968–1969. The Black population quadrupled from 4,200 in 1960 to 18,100 in 1970. Within city limits San Jose's Black population rose from 2,000 to 11,000 in the same period.[21] As with most U.S. communities, after 1970, the cost to buy and rent a home or an apartment in metropolitan San Jose became just as much a factor as race for residential segregation.[22] Census tract statistics and Census block data suggests that racism was a crucial dynamic in the makeup of most Santa Clara County communities (where San Jose resides), especially in traditional white neighborhoods in the western and southern peninsula sections of the region, such as Los Altos, Cupertino, and Los Gatos. Places in the county with a noticeable Black presence were San Jose, Milpitas, and Mountain View. In these communities the Black population of metropolitan San Jose grew phenomenally in the 1970s and 1980s. Most of the Black newcomers came to southwest suburban metropolises such as San Jose from central cities in search of social fairness, professional opportunities, better education for their children, single-family housing, safe neighborhoods, and mild weather. In short, African Americans have been seeking entrance to a pleasant middle-class lifestyle in the faster-growing cities in post–civil rights era America: Sunbelt metropolises such as San Jose that are in states like California that border Mexico. According to many standard markers of success in the United States, demographic data indicate that a large portion of Blacks in multiracial suburban metropolises like Arlington (Texas), Ontario (California), and San Jose were thriving.[23]

From 1970 to 1990, Blacks in the postsuburban West arguably were better integrated spatially and were more prosperous and educated than African Americans in most parts of the country. This most certainly was the case in San Jose, where the median income for Black households was about $43,500 compared with $46,200 for the general population.[24] More than 34 percent of San Jose area Blacks earned at least $50,000, whereas in California as a whole, only around 21 percent of the Black population was doing so. And in 1990 around 23.5 percent of African Americans were college graduates in metropolitan San Jose, compared with 9 percent nationwide and 15 percent in California as a whole.[25] Consequently what these figures indicate is that most Blacks in postsuburban Santa Clara County succeeded. Many had good jobs, educations, and homes in the suburbs—the prosperity that people identify with the American dream. But the original meaning of "the American dream" had as much to do with equal opportunity, fairness, and community as it did with prosperity.

Black Suburbanization in the Post–Civil Rights Era, 1968–1990

African American migration to the suburbs contributed to a demographic revolution within American communities in which suburban Black populations grew from 2.5 million people in 1960 to 11.9 million people by 2000, or from 13 percent to 34 percent of the national African American population.[26] To many people in the post–civil rights era, notable Black movement into the middle class and the suburbs symbolized America living up to its political creed that "all men are created equal."[27] In metropolitan San Jose this included most African Americans taking part in an ongoing freedom rights struggle (whether or not they saw it this way) by desegregating residential, educational, and employment spaces in pursuit of homeownership in middle-class, relatively low-density communities, while attempting to acquire comfortable incomes and professional occupations. Most of these African Americans, such as the Andersons, Dollarhydes, Garys, Grosses, and Jacksons, came from families that had modest middle-class aspirations and consciously looked to supplant race with class as the determinant of their life chances.[28]

African Americans came to metropolitan San Jose during a postwar period of rapid urban and high-tech industrial development, which in most areas was not noticeable until the South Bay, after 1971, became the computer and microelectronics capital of the United States, better known as "Silicon Valley." High-tech startups such as Apple Computer were able to make this so by relying more on venture capitalists to finance their companies than on the industry's military contracts and government purchases—which in the 1960s accounted for half of the semiconductor shipments, a pattern noticeably in notable decline in the 1970s.[29] This became an important factor in the local electronics industry's ability to surpass Boston as the most important chip-, hardware-, and software-producing area in the world.[30]

Many Western cities gradually adopted what historian Richard White called the Palo Alto–Stanford University industrial park model of urban growth. For example, after 1951 in Santa Clara County, Palo Alto rapidly transformed its rural acreage into neatly zoned industrial parks, strip malls, and single-family subdivisions. Key to this model was that—unlike traditional bedroom communities whose residents lived in the suburbs and worked in a central city such as San Francisco—by the late 1970s the high-tech suburb had its own economy and was retaining its workers. From this model emerged the Silicon Valley's version of postsuburbia.[31] By the mid-1990s, most of San Jose and the Santa Clara County became engulfed in this development, and soon the county had the largest population in the Bay Area and the fourth-largest population in California (behind Los Angeles, San Diego, and Orange Counties).[32] In the early 1990s, as recognition of this and the fact that top technology firms were moving their headquarters to San Jose, city and county officials began advertising San Jose as the "capital of Silicon Valley"—a pattern driven by industries of amusement, finance, high tech, medicine, and open-air malls, that have been replicated in suburban North Dallas–Fort Worth (aka "Silicon Prairie"), Santa Ana-Irvine/West Orange County (California) (aka "Silicon Coast"), West Austin (aka "Silicon Hills"); and since the mid-1990s, in older, industrial Western cities such as suburban North Denver (Colorado) (aka "Silicon Mountain"), San Francisco, West Los Angeles (aka "Silicon Beach"), West Portland (aka "Silicon Forest"), and West Seattle (aka "Silicon Canal").

Similar to the high tech cities listed, with the rise of Silicon Valley, metropolitan San Jose emerged as one of the fastest-growing regions in the United States. Its population grew from less than 650,000 in 1960 to almost 1.7 million in 2000. In that stretch of time, most urban populations in the country went into notable decline, and more than half of all Americans lived in suburbs for the first time in American history.[33] Similar to San Antonio (Texas), even though a small percent of San Jose's population lived in suburbs physically adjacent to the city (27 percent), such as Cupertino, Milpitas, and Santa Clara, most of its population lived in suburbs within the city limits, or in "inburbs" that date back to 1950 when strip annexation began.

Like other postwar Western metropolises, San Jose's phenomenal growth caught most of its residents by surprise. Prior to the 1970s, the region was still physically marked by apricot and cherry orchards, canneries, old farms, ranches, and sleepy towns, according to historian and Bay Area native Gordon Chang. What stood out for him was that there was very little ethnic diversity, in particular among Asian Americans, who since the 1990s have developed a dominant presence in both metropolitan San Jose and the Bay Area.[34] Mountain View resident Albert Jones said that the region's phenomenal physical transformation did not occur until the late-1970s—a period that loosely aligns with the testimony of most observers who migrated to the region from 1972–1977.[35] Other African American natives, such as Cass Jackson, say Greater San Jose grew exponentially from 1972 to 1980. But as much as the landscape had changed, other components had not, such as Blacks being scattered and having a weak sense of Black community, which Jackson had also experienced in the 1950s and 1960s, when Blacks started leaving clustered communities in Northside San Jose for the suburbanizing East San Jose.[36]

By 1980, Black flight, or the exodus of potential African American leaders and role models into the suburbs from central cities, hastened the gulf between the Black middle class and the Black working poor and was a major contributor to the post-1970 rise of "the truly disadvantaged." With the loss of its middle class, central cities such as Cleveland, San Jose, and Washington, DC, became the home of perpetually poor populations who were becoming increasingly poorer. Black business owners in many cases had moved out, taking jobs with them. So had many Blacks whose educational and professional successes might have led others to aspire to the same.[37] When so many of the high achievers moved out, it was as if they took with them the heart of the neighborhood, and the people who were left behind had to deal with the loss as best they could. But what they likely did not realize is that the loss cut both ways; the people who left the neighborhood had lost something, too. They went from being part of a Black community to simply representing a Black community everywhere they went. From 1970 to 1990, metropolitan San Jose's Black community had risen from a population of 18,100 to 56,200, which was its peak, from which it then gradually diminished and stabilized around 47,200 in 2000 and 46,400 in 2010. (See table 4.)[38]

The diminished impact that metropolitan San Jose's fragmented Black community could bring to bear on the ability of African Americans to feel connected to one another and the increased sense of living in social isolation was formally addressed in a public forum for the first time in February 1979, at a Black history conference titled, "The Crisis of the Black Spirit." This event was held at the Afro-American Center (later renamed the Afro-American Community Service Agency) in Northside San Jose, and was moderated by local Ann L. Bird, who was the West Coast regional chairwoman for the NAACP.

Seventy-five people attended lectures and workshops that addressed the state of Black America in Greater San Jose. They presented widely diverging ways to resolve the problems of how African Americans could become more politically active and overcome their dispersion throughout the region, ideas that ranged from encouraging greater involvement with the Black church to increased membership in political organizations like the San Jose NAACP—which was on decline due to a combination of Black flight and complacency. Bird accordingly echoed many of these sentiments when she stated that "Because Blacks in San Jose are not concentrated in one area, like many other cities, it's difficult for Blacks here to get a sense of community."[39] This problem was compounded by the rise of the Black middle class, many of whom were dissociating themselves from working-class communities of color through residential relocation to suburbs, hillsides, and disappearance from institutions that had the capacity to open communications "between the high and low income Blacks."[40]

Similar to Greater Anaheim (California), as metropolitan San Jose's Black population stabilized around 47,000 in the 2000s, its community seemed to become even more fragmented. Blacks with whom nurse and community activist Ellen Rollins (from Washington, DC) came into contact after 1989 were becoming comfortable with surviving and living fragmented, increasingly individualistic lives without either a stable sense of community or a local historical legacy because individuals were becoming socioeconomically diverse and broadly dispersed throughout the region.[41] In suburban metropolises without a Black center, interested African Americans in places such as Henderson

Table 4. The Thirty Most Populous Cities in 2010

Rank	City	State	2010 Pop	1950 Pop	Rank	1960 Pop	Rank
1	New York	NY	8,175,133	7,891,957	1	7,781,984	1
2	Los Angeles	CA	3,792,621	1,970,358	4	2,479,015	3
3	Chicago	IL	2,695,598	3,620,962	2	3,550,404	2
4	Houston	TX	2,099,451	596,163	14	938,219	7
5	Philadelphia	PA	1,526,006	2,071,605	3	2,002,512	4
6	Phoenix	AZ	1,445,632	106,818	99	439,170	29
7	San Antonio	TX	1,327,407	408,442	25	587,718	17
8	San Diego	CA	1,307,402	334,387	33	573,224	18
9	Dallas	TX	1,197,816	434,462	22	679,684	14
10	San Jose	CA	945,942	95,280	–	204,196	57
11	Indianapolis	IN	829,718	427,173	23	476,258	26
12	Jacksonville	FL	821,784	204,517	49	201,030	61
13	San Francisco	CA	805,235	775,357	11	740,316	12
14	Austin	TX	790,390	132,459	73	186,545	67
15	Columbus	OH	787,033	375,901	28	471,316	28
16	Fort Worth	TX	741,206	278,778	38	356,268	34
17	Louisville-Jefferson	KY	741,096	369,129	30	390,639	31
18	Charlotte	NC	731,424	134,042	70	201,564	59
19	Detroit	MI	713,777	1,849,568	5	1,670,144	5
20	El Paso	TX	649,121	130,485	76	276,687	46
21	Memphis	TN	646,889	396,000	26	497,524	22
22	Nashville-Davidson	TN	626,681	174,307	56	170,874	73
23	Baltimore	MD	620,961	949,708	6	939,024	6
24	Boston	MA	617,594	801,444	10	697,197	13
25	Seattle	WA	608,660	467,591	19	557,087	19
26	Washington	DC	601,723	802,178	9	763,956	9
27	Denver	CO	600,158	415,786	24	493,887	23
28	Milwaukee	WI	594,833	637,392	13	741,324	11
29	Portland	OR	583,776	373,628	29	372,676	32
30	Las Vegas	NV	583,756	24,624	–	64,405	–

Sources: National League of Cities, "The 30 Most Populous Cities" (http://www.nlc.org/build-skills-and-networks/resources/cities-101/city-factoids/the-30-most-populous-cities); *U.S. Bureau of the Census*, "Population of the 100 Largest Urban Places: 1950" (https://www.census.gov/population/www/documentation/twps0027/tab18.txt); *U.S. Bureau of the Census*, "Population of the 100 Largest Urban Places: 1960" (https://www.census.gov/population/www/documentation/twps0027/tab19.txt); *Las Vegas Convention and Visitors Authority*, "History of Las Vegas: Timeline" (http://www.lvcva.com/stats-and-facts/history-of-las-vegas/); *Metropolitan Transportation Commission, and Association of Bay Area Governments*, "Bay Area Census: City of San Jose" (http://www.bayareacensus.ca.gov/cities/SanJose50.htm).

(Nevada), Mesa (Arizona), and San Jose have found Black communities scattered geographically in Black churches, professional organizations, barber shops, beauty shops, sociopolitical organizations, and night spots. In Greater San Jose, James C. Dennis, an African American marketing communications director for Hewlett-Packard, found the Black community by making the extra effort to find Black barbershops, ethnic grocery stores, and nightclubs playing familiar music that could not be found in white and affluent Saratoga, where he lives. Dennis's wife, Tonya, thirty-eight, said that meeting Blacks in Silicon Valley required being bold about calling the friends of friends, inviting people to dinner, and introducing themselves to strangers.[42]

San Jose as Case Study for Restrictive Housing in the Postsuburban West, 1968–1990

Several studies in the late 1970s and early 1980s have charted African American suburbanization in Greater San Jose's housing market. Most of these studies focused on the rental market because most African Americans by the late 1970s were becoming renters. The most notable investigation was conducted in 1977 by *San Jose Mercury News* reporters Calvin Stovall and Bob Goligoski. Stovall was a Black man from the South. His parents and grandparents pushed him to go to college to broaden his employment opportunities and life options. When he came to the Santa Clara Valley in 1973, he had already lived in Arkansas, Mississippi, and Alabama, and he believed what he had been told back home about California: that people there do not judge other human beings by their race. This perspective changed for Stovall while he and Goligoski conducted their research, the topic of which was racial discrimination in rental housing in metropolitan San Jose.[43]

At first Stovall took the assignment lightly. That lasted no longer than his first day on the streets, when he actually started reporting. The first landlord he approached politely declined to rent to him, saying that there were no vacancies. Thirty minutes later, the same landlord, politely offered to rent an apartment to Goligoski, a white man, when he inquired about rentals. This sort of switch went on throughout Stovall and Goligoski's reporting. Of the thirty-four apartments surveyed, thirteen landlords "politely" declined to rent to Stovall but rented to Goligoski. The excuse usually given to Stovall was that "there was a long 'waiting list,' and no apartments would be vacant soon."[44] By the end of the report, Stovall no longer felt casual about the assignment.

> Suddenly, I saw the California apartment managers who discriminate as Southerners in disguise. . . . I realized that I preferred the direct discrimination I have faced for years in the South where whites told you if they didn't like you. I would rather have some of the managers call me a dirty nigger, and tell me they didn't rent apartments to darkies. . . . Even those racial slurs would not have hurt as much as the subtle lies. . . . The racial slurs at least let me know who my friends were.[45]

The newspaper report stunned the San Jose region and set a precedent for subsequent surveys that found housing discrimination in apartment rentals to be widespread throughout the metropolitan area up to 1990. Like Stovall, other Black researchers such as Marvin Conley, a member of the San Jose Human Relations Commission, were furious. Conley said he was "ready to buy torches and start burning things" after several landlords turned him down and later offered rentals to white members of the commission.[46] The commission estimated that discrimination existed in 27 percent of leased apartments in San Jose. The discrimination did not always mean barring someone from a rental; one European American participant was told by an apartment manager "that she raises the rent when Black persons inquire about apartments in order to keep Black people out of her apartment."[47]

Local governments usually responded to these surveys with indifference or superficial concern. The most notable example occurred in 1982 when the Mid-Peninsula Citizens for Fair Housing conducted a survey and concluded that African Americans had a much harder time renting apartments in Sunnyvale than did any other group of people. City officials such as City Councilman Larry Stone, by then embarrassed by more than a decade of complaints about unfair housing, went through the motions of developing a program that addressed housing discrimination. After several months of half-hearted effort, Sunnyvale abruptly dropped its plan to write a fair housing law, saying that federal and state laws were sufficient and that the city could better assist through "enforcement mechanisms" such as seminars and mailings to discourage discriminatory behavior. Marcia Fein, part of the complaining group, addressed Sunnyvale's resolution as typical of what was happening nationwide. She was shocked, however, by how many people thought that "because we have fair housing laws that the problem is solved."[48]

Although the enactment of state and federal fair housing laws sparked Black suburbanization, those laws were politically compromised and weakly enforced until the implementation of the National Housing

Act of 1988. This law broadened the scope of fair housing coverage, gave HUD direct enforcement powers, and empowered administrative law judges to render judgment in unfair housing court cases.[49] Prior to the National Housing Act of 1988, enforcement and investigation on both the state and national levels were hampered by a lack of enforcement powers. This put the responsibility for enforcement on the private citizen, who assumed the cost of litigation, which in some instances could last several years. California fair housing law under the Rumford Act was just as ineffectual. During the 1970s to 1980s, the law badly needed to be rewritten to fit the times and to omit the Proposition 14 compromises of the 1960s. Instead, as Dennis Keating writes in *The Suburban Racial Dilemma*, "Crowded dockets and less flexibility in the law [made] recourse to the Supreme Court, under California's Rumford Act . . . less attractive" to victims of housing discrimination.[50] Complainants usually bypassed government agencies and pursued lawsuits if they could afford to do so.

The best way for Blacks to avoid housing discrimination in Southwest Sun Belt cities such as San Jose was to become homeowners. According to a 1979 HUD report, Blacks stood a greater risk of being discriminated against in the rental market (85 percent) than in the homeownership market (48 percent).[51] Prior to the late 1970s, determination, rent discrimination, and the scarcity of rentals were the top contributing factors as to why more than 66 percent of African American families in Silicon Valley were homeowners.[52] Similar to postsuburban San Bernardino and Aurora (Colorado), Silicon Valley Blacks moved into relatively new homes (built from 1960 to 1980) in one of the youngest and fastest-urbanizing regions in America—a trend replicated in the post-1980 suburban South in Charlotte (North Carolina), Jacksonville (Florida), and Nashville (Tennessee), to name a few places.[53] After 1970, home buying by African Americans depended on the national and local economies, public policy, and fair housing practices. In the 1980s, for example, Black suburbanites were especially affected by the stagnation of the local housing market during economic recessions. Home buying by African Americans slumped from 1980 to 1984 and 1989 to 1990, whereas it increased by 66 percent from 1985 to 1988.[54] Still, by 1990, Black homeownership had slipped to slightly less than a third of Greater San Jose Blacks in an increasingly expensive Silicon Valley. The median value of a home rose from $23,400 in 1970 to $107,700 in 1980 to $289,400 in 1990, and was exceeded only in nearby San Francisco County, the most expensive place in the United States, followed by New York City.[55]

In the postsuburban West, the ramifications of housing inflation in places like the South Bay has over the decades arguably made cost more of an inhibiting factor than race for Blacks to live. And the decrease of homeownership has long-term effects on racial imbalances and on African Americans' chances to better themselves financially. Consider that in Greater San Jose, although 66 percent of Black households were homeowners before the late 1970s, that same percentage were renters by 1990, which means they were accumulating no land wealth, whereas 79 percent of whites (76 percent of the population) were homeowners earning equity and expanding their opportunities.[56]

Traditionally, Silicon Valley Blacks lived in the Northside of San Jose, East San Jose (after 1950), Northwest Milpitas (after 1957), downtown Palo Alto (in the 1920s), and unincorporated East Palo Alto (after 1950). During the post–civil rights era, much of this pattern held, but some African American households dispersed into surrounding communities of the region. This included sprinkles of Black people in formerly restricted communities in the very expensive and very white Mid-Peninsula area (i.e., Los Altos, Los Gatos, and Saratoga).[57] From 1970 to 1990, most metropolitan San Jose Blacks lived in diverse lower-middle-class and working-class communities in East San Jose, but sizable numbers resided in diverse middle-class high-tech suburbs in Milpitas, Mountain View, Palo Alto, Santa Clara, and Sunnyvale.[58] In some of the richer communities, however, entrée was difficult for Black people, even the most prominent ones.

In 1990, LaDoris Cordell, a Santa Clara County Superior Court judge, was planning to buy a home in Palo Alto. Or at least she was trying. "I became very frustrated because the racism was just so blatant," she said.

> I remember one instance I went to a home where a "For Sale" sign was up, and the person who answered the door was either a manager and/or a tenant, and I was told, immediately, that there was nothing available. And, of course, I checked, and it was actually available, and I went right back and confronted her. . . . I went into the house and was followed by the Realtor. She followed me everywhere, upstairs and downstairs. It was an open house, and there were a lot of other people there. The Realtor inquired what I was doing there and told me that this house was not for rent, it was for sale. The assumption was that I could not have been interested in buying a house. [This behavior] was a shock to me because I was in Palo Alto, and I'm thinking, "This is a somewhat enlightened city."[59]

Black Suburbanization during the Dot-Com Era, 1991–2000

Around the mid-1990s, the Silicon Valley engulfed most of the Greater San Jose and the Bay Area, just as the African American suburbanization in the region peaked and gradually began to decline. During this massive transformation, the South Bay started began to challenge San Francisco for the crown in the contest over which county was the most unaffordable U.S. area in which to live.[60] During this process of light-speed urban and industrial growth, most, if not all of the late-blooming metropolises have developed weak urban characters. (See figure 1.) This partly explains why many San Francisco Bay Area professional Blacks work in the Santa Clara County, and live in and around San Francisco or Oakland. For African American residents like Alissa Owens, the daughter of locally renowned educator and activist T. J. Owens, San Jose was the place she lived. Raised among European American youths in South San Jose, Alissa went to school with only a handful of Blacks in the early 1980s. While the public schools she attended were better than the San Jose schools in the northern section of the district, she was nevertheless culturally isolated from the people of the Northside among whom her father had been raised, where institutionally segregated schools existed. Years later, after graduating from the University of California at Berkeley, she chose to stay in the East Bay near Black culture and in a town that had "personality," in Point Richmond near Richmond. Before the passing of her father in 2005, she often commuted to South San Jose and Gilroy, where he lived. What pulled her to the region was family. Without family or a job, many middle-class Blacks like Owens left San Jose for nearby cities like Pittsburg and Manteca because there was not that much happening for African Americans from a recognizable Black community perspective.

During the dot-com era, the synergy of stagnated Black communities in postsuburban California coincided with the rapid growth of downtown and suburban Anaheim, Los Angeles, San Diego, San Francisco, and San Jose. During the hasty growth of these communities, Mexican American and Asian American population growth has been much larger than that of the region's African American population. In San Jose, most notable in its 1990s population growth was high-tech immigration from India and China, while a moderate decline in Black and white populations saw them resettled into affordable areas such as suburban Las Vegas and Phoenix.[61] In the 2000s, Asian Americans have gradually replaced whites in greater San Jose's most desirable places to live in West County, such as Palo Alto. Many have been drawn by proximity to Asia, nice weather, professional employment, great public schools, and nice neighborhoods from which whites have steadily moved due to death, retirement, and the lure of more affordable areas. The ramifications of San Jose's growth pattern have, on the one hand, resulted in the Silicon Valley becoming more international and sophisticated. Ethnicity was and is changing the character of the Valley, even as anti-immigrant sentiment constantly lurks below the surface of nonimmigrant residents, who were increasingly living paycheck-to-paycheck and in economic despair because their material expectations were not being

Figure 1. Some Black Communities in the Postsuburban U.S. West, 1950–2010

met.[62] On the other hand, this growth pattern sparked the demands of immigrants from the Global South for more resources, more press coverage, and more participation in the political-economic process as their populations increased.[63] Included in this massive growth in immigrant populations was substantial growth in metropolitan San Jose's African American population, which ended abruptly with the dot-com bubble burst in 2000.

Conclusion

Black suburbanization in the postwar and "postracial" U.S. West, based on the San Jose model, has been unique. This model of suburbanization has produced a different place for Blacks because unlike suburbs in the U.S. East, such as in white and affluent Fairfax County, and in the better known East Cleveland and Prince George's County—where the white population is peppered with the Black presence in the former model, and for the latter model, Black populations are large and often extend from the central city—suburban San Jose Black population has been small and resides within far more ethnically diverse communities. During the so-called postracial era this has resulted in Black communities modeled on San Jose having a much harder time developing a strong Black community, forming definable markers of their presence, and when confronted with de facto racial discrimination in fields such as housing, having a far more difficult time mobilizing and forming a consistent activist tradition. This has especially become problematic in the 2000s as deregulation of the Savings and Loan industry has resulted in rampant predatory and subprime lending practices that have disproportionately impacted the socioeconomic mobility of Black, Brown, and working poor people. Still, many Black residents in Greater San Jose have overcome social isolation and customary discrimination by participating in progressive activities and organizations centered on group interests and the needs of communities of color and their children. These priorities led to the creation of the recently opened African American Heritage House, the African American Parent Coalition, the Black Chamber of Commerce of Silicon Valley, and the Silicon Valley African American Cultural Center (still underway). Together with Juneteenth, the annual celebration of the end of slavery, these institutions are designed to build a stronger sense of Black community in the area and to relieve some of the de facto racialism and social isolation that African Americans have felt in what has been for most a difficult journey to feel like *welcomed* neighbors.

Notes

1. Social Explorer, *Census Tracts, 1970–2010: Population Density, Census 1970–2010, Census Bureau; Social Explorer,* http://old.socialexplorer.com/pub/maps/map3.aspx?g=0.

2. Sheryll Cashin, *The Failures of Integration: How Race and Class Are Undermining the American Dream* (New York: Public Affairs, 2005); Andrew Wiese, *Places of Their Own: African American Suburbanization in the Twentieth Century* (Chicago: University of Chicago Press, 2004); and Social Explorer, *Census Tracts, 1970–2010.*

3. See Robert E. Lang, and Patrick A. Simmons, "'Boomburbs': The Emergence of Large, Fast-Growing Suburban Cities in the United States," Fannie Mae Foundation Census Note 06 (June 2001), 1; "'Boomburbs': Fast-Growing Suburban Cities," in *Redefining Urban and Suburban America: Evidence from Census 2000*, eds. Bruce Katz, and Robert E. Lang (Washington, DC: Brookings Institution Press, 2003), 106; Social Explorer, *Census Tracts, 1970–2010*; Lawrence B. De Graaf, "African American Suburbanization in California, 1960 through 1990," in *Seeking El Dorado: African Americans in California*, ed. Lawrence B. De Graaf (Seattle, WA: University of Washington Press, 2001), 405–449; Matthew C. Whitaker, *Race Work: The Rise of Civil Rights in the Urban West* (Lincoln, NE: University of Nebraska Press, 2007). For San Antonio, Social Explorer Tables (SE), *Census 1980–2010, Census Bureau; Social Explorer.* In 1980, the tracts under investigation are 1209.1, 1211.1, 1212.1, 1212.2, 1214, 1215, 1218, 1315, 1316.2. In 1990–2010, they are: 1210, 1211.04, 1218.05, 1218.01, 1209.1, 1212.01, 1212.02, 1218.02–.04, 1215.01–.07, 1216.03, 1216.04, 1214.01–.04, 1315.01–.02, 1316.03–.07. Also see, Censusviewer.com, "Converse, Texas Population: Census 2010 and 2000 Interactive Map, Demographics, Statistics, Quick Facts," http://censusviewer.com/city/TX/Converse; Kirby, Texas Population," http://censusviewer.com/city/TX/Kirby; "Live Oak, Texas Population," http://censusviewer.com/city/TX/Live%20Oak; "Universal City, Texas Population," http://censusviewer.com/city/TX/Universal%20City; "Windcrest, Texas Population," http://censusviewer.com/city/TX/Windcrest). Suburban communities under examination are found in boomburb publications coauthored by Robert E. Lang. Boomburbs are late-blooming suburban towns that have accidentally grown into relatively large cities like Mountain View, the headquarters for Google. In 2000, forty-six out of fifty-three boomburbs existed mainly in the West as master-planned communities characterized by inadequate public transportation systems, industrial parks, small downtown cores, strip malls located by freeway exits, suburban sprawl, and large water districts that keep alive naturally dry and arid cities like Los Angeles. More important, this type of urbanization has "accounted for over half (51 percent) of the 1990s growth in cities with between 100,000 and 400,000 residents." In the Silicon Valley, even though there were only two cities accounting for over 100,000 people

in 2000 (San Jose and Santa Clara), the region as a whole has taken on the characteristics of the boomburb, or a string of accidental cities which still identify as towns that blend into one another and constitute a suburban metropolis.

4. Albert S. Broussard, *Black San Francisco: The Struggle for Racial Equality in the West, 1900–1954* (Lawrence, KS: University Press of Kansas, 1993); Cashin, *The Failures of Integration*; De Graaf, "African American Suburbanization in California, 1960 through 1990," 405–449; Emory J. Tolbert, and Lawrence B. de Graaf, "'The Unseen Minority': Blacks in Orange County," *Journal of Orange County Studies* 3, no. 4 (Fall 1989/Spring 1990): 54–61; Karyn R. Lacy, *Blue-Chip Black: Race, Class, and Status in the New Black Middle Class* (Berkeley: University of California Press, 2007); Thomas J. Sugrue, *The Origins of the Urban Crisis: Race and Inequality in Postwar Detroit* (Princeton, NJ: Princeton University Press, 1996); *Sweet Land of Liberty: The Forgotten Struggle for Civil Rights in the North* (New York: Random House, 2008); Quintard Taylor, *In Search of the Racial Frontier: African Americans in the West, 1528–1990* (New York: W. W. Norton, 1998); Quintard Taylor, *The Forging of a Black Community: Seattle's Central District, from 1870 through the Civil Rights Era* (Seattle: University of Washington Press, 1994); Joe William Trotter, *Black Milwaukee: The Making of an Industrial Proletariat, 1915–1945* (Urbana: University of Illinois Press, 1985); and Joe William Trotter, *The Great Migration in Historical Perspective: New Dimensions of Race, Class, and Gender* (Bloomington: Indiana University Press, 1991); Whitaker, *Race Work*; and Wiese, *Places of Their Own.*

5. See *Shelley v. Kramer*, 334 U.S. 1 (1948); W. Dennis Keating, *The Suburban Racial Dilemma: Housing and Neighborhoods* (Philadelphia: Temple University Press, 1994), 195, 214; Robert Self, *American Babylon* (Princeton, NJ: Princeton University Press, 2003), 116; John H. Denton, *Apartheid American Style* (Berkeley, CA: Diablo, 1968), 4; Mark Brilliant, *The Color of America Has Changed: How Racial Diversity Shaped Civil Rights* (Oxford: Oxford University Press, 2010), 125–156; Gerald Lee Klein, "Housing Discrimination in California: The Case of Proposition 14" (master's thesis, San Jose State College, 1968), 10.

6. U.S. Census Bureau, "Population of the 100 Largest Cities and Other Urban places in the Unites States: 1790–1990," http://www.census.gov/population/www/documentation/twps0027/twps0027.html; National Civic League, "Past Winners of the All-America City Award: Winning Communities, 1960," http://www.allamericacityaward.com/things-to-know-about-all-america-city-award/past-winners-of-the-all-america-city-award/past-winners-of-the-all-america-city-award-1960s/.

7. "Silicon Valley Hub Knocks off Detroit as 10th Largest City," *San Francisco Chronicle*, July 1, 2005; Associated Press, "Do You Know the Way to America's 10th Largest City? Does Anyone?" July 1, 2005; "To the Chagrin of Detroit, Top 10 No Longer," *New York Times*, June 29, 2005; Social Explorer,

Census Tracts, 1970–2010; and National League of Cities, "The 30 Most Populous Cities," http://www.nlc.org/build-skills-and-networks/resources/cities-101/city-factoids/the-30-most-populous-cities.

8. See Herbert G. Ruffin, "The Search for Significance in Interstitial Space: San Jose and Its Great Black Migration, 1941–1968," *Black California Dreamin': The Crises of California's African-American Communities* (Santa Barbara: UC Santa Barbara Center for Black Studies Research, December 2012), 19–56, http://www.escholarship.org/uc/item/63g6128j; Don Gagliardi, "Roots: The Northside Origins of San Jose's African American Community," *Northside* (Fall 2001): 19. Discriminatory real estate practices in the South Bay prior to the 1970s hampered not only African Americans, but also Mexican Americans, Japanese Americans, and Chinese Americans.

9. University of Virginia Library, *Historical Census Browser: County-Level* Results, 1850–1960 (University of Virginia Library: Geospatial and Statistical Data Center, 2005); U.S. Bureau of the Census, *1950 Census of Population:* Volume 11, *Characteristics of the Population*, Part 5, *California*, "Population of Urbanized Areas: 1950" (Washington, DC: U.S. Government Printing Office, 1952), 5–21; U.S. Bureau of the Census, *1970 Census of Housing*, Volume 1, *Housing Characteristics for States, Cavities, and Counties;* Part 6, *California* (Washington, DC: U.S. Government Printing Office, 1972), 7–10, 14–15, 453.

10. U.S. Bureau of the Census, *1970 Census of Housing*, 7–10, 14–15, 453; *U.S. Census of Population and Housing; 1970 Census Tracts*, table P-1. Homes with Black heads of household in metropolitan San Jose were 1.5 percent, which was well below the state average of 6.5 percent. However, Blacks in this area had a homeownership rate of 62 percent, significantly higher than the state average of 55 percent. Possible exclusive areas were Campbell, Cupertino, Fremont, Los Altos, Los Gatos, Santa Clara, Sunnyvale, and Saratoga—where rates of homes with Black heads of household were less than 0.7 percent. Milpitas, at 4.6 percent, was close to the state average, 6.5 percent. San Jose and Palo Alto had a small Black presence in their downtown areas at 1.3 percent to 2.4 percent. Santa Clara County and San Mateo County areas East Palo Alto and Menlo Park had Black homeownership populations well above the state average at 47.3 percent and 13 percent; however, Blacks were a mix of renters and owners. In Greater San Jose, Blacks were mostly owners, especially at Fremont, 75 percent; Los Altos, 84 percent; Milpitas, 79 percent; and Saratoga, 91 percent. The exception was Mountain View (34 percent), which was becoming an apartment city. Most metropolitan San Jose areas ranged between 55 percent and 66 percent owner occupancy. Palo Alto and Santa Clara were 55 percent—perhaps expensive areas, and many Blacks in this population were students and staff at Stanford and Santa Clara University. All-white areas in the county and surrounding areas were Campbell, Cupertino, Los Altos, Los Gatos, Santa Clara, Saratoga, Sunnyvale, and Fremont.

11. Garden City Women's Club, *History of Black Americans in Santa Clara Valley* (Sunnyvale, CA: Lockheed Missiles & Space Co., 1978), 152–154; "Trail Blazers in Open Housing, 1949–64," *The San Jose Chapter of the Links, Incorporated Files* (Research Library, History San Jose); *San Jose Mercury News*, October 29, 1986; and *San Jose Mercury News*, January 15, 1989.

12. Quote is in "Trail Blazers in Open Housing, 1949–64." Also see Edward P. Eichler, *Race and Housing: An Interview with Edward P. Eichler, President, Eichler Homes, Inc.* (1964), 16–17, 21; Garden City Women's Club, *History of Black Americans in Santa Clara Valley*, 152–154; Ned Eichler, *Eichler Insights* 2, no. 4 (Late Summer 1993): 5.

13. For more information on Milpitas see Herbert G. Ruffin, "Sunnyhills: Race and Working Class Politics in Postwar Silicon Valley, 1945–1968," *Journal of the West* 48, no. 4 (Fall 2009): 113–123. The San Jose movement for a fair housing ordinance is discussed in *San Jose Mercury News*, May 5, 1961; May 25, 1961; April 26, 1962; May 24, 1962; and November 30, 1963.

14. *Los Angeles Times*, December 4, 1964; Brilliant, *The Color of America Has Changed*, 125–156; De Graaf, "African American Suburbanization in California," 415; John H. Denton, *Apartheid American Style* (Berkeley, CA: Diablo, 1968), 40, 115; Herbert G. Ruffin, *Uninvited Neighbors: Black Life and the Racial Quest for Freedom in the Santa Clara Valley, 1777–1968* (Ann Arbor, MI: UMI Dissertation Publishing, 2007), 284–307; and *San Jose Mercury News*, November 30, 1963; March 14, 1964; March 22, 1964; March 23, 1964; April 6, 1965; September 10, 1964; October 14, 1964; October 16, 1964.

15. *San Jose Mercury News*, October 14, 1964.

16. Ocie Tinsley, interviewed by the author, San Jose, August 2010; "Affirmative Action," *Stanford Encyclopedia of Philosophy*, http://plato.stanford.edu/entries/affirmative-action/.

17. *Mulkey v Reitman*, 64 Cal 2d 529 (1966); and the U.S. Supreme Court decision, *Reitman v. Mulkey*, 387 U.S. 369 (1967); 1866 Civil Rights Act, 14 Stat. 27-30, April 9, 1866 A.D.; "1866 Civil Rights Act," in PBS, *Reconstruction: The Second Civil War*, http://www.pbs.org/wgbh/amex/reconstruction/activism/ps_1866.html. Also see Section 1 of the 14th Amendment states that: "No state shall make or enforce any law which abridges the privileges or immunities of citizens of the United States; nor shall any state deprive any person of life, liberty, or property without due process of law; nor deny any person within its jurisdiction the equal protection of the laws."

18. Ibid.

19. See "Civil Rights Act of 1968, Title 8 (Fair Housing Act of 1968)," http://www.usdoj.gov/crt/housing/title8.htm.

20. De Graaf, "African American Suburbanization in California," 415.

21. U.S. Bureau of the Census, 1970 *Census of Housing*, 7–10, 14–15, 453; University of Virginia Library, *Historical Census Browser*, 1960–1970; Metropolitan Transportation Commission (MTA), and the Association of Bay Area

Governments of Bay Area Governments (ABAG), *Bay Area Census—City of San Jose: 1890–2010, http://www.bayareacensus.ca.gov/cities/SanJose50.htm.*

22. U.S. Bureau of the Census, *1970 Census of Housing*, 7–10, 14–15, 453; and table P-1.

23. BlacksinDallas.com, "Arlington," http://blacksindallas.com/southern-suburbs/arlington/; Social Explorer Tables (SE), *Census 1980–2010, Census Bureau; Social Explorer.*

24. *San Jose Mercury News*, "Blacks Make Solid Leap," January 30, 1992.

25. See "San Jose Upstages Nation's Other Melting Pots," *San Jose Mercury News*, June 11, 1993; "Minorities Fare Better in County Than Nation: Income, Education Statistics Analyzed," *San Jose Mercury News*, October 28, 1992.

26. Weise, *Places of Their Own*, 255.

27. For more on the black middle class and their movement to the suburbs and the American symbolism involved see De Graaf, "African American Suburbanization in California, 1960 through 1990"; Karyn R. Lacy, *Blue-Chip Black: Race, Class, and Status in the New Black Middle Class* (Berkeley, CA: University of California Press, 2007); Weise, *Places of Their Own,* 257–258; and Whitaker, *Race Work.*

28. Some of the people interviewed by the author at San Jose, Los Altos, Mountain View, and Palo Alto in August 2010 and October 2011 include: Helen Anderson Gaffin (Dollarhyde); Orvella Stubbs (Dollarhyde); Patricia Perkins (Anderson and Dollarhyde); Kenneth Blackwell; Gloria Anderson (Dollarhyde); Charles Alexander; Mattie Briggs; and Charles Gary. Also see Ben Gross, interviewed by the author at UAW International, Detroit, December 2008; and Cass Jackson, interviewed by the author by phone at Monterey, California, June 25, 2012.

29. Sucheng Chan and Spencer Olin, *Major Problems in California History* (London: Wadsworth Publishing, 1996), 392; James J. Rawls, and Walton Bean, *California: An Interpretive History* (Boston: McGraw Hill, 2003), 511–514.

30. Chan and Olin, 393.

31. Richard White, *It's Your Misfortune and None of My Own: A New History of the American West* (Norman, OK: University of Oklahoma Press, 1991), 547.

32. Social Explorer Dataset (SE), *Census 1990, Social Explorer; U.S. Census Bureau*, "County Populations in California, 1990," http://www.socialexplorer.com/pub/reportdata/htmlresults.aspx?ReportId=R10291770&Page=1; "Silicon Valley Exodus: Thousands Leave Congested County as Others Move In," *San Jose Mercury News*, April 29, 1989.

33. Quoted from De Graaf, "African American Suburbanization in California," 405.

34. Gordon Chang, interviewed by the author at Palo Alto, October 2011. Other people who corroborate Chang's testimony include those interviewed by the author in October 2011: in Palo Alto, Albert Camarillo, Clayborne Carson, Jean Libby, Ken Lowe, and Steve Staiger (at Palo Alto Historical

Association, Palo Alto City Library), and the staff at the Stanford University Special Collections; in Mountain View, Barbara Kinchen (Mountain View Historical Association, Mountain View Public Library) and Monica Ramos (Mexican Heritage Corporation, San Jose); in Los Altos, Cazetta Gray; and at Cupertino, the staff at the California History Center at De Anza College.

35. See unpublished documentary on African Americans in Mountain View in Rosiland Bivings, *We Were Here, Too!* (Black history month documentary) (Mountain View, CA: Mountain View Public Library History Center, 1997).

36. Cass Jackson, interviewed by the author.

37. For more information on bifurcation in the black community, see "Prosperity Still Out of Reach for Many Blacks," *San Francisco Chronicle*, March 28, 1998; "Urban Racial Isolation Persists," *San Jose Mercury News*, April 9, 1991. Also see William Julius Wilson, *The Ghetto Underclass: Social Science Perspectives* (London: Sage Publications, 1993); Carl Husemoller Nightingale, "The Global Inner City: Toward a Historical Analysis," in *W. E. B. Du Bois, Race, and the City,* ed. Michael B. Katz and Thomas J. Sugrue (Philadelphia: University of Pennsylvania Press, 1998); WGBH Educational Foundation, *The Two Nations of Black America*, http://www.pbs.org/wgbh/pages/frontline/shows/race/economics/; WGBH Educational Foundation, *The Two Nations of Black America*, http://www.pbs.org/wgbh/pages/frontline/shows/race/interviews/wilson.html; Rawls and Bean, *California: An Interpretive History*, 463–467, 536; NPR, "Special Series: California in Crisis," http://www.npr.org/templates/story/story.php?storyId=106486189; "Fixing California," *Los Angeles Times*, http://theenvelope.latimes.com/la-me-state-budget-sg,0,6845417.storygallery; Grandmaster Flash and the Furious Five, "The Message" (12-inch single) (Englewood, NJ: Sugar Hill Records, 1982); The Stop the Violence Movement, "Self Destruction" (12-inch single and video; New York: Jive, 1989); *We're All in the Same Gang*, directed by West Coast All Stars (1990; Burbank, CA: Warner Brothers, 1990), VHS; *Boyz 'N the Hood*, directed by John Singleton (1991; Culver City, CA: Sony Pictures, 1991), DVD; *The Fire This Time: Why Los Angeles Burned*, directed by Randy Holland (1994; Los Angeles, CA: Rhino/Wea International, 1995), VHS.

38. U.S. Bureau of the Census, 1970 *Census of Housing*, 7–10, 14–15, 453; U.S. Bureau of the Census, *U.S. Census of Population and Housing*, 215; and Social Explorer Dataset (SE), *Census 1990-2010*, http://old.socialexplorer.com/pub/reportdata/htmlresults; http://old.socialexplorer.com/pub/reportdata/htmlresults.aspx?ReportId=R10536370; http://old.socialexplorer.com/pub/reportdata/htmlresults.aspx?ReportId=R10536341.

39. "Blacks in San Jose Lack a Sense of Community, Workshop Told," *San Jose Mercury News*, February 18, 1979.

40. Quoted from executive director of the Black Council on Alcoholism Hewitt Joyner Jr. in "Diversity Brings New Perspectives to Black Community," *San Jose Mercury News*, September 13, 1980.

41. Ellen Rollins, interviewed by the author at San Jose, October 2011.

42. See "In Silicon Valley, Blacks are Reaching out to Create their Community Feeling at Home," *San Jose Mercury News*, January 20, 1986.

43. "Black Apartment Hunter Encounters Waiting List," *San Jose Mercury News*, July 17, 1977.

44. Ibid.

45. Quoted from ibid.

46. "San Jose Race Bias Noted in Rentals," *San Jose Mercury News*, March 28, 1978.

47. Ibid.

48. "Apartment Bias in Sunnyvale," *San Jose Mercury News*, June 17, 1982.

49. Dennis Keating, *The Suburban Racial Dilemma: Housing and Neighborhoods* (Philadelphia, PA: Temple University Press, 1994), 196.

50. Ibid.

51. "Blacks Still Face Tremendous Discrimination in Housing," *San Jose Mercury News*, July 23, 1979; "Discrimination in Housing Still Rife in U.S.," April 17, 1978.

52. "Landlords Rarely Gave Same Stories to Black, White Applicants," *San Jose Mercury News*, January 28, 1979.

53. County of Santa Clara, Advance Planning Office, "Home Prices: California's Largest Counties, 1980–1990," Issue 92-5; and *National League of Cities*, "The 30 Most Populous Cities."

54. U.S. Bureau of the Census, *1990 Census of Population and Housing, San Jose PMSA* (Washington, DC: U.S. Government Printing Office, 1992), 1288–1289. Findings are based on sample tract with four hundred Black people in the county.

55. U.S. Bureau of the Census, *1970 Census of Housing*, 7–10, 14–15, 453; and U.S. Bureau of the Census, *1990 Census of Population and Housing, San Jose PMSA*, 1288–1289.

56. ABAG Regional Datacenter, "1990 Census STF1A" (May 1991).

57. Cazetta Gray and Jean Libby, interviewed by the author. The Palo Alto NAACP led by Muata Puryear was instrumental in getting hundreds of Blacks residential access into the white-affluent Mid-Peninsula region in the late 1960s to the 1970s.

58. "Diversity Brings New Perspectives to Black Community," *San Jose Mercury News*, September 13, 1980.

59. Quoted in "Color Separations," *Metro* (March 9–15, 2000): 26–27.

60. Performance Urban Planning, "8th Annual *Demographia* International Housing Affordability Survey: 2012—Ratings for Metropolitan Markets," http://www.demographia.com/dhi.pdf. According to this survey, San Jose is the most unaffordable place to live in the United States, and the fifth most unaffordable place to live in the world behind Hong Kong (China), Vancouver (Canada), Sydney (Australia), and Melbourne (Australia).

61. Milpitas Experiences Increase in Percent Growth" (Reference, Milpitas Community Library, Milpitas—Population); "Whites Aren't Majority and Region, Figures Show Asian, Latino Percentages Rise," *San Jose Mercury News*, March 30, 2001. Also see Ken Lowe, interviewed by the author, Palo Alto, October 2011; Gordon Chang interviewed by the author; Charles Gary interviewed by the author; and Steven Millner, interviewed by the author. In 2013, California out-migration was fueling part of the growth of suburban Oklahoma City (Oklahoma), and San Antonio and Austin (Texas).

62. "Whites Aren't Majority and Region, Figures Show Asian, Latino Percentages Rise," *San Jose Mercury News*, March 30, 2001; "'Them' Must Become 'Us' to Meet Valley's Needs," September 18, 1989.

63. "Asian-Americans Started Demanding Greater Political Role as Their Population Increased." *San Jose Mercury News*, May 12, 1991.

Bibliography

1866 Civil Rights Act. In PBS, *Reconstruction: The Second Civil War.* http://www.pbs.org/wgbh/amex/reconstruction.

1866 Civil Rights Act, 14 Stat. 27-30, April 9, 1866 A.D.

ABAG Regional Datacenter. "1990 Census STF1A" (May 1991).

"Affirmative Action." *Stanford Encyclopedia of Philosophy.* http://plato.stanford.edu/entries/affirmative-action/.

Associated Press. "Do You Know the Way to America's 10th Largest City? Does Anyone?" New York: Associated Press, July 1, 2005.

Bivings, Rosiland. *We Were Here, Too!* (Black History Month Documentary). Mountain View, CA: Mountain View Public Library History Center, 1997.

Boyz 'N the Hood, directed by John Singleton (1991; John. Culver City, CA: Sony Pictures, 1991), DVD.

Brilliant, Mark. *The Color of America Has Changed: How Racial Diversity Shaped Civil Rights*. New York: Oxford University Press, 2010.

Broussard, Albert S. *Black San Francisco: The Struggle for Racial Equality in the West, 1900–1954*. Lawrence: University Press of Kansas, 1993.

Cashin, Sheryll. *The Failures of Integration: How Race and Class Are Undermining the American Dream.* New York: PublicAffairs, 2005.

Censusviewer.com. "Texas Population in Converse: Census 2010 and 2000 Interactive Map, Demographics, Statistics, Quick Facts." http://censusviewer.com/city/TX/Converse.

———. "Texas Population in Kirby: Census 2010 and 2000 Interactive Map, Demographics, Statistics, Quick Facts." http://censusviewer.com/city/TX/Kirby.

———. "Texas Population in Live Oak: Census 2010 and 2000 Interactive Map, Demographics, Statistics, Quick Facts." http://censusviewer.com/city/TX/Live%20Oak.

———. "Texas Population in Universal City: Census 2010 and 2000 Interactive Map, Demographics, Statistics, Quick Facts." http://censusviewer.com/city/TX/Universal%20City.

———. "Texas Population in Wincrest: Census 2010 and 2000 Interactive Map, Demographics, Statistics, Quick Facts." http://censusviewer.com/city/TX/Windcrest.

Chan, Sucheng, and Spencer Olin, *Major Problems in California History*. London: Wadsworth Publishing, 1996.

Civil Rights Act of 1968, Title 8 (Fair Housing Act of 1968). 42 U.S.C., sec. 3601. Available at U.S. Department of Justice, Civil Rights Division Housing and Civil Enforcement Section. http://www.usdoj.gov/crt/housing/title8.htm.

"Color Separations." *San Jose Metro*. March 9–15, 2000.

County of Santa Clara, Advance Planning Office. "Home Prices: California's Largest Counties, 1980–1990." Issue 92-5.

De Graaf, Lawrence B., Kevin Mulroy, and Quintard Taylor. *Seeking El Dorado: African Americans in California*. Seattle: University of Washington Press, 2001.

Denton, John H. *Apartheid American Style*. Berkeley, CA: Diablo Press, 1968.

Eichler, Edward P. *Race and Housing: An Interview with Edward P. Eichler, President, Eichler Homes, Inc.*, 1964, 1–21.

Eichler, Ned. *Eichler Insights* 2, no. 4 (Late Summer 1993).

The Fire This Time: Why Los Angeles Burned. Directed by Randy Holland. 1994. Los Angeles: Rhino/Wea International, 1995. VHS.

Flash, Grandmaster, and the Furious Five. "The Message" (12-inch single). Englewood, NJ: Sugar Hill Records, 1982.

Gagliardi, Don. "Roots: The Northside Origins of San Jose's African American Community." *Northside* (Fall 2001): 16–19.

Garden City Women's Club (San Jose, CA). *History of Black Americans in Santa Clara Valley*. Sunnyvale, CA: Lockheed Missiles and Space Co., 1978.

Lang, Robert E., and Patrick A. Simmons. "'Boomburbs': The Emergence of Large, Fast-Growing Suburban Cities in the United States." Fannie Mae Foundation Census Note 06 (June 2001), 1–14.

Katz, Bruce, and Robert E. Lang, eds. Redefining Urban and Suburban America: Evidence from Census 2000. Washington, DC: Brookings Institution Press, 2003.

Katz, Michael B., and Thomas J. Sugrue, eds. *W. E. B. DuBois, Race, and the City: The Philadelphia Negro and Its Legacy*. Philadelphia, PA: University of Pennsylvania Press, 1998.

Keating, W. Dennis. *The Suburban Racial Dilemma: Housing and Neighborhoods*. Philadelphia, PA: Temple University Press, 1994.

Klein, Gerald Lee. "Housing Discrimination in California: The Case of Proposition 14." Master's thesis, San Jose State College, 1968.

Lacy, Karyn R. *Blue-Chip Black: Race, Class, and Status in the New Black Middle Class*. Berkeley, CA: University of California Press, 2007.

Metropolitan Transportation Commission (MTA), and the Association of Bay Area Governments of Bay Area Governments (ABAG). *Bay Area Census—City of San Jose: 1890–2010. http://www.bayareacensus.ca.gov/cities/SanJose50.htm.*

Mulkey v. Reitman, 64 Cal 2d 529 (1966).

National Civic League. "Past Winners of the All-America City Award: Winning Communities, 1960." http://www.allamericacityaward.com/things-to-know-about-all-america-city-award/past-winners-of-the-all-america-city-award/past-winners-of-the-all-america-city-award-1960s/.

NPR. "Special Series: California in Crisis." http://www.npr.org/templates/story/story.php?storyId=106486189.

Performance Urban Planning. "Eighth Annual *Demographia* International Housing Affordability Survey: 2012—Ratings for Metropolitan Markets." http://www.demographia.com/dhi.pdf.

Rawls, James J., and Walton Bean. *California: An Interpretive History*. Boston: McGraw Hill, 2003.

Reitman v. Mulkey, 387 U.S. 369 (1967).

Ruffin, Herbert G. "Sunnyhills: Race and Working Class Politics in Postwar Silicon Valley, 1945–1968." *Journal of the West* 48, no. 4 (Fall 2009): 113–123.

———. "The Search for Significance in Interstitial Space: San Jose and Its Great Black Migration, 1941–1968." In *Black California Dreamin': The Crises of California's African-American Communities*. Santa Barbara: UC Santa Barbara Center for Black Studies Research, December 2012.

———. "Uninvited Neighbors: Black Life and the Racial Quest for Freedom in the Santa Clara Valley, 1777–1968." Doctoral dissertation, Claremont Graduate University, 2007.

Self, Robert O. *America Babylon: Race and the Struggle for Postwar Oakland*. Princeton, NJ: Princeton University Press, 2003.

Shelley v. Kramer, 334 U.S. 1 (1948).

Social Explorer. "Census Tracts, 1970–2010: Population Density, Census 1970–2010." http://old.socialexplorer.com/pub/maps/map3.aspx?g=0.

Social Explorer Dataset (SE). *Census 1990, Social Explorer; U.S. Census Bureau*, "County Populations in California, 1990." http://old.socialexplorer.com/pub/reportdata/htmlresults; http://old.socialexplorer.com/pub/reportdata/htmlresults.aspx?ReportId=R10536370; http://old.socialexplorer.com/pub/reportdata/htmlresults.aspx?ReportId=R10536341.

Social Explorer Tables (SE). Census 1980–2010, Census Bureau; Social Explorer (for San Antonio).

Sugrue, Thomas J. *The Origins of the Urban Crisis: Race and Inequality in Postwar Detroit*. Princeton, NJ: Princeton University Press, 1996.

———. *Sweet Land of Liberty: The Forgotten Struggle for Civil Rights in the North*. New York: Random House, 2008.

Taylor, Quintard. *The Forging of a Black Community: Seattle's Central District, from 1870 through the Civil Rights Era*. Seattle, WA: University of Washington Press, 1994.

———. *In Search of the Racial Frontier: African Americans in the West, 1528–1990*. New York: W. W. Norton & Company, 1998.

The Stop the Violence Movement. "Self Destruction" (12-inch single and video). New York: Jive, 1989.

"To the Chagrin of Detroit, Top 10 No Longer." *New York Times*, June 29, 2005.

Tolbert, Emory J., and Lawrence B. de Graaf. "'The Unseen Minority': Blacks in Orange County." *Journal of Orange County Studies* 3, no. 4 (Fall 1989/Spring 1990): 54–61.

"Trail Blazers in Open Housing, 1949–64." *The San Jose Chapter of the Links, Incorporated Files*. Research Library, History San Jose.

Trotter, Joe William. *Black Milwaukee: The Making of an Industrial Proletariat, 1915–1945*. Urbana, IL: University of Illinois Press, 1985.

———. *The Great Migration in Historical Perspective: New Dimensions of Race, Class, and Gender.* Bloomington: Indiana University Press, 1991.

University of Virginia Library. *Historical Census Browser: County-Level Results for 1850–1960*. University of Virginia Library: Geospatial and Statistical Data Center, 2005. http://fisher.lib.virginia.edu/collections/stats/histcensus/.

U.S. Bureau of the Census. *1950 Census of Population*, Vol. 11, *Characteristics of the Population*, pt. 5, *California*. Washington, DC: U.S. Government Printing Office, 1952.

———. *1990 Census of Population and Housing, San Jose PMSA*. Washington, DC: U.S. Government Printing Office, 1992.

———. *Census of Housing, 1970*, Vol. 1, *Housing Characteristics for States, Cities, and Counties*, pt. 6, *California*. Washington, DC: U.S. Government Printing Office, 1972.

———. "Population of the 100 Largest Cities and Other Urban Places in the United States: 1790–1990." http://www.census.gov/population/www/documentation/twps0027/twps0027.html.

———. *U.S. Census of Population and Housing; 1970 Census Tracts*. Washington, DC: U.S. Government Printing Office, 1972. Table P-1. SMSA San Jose, California, Washington, DC: U.S. Government Printing Office, 1972.

We're All in the Same Gang, directed by West Coast All Stars (1990; Burbank, CA: Warner Brothers, 1990), VHS.

WGBH Educational Foundation. *The Two Nations of Black America.* http://www.pbs.org/wgbh/pages/frontline/shows/race/economics/.

Whitaker, Matthew C. *Race Work: The Rise of Civil Rights in the Urban West.* Lincoln, NE: University of Nebraska Press, 2007.

White, Richard. *It's Your Misfortune and None of My Own.* Norman, OK: University of Oklahoma Press, 1991.

Wiese, Andrew. *Places of Their Own: African American Suburbanization in the Twentieth Century.* Chicago, IL: University of Chicago Press, 2004.

Wilson, William Julius. *The Ghetto Underclass: Social Science Perspectives.* Newbury Park, CA: Sage Publications, 1993.

6

African American Economic Experiences

Income, Occupations, Savings, Investments, and Social Security Trends since 2000

LaToya T. Brackett

Introduction

The United States of America, as we know it today, was established by Europeans who wished for a new world with new ideals and new opportunities. Throughout America's growth into a nation, generations of whites immigrated to the United States for a better life. This same notion of a better life, or a so-called American Dream, continues to be pertinent today with people from all over the world. People enjoy hearing the stories of rags to riches, of humble beginnings and great success; no one wants to hear of the perpetual struggle of some groups. Sometimes, however, they forget that not everyone came to the United States willingly, with great expectations, and that without the Africans who were forced to build the new world, such stories of success may not have come to pass. The enslavement of Africans in the United States has greatly assisted whites, yet continually can be connected to the plight of some African Americans throughout American history, including today. A major variable in this plight revolves around the economic situation of African Americans.

Some African Americans are doing exceptionally well, but most continue to struggle even if their income establishes them as middle class. African Americans sometimes move from the lower class to the middle class, but it seems that this is where many of them stop. Angel L. Harris notes that

> in fact, black children from middle- and upper-middle class families experience a generational drop in income, which is in sharp contrast to the traditional American expectation that each generation will do better than the previous one; only 31% of middle class black children have greater family earnings than their parents compared to 68% of their white counterparts.[1]

Whites are doing better at more than twice the rate of African Americans when it comes to economic growth over generations. When one thinks of middle-class status for African Americans, the "status" may only refer to the educational status, rather than the income and assets.

Currently, African Americans are entering higher education at the highest rate ever. Although not all are attaining degrees, more are attaining them than before. In the United States, attaining education has become synonymous with economic success. This, however, is not necessarily true for all. The types of jobs that African Americans receive are not always in line with their educational attainment. A middle-aged, African American male with an MBA stated that it was difficult to see his college-educated friends working at places such as Walmart and Macy's. This continues to be the reality for many African Americans with a college degree.[2] Even when the jobs are level with their credentials, they earn less on the dollar than their white counterparts. African American men earn 72 percent of the average earnings of comparable white men, only making acquiring wealth through assets that much more difficult.[3] Furthermore, some African Americans have difficulty on jobs that are in predominately white businesses. Economic success in the United States is not only about income, but also about one's savings and investments. African Americans are saving at rates similar to whites, but because of lower income the accumulated savings are less as well. African Americans invest in options that are less risky, such as real estate and life insurance, which may not allow for as much economic success as whites, who take more risks and invest in stocks. Although 401(k) plans are accessible for some African Americans, they invest less and they cash out more often, leaving little to no savings for retirement. In 2011, their investments amounted to less than half of the rest of the nation. Three in ten African Americans with 401(k)s had borrowed or withdrawn from their accounts.[4] Could financial literacy have something to do with these investment differences, and how does this hurt African Americans? Because of the lack of assets, the lack of strong savings, and also retirement plans, African Americans rely on Social Security more than whites. African Americans receive a higher return in Social Security. In their retirement the earned Social Security benefits of African Americans are still less than whites. These economic situations and conditions all relate to the economic status of African Americans. This chapter examines jobs, income, wealth, savings, and investments and retirement options in regard to this group after the year 2000. It will show that the United States is not in a postracial society when, due to racial divisions and gaps, African Americans are still behind in economic stability and growth.

Income and Education and Status in America

According to David Hinson, the income of African Americans increased every year from 1980 until 2001, followed by a slight decline. In 2001, when the middle-class income was established to be between $32,000 and $49,000, the median African American household income was $29,470 before taxes, shutting them out of such a status. Even earning above the poverty line, which was drawn at $21,000 in 2001, African Americans were not living much better than someone below the poverty line. Hinson put forth that most people use 30 percent of their income on housing, spend roughly $8,000 on food, and dispense another $1,000 on fuel and transportation. This meant African Americans only had approximately $600 left per month to spend on tithing, clothing, child care, gas and electricity, medical and dental insurance, entertainment, repairs, personal grooming, and saving for retirement and their children's education.[5] The little money left over made median African American households living paycheck to paycheck with a financial security and lifestyle similar to those living below the poverty level. Can a median African American household move up to the middle class? Can their children move up economically?

Achieving a higher economic status is often viewed as important in the United States, as the aforementioned Horatio Alger–like stories are seen as the ideal American Dream, yet research reveals that such an occurrence is actually rare, especially for African Americans. Douglas Massey and Nancy Denton, authors of the pivotal text on the American underclass, *American Apartheid: Segregation and the Making of the Underclass*, reinforced this concept with the recognition that in families traits are passed down, increasing the likelihood that children will maintain a class status similar to their parents, rather than to move up. Massey and Denton specifically spoke about upper-class and middle-class children maintaining their economic status. "Children who enter the middle and upper classes through the accident of birth are more likely than other, equally intelligent children from other classes to acquire the schooling, motivation, and cultural knowledge required for socioeconomic success in contemporary society."[6] Nevertheless, such an experience does not rein true for African Americans. even when born into an upper class.

Melvin Oliver and Thomas Shapiro established the divide of racial wealth disparities in their essential text, *Black Wealth/White Wealth: A New Perspective on Racial Inequality*, and they explored the data regarding economic mobility within families, depending on established economic standing. They found that it was primarily a lack of wealth, not income, in Black families that created a major hindrance to maintaining higher economic status.[7] Over two-thirds of white American children of parents with upper-white-collar background occupations inherit and maintain this level, while "a little over one-third of the black parents from upper-white-collar backgrounds successfully transmit their status to their children."[8] These two texts began a conversation around the American Dream that placed a racial lens on it, which the remainder of this chapter will continue to do as well, with a more current lens.

In America, what is the current status of economic mobility? Examining income and wealth across generations, Jared Bernstein's research established that a poor family of four with two children would take nine to ten generations before achieving middle-class income, or over 200 years.[9] This slow upward mobility is not the case in some other prosperous nations around the world; it seems that the American system dissuades economic growth. Scandinavian countries and the United Kingdom are examples of places where impoverished individuals have a greater chance at doing better than their parents economically. "Using earnings levels from today's families, a son whose father earns about $16,000 a year has a 5 percent chance of earning over $55,000 per year," in the United States.[10] Five percent does not mean it is impossible, but it does mean that not even half of the lower-income children in this society will see their American Dream come to fruition. Perhaps they will simply be content with earning more than their parents. What road must these children take in order to get closer to earning $50,000 or more?

In the United States, education is seen as the leveling tool that would allow economic and status mobility. In 2012 President Barack Obama initiated education improvements, because he believed that "enhanced educational outcomes for African Americans will lead to more productive careers, improved economic mobility and security, and greater social well-being for all Americans."[11] Bernstein found that in the American system, it is harder to attain higher education if one is from a lower-income status, despite having similar merit as someone from a higher-income bracket. Children of parents who attended college are more likely to go to college themselves. Children of higher-income families are also more likely to attend any college and top-tier colleges; they are also more likely to graduate. Those status-establishing universities and colleges at the top tier that should be accessible to all, matriculates 70 percent of their students from families designated as high income. Only 3 and 6 percent of the students come from the lowest- and second-lowest income groups, respectively.[12] Is education accessible to all? There is no doubt that federal student aid has allowed for greater access, but it is apparent that what income bracket one belongs to establishes what school a student attends. Loans do come at a price, as African Americans with college education "are twice as likely to have student loan debt compared to all college educated Americans."[13]

Is the United States a meritocracy? When low-income, middle-income, and high-income eighth graders' math test scores were compared across low score, middle score, and high score in relation to college completion, it becomes apparent that merit alone does not stipulate higher education attainment, making a higher-income status that much more difficult. Those who scored low in general were less likely to complete college, while those scoring high were more likely to finish school. But throughout all levels of test scores, it was the income status that established the percentage of those who completed college; with those of low income being less likely to complete it, and those of high income more likely, despite the fact that both groups were in the same tier of test scores.[14] A low-income student who is brilliant is less likely than their high-income counterpart with the same academic ability to complete college.

There has been progress for African Americans in obtaining higher education. In 1940, only 1 percent and 2 percent of African American men and women held college degrees, respectively. In 2000, the percentages increased to 10 percent for African American men and 15 percent for African American women. Despite the increase in African Americans' completion of college, there still remains inequality in regard to obtaining employment. "[I]ncreased education has helped to narrow wage inequality between employed whites and blacks. What it hasn't done is close the unemployment gap."[15] This could be a reason why a child of someone making very little has the odds against him or her in attaining a much higher income, because however the American system works, it most often works to continue to keep people in the status they were born in, despite any hard work toward upward mobility.

Bernstein's research also evaluated the mobility of African American families. Most of his research was based on income; the low-income findings directly correlate to a great portion of African American households. "White families were almost two and a half times more upwardly mobile than black families, a statistically significant difference. And black families were twice as likely as whites to fall from the top to the bottom quartile."[16] In general, upward mobility in the United States is already very difficult, as established above, but it is more than twice as hard for African Americans. This lower-income status is perpetuated by the jobs African Americans have access to and the lack of occupational mobility. What jobs are African Americans partaking in? How are they being treated? If they have jobs on the similar level of their white counterparts, are they being paid equally? The discussion of occupation and pay will look at another aspect to the economic plight of African Americans.

Employment and Earnings

In 2012, the national unemployment rate was 9.1 percent, the white unemployment rate was 8 percent, yet the Black unemployment rate was 16.7 percent, more than twice the white rate.[17] Having a job is a major form of status in America, there is a strong divide between the employed and the unemployed. There is also a divide between those that work jobs paying minimum wage versus a salaried position. There is more to work than simply earning money. As Clifford L. Broman put it, "[w]ork provides people with an important sense of identity."[18] In other words, people put so much into their work that they base their views about themselves on how others perceive and recognize them. What then is someone's identity if they are not employed? African Americans are not only suffering because of the lack of earnings, but are also potentially having identity or mental health concerns due to employment status.

According to Kroll, African Americans were more likely to be unemployed even prior to the reduction of manufacturing jobs, the outsourcing of jobs, and the moving of companies out to the suburbs in the 1940s.[19] The higher rate of unemployment for African Americans is not new and is central in the economic plight of African Americans then and now. Remember that even with higher education, African Americans are still less likely to be employed even when African Americans and whites are compared based on the same level of degree attainment.[20] The saying in the Black community that "one must work twice as hard to make it just as far as their counterparts" seems to hold true with the data. A study conducted by the University of Chicago and Massachusetts Institute of Technology in 2001–2002 revealed that something as simple as a name could hinder a person from obtaining the chance to be hired for a position. Those with white-sounding names such as Emily and Greg, were 50 percent more likely to be called by a potential employer than those persons with African American–sounding names, such as Lakisha and Jamal.[21] It seems that even when African Americans take creativity and pride in a personal aspect of their life, the naming of their children, they should assess the potential future consequences, which in turn could hurt the future chances of an African American child in this American society. Despite hard work, it seems that African Americans are going to have difficulty obtaining work, especially work by which one would like to be identified.

Exploring the job situation for African Americans, Broman also states that they are more likely to be unemployed, but also underemployed where skills are underutilized in individuals' jobs. Unskilled occupations have a higher occurrence among African Americans, and with these jobs come low wages, poor working conditions, and job instability.[22] In a strong economy, African Americans are last to be hired, and in a recession, such as what recently occurred in the United States, they are the first to be let go.[23] But what types of jobs are African Americans active in? The move from manufacturing to service jobs has given fewer options to African Americans, with service jobs paying less.[24] This shift in job options has been a part of the discussion in the African American plight for decades due to its major impact on the community, and the way in which manufacturing jobs were once the uplift of the community, and now service is a major harm.[25] In a sample of North Carolina workers African Americans comprised 22 percent of the labor force, yet they represent 36 percent of service workers and only 8 percent of managers.[26] Of those African Americans working in North Carolina, 25 percent worked in jobs where the majority of the workers were also Black.[27]

Jobs that employ mostly African Americans occur due to location in the inner city where a great number of African Americans reside. Due to the location of the jobs the wages are also lower. A reason Browne stated the wages are lower is because of the high competition for jobs in the area—many people are in need of work and companies do not have to be competitive in pay.[28] Low wages can also occur due to the type of job, or its status in the American economy.[29] "Low-wage occupations are often service-oriented jobs that require few skills and offer little opportunities for training."[30] Some employers hire more African Americans because the majority of their customers are African Americans. James Button, Kelli Moore, and Barbara Rienzo stated, "[i]n order to minimize racial tension and boost minority business, employers tend to hire blacks to act as 'cultural brokers' with their black clientele."[31] African Americans are also more likely to be in Black jobs because of proximity, where commuting to the suburbs would create a barrier to better employment. Cynthia M. Hewitt also stated that this group tends to look for jobs that have a workplace culture resembling of Black culture.[32] Over the years jobs have also increased their skill requirement, which may require higher educational attainment, and thus would push out a good portion of African Americans as well. African American men have been hit hardest by this new requirement for jobs; they were more likely to be in declining industries than white men, they have low levels of skill, and they reside in areas that are changing most with economic transitions.[33] The jobs out there currently are either high paying with high educational requirement or low paying, dead-end jobs with minimal education requirements. Even in low-skilled jobs, there has been an increase in what employers look for.[34]

African American women suffer from two forms of discrimination: being Black and being female, not necessarily in that order or occurring separately. When it comes to employment, African American women seem to suffer more than white men, white women, and even African American men. Although African American men are more likely to be unemployed than African American women, the men have a higher median income than the women do.[35] African American women tend to "work in support positions, where there are fewer rewards and less opportunity for advancement or skill use; and work in jobs that are less secure than those held by men."[36] The sex-segregation theory states that because of being female, African American women are more accepted into jobs labeled as "women's work."[37] These jobs are not highly valued, which assists in the lower-wage earnings for the women in such positions.

To add to the lack of good jobs, when at work, African American women and men suffer in regard to workplace stress. "Discrimination in the workplace against Black, female workers comes in the form of stereotypes, excessive demands, an absence of mentoring, exclusions from work [office] cliques, being ignored and/or harassed, and assumptions that they are incompetent."[38] Such stereotypes that African American women have to contend with are being seen as welfare-dependent, and as strong-minded single mothers. Nevertheless, these women also have positive stereotypes that could explain in part why African American men are less likely to be employed than African American women.

These stereotypes are that African American women are more educated than the men, and that the women have better soft skills, like politeness and communication. These are the skills that are required in the many service jobs in which African Americans are highly populated.

In regards to the idea of hostility from African American women, Hall and Hamilton-Mason's research revealed a Black woman speaking on this very issue. They wrote, "[a]nd then there's the label of being hostile. It's like you don't have to open your mouth but walk into a situation and you're perceived as being hostile. I think that's in every environment that I've been in and it starts to wear on your own psyche. You start questioning stuff. Am I really hostile?"[39] Doubting herself, she only created an unhealthy self-image. Black men also suffer from stereotypes; employers may argue that people are afraid of African American males, that they are seen often as lazy, violent, and hostile like African American women, or that the men are seen as defensive and combative.[40] What would make an employer want to hire men or women with stereotypes such as the ones listed above?

African American women are very important in the African American community. Seventy-two percent of Black children are in households headed by African American women. African American women account for 44 percent of the breadwinners in families with children. What does it mean when they earn the least and have the least net worth?[41] The pay gap with their counterparts reveals even more struggle, as African American women earn 85 cents for every dollar white women earn, and only 63 cents for every dollar white men earn.[42] The overall pay gap rate for all women is 77 cents to every dollar a man earns.[43] Jobs inform income and income informs the ability to gain net worth, which is the market value of household assets minus the total liabilities.[44] Single African American women aged thirty-six to forty-nine have an average net worth of $5, while single white women of the same age range have an average net worth of $42,600.[45] These numbers reminds people that the United States is not a postracial society, and African American women have to struggle a great deal. They are central to the well-being of the African American people. Despite their importance, they are not gaining economic stability or upward mobility. A change needs to take place, but what besides fair pay acts can get to the bottom of this economic plight, which seems to most influence African American women but holds major determination for all African Americans.

The service jobs, into which African Americans seem to be categorized, such as retail stores and restaurants, are frequented by a diverse group of people. Such employers need to be more open in their hiring process to ensure that patrons feel comfortable. Other jobs such as banks, real estate, and insurance tend to be more segregated in employees.[46] Service jobs require fewer skills, and African American men average 22 percent of unskilled jobs, while African American women hold 19 percent of such jobs. When looking at managerial and high-level professional work, African American men only hold 8 percent of those positions and African American women only hold 6 percent of such higher-status jobs.[47] Perhaps one of the reasons why the women are paid less is because they are not in higher-paying jobs. Nonetheless, it is clear that employment opportunities for African Americans and their earnings levels are not equal to that of the majority in America. Such a situation has strong implications for what African Americans can say their family is worth.

Wealth, Net Worth, and Assets

According to David Hinson, a major reason why African Americans have difficulty accessing the status of middle class is because they lack accumulated wealth. In 2000, only 10.7 percent of African American families had a net worth exceeding $100,000. Almost three times as many had a net worth similar to what middle-aged single African American women had, as mentioned in the preceding section. A total of 29.1 percent of African American households had a zero or negative net worth, compared to only 12.7 percent of their white counterparts. White families with more than $100,000 in net worth were 41.8 percent, four times the rate of African Americans. In 2002, the median net worth of African American households was $6,000, which was $2,000 less than Latinos and $84,000 less than white households.[48] In order for African Americans to close such a gap, they would have to save their annual salaries for three consecutive years at least.[49] "Regardless of age, household structure, education, occupation, or income, black households typically have less than a quarter of the wealth of otherwise comparable white households."[50] Even in the working-poor economic status, African Americans only hold 2 percent of the wealth that working-poor whites have.[51] African Americans are hit harder by a recession than their white counterparts. According to Hamilton, in the 1999–2001 recession, the median household wealth fell 27 percentage points for African Americans, yet it grew by 2 percentage points for whites. When a difficult economic time for the entire country does not interact evenly with every group, then something needs to be done about the racial divisions in American society.

According to Maury Gittleman and Edward N. Wolff, two families with the same income but different wealth are certainly in different economic and social situations. "The wealthier family is likely to be in a neighborhood characterized by more amenities and lower levels of crime, to have greater resources that can be called upon in times of economic hardship and to have more influence in political life."[52] Gittleman and Wolff also found that over the decade of 1984 to 1994, wealth appreciation at the median for African Americans was only 6.1 percent in comparison to 35.4 percent for whites. Inheritance is another possibility for wealth growth, but it has not be studied over time and fully investigated. It would seem, based on the economic status of many African Americans, that there may not be as much inheritance for younger generations.

Building assets, helps one gain net worth, and net worth if positive along with a savings mentality can build wealth.[53] In the United States many people borrow in order to own, this allows for one to have a negative net worth, and borrowing seems very apparent for African Americans as their net worth is barely in comparison to whites. As will be discussed later, the debt is a relevant matter of concern in relation to net worth among African Americans. David W. Rothwell and Chang-Keun Han established the importance of owning assets over simply earning income in their study about assets and family stress.[54] "Income is vital for maintenance; assets are essential for development. Any benefits of asset holding are likely to occur because asset *stocks* are more permanent in nature than income *flows*."[55] Money is essential to everyday expenses but an asset is held onto and considered part of one's economic worth. Holding assets also relates to the overall well-being of a family due to their ability to dream and construct future plans for the family that will help with development.[56] Unemployed individuals have a hard time maintaining assets because families may use assets to compensate for job loss; with a higher unemployment rate, African Americans have a more difficult time establishing and maintaining assets.[57] Assets are necessary to build one's net worth and in turn gain wealth. So much stands in the way for African Americans to make progress in this economic aspect of their lives. Strides must be taken in several areas to propel African Americans in the right economic direction. Two very basic aspects to financial development must take place.

Savings and Investments

There are several means to save for long-term purposes, such as retirement or a child's educational expenses. The most popular employer assistance retirement plan is a 401(k). Some employees may have access to pensions through their work, although the idea of pensions has slowly faded over the years. There, of course, is the old-fashioned way of saving in a bank savings account. In order to save one must be disciplined, and if savings need to be used before the long-term event comes to pass, the savings must be used wisely. Where do African Americans stand in the process of saving?

As Americans work day in and day out, most hope for the day that they will retire comfortably and be able to enjoy their later years in life. African Americans feel less confident that they will have enough savings for retirement in comparison to whites. Forty-five percent of African Americans do not believe they will have enough money to live from in retirement, while only 37 percent of whites feel such a way.[58] Whether or not African Americans feel that they will have enough money in retirement relates to how they feel they are saving currently. In 2009, 33.3 percent of African Americans, but 41 percent of whites, felt that they saved regularly or saved a lot in regards to their retirement fund.[59] The rate of saving relates to the lack of confidence in retirement funds for African Americans. The lesser rate of saving in comparison to whites does not mean that African Americans would not save more if they were able. Leigh and Wheatley make reference to the fact that in 1998, only 46 percent of African Americans reported that they want to save but could not. But in 2009, the percentage raised to nearly 53.[60] Recalling the difficulties in acquiring work, in earning similar income as whites, and the lack of assets, there is no reason to wonder why African Americans are having difficulty in saving, despite their desire to do so. What makes the desire to save but inability to do so worse is the fact that in 1998, whites felt that same way at a rate of 43 percent but in 2009, the rate reduced to 35 percent.[61] A good return, despite the U.S. economic downturn, also occurred with median household wealth in 2001, as mentioned before. What aspect of American economic culture created such a negative result for African Americans, yet a positive result for whites?

The continued progression for whites and the decline for African Americans could revolve around the continuous hovering that many African American households maintain at the poverty level. M. Janice Hogan et al. stated that there are barriers hindering low-income families from being able to save to obtain assets. "Their low-wage jobs seldom have health insurance, retirement plans, and other benefits, and often they do not have the education or training to qualify for higher wage jobs," which is why many African Americans can only qualify for service jobs.[62] Despite the lack of pension and sometimes 401(k) opportunities for those individuals employed in lower-wage jobs, African Americans in 1998 were more likely than whites by 5 percentage points to expect employer-sponsored retirement options to be their major retirement income.[63] Yet in 2009, African Americans reduced their expectation by ten percentage point in regards to employer assistance.[64] In 2009, whites only lowered such an expectation by one percentage point.[65] Are African Americans realizing how much more difficult it is to secure jobs with such benefits? Or are they less likely to afford to participate in such employer-assistance programs because of their low earnings? It could be a little of both, as 61 percent of African Americans reported that their employers offered retirement savings plans, and 74 percent of those persons reported that they participated in these plans.[66] In 2009 African Americans were more likely to report that they could not afford to participate in the plans than their white counterparts, at a rate of 23 percent compared to 17 percent, respectively.[67] For African Americans, it seems to have been proven more difficult to save for retirement than the majority group.

Almost half of African Americans have access to employer retirement plans, such as a 401(k).[68] Eight in ten of those who have access participate in these plans, yet their savings and success are less, probably due to a lack of knowledge on how they work.[69] First, they tend to contribute less.[70] "Asian employees contributed 9.4% of their income to their plans, and whites 7.9%. Hispanics contributed 6.3% and African Americans 6%."[71] Out of the major racial groups, African Americans are contributing less to employer plans. In fact, "[m]any are not taking full advantage of employer retirement plans. Some 26% of those eligible for their employer's plan are contributing less than the amount matched by their employer or not at all; this is 10 points higher than the general population."[72] African Americans in 2011 had on average $9,000 in accounts such as 401(k)s, while the rest of the nation with access to such accounts had $20,000. African Americans are also more likely to take money out of their plans; approximately three in ten have barrowed or withdrawn from their accounts.[73] The main reason for these actions was debt. Nevertheless, 401ks are beneficial to this group. Aziz Gueye Adetemirin stated that 55 percent of African Americans who invest or save began saving because of such programs.[74] In comparison, only 47 percent of whites invest or save because of being introduced to 401(k)s or similar programs. African Americans and Hispanics tend to cash out of their accounts due to job loss, 60 percent of them to be exact.[75]

> When asked which is a bigger worry: day-to-day expenses or having enough money to retire, 41 percent of African Americans cited

> expenses and 59 percent cited retirement. In contrast, only 29 percent of whites cited expenses and 71 percent cited retirement. Among other findings, 56 percent of whites say retirement is their most important goal for saving and investing, but only 40 percent of African-Americans see retirement as their priority.[76]

Despite the difficulty, African Americans are more likely to retire earlier than the rest of the nation.[77] When they are retiring it is with fewer options. How can the attitudes toward such beneficial programs, such as a 401(k), be changed in this community? It seems to come down to increasing African Americans' education about their saving and investing options, and all possible actions that may occur with such accounts.

Research has shown that some reasoning behind the lack of saving and investing for African Americans is because of lack of financial literacy.[78] According to Annamaria Lusardi and Olivia S. Mitchell, in the 2009 National Financial Capability Survey, "both African-American and Hispanic respondents display lower levels of financial knowledge than do White/Asian respondents."[79] Yet no matter what people may or may not know about finances; in order to save money one must set some aside in a safe place. Nevertheless, in order to save, one must have that first form of monetary investment, and being in the lower rung of economic status African Americans are less likely to have an extra $2,000 every year to put into an Individual Retirement Account (IRA), which would constitute a full annual contribution.[80] For this group an extra $2,000 would probably be used for basic living expenses.

A profound reason African Americans do not save or save less has to do with assisting family members. They assist at nearly double the rate of the general population.[81] In this community, it is more likely for someone to expect to take care of their parents who are retired, as well. Forty-five percent of Blacks expect to support their parents, in comparison to only 29 percent of whites. African Americans earning over $25,000 annually are also more likely to be supporting someone who is unemployed.[82] Approximately six in ten African Americans give financial support to another person.[83] This community is a caring community, which is a virtue, not a fault, but it does not transfer into a monetary asset.

African American families may also use their savings for their children's education, which would be smart, as student loans are hitting this population hard.[84] African Americans also have difficulty saving for the long term due to their priority of "paying down debt, building an emergency fund and paying for children's needs. . . ."[85] Debt was considered the number one financial priority for African Americans in 2011. This includes the school loans that more and more African Americans are utilizing in attempts to move up in both economic and social status within the United States.[86] Once gaining that college degree, African Americans only reported saving one-third of what other college-educated Americans save.[87] Education should mean progress, where is the progress?

Educational debt is not the only debt they suffer from. Credit card and personal debt is also very high, as 94 percent of African Americans are in some sort of debt as of 2011. They have lower mortgage debt compared to the rest of Americans, yet the median household has $18,000 of debt, which is 50 percent more than the remaining population.[88] The general population is only 82 percent in debt.[89] Once again, the concern of having any leftover funds to save comes to light. Lusardi and Mitchell concluded that the lowest-paid and least-educated population knows less about finances, and because of this, are more vulnerable to making poor financial decisions.[90] Could the lack of savings, especially in regard to retirement be due to a lack of knowledge about finances? It seems so, but how much will information help if the information does not pertain to the group, because the group does not have access to a surplus in earnings to make such investment decisions. In actuality, Darrick Hamilton stated that in 2004, Blacks save at a moderately higher rate than whites when adjusting for income differences. But as listed above they have fewer less resources in order to save more.[91] If there was more equality for African Americans in the education and job realm, would savings disparities remain different?

African Americans are less likely to save by more independent means. In 2009, 51 percent of African Americans compared to 72 percent of whites report having money in savings accounts, certificates of deposits, or money market accounts.[92] In that same year, 28 percent of African Americans report having invested money in an IRA or Keogh plan, compared to 47 percent of whites.[93] Twenty-seven percent of African Americans reported owning stocks or mutual fund shares in comparison to 49 percent of whites.[94] Twenty-seven percent of whites and only 17 percent of African Americans reported owning bonds.[95] The greatest difference in these before-mentioned statistics between whites and African Americans is that the minority group is less likely to have any savings, let alone savings that require broker assistance.

Hogan mentioned some of the reasons working poor are unable to gain financial security; "lack of affordable housing, inadequate health insurance, balancing employment and parenting demands, lack of affordable quality child care, and inflexible jobs."[96] Other reasons, according to Hogan, that African American women in particular have financial vulnerability are due to "unemployment or underemployment, unreliable vehicles, health problems, childcare costs, or lack of child support payments," which were established by studying such women in a program to build Individual Development Accounts (IDA).[97] But one must not forget that despite these issues, African American women, who raise a majority of their children on their own, still manage to survive. Some women make reference to their survival with such statements as: "'keeping us above water . . ., 'nothing has been cut off—a lot of threats—but I'm still with lights and water and gas . . .,' and 'I'm doing OK, enough to get by.'"[98] These women continue to try to look on the brighter side of things, despite obvious struggles. This type of resiliency could be an asset in trying to move African Americans forward in economic growth. African Americans are more likely to suffer from such circumstances than persons belonging to the majority racial group, due to their status in the American economy. Nevertheless, there are African Americans benefiting from such savings and investment opportunities. What is the most common investment for African Americans?

Life insurance and real estate is the most common form of investment made by African Americans who have the means to do so.[99] There seems to be an association of less risk taking in both real estate and life insurance options.[100] Bill Thomason stated that historically Blacks have seen owning property as a sign of financial freedom. Those who have the ability to invest in more than their own property may invest in rental real estate, which Thomason labeled as a conservative investment.[101] "Blacks show a greater preference for real estate as an investment than whites, with 45 percent of Blacks and 34 percent of whites saying it is the 'best investment overall.'"[102] But whites are more likely to own their homes than African Americans nonetheless; African Americans hold more of their wealth in their home by almost twice that of whites.[103] In Minnesota, even when attempting to gain assets by buying a home, African Americans with more than three times the amount of income as whites are twice as likely to be denied a home loan.[104] When these African Americans are approved for a loan they are three times more likely to have a subprime loan.[105] Perhaps the subprime loan is the reason African Americans do not own their homes at a similar rate as whites, despite their heavy desire to do so.

Real estate could be less risky for the typical mortgage applicant, but is it not risky for African Americans due to loan inconsistencies. What is a more secure, conservative form of investment for this community? According to Gutter and Hatcher, "[t]hose not willing to take investment risks were more likely to own life insurance."[106] African Americans have strong beliefs in life insurance as an economic profit. Life insurance is meant to assist a household economically if a financially contributing member of a household dies. Since the late 1800s African Americans have been seeking life insurance, but were being denied or paying very high rates in comparison to whites. Insurance companies established that because of a higher mortality rate, African Americans did not deserve the same coverage. Even in the 1940s, there were discrepancies with life insurance companies and issuing policies to African Americans.[107] Despite this negative history with life insurance companies, today African Americans are more receptive to buying life insurance and have a more positive attitude toward the companies than the general population does.[108] The "[l]evel of life insurance protection counts twice as much in African Americans' financial confidence than for the general population (22 percent v. 11 percent)."[109] They are more confident about their finances if they know they have life insurance. But to their own dismay, African Americans tend to insure less human capital in the household in comparison to whites; they think highly of life insurance but probably because of lack of education they do not buy enough insurance.[110] If the most valuable person passes, will there be enough life insurance coverage to compensate for what the household will now be lacking? Once again, education seems to be a potential form of assistance needed.

Social Security Benefits

African Americans are saving in different options at lower rates, and especially lower amounts than whites. What will they rely on for their retirement? African Americans rely on Social Security heavily because of the saving and investment circumstances stated above. In 2013, 58 million people will receive $816 billion in Social Security benefits.[111] Over the age of 65, nearly nine out of ten individuals receive Social Security benefits. The majority of Social Security benefits account for retired workers income, 74 percent, and 16 percent for disabled workers, and the remaining 10 percent goes to survivors of deceased workers.[112] African Americans rely on Social Security more than whites in regard to the use of it in retirement. In 1998, 35 percent of African Americans expected that Social Security would be their major source of income in retirement, in comparison to 17 percent of whites. In 2009, instead of

African Americans greatly increasing in their belief that Social Security would be their major source of income, their percentage only went up by two points. It was in the white community that there was a significant increase in reliance on Social Security, with their percentage moving up to 27 percent.[113] In this instance the American economic status did not harm African Americans more as it had done in some instances mentioned above.

Because Social Security is an insurance plan for all working Americans, it is guaranteed that Social Security savings will be there when one retires, becomes disabled, or if a worker passes away and leaves behind dependent survivors. It is a sure way to save one's own earnings, and unlike employer-assisted programs, one cannot borrow from Social Security. If people are employed, there is no way they can hinder their Social Security benefits. But one must think how many African Americans are not paying into this social insurance because they are not employed? African Americans earn less than white Americans when it comes to Social Security benefits, despite the way the system is set up to benefit those low earners with a higher return on their contributions. "Since African Americans have lower lifetime earnings than whites, on average, they benefit disproportionately from this aspect of Social Security."[114] Spriggs and Furman explain this mechanism. For example, in 2003, persons who on average earned no more than $606 a month received 90 percent of those earnings in retirement—still not the full amount, which back then was definitely not enough to live off. The disproportion comes when very high income earners only received 25 percent of their average earnings when collecting Social Security. This is very positive for all low-income earners, yet it still does not bridge the divide between the rich and the poor.

Even with assistance from Social Security, African Americans in retirement are only receiving 85 percent of the average benefit of whites who are retired.[115] On average, African Americans are only earning, prior to retirement, 73 percent of what whites earn. Social Security helps bridge the divide, but there is still a great disproportion. Only half of those African Americans receiving Social Security receive it for retirement, the other half are receiving it for disability or survivor's benefits.[116] These other two benefits are more likely to be received by African Americans, as they are more likely to become disabled or to die before being eligible to retire.[117] In 2011, of those African Americans receiving Social Security benefits, 23 percent were elderly married couples, but the greatest portion at the rate of 56 percent were unmarried elderly African Americans.[118] These single elderly persons rely on Social Security for 90 percent of their retirement income; if they earned very little when working, they will earn even less in retirement.[119] One also has to remember that African Americans are not as secure economically when retiring, based on the evidence of savings and other retirement plans. African American men sixty-five years or older received $13,458 in Social Security income in 2011, and African American women received $12,173.[120] This would mean that whites are earning around $16,000 in their benefits, plus all of the personal savings, employer-assisted program savings, and any other brokered assets. Even a secure system like Social Security cannot even the economic ground for African Americans in elder years. How secure is Social Security? Spriggs and Furman state that "[p]roposals to scale back the traditional Social Security system and replace a portion of it with private accounts are unlikely to maintain" the little protection it has for African Americans.[121] The discussion to overhaul Social Security in a direction of privatization needs to be a discussion to overhaul it in ways to protect all workers, no matter what their earnings are, to ensure that when in retirement they are not in poverty. In 2010, 19.3 percent of African American seniors were living in poverty compared to 7.4 percent of white seniors.[122] We must find a way to strengthen Social Security, not to dismantle it.

Conclusion

African Americans have a more negative relationship with the American economy than a positive one in numerous areas of concern. Their median income is less than the majority racial group, yet according to Prudential it has greatly increased since the year 2001.[123] African Americans hold less education, despite the growth in matriculation into higher education. But because of a lower income and lower status in the United States, African Americans are less likely to graduate from these higher-education institutions. It is apparent that America is not a meritocracy, due to the difficulty of educational attainment. In the United States there is also less upward mobility for families, as someone whose parent earned less than $20,000 in a year has only a 5 percent chance of earning more than $50,000. Upward mobility is almost twice as difficult for African Americans.

The unemployment rate for African Americans has repeatedly been higher than white Americans, throughout U.S. history. Something as simple as a Black-sounding name could hinder African Americans from gaining any type of employment. They are also more likely to be in service or unskilled types of jobs. The fight for employment is influenced by stereotypes others have about both male and female African Americans. While for men, stereotypes are a great hindrance, for women, some help them gain employment. African American women are more likely to be employed than African American men, although the men have a higher median income. African American women are essential to the well-being of the African American community, but they seem to suffer more in economic situations.

African Americans have a lower level of wealth and net worth, and fewer assets than whites; a significant reason for this is their lower earnings in the jobs they do have access to. African Americans have less money in their savings, despite the acknowledgment that they could be saving at a similar rate to whites; this needs to be investigated further. They tend to be more conservative with their investments, remaining loyal to life insurance and real estate, if they have such means. When assisted by employers, African Americans participate in 401(k) plans less, and tend to withdraw from them more than their white counterparts. They also assist family members more with monetary help than whites do. This would negate the desire to save. Paying off debts, which African Americans have more of, is another reason saving is more difficult for this community. One thing working well in saving for retirement is Social Security, yet even this federal program is not bridging the earnings gap between African Americans and whites.

African Americans are in a fight for their livelihoods. Nevertheless, "nearly half of African Americans say their financial situation now is better than it was five years ago, 23 percent say it is worse."[124] They also have a more optimistic outlook for the next two years in regard to their finances than the general population.[125] This positivity reminds one of how resilient African Americans are despite their status in a country built on racist notions. What can assist in this economic plight? As seen throughout this paper, education about finances seems to be lacking.

Recommendations

The United States seems to be built on the notion that education can solve any problem. Despite the fact that education does not seem to solve the economic divide between African Americans and whites, perhaps a different type of education can help in closing such a gap. A little insight on how African Americans view those in finance professions reveals that only 26 percent of African Americans feel as though financial services companies have shown support and engaged their community.[126] No matter what economic status, "African Americans receive 13% less contact from financial advisors than members of the general population."[127] There is some action in the African American community in regard to sharing knowledge on economic prospects, and perhaps it is helping those African Americans that are doing well, but how can those suffering also be reached?

Local organizations, including nonprofits with a focus on financial literacy or even on overall well-being of a community, can go into African American communities and share their knowledge. Although there are existing projects of this kind, the approach may need to be revised. When teenagers get their first jobs, someone needs to talk to them about the purpose of a bank account, how to balance an account, and why one should begin the habit of saving. Perhaps a teenager only learns to save up for something he or she wishes to purchase nonetheless, it instills the notion of saving for a purpose. When that first paystub comes home, someone needs to explain what taxes are, the purposes of them, and especially the Social Security tax. When someone turns eighteen or goes off to college and begins receiving inquiries about credit cards, someone needs to discuss the pros and cons of a credit card, and explain what an interest rate is, and how it relates to one's purchases. This is also the prime time to discuss credit scores, and credit history. Someone who has probably not been taught these things by watching their parents, or asking them questions needs to know that from the moment they sign up for a credit card, and even their bank account, every purchase, withdrawal, overdraft, and missed payment relates to what their credit score will be. And what does a credit score do for you? Explain how when one needs a loan for a car and later on a house their credit score really counts. A poor credit score can stipulate what kind of buying power one will have, and can determine the type of economic life one will live.

When someone gains employment with benefits, such as an employer-assisted savings account, someone needs to be there to explain the pros and cons of all actions. What does it mean to put in the very minimum, versus a larger amount? What does it mean to borrow from it, or completely withdraw? Someone needs to sit down with this person and lay out how this 401(k) can help in his or her retirement future. There needs to be a blatant discussion about where this person wants to be in his or her retirement years and how to go about getting there. Will Social Security benefits be enough? As seen above, the answer is most likely no.

With continued communication, on the level of the client, one can go even further into buying life insurance, or getting in the proper position to buy a home. These two options are important to African Americans and still requires guidance in such endeavors, because even real estate still has loan discrimination. And when the relationship has gained trust, someone should talk to about brokered options, such as stocks and bonds. It would be important not to push at this moment, and it may help to have an African American broker, or stories from other African Americans who have invested. These are just some ideas on how to help educate and hopefully assist in this fight for economic equality.

When it comes to Social Security adjustments, this will not be a one-on-one intervention; it will have to come from officials influenced by the advice of their constituents. Some organizations are working to strengthen Social Security. The Center for Community Change in New York City believes that there needs to be adequate benefits for the lowest-income earners. This could happen by raising the minimum benefit to 125 percent of the poverty line. Too many elderly qualify as impoverished by the poverty-level standards, especially African Americans.

Currently, survivor's benefits are given to children of disabled or deceased Social Security earners until the age of eighteen; it used to be that from 1965 to 1981, these children would receive benefits until the age of twenty-two.[128] The Center for Community Change, along with other organizations like Virginia Organizing out of Charlottesville, Virginia, believes that raising the age to twenty-four, when more students are graduating from college, would be most beneficial. A lot of low-income students have to work, while they are pursuing a higher education, which can necessitate taking fewer classes at a time, or even to take time off. The benefit would give them funds to help stop such instances, such as working while in school or having to take time off, because they would receive the benefits until after the average college graduation age. Most importantly, these benefits should not be counted as income when students apply for financial aid.

Another way to strengthen Social Security is to implement a Caregiver Credit. This is for those who stopped working and took care of a family member who could no longer take care of him- or herself. The time someone spends taking care of another without pay is zero income for Social Security. These years could be averaged into this person's benefits numbers when it comes time to retire. The Center of Community Change suggests up to five years of credit, with a credit to their Social Security earnings of half of an average yearly wage of all covered workers. These are three current suggestions for making Social Security better; indeed taking some of these actions could assist African Americans when it comes time to retire, or receive benefits due to the loss of a worker.

There needs to be more focus on the economic situation of African Americans. It is important to have the numbers that give raw data on what their situation is in this American economy. But as some of the research references in this chapter suggest, it is important to gain insight by doing qualitative research in the African American community as well. Some of the aforementioned recommendations should be further fleshed out and implemented in small samples of the African American community, to see if those participating gain from the approach. This sample also needs to be followed over years to see if there is progress. Perhaps more research should be completed on the social programs implemented by the government as well. To what extent do these programs help or hinder this population economically? Social Security has greatly benefited African Americans, but so much more can be done with the program. Perhaps it is time to organize this community to take action to help strengthen this program that has been very helpful, despite its flaws. This chapter touches on numerous aspects of the economic well-being of African Americans, but there is so much more to be investigated.

Notes

1. Angel L. Harris, "The Economic and Educational State of Black Americans in the 21st Century: Should We Be Optimistic or Concerned?" *Review of Black Political Economy* 37 (2010): 242.

2. Zack Burgess, "Blacks Still Struggling in Job Market," *Philadelphia Tribune* (2012), http://www.phillytrib.com/newsarticles/item/3459-blacks-still-struggling-in-job-market.html

3. Williams Rodgers III, "Understanding the Black-White Earnings Gap," *The American Prospect* (2008), http://prospect.org/article/understanding-black-white-earnings-gap.

4. Ibid.; Anonymous, "Discrimination—Racial Disparities in 401(K) Participation and Contribution—Fiduciary Duty—Plan Design," *Benefits Quarterly* 26, no. 4 (2010): 67.

5. David Hinson, "Middle-Class Income Isn't a Viable Choice for African-Americans (Part One of Two)," *Network Journal* 11, no. 3 (2004): 2.

6. Massey, Douglas S., and Nancy A. Denton. *American Apartheid: Segregation and the Making of the Underclass* (Cambridge: Harvard University Press, 1993), 149.

7. Oliver, Melvin L., and Thomas M. Shapiro. *Black Wealth/White Wealth: A New Perspective on Racial Inequality* (New York: Routledge, 1995), 157–158

8. Ibid., 158.

9. Jared Bernstein, "You Can Take It with You: Income and Wealth across Generations," in *All Things Being Equal: Instigating Opportunity in an Inequitable Time*, ed. Brian D. Smedley, and Alan Jenkins, (New York: New Press, 2007), 20.

10. Ibid., 22–23.

11. The White House, "President Obama Signs New Initiative to Improve Educational Outcomes for African Americans" (2012), http://www.whitehouse.gov/the-press-office/2012/07/26/president-obama-signs-new-initiative-improve-educational-outcomes-africa

12. Bernstein, 27.

13. The Prudential Insurance Company, "The African American Financial Experience," (2013), 5.

14. Bernstein, 27–28.

15. Andy Kroll, "What We Don't Talk about When We Talk about Jobs: The Continuing Scandal of African-American Joblessness," *New Labor Forum* 21, no. 1 (2012): 51.

16. Bernstein, 35.

17. Kroll, 51.

18. Clifford L. Broman, "Work Stress in the Family Life of African Americans," *Journal of Black Studies* 31 (2001): 835.

19. Kroll, 50–51.

20. Ibid., 51.

21. Marianne Bertrand and Sendhil Mullainathan, "Are Emily and Brendan More Employable Than Lakisha and Jamal? A Field Experiment on Labor Market Discrimination," *American Economic Review* 94, no. 4 (September 2004): 991–1013.

22. Broman, 836; Kroll, 50.

23. Broman, 836.

24. Irene Browne, Cynthia Hewitt, Leann Tigges, and Gary Green, "Why Does Job Segregation Lead to Wage Inequality among African Americans? Person, Place, Sector, or Skills? " *Social Science Research* 30, no. 3 (September 2001): 479.

25. Massey and Denton, 117.

26. Ibid., 475.

27. Ibid.

28. Ibid., 476.

29. Ibid., 477.

30. Ibid., 479.

31. James Button, Kelli N. Moore, and Barbara A. Rienzo, "Supporting Diversity Works: African American Male and Female Employment in Six Florida Cities," *Western Journal of Black Studies* 30, no. 3 (2006): 135.

32. Cynthia M. Hewitt, "African-American Concentration in Jobs: The Political Economy of Job Segregation and Contestation in Atlanta," *Urban Affairs Review* 39, no. 3 (January 2004): 334.

33. Browne et al., 479.

34. Ibid.

35. Julianne Malveaux, "Still Slipping: African-American Women in the Economy and in Society," *Review of Black Political Economy* 40, no. 1 (March 2013): 15; Button, Moore, and Rienzo, 136; Linda Loubert, "The Plight of African American Women: Employed and Unemployed," *Review of Black Political Economy* 39, no. 4 (2012): 375.

36. J. Camille Hall, Joyce E. Everett, and Johnnie Hamilton-Mason, "Black Women Talk about Workplace Stress and How They Cope," *Journal of Black Studies* 43, no. 2 (2012): 208.

37. Button, Moore, and Rienzo, 134.

38. Hall, Everett, and Hamilton-Mason, 211.

39. Ibid., 213.

40. Button, Moore, and Rienzo, 134.

41. Malveaux, 16.

42. Ibid.

43. Ibid.

44. Andrew F. Brimmer, "Building Wealth and Assets," *Black Enterprise* 21, no. 12 (1991): 31.

45. Malveaux, 16.

46. Button, Moore, and Rienzo, 134.

47. Ibid., 136.

48. Darrick Hamilton, "Race, Wealth, and Intergenerational Poverty," *The American Prospect* (2009), http://prospect.org/article/race-wealth-and-intergenerational-poverty.

49. Ibid.

50. Ibid.

51. Ibid.

52. Maury Gittleman, and Edward N. Wolff, "Racial Differences in Patterns of Wealth Accumulation," *Journal of Human Resources* 39, no. 1 (Winter 2004): 194.

53. Wealth, according to Hinson, is the creation of resources rather than the consumption of them by using one's money. Net worth is the total assets minus total liabilities as mentioned before. Assets are things that can be owned that holds positive value; there are liquid assets such as bank accounts and nonliquid assets such as property.

54. David W. Rothwell, and Chang-Keun Han, "Exploring the Relationship between Assets and Family Stress among Low-Income Families," *Family Relations* 59, no. 4 (September 2010): 396–407.

55. Ibid., 397.

56. Ibid., 398.

57. Ibid., 404.

58. Wilhelmina A. Leigh, and Anna L. Wheatley, "Retirement Savings Behavior and Expectations of African Americans: 1998 and 2009" (Joint Center for Political and Economic Studies, 2010), 2.

59. Ibid.

60. Ibid.

61. Ibid., 2–3.

62. M. Janice Hogan, Catherine Solheim, Susan Wolfgram, Busisiwe Nkosi, and Nicola Rodrigues, "The Working Poor: From the Economic Margins to Asset Building," *Family Relations* 53, no. 2 (March 2004): 229.

63. Leigh and Wheatley, 3.

64. Ibid.

65. Ibid.

66. Ibid.

67. Ibid.

68. The Prudential Insurance Company, 5.

69. Ibid.

70. Anonymous.

71. Ibid.

72. The Prudential Insurance Company, 17.

73. Ibid. Anonymous, "Discrimination—Racial Disparities in 401(K) Participation and Contribution—Fiduciary Duty—Plan Design."

74. Aziz Gueye Adetemirin, "Personal Finance," *Network Journal* 15, no. 8 (2008): 10.

75. Enskat & Associates, "Gender and Race Inequalities in Retirement Savings—Changing the Future," (2012).

76. Adetemirin, "Personal Finance."

77. The Prudential Insurance Company, 17.

78. Bill Thomason, "African Americans and Retirement Savings," *Hyde Park Citizen* 2002.

79. Annamaria Lusardi, and Olivia S. Mitchell, "Financial Literacy and Retirement Planning in the United States," *Journal of Pension Economics and Finance* 10, no. 4 (2011): 515.

80. Thomason.

81. Ibid. The Prudential Insurance Company, 4.

82. "The African American Financial Experience," 7.

83. Ibid., 10.

84. Thomason.

85. The Prudential Insurance Company, 4.

86. Ibid., 5.

87. Ibid., 12.

88. Ibid., 13.

89. Ibid.

90. Lusardi and Mitchell, 523.

91. Hamilton.

92. Leigh and Wheatley, 4.

93. Ibid.

94. Ibid.

95. Ibid.

96. Hogan et al., 230.

97. Ibid., 236.

98. Marcia A. Shobe, and Kameri Christy-McMullin, "Savings Experiences Past and Present: Narratives from Low-Income African American Women," *Affilia* 20, no. 2 (Summer 2005): 229.

99. The Prudential Insurance Company, 4.

100. Michael S. Gutter, and Charles B. Hatcher, "Racial Differences in the Demand for Life Insurance," *Journal of Risk and Insurance* 75, no. 3 (September 2008): 679.

101. LIMRA, "LIMRA Study: African Americans Value Life Insurance Protection More than General Population" (2013), http://www.limra.com/Posts/PR/News_Releases/LIMRA_Study_Finds_African_Americans_Place_More_Value_on_Life_Insurance_Protection_Compared_to_Total_Population.aspx.

102. Adetemirin.

103. Hamilton.

104. Ibid.

105. Ibid.

106. Gutter and Hatcher, 683.

107. Jr. John S. Haller, "Race, Mortality, and Life Insurance: Negro Vital Statistics in the Late Nineteenth Century," *Journal of the History of Medicine and Allied Sciences* 25, no. 3 (July 1970): 247–261.

108. LIMRA, "LIMRA Study: African Americans Value Life Insurance Protection More than General Population" (2013).

109. The Prudential Insurance Company, 9.

110. Gutter and Hatcher, 685.

111. Social Security Administration, "Fact Sheet: Social Security," http://www.socialsecurity.gov/pressoffice/factsheets/colafacts2013.pdf.

112. Ibid.

113. The Prudential Insurance Company, 3.

114. William Spriggs and Jason Furman, "African Americans and Social Security: The Implications of Reform Proposals" (Washington, DC: Center on Budget and Policy Priorities, 2006), 2.

115. Ibid., 3.

116. Ibid., 2.

117. Ibid., 1.

118. Social Security Administration, "Social Security Is Important to African Americans," http://www.ssa.gov/pressoffice/factsheets/africanamer.htm.

119. Ibid.
120. Ibid.
121. Spriggs and Furman, "African Americans and Social Security: The Implications of Reform Proposals," 1.
122. Center for Community Change, "Strengthening Social Security: Adequate Benefits for the Lowest-Income Earners," ed. Center for Community Change (2012).
123. The Prudential Insurance Company, 12.
124. Ibid., 7.
125. Ibid., 8.
126. Ibid., 18.
127. Ibid., 8.
128. Center for Community Change.

Bibliography

Adetemirin, Aziz Gueye. "Personal Finance." *Network Journal* 15, no. 8 (2008): 10–11.

Anonymous. "Discrimination—Racial Disparities in 401(K) Participation and Contribution—Fiduciary Duty—Plan Design." *Benefits Quarterly* 26, no. 4 (2010).

Bernstein, Jared. "You Can Take It with You: Income and Wealth across Generations." In *All Things Being Equal: Instigating Opportunity in an Inequitable Time*, edited by Brian D. Smedley and Alan Jenkins. New York: New Press, 2007.

Bertrand, Marianne, and Sendhil Mullainathan. "Are Emily and Brendan More Employable Than Lakisha and Jamal? A Field Experiment on Labor Market Discrimination." *American Economic Review* 94, no. 4 (September 2004): 991–1013.

Brimmer, Andrew F. "Building Wealth and Assets." *Black Enterprise* 21, no. 12 (1991): 31–34.

Broman, Clifford L. "Work Stress in the Family Life of African Americans." *Journal of Black Studies* 31 (2001): 835–846.

Browne, Irene, Cynthia Hewitt, Leann Tigges, and Gary Green. "Why Does Job Segregation Lead to Wage Inequality among African Americans? Person, Place, Sector, or Skills?" *Social Science Research* 30, no. 3 (September 2001): 473–495.

Burgess, Zack, "Blacks Still Struggling in Job Market," *Philadelphia Tribune* (2012), http://www.phillytrib.com/newsarticles/item/3459-blacks-still-struggling-in-job-market.html.

Button, James, Kelli N. Moore, and Barbara A. Rienzo. "Supporting Diversity Works: African American Male and Female Employment in Six Florida Cities." *Western Journal of Black Studies* 30, no. 3 (2006): 133–141.

Center for Community Change. "Strengthening Social Security: Adequate

Benefits for the Lowest-Income Earners." edited by Center for Community Change, 2012.

Enskat & Associates. "Gender and Race Inequalities in Retirement Savings—Changing the Future." (2012).

Gittleman, Maury, and Edward N. Wolff. "Racial Differences in Patterns of Wealth Accumulation." *Journal of Human Resources* 39, no. 1 (Winter 2004): 193–227.

Gutter, Michael S., and Charles B. Hatcher. "Racial Differences in the Demand for Life Insurance." *Journal of Risk and Insurance* 75, no. 3 (Sep. 2008): 677-89.

Hall, J. Camille, Joyce E. Everett, and Johnnie Hamilton-Mason. "Black Women Talk about Workplace Stress and How They Cope. " *Journal of Black Studies* 43, no. 2 (2012): 207–226.

Hamilton, Darrick. "Race, Wealth, and Intergenerational Poverty." *The American Prospect* (2009). Published electronically August 14, 2009. http://prospect.org/article/race-wealth-and-intergenerational-poverty.Harris, Angel L. "The Economic and Educational State of Black Americans in the 21st Century: Should We Be Optimistic or Concerned?" *Review of Black Political Economy* 37 (2010): 241–252.

Hewitt, Cynthia M. "African-American Concentration in Jobs: The Political Economy of Job Segregation and Contestation in Atlanta." *Urban Affairs Review* 39, no. 3 (Jan. 2004): 318-41.

Hinson, David. "Middle-Class Income Isn't a Viable Choice for African-Americans (Part One of Two)." *Network Journal* 11, no. 3 (2004).

Hogan, M. Janice, Catherine Solheim, Susan Wolfgram, Busisiwe Nkosi, and Nicola Rodrigues. "The Working Poor: From the Economic Margins to Asset Building." *Family Relations* 53, no. 2 (March 2004): 229–236.

John S. Haller, Jr. "Race, Mortality, and Life Insurance: Negro Vital Statistics in the Late Nineteenth Century." *Journal of the History of Medicine and Allied Sciences* 25, no. 3 (July 1970): 247–261.

Kroll, Andy. "What We Don't Talk About When We Talk About Jobs: The Continuing Scandal of African-American Joblessness." *New Labor Forum* 21, no. 1 (2012): 49–55, 119.

Leigh, Wilhelmina A., and Anna L. Wheatley. "Retirement Savings Behavior and Expectations of African Americans: 1998 and 2009." 1–4: Joint Center for Political and Economic Studies, 2010.

LIMRA, "LIMRA Study: African Americans Value Life Insurance Protection More than General Population" (2013), http://www.limra.com/Posts/PR/News_Releases/LIMRA_Study_Finds_African_Americans_Place_More_Value_on_Life_Insurance_Protection_Compared_to_Total_Population.aspx.

Loubert, Linda. "The Plight of African American Women: Employed and Unemployed." *Review of Black Political Economy* 39, no. 4 (2012): 373–380.

Lusardi, Annamaria, and Olivia S. Mitchell. "Financial Literacy and Retirement Planning in the United States." *Journal of Pension Economics and Finance* 10, no. 4 (2011): 509–525.

Malveaux, Julianne. "Still Slipping: African-American Women in the Economy and in Society." *Review of Black Political Economy* 40, no. 1 (March 2013): 13–21.

Rodgers, Williams, III, "Understanding the Black-White Earnings Gap," The American Prospect (2008), http://prospect.org/article/understanding-black-white-earnings-gap.

Rothwell, David W., and Chang-Keun Han. "Exploring the Relationship between Assets and Family Stress among Low-Income Families." *Family Relations* 59, no. 4 (September 2010): 396–407.

Shobe, Marcia A., and Kameri Christy-McMullin. "Savings Experiences Past and Present: Narratives from Low-Income African American Women." *Affilia* 20, no. 2 (Summer 2005): 222–237.

Social Security Administration. "Fact Sheet: Social Security." http://www.socialsecurity.gov/pressoffice/factsheets/colafacts2013.pdf.

———. "Social Security Is Important to African Americans." http://www.ssa.gov/pressoffice/factsheets/africanamer.htm.

Spriggs, William, and Jason Furman. "African Americans and Social Security: The Implications of Reform Proposals." 1–14. Washington, DC: Center on Budget and Policy Priorities, 2006.

The Prudential Insurance Company. "The African American Financial Experience," 2013, 1–20.

Thomason, Bill. "African Americans and Retirement Savings." *Hyde Park Citizen*, 2002.

7

Confronting an Enduring Legacy

Health-Care Workforce Disparity

Costellia H. Talley and Henry C. Talley

"No Black Nurses to Take Care of This Baby."[1]

Reading a headline like this, one would think that it was made during the Jim Crow era. Jim Crow racial segregation laws were legally sanctioned until the passing of legislation in the mid-1960s, namely the Title VI of the 1964 Civil Rights Act. However, the headline above was actually published in February 2013.[2] In this news story, a father made a request to the charge nurse that "no *Black* nurses" care for his infant who was receiving care in the neonatal intensive care unit. While making this request of the charge nurse, he pulled up his sleeve to reveal what was thought to be a tattoo of a swastika. Hurley Medical Center in Flint, Michigan, allegedly granted the father's request (father's name was not included in the complaint). Analogous scenarios of racism and insensitivity toward African Americans in health care continue to play out in other parts of the United States, such as Georgia and Hawaii, as well as outside the country, including Canada and the U.K.[3]

A similar scenario occurred at Abington Memorial Hospital in Philadelphia, Pennsylvania. [4] A pregnant white woman was admitted for a caesarian section, and her male partner requested that no African Americans be involved in the delivery of their child or enter her room. The hospital did not allow African American employees to care for the woman. The employees claimed racial discrimination and asked the court to issue an order permanently prohibiting racial discrimination against African American employees of the hospital and payment for damages, attorney's fees and court costs. These news stories demonstrate how deeply race/racism is embedded in society, and is a staunch reminder that racism, thought to be a thing of the past, is still alive and well. The most nefarious aspect of these encounters is that overt incidences of racism and aggression toward African American nurses continue to occur; at both the institutional and interpersonal level.

Despite the belief that we are currently in a postracial society because of the strides that have been made, election of the first African American president, fall of apartheid, and a series of African American achievements, racism continues to exist.[5] Bobo asserts that at the end of the twentieth century, racism was more subtle, "laissez-faire racism" or "covert" and steeped in negative stereotypes and the belief that African Americans were prone to violence, on welfare, and less intelligent.[6] This form of racism was adopted by whites as they do not want to be seen or thought of as racist because of its negative connotation. Laissez-faire form of racism is "subtle, subversive, and deliberate, informal and formal mechanisms that allow differential access to rewards, prestige, sanctions, status, and privileges based on racial hierarchies."[7] Subtle racism is often unconscious and unintentional, but it has the same effect as overt racism-distrust-miscommunication. Discrimination is justified based on some other factor rather than race. African Americans indicate that subtle racism causes them to ruminate for days and causes them to have physiological symptoms, for example, blood pressure increase, headaches, and/or experience painful tightness in the neck and shoulders. Whites also often deny that they notice race. They like to claim to be color blind. In some instances, this notion of color blindness may alienate minority group members and increase distrust because minorities often seek acknowledgment of their racial identity. The ideology of color blindness reflects an attempt to deny, minimize/distort the fact that racism occurs and to avert a discussion about race (which is uncomfortable for many). Some suggest that color blindness itself is a manifestation of racial discrimination.[8]

In a society that supports the ideology of color blindness, health disparities are more likely to be overlooked; thereby, increasing the health disparities gap. A substantive body of research demonstrates that workforce diversity is a key strategy for improving cultural competence, increasing access to high-quality health care, providing for optimal management of the health-care system, and strengthening the nursing research agenda.[9] A diverse workforce improves communication, tolerance, trust, and patients' outcomes. Health-care providers who come from diverse, economically disadvantaged backgrounds are more likely to go back to those communities to provide care, increasing access to care. The health of a society is intricately entwined with the health of racial/ethnic minority populations. With the anticipated increase in racial/ethnic minority populations, the health disparities gap between whites and other minority populations will be a challenge for health-care providers.

A health-care work environment that supports workforce diversity is essential to reduce health disparities. Institutions must change the way they respond to and value diversity and these changes must be systematic and comprehensive.[10] The institutional climate plays an important role within the context of diversity. Diversity in institutions is influenced by the historical legacy of inclusion and exclusion of people of color, the psychological climate (degree of racial tension and discrimination), and behavioral dimensions (quality and quantity of interaction).[11] This chapter focuses on African American health-care workforce disparities, within the context of nursing. This chapter has four main sections: (1) An overview of the health-care workforce disparities of African Americans within a historical context; (2) the current state of health-care workforce diversity; (3) challenges to improving health-care workforce diversity; and (4) strategies and recommendations to improve health-care workforce diversity. Although the focus of this paper is on nursing workforce diversity, many other health-care professions lack diversity (e.g., MD, allied health professionals), which includes difficulty in recruiting and retaining an adequate numbers of students to achieve optimum diversity (educational pipeline).

Historical Roots of Health-Care Workforce Disparities

Historically, nurses in general have been victims of verbal, emotional, and physical abuse in their work environment.[12] Abuse is often underreported because of fear of retaliation, belief that nothing will be done and that it is "part of the job" and fear of being labeled as a troublemaker. The sources of nurses' abuse have been from patients, families, other nurses, and physicians. In 2009, over 50 percent of emergency center nurses reported being verbally and physically abused by patients and/or family members and no written reports were filed.[13] The American Nurses Association (ANA) issued a statement on workplace violence that nursing personnel have the right to work in healthy work environments free of abusive behavior such as bullying, hostility, lateral abuse and violence, sexual harassment, intimidation, abuse of authority and position, and reprisal for speaking out against abuses. In 2012, the ANA Petitioned the U.S. Occupational Safety and Health Administration to develop workforce violence prevention programs. Some states have implemented laws requiring comprehensive workplace violence prevention (e.g., California, New York, New Jersey, and Connecticut).

African American nurses face double jeopardy due to their race and the nursing role. There has been a historical antipathy toward African Americans as health-care providers, which has been supported by discriminatory policies and practices. Health-care provider disparities occur within the context of health-care provider support, professional support, and racial bias. Health-care providers see the interplay of diversity, health disparities, and social determinants on a daily basis.[14] African American health-care providers often experience prejudice from multiple sources, including coworkers, managers, patients, professional organizations, and educational systems.

African Americans have historically been underrepresented in the health-care workforce and professional organizations. According to the *Sullivan Report*, Schools of Medicine, Nursing, and Dentistry were the last to integrate their classrooms and organizations.[15] During the time of Jim Crow, patterns of segregation and inferiority were sanctioned for African American health care providers. The *Flexner Report* stated, "Medical Education in the United States and Canada" of 1910 reorganized medical education, while strengthening the belief in segregated education for African Americans.[16] Although the goal of the *Flexner Report* was to improve educational standards in medical schools, it had a tremendous effect on the education of African American physicians. Flexner suggested that all but two of the seven predominantly African American medical schools (Meharry Medical College and Howard University) should be closed. Between 1910 and 1970, these two medical schools were the only schools that educated African American physicians. Dr. Abraham Flexner in his report stated that "the Negro should only be trained as sanitarian to protect whites from disease because Negros was a source of contagion and infection.[17] For over 100 years after the Flexner's report, African Americans continue to be underrepresented in health professions.[18]

A similar report, the *Ethel Johns Report: African American Women in the Nursing Profession, 1925*, was completed in nursing, exposing racial inequities.[19] The report, financed by the Rockefeller Foundation, aimed to identify the training available for African American nurses, and describe African American nurses' employment and their opportunities for employment. The findings of the report were so egregious that it went unpublished for almost sixty years. Johns's report maintained that certain doors were closed to African American nurses regardless of their training and skill, she went on to say that she found nowhere in the country that African American nurses were allowed to practice equally to white nurses. African American nurses experience open hostility from patients and physicians, and that physicians regarded African American nurses as inferior. White nurses were resentful of African American nurses and blocked their advancement to supervisory roles. Johns noted that often the medical profession declared a preference for African American nurses, but this was because it was easier to exploit African American nurses than white nurses due to lack of power, and African American nurses performed duties and services that were loathed by white nurses. The notion of exploitation brings to mind the statement made by Eunice Rivers, an African American nurse involved in the Tuskegee Syphilis Study, who said, "we were taught to never question the doctors order, we never prescribe; we follow the doctors' orders." The idea of passive obedience, unquestionably carrying out the orders of physicians, was customary among African American nurses during this time. The Johns Report also contended that white superintendents of the nursing schools maintained that they preferred younger African American women (under 18 years old) in their programs, because African American women older than this were too "uppity," "troublesome," and "hard to manage." In the report, Johns stated that "the nursing problem interesting as it may be, is insignificant in comparison to the whole Negro situation in relation to health, especially those phases which bear on hospital services and the practice of medicine by Negroes."[20]

For over a century, some medical and professional organizations actively reinforced and/or passively permitted the exclusion of African Americans from their organizations. To become a member of the national organization, an individual was required to first be a member of their local state organization. Several states refused to allow African Americans to join their local chapters, thereby preventing them from becoming a member of the larger national organization. This was true for organizations such as the American Medical Association (AMA), American Nurses Association (ANA), National League of Nursing Education, and National Organization of Public Health Nurses. Disenfranchised African American physicians and nurses formed their own national professional organizations such as the National Medical Association (1895), National Dental Association (1932), Old North State Medical Society (1887), and National Association of Colored Graduate Nurses (1908).[21]

The AMA was formed in 1846 to standardize the requirements for obtaining a Medical Degree. The current mission of the AMA is "to promote the art and science of medicine and the betterment of public health.[22] However, for over one hundred years, African American physicians were often denied membership into the AMA. In 2005, the AMA Institute for Ethics convened a panel to examine the historical divide between African American and white physicians.[23] This led to the AMA formal apology to African American physicians for their discriminatory practices and racial inequality.[24] Similar to the AMA, it was not until 1965 that the American Dental Association admitted African American dentist, and in 1948 that African American nurses were authorized to apply for membership in the ANA.[25] The ANA was the first health organization to admit African Americans.

African American Health-Care Workforce

The United States is rapidly becoming more diverse. Reports indicate that by the year 2050, the number of African Americans in the United States will almost double and the number of Hispanic and Asian population will triple.[26] For example, the African American population will increase from 41.2 million in 2012 to 61.8 million in 2060, and the Hispanic population will increase from 53.3 million in 2012 to 128.8 million in 2060.[27] The projected shift in the demographic composition of the U.S. population and the increasing health disparities and poor health outcomes among ethnic minority populations indicate that there is a need to increase the diversity of the health-care workforce to meet the needs of the population. The underrepresentation of racial/ethnic minorities in the health-care workforce is expected to continue, most likely leading to an ill-prepared health-care workforce. National organizations and health-care leaders have indicated that a diverse health-care workforce is crucial to decreasing health disparities.[28]

Data indicates that African Americans are underrepresented in most of the health-care professions. For example, African American nurses account for 5.4 percent of the U.S. nursing workforce, and African American physicians account for 3.8 percent of the U.S. physician workforce, notwithstanding the fact that African Americans represent 12.8 percent of the U.S. population.[29] African Americans are also underrepresented in the allied health professions. For example, 66.9 percent of physical therapists are white compared to 3.9 percent African American.[30]

The number of African American physicians entering academic medicine is also low. Approximately 4 percent of medical school faculty is an underrepresented minority and 20 percent of this group is at Howard University, Morehouse School of Medicine, Meharry Medical College, and three medical schools in Puerto Rico.[31] African American physicians are five times more likely than other physicians to practice in areas where there is a large amount of African American residents. Approximately 50 percent of the patients seen by African American physicians are Medicaid or uninsured. African American physicians are more likely to conduct research related to reducing health disparities than other physicians. The Association of American Medical Colleges projects that by the year 2020, there will be a shortage of over 90,000 physicians needed to provide primary care and specialty services.[32]

African American nurses face some of the same challenges as African American physicians. African American nurses report that they do not feel that they are accepted as being equal to their white nurse colleagues, providers, or patients. The nursing workforce has historically been dominated by white females, and it continues to be dominated by white females. Although there has been an increase in the number of African American nurses, the progress has been slow and the numbers are not reflective of the population.

Nurses are the largest segment of the health-care occupations. It is projected that by the year 2020, the nursing shortage will reach over one million.[33] This shortage will be partially due to the number of nurses reaching retirement age. A 2013–2014 American Association of Colleges of Nursing report indicated that nursing schools turned away 78,089 qualified applicants from baccalaureate and graduate nursing programs in 2013, due largely to insufficient number of faculty.[34] Combine this factor with the current limited enrollment of African American students, increases the potential for continued underrepresentation of African Americans in nursing.

The IOM report recommended higher levels of education to meet the needs of sicker patients and sophisticated technology used in health care.[35] The goal is to increase the proportion of nurses with a Bachelor's degree to 80 percent by 2020. A report by Health Resources and Services Administration (HRSA) indicates that over a nine-year period there was only a small increase in the number of nurses with a bachelors or graduate degree; approximately five percentage points.[36]

Allied health-care professionals workforce diversity mirrors that of physicians and nurses.[37] Allied health professionals are "the segment of the workforce that delivers services involving the identification, evaluation and prevention of diseases and disorders; dietary and nutrition services; and rehabilitation and health systems management."[38] Included in this category of health-care professionals are: dental hygienists, diagnostic medical sonographers, dietitians, medical technologists, occupational therapists, physical therapists, radiographers, respiratory therapists, and speech language pathologists. Allied health-care professionals make up 60 percent of the health-care workforce.

Grumbach and Medndoza suggest that the underrepresentation of racial/ethnic minorities in the health-care workforce is a public health problem.[39] The underrepresentation of racial/ethnic minorities in the health-care workforce contributes to health disparities. Health disparities are a "chain of events that are signified by a difference in: (a) environment; (b) access to, utilization of, and quality of care; (c) health status; or (d) a particular health outcome that deserves scrutiny."[40] There is clear and compelling evidence that African Americans experience higher levels of disparities in health status than whites, and that these health disparities contribute to higher morbidity and mortality rates.[41] African Americans are more likely to receive low-quality care and less likely to receive routine preventive care.[42] African Americans report poor patient-provider communication, lack of trust, and less respect from their health-care provider.[43]

The health status of African Americans has been linked to the social determinants of health (racism, environment, and socioeconomic status), health disparities, and workforce diversity (3D).[44] Race matters in health-care whether viewing health care from the history and legacy of discrimination in medical care,[45] discriminatory barriers to entry into health professions, unfair and bias treatment after becoming a health-care professional,[46] the quality of care and clinical decisions made by physicians based on racism,[47] or scientific racism. Evidence of bias, discrimination, and stereotyping by health-care professionals has been reported by researchers. Health disparities have broad implications for health-care professionals. Health providers must be knowledgeable about the effects of health disparities.

There are several advantages to having a diverse workforce. Diversity among health-care providers is associated with improved access to care for underserved racial and ethnic minority patients, better patient satisfaction, greater patient choice, and enhanced educational experiences for students and improve cultural competence.[48] Some studies suggest that increased diversity in the health-care workforce may decrease distrust of the health-care system.[49] Additionally, a diverse workforce will assist in reducing the health-care shortages. Minority health-care professionals tend to disproportionately work in areas with minority and underserved populations. Race is a strong predictor of likelihood that healthcare providers will treat the underserved. Racial concordance between patients and health-care providers has also been shown to improve interpersonal care. Similarly, health-care providers from minority populations are more likely to advocate on behalf of underserved and vulnerable populations.

LaVeist and Pierre suggest that there are six public health benefits to a diverse health-care workforce.[50] These benefits include: (a) improvement in overall quality of care as a result of better patient satisfaction and trust; (b) improvement in the level of cultural competency in health care by improving patient-provider relationships (which is associated with better patient-provider communication, and the "overall influence minority providers exert on their white colleagues and health-care organizations to provide culturally sensitive and appropriate care for minority patients"); (3) increased access to and utilization of health services and improved health outcomes; (d) "increased access to care for geographically underserved minority and white communities, because minority physicians are more likely to locate in underserved communities; (e) improve health and health-care research by enhancing the breadth and scope of research with a broader range of racial/ethnic perspectives and by encouraging greater inclusion of racial/ethnic minority patients/subjects in biomedical and clinical trials research; and (f) yield other societal benefits, including minority providers operating their own practice."[51]

Challenges to Achieving a Diverse Workforce

Recent reports have identified multiple factors that contribute to the underrepresentation of African Americans in health care.[52] Discriminatory practices based on racist ideology create barriers and burdens for African American nurses. Two major areas deserve particular attention; institutional climate/culture and educational pipeline.

Institutional Climate/Culture

The Sullivan Commission defines institutional climate as "the collective social, cultural, and psychological attitudes and values that prevail within an institution and which demonstrate—particularly as seen from the viewpoint of minority students and faculty—whether the institution truly welcomes minorities."[53] A factor that contributes to an unwelcoming institutional climate is that African Americans are viewed as being lesser than-marginal. When African American nurses are perceived as marginal, they are viewed as "someone who can be subordinated, disadvantaged, restricted, silenced, not told about opportunities nor given cooperation for control."[54] The ideology of marginalization contributes to underrepresentation of African American health-care professionals in academia, inequity in tenure and promotion and higher attrition for nursing students.[55]

Health-care faculty and health-care providers' practices are intertwined, as health-care education exists to prepare students for professional practice.[56] Although the percentage of minority faculty has increased, the greatest gains have been as nontenured faculty and lecturer (109 percent) versus the tenure track (37 percent).[57] Discrimination in the promotion process has been identified as one of the reasons for the underrepresentation of African Americans in academia.[58] A twelve-year retrospective review examining the trends in academic appointment of underrepresented minorities in medicine reported that academic progression is more difficult for minorities.[59] African Americans had the least progression overall, particularly at the professor and chairperson rank. The study found that African Americans represented 1.25 percent of professors, 2.69 percent of chairpersons, and 4.94 percent of deans compared to 84.76 percent of professors, 88.26 percent of chairpersons, and 91.28 percent of deans for whites. African Americans are the least likely to receive federal grant funding (whites 69.9 percent; African Americans 1.4 percent).[60] Grant funding is an important component of scholarship and promotion for tenure-track faculty. Difficulty in successfully establishing a program of research is the most common reason that faculty is denied promotions and tenure. These issues, combined with teaching, preparation, and demands to publish and prepare grant and conference proposals, causes many faculty to leave academe.

African Americans in academia face many challenges, including lack of diversity in the institutional climate and/or discrimination, problems finding mentors who can lessen the difficulties of entry into the established research infrastructure, institutional bias, and lack of institutional support.[61] African American faculty members report that communication about resources on campuses and diversity initiatives are extremely uneven and idiosyncratic.[62] African American physicians also reported limited mentorship as junior faculty and as medical students, which is related to limited numbers of underrepresented faculty. African American women in academia face an interlocking system of race and sex bias.[63] Their scholarship and teaching approaches are questioned by faculty, students, and administration.[64] Women of color in academia report episodes of microaggression and humiliation, personal struggles with their identity, and painful loss of self-confidence.[65] Diversity of faculty is essential to the recruitment of African Americans into health care.[66] African American physicians are less satisfied with their medical school and its social environment, medical career, professional and research activities, and achievements than white physicians.[67]

Educational Pipeline

In addition to maintaining the current African American health-care workforce, it is important to increase the enrollment and graduation rates of African American students in the health-care professions.[68] In 2013, African Americans accounted for 9.6 percent of students entering the nursing baccalaureate programs, which is slightly down from the 2013 entry rate of 10.9 percent.[69] The low rate of admissions is also mirrored in other health-care professions. Nursing schools have a larger number of underrepresented minority students than any other health-care profession.

Historically Black Colleges and Universities (HBCUs) have played an important role in increasing the diversity of the workforce; however, these colleges are small and are admitting an increasing number of white students.[70] HBCUs have provided education for nurses, baccalaureate education for physicians and dentist, and other allied health professions.[71] To meet the future needs of the African American population will require that African American students also attend predominantly white institutions. The recruitment and graduation of a diverse student population will require a culture that is conducive to change and the implementation of diversity initiatives.[72] To meet these goals will require commitment from the leadership and a formal commitment to cultural competence, diversity, and reducing health disparities.

African American students' experiences in predominantly white institutions mirror that of African American faculty. African American nursing students report feelings of being treated differently in classrooms and being marginalized, and feeling that the institution supported the culture of racism by ignoring or denying that it existed.[73] Minority students also report feeling that they had to prove themselves against the negative stereotypes while attending class or clinical practice experience, which leads them to feeling lonely and depressed.[74] African American nursing students report feelings of being treated differently in classrooms and being marginalized, and feeling that the institution supported the culture of racism by ignoring or denying that it existed.[75]

Racism and the African American Health-Care Workforce

Researchers have argued that racism is the main cause of health-care workforce disparities.[77] Racism is not limited to individuals, but can also be a system of structures, policies, practices, ideologies, and customs that generate or perpetuate unduly disparate patterns of exclusion and unequal treatment based on race or ethnicity.[78] According to the Sullivan Commission Report: Missing Persons: Minorities in the Health Professions describe acts of racism in health care in the following ways:

- whenever one race or ethnic group neglects to share system governance or institutional power with certain other groups;
- whenever opportunities and resources for health professions education, training, or practice unduly favor a certain racial or ethnic group;
- whenever opportunities and resources for faculty appointment, leadership, and research unduly favor a certain racial or ethnic group;
- whenever health-care providers unduly deliver diagnostic and treatment services disparately to certain racial and ethnic groups;
- whenever health-care institutions or health professions schools maintain unresponsive and inflexible policies, procedures, and practices that perpetuate the exclusion of certain racial and ethnic groups from health-care education or practice; and
- whenever health-care institutions or health professions schools impose ethnocentric culture on any other race or ethnic group to that group's detriment.[79]

Several organizations and groups have worked to improve the access of African American students to health-care professions; however, less attention has been focused on institutional barriers and policies that African Americans confront as they attempt to enter the health profession. Typically issues of racism and discrimination in health-care are examined as individual acts.[80] However, there are three levels of racism encountered in health-care systems: institutional, personally mediated, and internalized.[81] Institutional racism in health-care is defined "as that system of structures, policies, practices, and customs that together result in health care disparities or unduly constricted access to health care professions education and the health care careers for racial and ethnic minorities."[82] It leads to inequity in health-care professions and health-care delivery. This form of racism can be intentional or unintentional.

Personally mediated racism in health care is based on stereotypes, prejudice, and bias. This form of racism can occur in a variety of encounters in health care: faculty-student, student-student, faculty-faculty, patient-provider, and coworker-coworker. Personally mediated racism may manifest as disrespect and failure to communicate options. Personally mediated racism can be intentional or unintentional. Internalized racism occurs when the person believes the perceptions of others. The perceptions are based on negative messages about their abilities, potential and their worth as an individual. These negative messages can be communicated by health-care coworkers, faculty, peers, media, and/or parents.

There is no consensus on how to measure racism in health care.[83] Most researchers use self-perceived measures. Critics suggest that this method has disadvantages because perceived acts of racism may be misinterpreted. However, these perceptions are the individual's reflections on the interaction and are important to consider when examining the effects of discrimination on health. African Americans who were born prior to desegregation, health-care encounter experiences may be shaped within the context of their historical health-care experiences.

Experiences of racism and discrimination leads to chronic stress and this chronic stress may affect health.[84] Chronic exposures to racism and discrimination among African Americans are associated with coronary artery calcification and elevated C-reactive protein.[85] C-reactive protein, a marker of systemic inflammation, is a precursor to cardiovascular disease and is linked to poor cardiovascular health outcomes and depression. Studies have shown that C-reactive protein in consistently higher in African Americans than whites. Chronic discrimination leads to high-blood pressure, increased carotid intima media thickness.[86] Carotid intima media thickness is a marker of atherosclerosis, a precursor of coronary artery disease and/or stroke.

Racism in health care has undergone a transformation and is manifested in a more disguised and covert way. The Sullivan Commission report indicates that racism and discrimination must be recognized, because today's racism is more subtle. Subtle racism can manifest itself in many forms. A subtle form of racism that is receiving increased attention is the concept of racial microaggression.[87] Racial microaggressions are "brief and commonplace daily verbal, behavioral, or environmental indignities, whether intentional or unintentional, that communicate hostile, derogatory, or negative racial slights and insults toward people of color."[88] Some argue that racial microaggressions have a greater impact on racial anger, frustration, and self-esteem than overt racism.[89] Racial microaggressions contribute to cumulative stress.[90] When the microaggression is directed toward an employee by a supervisor, the effects are more damaging, particularly if it's a racial/ethnic minority.[91]

According to the concept, most people have unconscious biases and prejudices that may be expressed in their interactions. These unconscious biases are most often intergenerational and based on insidious stereotypes and fears taught during childhood that continue throughout life—social conditioning. Health-care providers must be aware of their personal bias. Researchers agree that invisible racism needs to be made visible, particularly in health care.

The American Public Health Association suggests that aggressive methods need to be undertaken to reduce disparities in the health-care workforce. Several initiatives and strategies have been implemented to support the recruitment of minority students. For example, the Association of American Medical Colleges (AAMC) implemented a project in 1990 called the 3000 by 2000, aimed at increasing the annual enrollment of underrepresented minority medical students to 3000 by the year 2000.[92] The project was successful in increasing enrollment, but did not meet its goal.

Where Do We Go from Here?

The current shift in demographics, coupled with the ongoing disparities in health care and health outcomes, will warrant our ongoing attention and action. As within all health professions, concerted efforts are needed to diversify the nation's health-care workforce. It is imperative that we find ways to develop and maintain ethnic minority populations in the health-care workforce. One of the debates in public health is how to address health inequalities and inequities. The reduction and/or elimination of health-care disparities will require efforts to address avoidable inequities, historical racism, and contemporary injustice (subconscious bias, health inequality). To do this, we must raise awareness of health-care workforce disparities and the continual widening of the health disparities gap in specified areas through national and local educational campaigns. It is important to include all racial/ethnic groups in the conversations because not only are some racial/ethnic groups not aware of the issues around health disparities, some African Americans are not aware of the health disparities. For example, Benz and colleagues reported that only 59 percent of Americas were aware of health disparities experienced by African Americans and Latinos.[93] Awareness of health disparities only increased by 4 percent from 1999 to 2010 (59 percent versus 55 percent).[94] When disaggregated by race,

89 percent of African Americans were aware of health disparities between African Americans compared to 55 percent of whites. Most perplexing was the low level of awareness of health disparities seen in African Americans as relates to common specific diseases such as diabetes and hypertension (37 percent and 44 percent, respectively). Not only is it important to educate the public about health disparities, it is also important to educate the public about disease prevention, risk reduction, health promotion, treatment, and management of disease. By increasing the public awareness of health disparities and educating them on self-management of disease (e.g., medications, screening exams), it is anticipated that it will lead to support for interventions to reduce disparities.

Health-care providers must also be educated about health-care disparities, including race/ethnicity, socioeconomic status, and historical racism. In addition to education about health disparities, it is important that health-care providers are educated regarding cultural competence/sensitivity. Health-care providers must be aware that their behavior and clinical decisions along with health system–related factors (e.g., lack of access and/or availability of services, gaps in care related to health insurance, prior experiences of racism) are often associated with a negative history. These barriers will need to be overcome with an attempt to work in partnership with patients and their families. The perspective of patients and the perspectives of health-care providers are often different. For physicians, it is a disease with physiological disturbances that is understood and treated using a biomedical model.[95] For patients, it is personal and individual. At the core of cultural competence for health-care providers should be the notion of justice: "to treat all patients as individuals—with all the emotional, experiential, cultural richness and depth that comprises an individual's identity—with fairness and compassion.[96]

To address health disparities, there must be an increase in the diversity of health-care providers at all levels. To increase the number of minorities in health care will require an evaluation of methods that colleges and universities have used for recruitment and retention to determine which methods are most effective. One strategy may be an alliance between minority and majority colleges/universities. Alliances between universities will be beneficial for faculty and students at both institutions. In addition to recruiting minorities into health professions, there is a need to support long-term career trajectories through career development. Many minorities are often the first in their family to enter the health-care field, so they have no reference point as to what should be done as far as career development goes. This brings to mind a discussion that I had with a student several years ago. The student pointed out that when African Americans attend majority universities, they are often the first in the family or the only African American student in their class. Whereas, white students often are able to obtain previous exams, papers, and other documents from prior students, African American students are not able to obtain these documents, because very few African American students have gone on before them. Another student said, "I wasn't embraced as a minority . . . if they do reach out to the minorities it's one or two minorities and that's all that's in the program, and we're done with that." Minority students also place a high value on mentorship. One student commented, "as an African American male nursing student, we are limited, as to that culture, we are limited to resources, and role models are a great part of some of our lives especially in some of that culture. If you've got a blue print of a mentor or someone that has already accomplished that, that will give you a better pathway to get there but I think role models play a really big part in life." This statement was made during a focus group that examined why minorities did not seek specific advanced degrees in nursing.

Systems Approach

To address the inequalities and inequities in health care will require a systems approach. This includes hospital associations, community members, health-care providers, stakeholders, politicians, and policy makers. Some of the existing policies that influence access and outcomes in minority and underserved populations need to be examined with input from stakeholders. To improve the inequity and inequality in health care of families and communities will require more than addressing their present illness or the outcome of their health risk. It must include issues around the social determinants of health, such as premature death, the underlying causes of illness, and disability.

Health and health-care outcomes are related to multiple interacting factors; therefore, it requires a systems approach. It is important that the approach include the community because this will allow input from the community and improve the problem-solving capacity of the community, its skills and assets, and ensure that the community is actively engaged in reducing health disparities. We know that these communities have deficits; however, the conversation must start with the identification of the assets, skills, and capacity of the community.

This process will include assets mapping, building relationships, mobilizing for economic development and convening the community to develop a vision and plan, and leveraging outside resources to support locally driven development. Inclusion of the community will support the ideals of the IOM report.

Communities and community organizations can be vital contributors to the resources and capacity of a public health system. A community's right to self-determination, its knowledge of local needs and circumstances and its human, social, and cultural assets, including the linkages among individuals, businesses, congregations, civic groups, schools, and innumerable others, are all important motivations for community health action. In cases in which community health promotion and protection activities are initiated by a health department or an organization, engaging the community is a primary responsibility. Realizing the vision of healthy people in healthy communities is possible only if the community, in its full cultural, social, and economic diversity, is an authentic partner in changing the conditions for health.[97]

The conversation should also include the determination of strategies to reduce health disparities. The current most effective method to reduce health disparities is to address multiple determinants of health. Interventions must be based on adherence to established evidence-based guidelines when providing care for all patients. Further research is needed to identify sources of health disparities and to develop interventions. The impact of interventions to reduce health disparities must be measured and monitored. This includes monitoring progress toward benchmarks and identification of best practices for data collection.

Notes

1. Robin Erb, "Nurse Sues, Says Hospital Backs Dad's Request that No Blacks Treat His

Newborn," *Detroit Free Press*, February 19, 2013, accessed December 12, 2014, http://archive.freep.com/article/20130219/NEWS06/302190075/Nurse-sues-says-hospital-backs-dad-s-request-that-no-blacks-treat-his-newborn.

2. Ibid.

3. Christina Ng, "Georgia Company Sued for Alleged Nurse Discrimination," *ABC News*, accessed September 1, 2013, http://abcnews.go.com/blogs/headlines/2011/11/georgia-company-sued-for-alleged-nurse-discrimination/.

4. Prichard O. "Three Workers Sue Abington Hospital over Racist Incident: Supervisors Obliged a 2003 Demand for Only White Staff in a Delivery," *Philadelphia Inquirer*, accessed December 12, 2014, http://articles.philly.com/2005-09-16/news/25429798_1_nursing-racial-slur-obstetrical-resident.

5. Polycarp Ikuenobe, “Conceptualizing Racism and Its Subtle Forms,” *Journal for the Theory of Social Behaviour* 41, no. 2 (2011): 161–181.

6. Lawrence D. Bobo, “Racial Attitudes and Relations at the Close of the Twentieth Century,” in *America Becoming: Racial Trends and Their Consequences*, eds. Neil J. Smelser, William Julius Wilson, and Faith Mitchell (Washington, DC: National Academy Press, 2001), 264–301.

7. Ikuenobe, “Conceptualizing Racism”; Rodney D. Coates, “Covert Racism in the USA and Globally,” *Sociology Compass* 2, no. 1 (2008): 208–231.

8. American Psychological Association, “Dual Pathways to a Better America: Preventing Discrimination and Promoting Piversity,” American Psychological Association, http://www.apa.org/pubs/info/reports/promoting-diversity.aspx; Helen A. Neville et al., “Color-blind Racial Ideology: Theory, Training, and Measurement Implications in Psychology,” *American Psychologist* 68, no. 6 (2013): 455-466.

9. Jordan J. Cohen, Barbara A. Gabriel, and Charles Terrell, “The Case for Diversity in the Health Care Workforce,” *Health Affairs* 21, no. 5 (2002): 90–102.

10. Institute of Medicine, *In the Nation’s Compelling Interest: Ensuring Diversity in the Health Care Workforce* (Washington, DC, 2004).

11. Ibid.

12. M. Michelle Rowe, and Holly Sherlock, “Stress and Verbal Abuse in Nursing: Do Burned Out Nurses Eat Their Young?” *Journal of Nursing Management* 13, no. 3 (2005): 242–248.

13. Deborah, D. May, and Laurie M. Brubbs, “The Extent, Nature, and Precipitating Factors of Nurse Assault among Three Groups of Registered Nurses in a Regional Medical Center,” *Journal of Emergency Nursing* 28, no. 1 (2002): 11–17.

14. Erin D. Maughan, and Beth M. Barrows, “The ‘3 Ds’ of School Nursing: Diversity, Determinants, and Disparities,” *NASN School Nurse* 28, no. 3 (2013): 156–160.

15. The Sullivan Commission, *Missing Persons: Minorities in the Health Professions* (Atlanta, GA, 2004).

16. Abraham Flexner, *Medical Education in the United States and Canada: A Report to the Carnegie Foundation for the Advancement of Teaching* (New York, NY, 1910).

17. Ibid; W. Michael Byrd, and Linda A. Clayton, “Race, Medicine, and Health Care in the United States: A Historical Survey,” *Journal of the National Medical Association* 93, no. 3 (2001): 11S–34S.

18. Louis W. Sullivan, and Ilana Suez Mittman, “The State of Diversity in the Health Professions: A Century after Flexner,” *Academic Medicine: Journal of the Association of American Medical Colleges* 85, no. 2 (2010): 246–253.

19. Darlene Clark Hine, “The Ethel Jones Report: Black Women in the Nursing Profession, 1925,” *The Journal of Negro History* 67, no. 3 (1982): 212–228.

20. Ibid.

21. National Association of Colored Graduate Nurses, *National Association of Colored Graduate Nurses Records,* Culture SCfRiB, New York Public Library, 1951; National Medical Association, *History: The Founders Early Years Later Years Recent and Current Years*, accessed November 8, 2013, http://www.nmanet.org/index.php?option=com_content&view=article&id=3&Itemid=4.

22. American Medical Association.

23. Robert B. Baker, Harriet A. Washington, Ololade Olakanmi, et al., "African American Physicians and Organized Medicine, 1846–1968: Origins of a Racial Divide," *The Journal of the American Medican Association* 300, no. 3 (2008): 306–313.

24. CNN. "AMA Apologizes for Racially Biased Policies," *CNN.com Health*, accessed December 12, 2014, http://edition.cnn.com/2008/HEALTH/07/10/ama.racism/index.html.

25. The Sullivan Commission, "Missing Persons: Minorities in the Health Professions," *A Report of the Sullivan Commission on Diversity in the Healthcare Workforce* (Kellogg Foundation, 2004).

26. U.S. Department of Commerce, *The Emerging Minority Marketplace* (Washington, DC, 1999).

27. J. M. Phillips, and B. Malone, "Increasing Racial/Ethnic Diversity in Nursing to Reduce Health Disparities and Achieve Health Equity," *Public Health Reports* 129, no. 2 (2014): 45–50.

28. Institute of Medicine, *In the Nation's Compelling Interest*; The Sullivan Commission; Association of American Medical Colleges, *Diversity in the Physician Workforce: Facts and Figures 2010* (Washington, DC, 2010); Institute of Medicine, *Unequal Treatment: Confronting Racial and Ethnic Disparities in Healthcare* (Washington, DC: National Academies Press, 2003); American Association of Colleges of Nursing, *Enhancing Diversity in the Workforce. 2014*, accessed October 1, 2014, http://www.aacn.nche.edu/media-relations/fact-sheets/enhancing-diversity.

29. The Sullivan Commission.

30. Health Resources and Services Administration, *The U.S. Health Workforce Chartbook—Part IV*, accessed September 30, 2014, http://bhpr.hrsa.gov/healthworkforce/supplydemand/usworkforce/chartbook/chartbook-part4.pdf.

31. Association of American Medical Colleges, *Diversity in the Physician Workforce*; Association of American Medical Colleges, *Striving Toward Excellence: Diversity in Medical Education* (Washington, DC, 2009).

32. Association of American Medical Colleges, *Diversity in the Physician Workforce.*

33. American Association of Colleges of Nursing, *Enhancing Diversity in the Workforce.*

34. American Association of Colleges of Nursing, *2013–2014 Enrollment*

and Graduations in Baccalaureate and Graduate Programs in Nursing (Washington, DC, 2014).

35. Institute of Medicine, *The Future of Nursing: Leading Change, Advancing Health* (Washington, DC, 2011).

36. Health Resources and Services Administration, Bureau of Health Professions, National Center for Health Workforce Analysis, *The U.S. Nursing Workforce: Trends in Supply and Education* (Washington, DC, 2013).

37. Institute of Medicine, *Allied Health Workforce and Services:Workshop Summary* (Washington, DC, 2011).

38. Association of Schools of Allied Health Professionals, *Allied Health Prosessions*, accessed Oct. 2, 2014, http://www.asahp.org/wp-content/uploads/2014/08/Health-Professions-Facts.pdf.

39. Kevin Grumbach, and Rosalia Mendoza, "Disparities in Human Resources: Addressing the Lack of Diversity in the Health Professions," *Health Affairs* 27, no. 2 (2008): 413–422.

40. Olivia Carter-Pokras, and Claudia Baquet, "What Is a Health Disparity?" *Public Health Reports* 117, no. 5 (2002): 426–434.

41. Institute of Medicine, *Unequal Treatment.*

42. Institute of Medicine, *In the Nation's Compelling Interest: Ensuring Diversity in the Health-Care Workforce* (Washington, DC, The National Academies Press, 2004).

43. Robert J. Blendon, Tami Buhr, Elaine F. Cassidy, Debra J. Perez, Tara Sussman, John, M. Benson, and Melssa J. Herrmann, "Disparities in Physician Care: Experiences and Perceptions of a Multi-ethnic America," *Health Affairs* 27, no. 2 (2008): 507–517.

44. Peter A. Clark, "Prejudice and the Medical Profession: Racism, Sometimes Overt, Sometimes Subtle, Continues to Plague U.S. Health Care," *Health Progress* 84, no. 5 (2003):12–23; Peter A. Clark, "Prejudice and the Medical Profession: A Five-year Update," *The Journal of Law, Medicine & Ethics* 37, no. 1 (2009): 118–133; G. C. Dennis, "Racism in Medicine: Planning for the Future," *Journal of the National Medical Association* 93, no. 3 (2001): 1S–5S; Megan-Jane Johnston, "Nurses Must Take a Stand Against Racism in Health Care," *International Nursing Review* 53, no. 3 (2006): 159–160; Thomas A. LaVeist, and Geraldine Pierre, "Integrating the 3Ds—Social Determinants, Health Disparities, and Health-Care Workforce Diversity," *Public Health Reports* 129, no. 2 (2014): 9–14.

45. W. Michael Byrd, "Race, Medicine, and Health Care in the United States"; W. Michael Byrd, and Linda Clayton, *An American Health Dilemma, Volume One: A Medical History of African Americans and the Problem of Race: Beginnings to 1900* (New York: Routledge, 2000).

46. Institute of Medicine, *Unequal Treatment.*

47. Michelle van Ryn, and Jane Burke, "The Effect of Patient Race and Socio-Economic Status on Physicians' Perceptions of Patients," *Social Science & Medicine* 50, no. 6 (2000): 813–828.

48. Institute of Medicine, *In the Nation's Compelling Interest.*

49. U.S. Department of Health and Human Services, Health Resources and Services Administration Bureau of Health Professions, *The Rationale for Diversity in the Health Professions: A Review of the Evidence* (Washington, DC, 2006).

50. LaVeist and Pierre.

51. Ibid.

52. Brian D. Smedley, Adrienne Stith Butler, and Lonnie R. Bristow, "In the Nation's Compelling Interest: Ensuring Diversity in the Health Care Workforce," ed. Institute of Medicine (Washington, DC, 2004); the Sullivan Commission, "Missing Persons: Minorities in the Health Professions: A Report of the Sullivan Commission on Diversity in the Healthcare Workforce," Kellogg Foundation, http://www.aacn.nche.edu/search-results?cx=004745212939755731071%3A9ffni8oukg8&cof=FORID%3A11&ie=UTF-8&q=sullivan+report&sa.x=14&sa.y=11&siteurl=www.aacn.nche.edu%2F&ref=&ss=3980j1188216j15.

53. The Sullivan Commission, "Missing Persons: Minorities in the Health Professions: A Report of the Sullivan Commission on Diversity in the Healthcare Workforce."

54. Rebecca Hagey, et al., "Immigrant Nurses' Experience of Racism," *Journal of Nursing Scholarship* 33, no. 4 (2001): 390.

55. D. Hassouneh, et al., "Exclusion and Control: Patterns Aimed at Limiting the Influence of Faculty of Color," *Journal of Nursing Education* 51, no. 6 (2012).

56. Cornelia P. Porter, and Evelyn Barbee, "Race and Racism in Nursing Research: Past, Present, and Future," *Annual Review of Nursing Research* 22 (2004): 9–37.

57. Mikiyung Ryu, *Minorities in Higher Education 2010: Twenty-Fourth Status Report* (Washington, DC: American Council on Education, 2010).

58. American Association of Colleges of Nursing, *Enhancing Diversity in the Workforce*; Marcella Nunez-Smith, Maria M. Ciarleglio, Terasa Sandoval-Schaefer, Johanna Elumn, Laura Castello-Page, Peter Peduzzi, and Elizabeth H. Bradley, "Institutional Variation in the Promotion of Racial/Ethnic Minority Faculty at US Medical Schools," *American Journal of Public Health* 102, no. 5 (2012): 852–858; Christin U. Liu, and Hershel Alexander, "Promotion Rates for First-Time Assistant and Associate Professors Appointed from 1967 to 1997," *AAMC Analysis in Brief* 9, no. 7 (2010): 2.

59. Peter T. Yu, Pouria V. Parsa, Omar Hassanein, Selwyn Rogers, David C. Chang, "Minorities Struggle to Advance in Academic Medicine: A 12-Year Review of Diversity at the Highest Levels of America's Teaching Institutions," *The Journal of Surgical Research* 182, no. 2 (2013): 212–218.

60. Donna K. Ginther, Walter T. Schaffer, Joshua Schnell, Beth Masimore, Faye Liu, Laurel L. Haak, and Raynard Kington, "Race, Ethnicity, and NIH Research Awards," *Science* 333, no. 6045 (2011):1015–1019.

61. Megan R. Mahoney, Elisabeth Wilson, Kara L. Odom, Loma Flowers, and Shelley R. Adler, "Minority Faculty Voices on Diversity in Academic

Medicine: Perspectives from One School," *Academic Medicine: Journal of the Association of American Medical Colleges* 83, no. 8 (2008): 781–786; Marcella Nunez-Smith, Leslie A. Curry, JudyAnn Bigby, David Berg, Harlan M. Krumholz, and Elizabeth H. Bradley, "Impact of Race on the Professional Lives of Physicians of African Descent," *Annals of Internal Medicine* 146, no. 1 (2007): 45–51; Neeraja B. Peterson, Robert H. Friedman, Arlene S. Ash, Shakira Franco, and Phyllis L. Carr, "Faculty Self-Reported Experience with Racial and Ethnic Discrimination in Academic Medicine," *Journal of Internal Medicine* 19, no. 3 (2004): 259–265; Eboni G. Price, Neil R. Powe, David E. Kern, Sherita Hill Golden, Gary S. Wand, and Lisa A. Cooper, "Improving the Diversity Climate in Academic Medicine: Faculty Perceptions as a Catalyst for Institutional Change," *Academic Medicine* 84, no. 1. (2009): 95–105.

62. Caroline Sotello Viernes Turner, Juan Carlos Gonzalez, and Kathleen Wong, "Faculty Women of Color: The Critical Nexus of Race and Gender," *Journal of Diversity in Higher Education* 4, no. 4 (2011): 199–211.

63. Caroline Sotello Viernes Turner, "Women of Color in Academe: Living with Multiple Marginality," *The Journal of Higher Education* 73, no. 1 (2002): 74–93; John H. Gartland, Mohammadreza Hojat, Edward B. Christian, Clara A. Callahan, and Thomas J. Nasca, "African American and White Physicians: A Comparison of Satisfaction with Medical Education, Professional Careers, and Research Activities," *Teaching and Learning in Medicine* 15, no. 2 (2003): 106–112.

64. George Yancy, and Maria del Guadalupe Davidson, *Race in Predominately White Classrooms: Scholars of Color Reflect* (New York, NY: Routledge, 2013).

65. Gabriella Gutierrez y Muhs, Yolanda Flores Niemann, Carmen G. Gonzalez, and Angela P. Harris, *Presumed Incompetent: The Intersections of Race and Class for Women in Academia* (Boulder, CO: University Press of Colorado; 2012).

66. Gartland, Hojat, Christian, Callahan, Nasca.

67. Ibid.

68. Billy Thomas, "Health and Health Care Disparities: The Effect of Social and Environmental Factors on Individual and Population Health," *International Journal of Environmental Research and Public Health* 11, no. 7 (2014): 7492–7507.

69. American Association of Colleges of Nursing, *2013–2014 Enrollment and Graduations*.

70. Sarah Butrymowicz S, "Historically Black Colleges Are Becoming More White," *Time*, accessed December 13, 2014, http://time.com/2907332/historically-black-colleges-increasingly-serve-white-students/.

71. Sullivan, and Suez Mittman.

72. Institute of Medicine, *In the Nation's Compelling Interest*; The Sullivan Commission. "Missing Persons."

73. Lilita Chappel Aiken, Ronald M. Cervero, and Juanita Johnson-Bailey,

"Black Women in Nursing Education Completion Programs: Issues Affecting Participation," *Adult Education Quarterly* 51, no. 4 (2001): 306–321.

74. Nancey France, Annazette Fields, and Kary Garth, "'You're Just Shoved to the Corner': The Lived Experience of Black Nursing Students Being Isolated and Discounted, A Pilot Study," *Journal of Rogerian Nursing Science* 12, no. 1 (2004): 28–36; Jannelle Gardner, "Barriers Influencing the Success of Racial and Ethnic Minority Students in Nursing Programs," *Journal of Transcultural Nursing* 16, no. 2 (2005): 155–162.

75. Aiken, Cervero, and Johnson-Bailey.

76. France, Fields, and Garth; Gardner.

77. Joe R. Feagin, and Karyn D. McKinney, *The Many Costs of Racism* (Lanham, MD: Rowman and Littlefield Publishers, 2005); Nancy Krieger, "The Ostrich, the Albatross, and Public Health: An Ecosocial Perspective—or Why an Explicit Focus on Health Consequences of Discrimination and Deprivation Is Vital for Good Science and Public Health Practice," *Public Health Reports* 116, no. 5 (2001): 419–423; James Y. Nazroo, "The Structuring of Ethnic Inequalities in Health: Economic Position, Racial Discrimination, and Racism," *American Journal of Public Health* 93, no. 2 (2003): 277–284.

78. The Sullivan Commission, *Missing Persons*.

79. Ibid., 40.

80. Feagin and McKinney.

81. Camera P. Jones, "Levels of Racism: A Theoretic Framework and a Gardener's Tale," *American Journal of Public Health* 90, no. 8 (2000): 1212–1215.

82. The Sullivan Commission, *Missing Persons*.

83. Nancy R. Kressin, Kristal L. Raymond, and Meredith Manze, "Perceptions of Race/Ethnicity-Based Discrimination: A Review of Measures and Evaluation of Their Usefulness for the Health Care Setting," *Journal of Health Care for the Poor and Underserved* 19, no. 3 (2008): 697–730.

84. Elliot M. Friedman, David R. Williams, Burton H. Singer, and Carol D. Ryff, "Chronic Discrimination Predicts Higher Circulating Levels of E-selectin in a National Sample: The MIDUS Study," *Brain, Behavior, and Immunity* 23, no. 5 (2009): 684–692.

85. Tene T. Lewis, Allison E. Aiello, Sue Leurgans, Jeremiah Kelly, and Lisa L. Barnes, "Self-reported Experiences of Everyday Discrimination are Associated with Elevated C-Reactive Protein Levels in Older African-American Adults," *Brain, Behavior, and Immunity* 24, no. 3 (2010): 438–443; Tene T .Lewis, Susan A. Everson-Rose, Lynda H. Powell, Karen A. Matthews, Charlotte Brown, Kelly Karavolos, Kim Sutton-Tyrrell, Elizabeth Jacobs, and Deidre Wesley, "Chronic Exposure to Everyday Discrimination and Coronary Artery Calcification in African-American Women: The SWAN Heart Study," *Psychosom Medicine* 68, no. 3 (2006): 362–368.

86. Maz Guyll, Karen A. Matthews, and Joyce T. Bromberger, "Discrimination and Unfair Treatment: Relationship to Cardiovascular Reactivity among African American and European American Women," *Health Psychology* 20, no. 5 (2001): 315–325; Wendy M. Troxel, Karen A. Matthews, Joyce T. Bromberger,

and Kim Sutton-Tyrrell, "Chronic Stress Burden, Discrimination, and Subclinical Carotid Artery Disease in African American and Caucasian Women," *Health Psychology* 22, no. 3 (2003): 300–309.

87. George C. Bond, "Racism in the Academy: Ideology, Practice, and Ambiguity," in *Racism in the Academy: The New Millinieum*, eds. Audrey Smedley, andJanis Faye Hutchinson (Arlington, VA: American Anthropological Association, 2012), 178.

88. Derald Wing Sue, Christina M. Capodilupo, Gina C. Torino, Jennifer M. Bucceri, Aisha M. B. Holder, Kevin L. Nadal, and Marta Esquilin, "Racial Microaggressions in Everyday Life: Implications for Clinical Practice," *American Psychologist* 62, no. 4 (2007): 271–286.

89. Daniel Solorzano, Miguel Soja, and Tara Yasso, "Critical Race Theory, Racial Microaggressions, and Campus Racial Climate: The Experiences of African American College Students," *Journal of Negro Education* 69, no. 1–2 (2000): 60–73.

90. Sue, Capodilupo, Torino, et al.; Derald Wing Sue, *Microagressions in Everyday Life: Race, Gender, and Sexual Orientation* (Hoboken, NJ: John Wiley & Sons, 2014); Derald Wing Sue, Annie I. Lin, Gina C. Torino, Christina M. Capodilupo, and David P. Rivera, "Racial Microaggressions and Difficult Dialogues on Race in the Classroom," *Cultural Diversity & Ethnic Minority Psychology* 15, no. 2 (2009): 183–190.

91. Sue, *Microaggressions in Everyday Life*.

92. Charles Terrell, and James Beaudreau, "3000 by 2000 and Beyond: Next Steps for Promoting Diversity in the Health Professions," *Journal of Dental Education* 67, no. 9 (2003): 1048–1052.

93. Jennifer K. Benz, Oscar Espinosa, Valerie Welsh, and Angela Fontes, "Awareness of Racial and Ethnic Health Disparities Has Improved Only Modestly Over a Decade," *Health Affairs* 30, no. 10 (2011): 1860–1867.

94. Ibid.

95. Arno K. Kumagai, "The Patient's Voice in Medical Education: The Family Centered Experience Program," *Virtual Mentor* 11, no. 3 (2009): 228–231.

96. Arno K. Kumagai, and Monica Lypson, "Beyond Cultural Competence: Critical Consciousness, Social Justice, and Multicultural Education," *Academic Medicine* 84, no. 6 (2009): 782–787.

97. Institute of Medicine, *Unequal Treatment*.

Bibliography

Agency for Healthcare Research and Quality. *National Healthcare Disparities Report 2012*. Rockville, MD, 2013.

Aiken, Lolita Chappel, Ronald M. Cervero, and Juanita Johnson-Bailey. "Black Women in Nursing Education Completion Programs: Issues Affecting Participation." *Adult Education Quarterly* 51 (2001): 306–321.

American Association of Colleges of Nursing. *2013–2014 Enrollment and*

Graduations in Baccalaureate and Graduate Programs in Nursing. Washington, DC, 2014.

———. *Enhancing Diversity in the Workforce*. Washington, DC, 2014.

American Medical Association. "AMA: Mission & Guiding Principles." *AMA*. Accessed February 11, 2014. http://www.ama-assn.org/ama/home.page?.

American Psychological Association. "Dual Pathways to a Better America: Preventing Discrimination and Promoting Diversity." American Psychological Association, http://www.apa.org/pubs/info/reports/promoting-diversity.aspx.

Association of American Medical Colleges. *Striving Toward Excellence: Diversity in Medical Education*. Washington, DC, 2009.

———. *Diversity in the Physician Workforce: Facts and Figures 2010*. Washington, DC, 2010.

American Nurses Association. "Code of Ethics for Nurses." *American Nurses Associtation*. Accessed February 11, 2014. http://nursingworld.org/MainMenuCategories/ThePracticeofProfessionalNursing/EthicsStandards/CodeofEthics.aspx.

Association of Schools of Allied Health Professionals. *Allied Health Professions*. Washington, DC: ASAHP, 2014.

Baker, Robert B., Harriet A. Washington, Ololade Olakanmi, Todd L. Savitt, Elizabeth A. Jacobs, Eddie Hoover, and Matthew K. Wynia. "African American Physicians and Organized Medicine, 1846–1968: Origins of a Racial Divide." *Journal of American Medical Association* 300, no. 3 (2008): 306–313.

Benz, Jennifer K., Oscar Espinosa, Valerie Welsh, and Angela Fontes. "Awareness of Racial and Ethnic Health Disparities Has Improved Only Modestly over a Decade." *Health Affairs* 30, no. 10 (Oct 2011): 1860–1867.

Blendon, Robert J., Tami Buhr, Elaine F. Cassidy, Debra J. Pérez, Tara Sussman, John M. Benson, and Melissa J. Herrmann. "Disparities in Physician Care: Experiences and Perceptions of a Multi-Ethnic America." *Health Affairs* 27, no 2 (2008): 507–517.

Bobo, Lawrence D. "Racial Attitudes and Relations at the Close of the Twentieth Century." In *America Becoming: Racial Trends and Their Consequences*. Edited by Neil J. Smelser, William Julius Nelson, and Faith Mitchell. Washington, DC: National Academy Press, 2001, 264–301.

Bond, George Clement. "Racism in the Academy: Ideology, Practice, and Ambiguity," In *Racism in the Academy: The New Millinieum*. Edited by Audrey Smedley, and Janice F. H. Hutchinson. Arlington, VA: American Anthropological Association, 2012.

Butrymowicz, Sarah. "Historically Black Colleges Are Becoming More White." *Time*: Accessed December 13, 2014. http://time.com/2907332/historically-black-colleges-increasingly-serve-white-students/.

Byrd, W. Michael, and Linda A. Clayton. *An American Health Dilemma, Volume One: A Medical History of African Americans and the Problem of Race: Beginnings to 1900.* New York: Routledge, 2000.

Byrd, W. Michael, and Linda A. Clayton. "Race, Medicine, and Health Care in the United States: A Historical Survey." *Journal of National Medical Association* 93, no. 3 (March 2001): 11S–34S.

Carter-Pokras, Oliva, and Claudia Baquet. "What Is a Health Disparity?" *Public Health Report* 117, no. 5 (2002): 426–434.

Centers for Disease Control and Prevention. 2014. *Black or African American Populations.* Accessed October 3, 2014. http://www.cdc.gov/minority-health/populations/remp/black.html.

Clark, Peter A. "Prejudice and the Medical Profession. Racism, Sometimes Overt, Sometimes Subtle, Continues to Plague U.S. Health Care." *Health Progress* 84 (2003): 12–23.

———. "Prejudice and the Medical Profession: A Five-Year Update." *Journal of Law, Medicicne & Ethics* 37 (2003): 118–133.

CNN. "AMA Apologizes for Racially Biased Policies." *Black in America 2*. Accessed December 12, 2014. http://www.cnn.com/2008/HEALTH/07/10/ama.racism/index.html?eref=bia_all.

Coates, Rodney D. "Covert Racism in the USA and Globally." *Sociology Compass* 2 (2008): 208–231.

Cohen, Jordan J., Barbara A. Gabriel, and Charles Terrell. "The Case for Diversity in the Health Care Workforce." *Health Affairs* 21, no. 5 (2002): 90–102.

Dennis, Gary C. "Racism in Medicine: Planning for the Future." *Journal of the National Medical Association* 93 (2001): 1S–5S.

Erb, Robin. "Nurse Sues, Says Hospital Backs Dad's Request That No Blacks Treat His Newborn." *Detroit Free Press*. Accessed February 12, 2014. http://archive.freep.com/article/20130219/NEWS06/302190075/Nurse-sues-says-hospital-backs-dad-s-request-that-no-blacks-treat-his-newborn.

Feagin, Joe R. and Karyn D. McKinney. *The Many Costs of Racism.* Lanham, MD: Rowman and Littlefield Publishers, 2005.

Flexner, Abraham. *Medical Education in the United States and Canada: A Report to the Carnegie Foundation for the Advancement of Teaching.* New York City, 1910.

France, Nancey, Annazette Fields, and Katy Garth. "You're Just Shoved to the Corner: The Lived Experience of Black Nursing Students Being Isolated and Discounted: A Pilot Study." *Journal of Rogerian Nursing Science* 12 (2004): 28–36.

Friedman, Elliot M., David R. Williams, Burton H. Singer, and Carol D. Ryff. "Chronic Discrimination Predicts Higher Circulating Levels of E-selectin in a National Sample: The MIDUS Study." *Brain, Behavior, and Immunity* 23 (2009): 684–692.

Gardner, Janelle. "Barriers Influencing the Success of Racial and Ethnic Minority Students in Nursing Programs." *Journal of Transcultural Nursing* 16 (2005): 155-162.

Gartland, John J., Mohammadreza Hojat, Edward B. Christian, Clara A. Callahan, and Thomas J. Nasca. "African American and White Physicians: A Comparison of Satisfaction with Medical Education, Professional Careers, and Research Activities." *Teaching and Learning in Medicine* 15 (2003): 106–112.

Ginther, Donna K., Walter T. Schaffer, Joshua Schnell, Beth Masimore, Faye Liu, Laurel L. Haak, and Raynard Kington. "Race, Ethnicity, and NIH Research Awards." *Science* 333 (2011): 1015–1019.

Grumbach, Kevin, and Rosalia Mendoza. "Disparities in Human Resources: Addressing the Lack of Diversity in the Health Professions." *Health Affairs* 27 (2008): 413–422.

Gutiérrez y Muhs, Gabriella, Yolanda F. Neimann, Carmen G. González, and Angela P. Harris. *Presumed Incompetent: The Intersections of Race and Class for Women in Academia*. Boulder, CO: University Press of Colorado. 2012.

Guyll, Max, Karen A. Matthews and Joyce T. Bromberger. "Discrimination and Unfair Treatment: Relationship to Cardiovascular Reactivity Among African American and European American Women." *Health Psychology* 20 (2001): 315–325.

Hagey, Rebecca, Ushi Choudhry, Sepali Guruge, Jane Turrittin, Enid Collins, and Ruth Lee. "Immigrant Nurses' Experience of Racism." *Journal of Nursing Scholarship* 33, no. 4 (2001): 389–394.

Hassouneh, Dena, Jen Akeroyd, Krisitin F. Lutz, and Ann K. Beckett. "Exclusion and Control: Patterns Aimed at Limiting the Influence of Faculty of Color." *Journal of Nursing Education* 51 (2012): 314–325.

Health Resources and Services Administration. *The U.S. Health Workforce Chartbook—Part IV.* Washington, DC: Department of Health and Human Services, 2013.

Health Resources and Services Administration, Bureau of Health Professions & National Center for Health Workforce Analysis. *The U.S. Nursing Workforce: Trends in Supply and Education,* 2013.

Hine, Darlene C. "The Ethel Jones Report: Black Women in the Nursing Profession." *Journal of Negro History* 67 (1982): 212–228.

Ikuenobe, Polycarp. "Conceptualizing Racism and Its Subtle Forms." *Journal for the Theory of Social Behaviour* 41 (2011): 161–181.

Institute of Medicine. *Unequal Treatment: Confronting Racial and Ethnic Disparities in Health Care*, Washington, DC: National Academies Press, 2003.

———. *In the Nation's Compelling Interest: Ensuring Diversity in the Health Care Workforce*. Washington, DC: The National Academies Press, 2004.

———. *Allied Health Workforce and Services: Workshop Summary*. Washington, DC: National Academies Press, 2011.

———. *How Far Have We Come in Reducing Health Disparities? Progress since 2000: Workshop Summary*. Washington, DC: National Academies Press, 2012.

———. *The Future of Nursing: Leading Change, Advancing Health*. Washington, DC: National Academies Press, 2011.

Institute of Medicine, Board on Health Sciences Policy, Committee on Institutional Policy-Level Strategies for Increasing the Diversity of the U.S. Healthcare Workforce. *In the Nation's Compelling Interest: Ensuring Diversity in the Health-Care Workforce*. Washington, DC: National Academies Press, 2004.

Johnstone, Megan-Jane. "Nurses Must Take a Stand Against Racism in Health Care." *International Nursing Review* 53 (2006): 159–160.

Jones, Camara P. "Levels of Racism: A Theoretic Framework and a Gardener's Tale." *American Journal of Public Health* 90 (2000): 1212–1215.

Krieger, Nancy. "The Ostrich, the Albatross, and Public Health: An Ecosocial Perspective—or Why an Explicit Focus on Health Consequences of Discrimination and Deprivation Is Vital for Good Science and Public Health Practice." *Public Health Reports* 116 (2000): 419–423.

Kumagai, Arno K. "The Patient's Voice in Medical Education: The Family Centered Experience Program." *Virtual Mentor* 11 (2009): 228–231.

Kumagai, Arno K., and Monica L. Lypson. "Beyond Cultural Competence: Critical Consciousness, Social Justice, and Multicultural Education." *Academic Medicine* 84, no. 6 (2009): 782–787.

LaVeist, Thomas, and Geradine Pierre. "Integrating the 3Ds—Social Determinants, Health Disparities, and Health-Care Workforce Diversity. *Public Health Reports* 129, no. 2 (2014): 9–14.

Lewis, Tené T., Susan A. Everson-Rose, Lynda H. Powell, Karen A. Matthews, Charlotte Brown, Kelly Karavolos, Kim Sutton-Tyrrell, Elizabeth Jacobs, and Deidre Wesley. "Chronic Exposure to Everyday Discrimination and Coronary Artery Calcification in African-American Women: The SWAN Heart Study." *Psychosomatic Medicine* 68 (2006): 362–368.

Lewis, Tené T., Allison E. Aiello, Sue Leurgans, Jeremiah, and Lisa L. Barnes. "Self-Reported Experiences of Everyday Discrimination Are Associated with Elevated C-Reactive Protein Levels in Older African-American Adults." *Brain, Behavior, and Immunity* 24 (2006): 438–443.

Liu, Christine Q., and Hershel Alexander. "Promotion Rates for First-Time Assistant and Associate Professors Appointed from 1967 to 1997." *AAMC Analysis in Brief*. Washington, DC: Association of American Medical Colleges, 2010.

Mahoney, Megan R., Elisabeth Wilson, Kara L. Odom, Loma. Flowers, and Shelley R. Adler. Minority Faculty Voices on Diversity in Academic

Medicine: Perspectives from One School. *Academic Medicine* 83 (2008): 781–786.

Maughan, Erin D., and Beth M. Barrows. 2013. "The "3 Ds" of School Nursing: Diversity, Determinants, and Disparities." *NASN School Nurse* 28 (2013):156–160.

May, Deborah D., and Laurie M. Grubbs. "The Extent, Nature, and Precipitating Factors of Nurse Assault Among Three Groups of Registered Nurses in a Regional Medical Center." *Journal of Emergency Nursing* 28 (2002): 11–17.

Michelle Rowe, M., and Holly Sherlock. "Stress and Verbal Abuse in Nursing: Do Burned Out Nurses Eat Their Young?" *Journal of Nursing Management* 13 (2005): 242–248.

National Association of Colored Graduate Nurses. *National Association of Colored Graduate Nurses Records*. Schomburg Center for Research in Black Culture. New York: New York Public Library, 1951.

National Medical Association. *History: The Founders Early Years Later Years Recent and Current Years*, 2013. Accessed November 8, 2013. http://www.nmanet.org/index.php?option=com_content&view=article&id=3&Itemid=4.

Nazroo, James V. "The Structuring of Ethnic Inequalities in Health: Economic Position, Racial Discrimination, and Racism. *American Journal of Public Health* 93 (2003): 277–284.

Neville, Helen A., Germine H. Awad, James E. Brooks, Michelle P. Flores, and Jamie Bluemel. "Color-Blind Racial Ideology: Theory, Training, and Measurement Implications in Psychology." *American Psychologist* 68, no. 6 (2013): 455–466.

Ng, Christinia. "Georgia Company Sued for Alleged Nurse Discrimination." *ABC News*. Accessed September 1, 2013. http://abcnews.go.com/blogs/headlines/2011/11/georgia-company-sued-for-alleged-nurse-discrimination/.

Nunez-Smith, Macella, Leslie A. Curry, JudyAnn Bigby, David Berg, Harlan M. Krumholz, and Elizabeth H. Bradley. "Impact of Race on the Professional Lives of Physicians of African Descent." *Annals of Internal Medicine* 146, no. 1 (2007): 45–51.

Nunez-Smith, Marcella, Maria M. Ciarleglio, Teresa Sandoval-Schaefer, Johanna Elumn, Laura Castillo-Page, Peter Peduzzi, and Elizabeth H. Bradley. "Institutional Variation in the Promotion of Racial/Ethnic Minority Faculty at US Medical Schools." *American Journal of Public Health* 102 (2012): 852–858.

Peterson, Neeraja B., Robert H. Friedman, Arlene S. Ash, Shakira Franco, and Phyllis L. Carr. "Faculty Self-Reported Experience with Racial and Ethnic Discrimination in Academic Medicine." *Journal of General Internal Medicine* 19 (2004): 259–265.

Phillips, Janice M., and Beverly Malone. "Increasing Racial/ethnic Diversity in Nursing to Reduce Health Disparities and Achieve Health Equity." *Public Health Reports* 129, no. 2, (2014): 45–50.

Porter, Cornelia P., and Evelyn Barbee. "Race and Racism in Nursing Research: Past, Present, and Future." *Annual Review of Nursing Research* 22 (2004): 9–37.

Price, Eboni G., Neil R. Powe, David E. Kern, Sheritta H. Golden, Gary S. Wand, and Lisa A. Cooper. "Improving the Diversity Climate in Academic Medicine: Faculty Perceptions as a Catalyst for Institutional Change." *Academic Medicine* 84 (2009): 95–105.

Prichard, Oliver. "Three Workers Sue Abington Hospital over Racist Incident Supervisors Obliged a 2003 Demand for Only White Staff in a Delivery: The Suits Follow a Federal Ruling." *Philadelphia Inquirer*. Accessed February 14, 2014. http://articles.philly.com/2005-09-16/news/25429798_1_nursing-racial-slur-obstetrical-resident.

Raymond, Kristal L. "Perceptions of Race/Ethnicity-Based Discrimination: A Review of Measures and Evaluation of Their Usefulness for the Health Care Setting." *Journal of Health Care for the Poor and Underserved* 19, no. 3 (2008): 697–730.

Rowe, M. Michelle, and Holly Sherlock, "Stress and Verbal Abuse in Nursing: Do Burned Out Nurses Eat Their Young?" *Journal of Nursing Management* 13, no. 3 (2005): 242–248.

Ryu, Mikyung. "American Council on Education." *Minorities in Higher Education 2010: Twenty-Fourth Status Report*, 2010.

Solorzano, Daniel. "Critical Race Theory, Racial Microaggressions, and Campus Racial Climate: The Experiences of African American College Students." *Journal of Negro Education* 69, no. 1/2 (2000): 60–73.

Sue, Derald W. *Microagressions in Everyday Life: Race, Gender, and Sexual Orientation*. Hoboken, NJ: John Wiley & Sons, 2014.

Sue, Derald W., Christina M. Capodilupo, Gina C. Torino, Jennifer M. Bucceri, Aisha M. Holder, Kevin L. Nadal, and Marta Esquilin. "Racial Microaggressions in Everyday Life: Implications for Clinical Practice." *American Psychologist* 62, no. 4 (2007): 271–286.

Sue, Derald W., Annie I. Lin, Gina C. Torino, Christinia M. Capodilupo, and David P. Rivera. "Racial Microaggressions and Difficult Dialogues on Race in the Classroom." *Cultural Diversity Ethnic Minority Psychology* 15 (2009): 183–190.

Sullivan, Louis W, and Ilana Suez Mittman. "The State of Diversity in the Health Professions a Century after Flexner." *Academic Medicine* 85 (2010): 246–253.

Terrell, Charles, and James Beaudreau. "3000 by 2000 and Beyond: Next Steps for Promoting Diversity in the Health Professions." *Journal of Dental Education* 67, no. 9 (2003): 1048–1052.

The Sullivan Commission. *Missing Persons: Minorities in the Health Professions*:

A Report of the Sullivan Commission on Diversity in the Healthcare Workforce. Kellogg Foundation, 2004.

Thomas, Billy. "Health and Health Care Disparities: The Effect of Social and Environmental Factors on Individual and Population Health." *International Journal of Environmental Research in Public Health* 11, no. 7 (2014): 7492–7507.

Troxel, Wendy M., Karen A. Matthews, Joyce T. Brombergerm, and Kim Sutton-Tyrrell. "Chronic Stress Burden, Discrimination, and Subclinical Carotid Artery Disease in African American and Caucasian Women." *Health Psychology* 22, no. 3 (2003): 300–309.

Turner, Caroline Sotello Viernes. "Women of Color in Academe: Living with Multiple Marginality." *Journal of Higher Education* 73 (2002): 74–93.

Turner, Caroline Sotello Viernes, Juan Carlos González, and Kathleen Wong. "Faculty Women of Color: The Critical Nexus of Race and Gender." *Journal of Diversity in Higher Education* 4 (2002): 199–211.

U.S. Department of Commerce. *The Emerging Minority Marketplace.* Washington, DC: U.S. Census Bureau, 1999.

U.S. Department of Health and Human Services and Health Resources and Services Administration Bureau of Health Professions. *The Rationale for Diversity in the Health Professions: A Review of the Evidence*, 2006.

van Ryn, Michelle, and Jane Burke. "The Effect of Patient Race and Socio-Economic Status on Physicians' Perceptions of Patients." *Social Science & Medicine* 50, no. 6 (2000): 813–828.

Yancy, George, and Maria del Guadalupe Davidson. *Exploring Race in Predominately White Classrooms: Scholars of Color Reflect.* New York: Routledge, 2013.

Yu, Peter T., Pouria V. Parsa, Omar Hassanein, Selwyn O. Rogers, and David C. Chang. "Minorities Struggle to Advance in Academic Medicine: A 12-Year Review of Diversity at the Highest Levels of America's Teaching Institutions." *Journal of Surgical Research* 182, no. 2 (2013): 212–218.

part 3

African American Youth

8

Sustained Inequality

African American Education in a "Postracial" Nation

Daniel R. Davis

> Education then, beyond all other devices of human origin, is a great equalizer of the conditions of men,—the balance wheel of the social machinery.
>
> —Horace Mann, "Horace Mann on Education and National Welfare: 1848"

Introduction

In 1870, five years after their emancipation from bondage, 80 percent of African Americans were illiterate compared to just 12 percent of whites. By 1940, despite their illiteracy rate decreasing to only 12 percent, African Americans were still six times more likely than whites to lack the ability to read and write.[1] After the landmark *Brown v. Board of Education* decision in 1954, which ended de jure segregation in United States' schools, African Americans continued to endure de facto segregation and educational inequalities that perpetuated the continuance of wide gaps in educational achievement. In his critically acclaimed work, *The Silent Majority,* Mathew Lassiter details the widespread change from legal segregation based on race, to a form of segregation, just as pronounced, under the guise of "suburban innocence" and "suburban exclusion" in the wake of the civil rights movement.[2] Beneath this veil of racist denial, African American students continued to suffer substandard and unequal education largely in inner-city urban communities compared to suburban whites mainly because of residential factors. These sentiments are largely shared by Douglas Massey and Nancy Denton in their heralded work *American Apartheid.* In it they similarly argue that segregation, particularly housing segregation, is the main cause of continued racial disparities in multiple categories of life, including poverty rates and educational quality.[3] Jonathan Kozol, in his influential book *Savage Inequalities*, which detailed the educational conditions of various school districts across the United States in the 1980s, spoke to this point:

> What startled me most—although it puzzles me that I was not prepared for this—was the remarkable segregation that persisted almost everywhere. Like most Americans, I knew that segregation was still common in the public schools, but I did not know how much it had intensified. The Supreme Court decision in *Brown v. Board of Education* 37 years ago, in which the court had found that segregated education was unconstitutional because it was "inherently unequal," did not seem to have changed very much for children in the schools I saw. . . .[4]

Further, in 1971, African American students, ages nine, thirteen, and seventeen scored 44, 39, and 52 points lower, respectively, than whites on reading assessments on a 0–500-point scale.[5] Sadly, discrepancies such as this were nearly duplicated in math and science assessments from the 1970s until present day.

This chapter focuses on the continued educational achievement gaps between African American or Black students and white students in the allegedly "postracial" United States. *Postracial* is a term used to define this mythical contemporary period in the United States, which has elevated above the archaic standard practices of discrimination and social stratification based on racial identifiers. This fictional historic epoch conveniently highlights the economic (Oprah Winfrey), occupational (Black Professionals), educational (Black Intelligentsia), and political (Barack Obama) advancements of people of color, and uses these sporadic progressions as skewed evidence that one's race will no longer stifle a person's access to the American Dream. Loosely estimated, this utopian era began at the dawn of the new millennium, validated itself in 2008 with the election of Barack Obama, and optimistically, it will last until the end of time.

In stark defiance of this postracial notion, this chapter examines the magnitude of the persisting educational inequalities confronting African American students in comparison to their white peers. These embarrassingly conspicuous deficits in educational achievement, access to quality teachers, academic resources, and socioeconomic status along racial lines cogently negate the assertion that race is no longer a significant American issue. Understandably, the entirety of this problem is far too vast and complex to respectfully examine within the confines of a single chapter, therefore, particular attention is given to the educational disparities in the northeastern region of the United States. As the statistics will show, virtually any region of the United States would suffice for the purpose of this chapter; however, the northeastern region is home to New York City, which hosts the highest concentration of African Americans in comparison to any other city. Further, the northeastern region is home to several other large African American school districts and populations in metropolises such as Philadelphia, Baltimore, and Washington, DC. Additionally, brief statistical illustrations of similar inequalities and fissures in educational achievement from the Midwestern, western, and southern United States are also presented.

National Trends

Nationally, in 2007, white students had average scores at least 26 points higher than African American students in each standardized test subject on a 0–500 scale.[6] In 2012, African American students at ages nine, thirteen, and seventeen years of age scored 23, 23, and 26 points lower, respectively, than their white counterparts on standardized reading assessments. Even more disheartening, despite significant increases in African Americans' assessment scores at each age level and moderate increases by white students, African Americans' 2012 reading assessment scores remained lower than white students' assessment scores in 1971. (See table 1.) This trend is true for mathematics as well. In 2012, African American students at each age level (9, 13, and 17) increased their math assessment scores at a higher rate than white students since 1973, yet they continued to score 25, 28, and 26 points lower than whites at ages nine, thirteen, and seventeen, respectively. Similar to their reading assessment scores, despite significant improvements over forty years, African American students' 2012 math assessment scores remained lower than whites' scores in 1973, except for nine-year-old children, whose assessment scores were only one point higher than whites' 1973 scores. (See table 2.)[7]

These statistics provide startling evidence that counters the narrative that the educational gap is closing. Yes, African Americans have clearly shown substantial growth in their academic performance over the last four decades, yet they remain over forty years behind their white counterparts. There must be a concerted effort from educators, policy makers, parents, and scholars to address this disconsolate truth.

Table 1. Reading Scores of Black and White Nine-, Thirteen-, and Seventeen-Year-Olds in 1971 and 2012[8]

Year	Black Age 9	White Age 9	Black Age 13	White Age 13	Black Age 17	White Age 17
1971	170	214	222	261	239	291
2012	206	229	247	270	269	295

Table 2. Mathematics Scores of Black and White Nine-, Thirteen-, and Seventeen–Year-Olds in 1973 and 2012[9]

Year	Black Age 9	White Age 9	Black Age 13	White Age 13	Black Age 17	White Age 17
1973	190	225	228	274	270	310
2012	226	252	264	293	288	314

Theories attempting to explain African Americans' struggles with education range from racist to historical. Bigoted notions such as those presented by the late Richard Herrnstein and Charles Murray in *The Bell Curve* argue that African Americans are genetically predisposed to lag whites in educational and occupational achievement.[10] Graziella Bertocchi and Arcangelo Dimico postulate that the present educational gap between whites and African Americans is a result of slavery. They conclude that "the contemporaneous degree of racial inequality in education is indeed affected by slavery through its effect on the level of the gap at the eve of World War Two."[11] Regardless of the explanation, the sad reality is that the educational systems of America continue to perpetuate privilege for white students and disadvantage for African American students.

The depth of the educational injustices suffered by African American students must be understood in a larger context than just the classroom. This idea was plainly stated by Gregory Lewis Bynum, who powerfully stated that the United States' unequal treatment of African Americans in education is more than just an educational, economic, and occupational detriment; it is a human rights violation. Bynum argued that:

> Sadly, as a nation the United States has not been able to answer "yes" to the question of whether African American students have been accorded the human right to education as defined by international human rights documents. Specifically at issue here are the statement in the Universal Declaration of Human Rights that education "shall promote understanding, tolerance, and friendship among all . . . racial . . . groups"; the statement in the International Covenant on Economic, Social, and Cultural Rights that education "shall be directed to the full development of the human personality and the sense of its dignity"; and the statement in the Convention on the Rights of the Child that the "education of the child shall be directed to . . . the development of respect for the child's . . . own cultural identity, language and values."[12]

It is more than a mere oversight to overlook or underacknowledge the existing inequalities in education between whites and African Americans—it is unequivocally criminal.

Nationally, African American students are enduring a myriad of factors that are hindering their academic success—including racism, low self-esteem, broken homes, a lack of culturally relevant curriculum, sub-par instruction, and perhaps most importantly, poverty. In 2010, more than twice as many Black children were living in poverty than white children. Specifically, although African Americans comprise only 12 percent of the United States population, 38 percent of Black children were living in poverty compared to only 17 percent of white children.[13] That same year, 37 percent of Black students were attending high poverty schools compared to only six percent of whites.[14] In 2009, 74 percent of Black students were eligible for free or reduced-priced lunch compared to only 29 percent of Whites.[15]

Unfortunately, there is a high correlation between schools with high levels of poverty and inadequate school resources, such as high-quality teachers, current textbooks, up-to-date technology, and general building upkeep. According to the United States Department of Education, in 2009, 40 percent of low-income schools received "less than their fair share" of state and federal funds. Tellingly, this reality exists despite the fact that it would only cost an average of 1 to 4 percent of each institution's total school-level expenditures to resolve this inequality.[16] Clearly, there is a nationwide inclination to accept low-income school's unequal access to resources. This is particularly consequential for African American students, since nearly four of every ten attends a high-poverty school. Black students are "less likely to have access to early education, highly effective teachers, tutors, and well stocked libraries."[17] This imbalanced allocation of funds unquestionably has a negative impact on these students' education due to many resulting factors, and perhaps most significantly, far too many African American students are receiving inadequate instruction from teachers at high-poverty schools.

Low-income students, particularly African American students, "often are taught by less-experienced teachers, as well as by teachers who received their degrees from less-competitive colleges."[18] Students in high-poverty schools are twice as likely as students in low-poverty schools to be taught by an "out-of-field" teacher. An out-of-field teacher is one who is teaching a subject without possessing a degree or certification in that area. "One in four core classes (25.1 percent) in high-poverty suburban schools has an out-of-field teacher compared with one in nine (10.6 percent) in low-poverty schools."[19] In 2008, 25 percent of secondary mathematics teachers at majority African American schools did not have a major or certification in mathematics compared to only 8 percent of mathematics teachers at majority white schools.[20] Perhaps these conditions, among a constellation of other factors, contribute to the increased likelihood that African Americans will drop out of high school in comparison to white students. Despite steadily decreasing high school drop-out rates for African Americans, in 2010, similar to twenty-five years ago, they remain over 50 percent more likely than whites to not finish secondary school in four years.

Some may argue that African Americans' lagging student achievement is solely caused by poverty and that race is simply a latent reality. This argument ignores the impact that negative preconceived notions by teachers, stereotyping, and low self-esteem has on students' academic achievement. The burden of being an African American student within an educational structure designed and executed by whites can become a "racial baggage" which "often takes the form of fear of reinforcing stereotypes" among other debilitating causalities.[21] Stanford University professor Claude Steele succinctly stated that societal pressures and racial stereotypes about African American students "dramatically depress standardized test scores" and cause "disidentification with school."[22] Dr. Steele utilizes the domain identification theory described as a theory that:

> begins with an assumption: that to sustain school success one must be identified with school achievement in the sense of its being a part

of one's self-definition, a personal identity to which one is self-evaluatively accountable. This accountability—that good self-feelings depend in some part on good achievement—translates into sustained achievement motivation. For such an identification to form, this reasoning continues, one must perceive good prospects in the domain, that is, that one has the interests, skills, resources, and opportunities to prosper there, as well as that one belongs there, in the sense of being accepted and valued in the domain.[23]

He continues to say that when discussing the perils of students regarding the education gap researchers must ask what "might frustrate their identification with all or certain aspects of school achievement?"[24] Considering the plethora of negative stereotypes attached to African Americans' temperament, intellectual capacity, work ethic, and youth culture, the domain identification theory identifies race as the key factor influencing the education gap between whites and African Americans. Adding credence to this position is the reality that 83 percent of primary and secondary school teachers are white and only 7 percent are African American.[25] Therefore, African American students are far more likely to have a white teacher than an African American teacher, which increases the possibility of suffering racial discrimination, cultural disharmony, and potential detachment from their "domain."

This theory was supported by an African American student from Oakland, California, during a 2011 CBS News story about the education gap; the student stated that he felt disenchantment with his school because "people always like have expectations of us that we don't have of ourselves like 'they aren't gonna live that long' and like all kids are outside always selling drugs and all that."[26] An East Coast youth empowerment group called "The Club" also has identified the value of students feeling connected and welcomed regarding their academic achievement. Program leaders focus on creating a safe and welcoming space for African American students to create separation from their usual educational environment plagued by "alienation" and "failure." The program believes that creating this type of "critical space increases self-esteem, maturity, and confidence allowing young people to find and pursue a positive purpose in schools."[27] This environment runs counter to the far too prevalent damaging school atmosphere disproportionately experienced by African American students. In North Carolina, researchers examined the attitudes of teachers and administrators at a 99 percent African American high school; they concluded that "school personnel overwhelmingly blamed students, their families, and their communities for the minority achievement gap. In short, the school was pervaded by a culture of defeat and hopelessness."[28]

The alarming statistics and discussions detailed above present a dismal outlook for the futures of many African American children, because there are direct correlations between educational achievement, school resources, teacher quality, and income level. Further, today's primary and secondary school students will be entering a far more global society than any preceding generation. Therefore, these students will be competing against educationally advanced fellow American citizens, foreign-born residents, and individuals from foreign countries all over the world. Globally, American students from the top 25 percent of affluent families ranked twenty-third against students from similar socioeconomic backgrounds among the thirty most developed nations.[29] This means that even America's most privileged students are resting in the 25th percentile of the worlds' most educated. Where then does this status place impoverished African American children who remain decades behind America's most advanced students?

Sadly, the occurrence of unequal treatment and below-average achievement by African American students is not concentrated in small pockets of the United States. The vast inequalities burdening African American students, and the resulting lag in achievement, are present in every region of the country. Amazingly, the incongruent achievement between white and Black students exists nationwide in a fairly consistent nature. Despite variations in other cultural norms based on region such as language, music, residential landscapes, and even food, the educational achievement gap between African Americans and whites remains startlingly consistent.

Gaps in Proficiency on State Assessments

Northeastern United States

Standardized state assessment tests and accompanying standardized college entry exams such as the SAT and ACT, are highly valued by governmental policy makers and higher-learning institutions. Since the No Child Left behind Act of 2002, which essentially decreased funding and resources to schools that failed to reach proficiency goals, students most desperately in need of extra resources and support receive just the opposite. This creates a self-fulfilling prophecy that "certain" students will invariably fail academically; far too often this hypothesis is directed toward African American students.

Nationally, African American students faired far worse on all

National Assessment of Educational Progress (NAEP) assessments than white students. Only 18 percent of Black fourth-grade students were proficient in reading compared to 46 percent of white students.[30] This trend holds true for eighth graders as well. A mere 17 percent of Black eighth graders were proficient in reading compared to 46 percent of whites. Sadly, mathematics assessments revealed similarly disheartening results. Only 18 percent of Black fourth graders were proficient in math compared to 54 percent of whites. Among eighth graders, only 14 percent of Black students were math proficient while 45 percent of whites reached proficiency. (See table 3.)[31]

Table 3. National Percentages of Black and White Fourth and Eighth Graders Who Reached Proficiency in Reading and Math

	4th Grade Reading	4th Grade Math	8th Grade Reading	8th Grade Math
Black	18	18	17	14
White	46	54	46	45

In 2012, in the 85 percent African American, Baltimore City School District, Black students, grades three through eight, were significantly less likely than whites to meet proficiency to advanced proficiency standards on Maryland School Assessments' (MSA) reading, science, and mathematics assessments, although they scored higher than national averages across subject and racial lines. (See table 4.) Specifically, eighth-grade African Americans were 39 percent less likely than whites to meet proficient standards in algebra, 28 percent less likely than whites to meet proficiency standards in English, and 50 percent less likely than whites to meet proficiency standards in biology. (See table 5.) Fifth-grade students, the only third-through seventh- grade-level tested, were 75 percent less likely than white students to meet proficiency standards in science.[32] By eighth grade, nearly two-thirds of Baltimore City Public Schools' African American population was not proficient in mathematics. (See table 6.) Each of these subject gaps is telling and in desperate need of further examination. Particularly, the proficiency margins in science, which illustrate the largest divide, are worthy of advanced inquiry.

Table 4. Percentage of Students Who Met Proficiency to Advanced Proficiency Standard on MSA Reading Assessments for Grades Three through Eight, Baltimore City School District (2012)[33]

Grade	3rd	4th	5th	6th	7th	8th
Black	63	71	72	65	65	61
White	81	80	84	80	82	76

*Percentages rounded to the nearest whole number.

Table 5. Percentage of Eighth-Grade Students Who Met Proficiency to Advanced Proficiency Standards on MSA Algebra, English, and Biology Assessments, Baltimore City School District (2012)

Subject	Algebra	English	Biology
Black	56	60	53
White	78	77	80

*Percentages rounded to the nearest whole number.

Table 6. Percentage of Students Who Met Proficiency to Advanced Proficiency Standard on MSA Mathematics Assessments for Grades Three through Eight, Baltimore City School District (2012)

Grade	3rd	4th	5th	6th	7th	8th
Black	66	74	63	55	43	35
White	83	90	79	76	67	56

*Percentages rounded to the nearest whole number.

Unfortunately, virtually every other major school district in the eastern United States is perpetuating these inequalities and presenting these startling gaps in educational achievement between African American and white students. In the state of New York—whose capital, New York City, is the most highly populated city in the United States and home to the highest concentration of African Americans in any metropolis—the achievement gap between African American and white students is upsetting. In 2012, on a 1-to-4 scale, in which 1 = below standard, 2 = meets basic standard, 3 = meets proficiency standard, and 4 = exceeds proficiency standard, white eighth-grade students were twice as likely to score a 3–4 in English on New York State Testing Program's (NYSTP) assessments. Similarly, in science and mathematics, white eighth-grade students scored 3–4 at a rate 75 percent higher than African American students.[34] On this statewide assessment, white students at every grade level (grades 3–8) met or exceeded proficiency standards in English, mathematics, and science at rates at least 50 percent higher than African Americans.[35] Despite scoring higher than the national averages in reading and math, this proficiency gap in New York is alarming. (See table 7.)

Table 7. Percentage of New York's Eight-Grade Students Who Met or Exceeded Proficiency Standards on New York State Testing Program (NYSTP) Assessments (2012)[36]

Subject	English	Science	Math
Black	30	48	41
White	63	85	71

In Philadelphia, Pennsylvania, the eastern regions second-most populous city, among students in grades three to eight and eleven combined, white students met or exceeded Pennsylvania's proficiency standards in reading and mathematics at a rate 62 percent higher than African Americans.[37] In Boston, Massachusetts, according to the 2012 Massachusetts Comprehensive Assessments Systems (MCAS) results, white third-grade students were twice as likely to meet the proficiency standard in English Language Arts as African American students. White fourth-grade students were over three times more likely to meet or exceed the proficiency standard in math in comparison to African American students. Among fifth graders, white students were over four times more likely than African American students to meet or exceed the proficiency standard in science and technology/engineering assessments, with only 9 percent of Black students reaching that goal.[38] Of all the daunting statistical evidence of African Americans' lag in academic achievement on the eastern section of the United States, perhaps the most disturbing and symbolic substantiation of America's educational deformity resides in the school district of the nation's capital.

The District of Columbia School District shamefully hosts some of the widest achievement gaps in educational proficiency in the United

States. In 2011, white elementary school students were two and a half times more likely to meet or exceed the proficiency standard in reading and nearly three times more likely to meet or exceed the proficiency standard in mathematics than African American students. (See table 8.) The DC Comprehensive Assessment System's goal was to have 73 percent of all elementary students meet or exceed the proficiency standard in reading and 70 percent to do so in mathematics; only 36 percent of African American students met or exceeded the proficiency standard in reading, and 33 percent met or exceeded the proficiency standard in mathematics. Frankly, much like virtually every other major city school district in the United States, the DC public schools failed their African American students miserably, despite reaching proficiency above national averages. That same year among secondary school students, whites were more than twice as likely to meet or exceed proficiency standards in reading and mathematics. For secondary school students, the district goal was to have 72 percent of students meet or exceed the proficiency standard in reading—only 38 percent of African Americans achieved this goal. In mathematics, the district goal was for 70 percent of students to meet or exceed the proficiency standard in mathematics—only 40 percent of African Americans accomplished this feat. (See table 9.)[39]

Table 8. Percentage of Elementary School Students Who Met or Exceeded Proficiency Standard in Reading and Math on the Washington, DC Comprehensive Assessment System (2011)[40]

Subject	Reading	Math
Black	36	33
White	90	89
*District goal	*73	*70

Table 9. Percentage of Secondary School Students Who Met or Exceeded the Proficiency Standard in Reading and Math on the Washington, DC Comprehensive Assessment System (2011)

Subject	Reading	Math
Black	38	40
White	87	89
*District goal	*72	*70

In sum, the aforementioned examples of northeastern state assessment achievement gaps are but a microcosm of a clear national pandemic. African American students are simply not achieving in school at nearly the same rate as their white counterparts. These wide and consequential gaps in assessment scores are duplicated in every region of the United States.

Nationwide Snapshots

Long heralded as one the worst and unequal school districts in the United States, Chicago Public Schools (CPS) possess some of the largest gaps in achievement in the country along racial lines. In 2012, African American students in all grade levels (3–8 and 11) were far less likely than whites to meet or exceed proficiency standards in each of the subjects tested via the Illinois Standard Achievement Test (ISAT)—reading, mathematics, science, and writing. Particularly, the proficiency gap among eleventh-grade students was the most pronounced.

In 2012, white eleventh graders were nearly three times more likely to meet or exceed proficiency standard in reading, more than three times more likely to meet or exceed proficiency standard in mathematics, and nearly four times more likely to meet or exceed proficiency standard in science than African American students. (See table 10.) In 2011, the most recent statistics reported, white eleventh graders were nearly three times more likely than African American students to meet or exceed the proficiency standard in writing.[41]

Table 10. Percentage of Chicago Public Schools (CPS) Students Who Met or Exceeded Proficiency Standard in Reading, Math, Science, and Writing on the 2012 Illinois Standard Achievement Test (ISAT)[42]

	Reading	Math	Science	Writing*
Black	23	20	17	25
White	65	63	65	70

*Percentages from (2011) ISAT.

Within St. Louis, Missouri's St. Louis City School District African American students are achieving proficiency at much lower rates than whites on the Missouri Assessment Program assessments.

Among eighth graders, whites are more than twice as likely as African Americans to meet or exceed proficiency standard in communication arts and math. (See table 11.) At this grade level, whites are nearly three times more likely than African Americans to meet or exceed proficiency standard in science. This subject illustrates the largest achievement gap in proficiency—a trend that that holds true throughout the United States.[43]

Table 11. Percentage of St. Louis City School District Eighth-Grade Students Who Met or Exceeded Proficiency Standard in Communication Arts, Math, and Science on the Missouri Assessment Program (MAP) (2012)[44]

	Communication Arts	Math	Science
Black	21	20	12
White	49	49	35

*Percentages rounded to the nearest whole number.

Two of the largest school districts in the southern United States, Houston Independent School District (Houston ISD) and Atlanta Public Schools, continued this trend of gaping holes in achievement between African American and white students on state assessments. In 2012, in Houston ISD, African American tenth graders were nearly three times more likely than whites to *not* meet the proficiency standard in language arts, three times more likely to *not* meet the proficiency standard in mathematics, and nearly four times more likely to *not* meet the proficiency standard in science on Texas's No Child Left Behind (NCLB) assessments. (See table 12.)[45] Among Atlanta Public School fourth graders in 2011, the achievement gaps on the Georgia Criterion-Referenced Competency Tests (CRCT) were perhaps the most awe striking in the United States. In English/Language Arts, African American students were astonishingly eleven times more likely to *not* meet the proficiency standard. In mathematics and science, African American students were nearly ten times more likely to *not* meet the proficiency standard. Most outrageously, African American students were over twelve times more likely to *not* meet the proficiency standard in social studies, and twenty-four times more likely to *not* meet the proficiency standard in reading. (See table 13.)[46]

Table 12 Percentage of Houston Independent School District (Houston ISD) Tenth-Grade Students Who Did Not Meet the Proficiency Standard in Language Arts, Math, and Science on the Texas No Child Left Behind (NCLB) assessments (2012)[47]

	Language Arts	Math	Science
Black	16	36	38
White	6	13	10

Table 13. Percentage of Atlanta Public School District Fourth-Grade Students Who DN Meet the Proficiency Standard in Language Arts, Math, Science, Social Studies, and Reading on the Georgia Criterion-Referenced Competency Tests (CRCT) (2011)[48]

	Language Arts	Math	Science	Reading	Social Studies
Black	22	39	39	24	37
White	2	4	4	1	3

California, the United States' most populous state, represents more blatant discrepancies in student achievement along racial lines. Particularly, the cities of Oakland and Los Angeles are clear examples of this disheartening reality. Like every other major city and school district discussed, African Americans are distressingly less likely to be proficient in every academic category than white students. Even without comparison to their white counterparts, the proficiency percentages for African American students in Oakland are alarming. In 2013, only 14 percent of Oakland Unified School District's African American sixth graders and 13 percent of its seventh graders reached the proficiency standard in mathematics. (See table 14.) Combined, approximately six out of every seven African American sixth and seventh graders did *not* meet the proficiency standard in math. Among this same specific subset, white students were more than four times more likely to meet the proficiency standard in mathematics. In science, only one out of five African American tenth graders met the proficiency standard. (See table 15.) White tenth graders were nearly four times more likely to meet the proficiency standard.[49]

In the Los Angeles Unified School District, although African Americans showed greater proficiency in virtually every subject and grade level than in Oakland, they still achieved at much lower rates than whites in every category. African American sixth and seventh graders in Los Angeles were more than twice as likely to meet the proficiency standard in math as their Oakland peers; yet, they remained less than half as likely as their white counterparts to meet the proficiency standard. Consistent with status quo, African American students in the Los Angeles Unified School District categorically met the proficiency standard at far lower rates than whites.[50]

Table 14. Percentage of Oakland Unified School District Sixth and Seventh Grade Students Who Met or Exceeded the Mathematics Proficiency Standard on California Standards Tests (2013)[51]

	Black	White
6th Grade	14	71
7th Grade	13	43

Table 15. Percentage of Oakland Unified School District Students Who Met or Exceeded the Science Proficiency Standard on California Standards Tests (2013)

	Black	White
5th Grade	30	84
8th Grade	36	82
10th Grade	20	76

Closing the Gap

"You cannot change racial inequality if you pretend that race isn't there."[52] This simplistically profound statement was made by Charles Payne during a 2005 speech about racism and inequalities in Chicago's school system. This statement spoke to the point that despite feelings of discomfort, before any theoretical discussions take place regarding the "eight hundred pound gorilla of race," concerned parties must fully respect and acknowledge this fundamental and basic principal—racism exists. The myth, and covertly racist, ideology of *color blindness* is a futile attempt by some to move beyond the race issue in education. As effectively noted by Lassiter, middle-class white Americans chose—and were heavily persuaded—to believe that "meritocratic individualism" *not* racism, was the reason for the glaring differences in neighborhood quality, economic status, and educational conditions along racial lines.[53] This dogma perpetuates Eurocentric cultural norms as the default mode of existence and ignores the values, traditions, and perspectives of other racial and ethnic groups. Therefore, educational institutions must not approach the lagging achievement of African Americans from this purview. Although it is imperative that one's race and culture be acknowledged, it is of paralleled importance that African American students are held to high standards equal to all other students.

Certainly, adjustments must be made in public policy, by school administrators, and by classroom teachers regarding race, but school districts must not adopt the practice of lowering expectations for African American students. "Pobrecito syndrome," a condition caused by sympathy for disadvantaged students that promotes leniency and lowered expectations in achievement is a dangerous reaction to the racial achievement gap.[54] For example, "The Florida Board of Education set the 2018 goal for reading at grade level at 90 percent for Asian students and 88 percent for white students, while expecting only 81 percent of Hispanic and 74 percent of African American students to do so. Similar goals were set for math."[55] Regardless of motivation—racist, sympathetic, or practical—policies such as this are harmful and misguided, and inevitably these initiatives will encumber these students' academic growth. Further, ingenuities such as this send the wrong message to all audiences. It tells African American students that they are not capable of keeping pace with other races and potentially wounds their self-esteem. To the majority population, these practices perpetuate the centuries-old bigoted belief that African American students are unable to perform intellectually at the same rate as other students. Rather, administrators, teachers, and district board members must make honest efforts to understand racial and cultural differences to guide pedagogical adjustments.

To ignore the value of cultural acknowledgment in the classroom is to also disregard the benefit white students' gain by consistently having their norms and behaviors encouraged and validated. As noted by social justice educator and writer Paul Kivel, concerning African American students educators must "understand and give credence to their experiences."[56] Precedent has been established to allow African American cultural traits to influence instructional practices. In Ann Arbor, Michigan, a 1979 court ruling "established the legitimacy of African American Language/"Black English" within a legal framework. . . ."[57] Thus, the often ridiculed verbal patterns and diction of African Americans has been legally accepted as a distinct language. Further, the Oakland Unified School District recognized African American Language or "Ebonics" as the primary language used by African American students, and mandated its use to facilitate English language instruction via the Oakland Ebonics Resolution in 1996.[58] In theory, this racial and cultural acknowledgment should have created an environment of understanding and acceptance for racial differences, while simultaneously providing educators with a knowledge base from which they can educate their students. Sadly, these precedents have not been duplicated throughout the United States, and these initiatives have not received spirited follow-up efforts. However, pedagogical adjustments based on cultural acknowledgment such as this are certainly what is needed and steps in the right direction.

There is also a desperate need for more Afrocentric curriculum for African American students. This curriculum will place African Americans' traditions, culture, history, and experiences at the center of the curriculum. As suggested by Professor Molefi Asante, Afrocentrism's most noted proponent, "by centering their students of color, teachers can reduce feelings of dislocation engendered by our society's predominately white self-esteem curriculums."[59] This effort will take strides toward diminishing the damage imposed in the previously discussed "domain identification theory."

Clearly, poverty and unequal distributions of school resources continue to prove detrimental to the educational achievement of African American students. As highlighted exceptionally well by Massey and Denton, residential segregation is perhaps the most significant factor regarding the Black/white achievement gap and quality of life along racial lines overall. In most cases, property taxes greatly influence the budgets of area schools. By default, schools located in more affluent neighborhoods will reap the benefits economically and inevitably academically. Conversely, schools located in poorer areas suffer from numerous inequalities, as aforementioned. There must be a collective outcry by parents and concerned residents to state and local officials for this blatantly unfair reality to be properly addressed.

Without governmental efforts, spearheaded by the municipality, to serve as an equalizer regarding school funding, this issue will not disappear. Tactics such as zoning and the eradication of bussing in some districts perpetuate these inequalities and must be confronted.

Lastly, the families of these underachieving students must accept responsibility for their children's education. There is no institutional, governmental, or economic substitution for parental involvement in a student's education. Despite hurdles related to racism, poverty, and school incompetence, parents and guardians must understand these challenges and execute plans to overcome them for the sake of their children.

Conclusion

This disease of gaping achievement gaps along racial lines is undoubtedly evidence of the insidious inequalities endured by African American students and the privilege bestowed on white students. In a national educational system outwardly dedicated to "college readiness," these realities are devastating. As they enter high school, African American students are beginning at a disadvantage. Additionally, as discussed, African American students are disproportionately more likely to attend high-poverty high schools, which have proven themselves ill equipped to restore such large deficits in proficiency. Today's job market is more competitive than at any other time in United States' history. There are more college graduates both employed and seeking employment than ever before, and more students are enrolled in college courses than in any previous generation. Any concerned party must ask him- or herself, "how are these students supposed to compete in such a competitive and increasingly educated society while boasting such humble credentials in key areas of academic measure?" The answer to such inquiry is indeed bleak, and at the very least desperately frustrating.

As noted in a 2013 article in *USA Today*, "Racial Wealth Gap Widening," "in the past 25 years, education has failed to be the great equalizer that many expected." In 2009, the median income for African American households was $32,584 compared to $51,861 for whites. It is reasonable to assume that the continuing gap in educational achievement between whites and African Americans may play a major role in this economic reality. This illustrates the importance of one's education regarding lifestyle and standard of living that further highlights the magnitude of the great injustice being served to African Americans. Across the United States, regardless of region, African American students are scoring far lower on state assessments and are far less likely to reach proficiency standards than white students in all subject areas. This unfortunate truth persists regardless of sex or grade level.

Numerous theories exist that attempt to identify and address the causal factors for the African American/white educational achievement gap. Among them, a common theme persists—race. It is clear that in addition to poverty, race and issues related to it—cultural irrelevancy, school resource inequities, student disidentification—are largely responsible for the embarrassing gaps in educational achievement between Blacks and whites.

Admittedly, there is no clear answer for such a complex and gargantuan problem. However, there are practical and justifiably ambitious efforts that can be executed to this end. There must be concerted efforts by school districts to include culturally relevant curriculum for African American students. Teachers must be educated about cultural sensitivity and understand that different is not "wrong." School, local, and state officials must recognize the inequalities perpetuated by allowing school resources to coincide with local property taxes and prohibit practices that dissuade parents from enrolling their children into the schools of their choice. Most importantly, parents and guardians must accept the challenges of our imperfect society and educational systems, and decide that their children will succeed—period.

Notes

1. "120 Years of Literacy," *National Assessment of Adult Literacy (NAAL), National Center for Education Statistics*, accessed August 13, 2013, http://nces.ed.gov/naal/lit_history.asp#educational.

2. Mathew Lassiter, *The Silent Majority: Suburban Politics in the Sunbelt South* (Princeton, NJ: Princeton University Press, 2007), 1.

3. Douglas S. Massey and Nancy A. Denton, *American Apartheid: Segregation and the Making of the Underclass* (Cambridge: Harvard University Press, 1993).

4. Jonathan Kozol, *Savage Inequalities: Children in America's Schools* (New York: Crown Publishers, 1991), 2–3.

5. "The Black White Achievement Gap: When Progress Stopped," *Educational Testing Service,* accessed August 13, 2013, http://www.ets.org/Media/Research/pdf/PICBWGAP.pdf.

6. A. Vanneman, L. Hamilton, Anderson J. Baldwin, and T. Rahman, "Achievement Gaps: How Black and White Students in Public Schools Perform in Mathematics and Reading on the National Assessment of Educational Progress," *National Center for Education Statistics, Institute of*

Education Sciences, U.S. Department of Education (2009), accessed August 7, 2013, http://nces.ed.gov/nationsreportcard/pdf/studies/2009455.pdf.

7. "NAEP 2012 Trends in Academic Progress: Reading 1971–2012 and Mathematics 1973–2012," *National Center for Education Statistics, United States Department of Education* (2012), accessed August 7, 2013, http://nces.ed.gov/nationsreportcard/subject/publications/main2012/pdf/2013456.pdf.

8. Ibid.

9. Ibid.

10. Richard J. Herrnstein and Charles Murray, *The Bell Curve: Intelligence and Class Structure in American Life* (New York: Free Press, 1994).

11. Graziella Bertocchi and Arcangelo Dimico, "The Evolution of the Racial Gap in Education and the Legacy of Slavery," *Institute for the Study of Labor* (2011), accessed August 12, 2013. https://www.econstor.eu/dspace/bitstream/10419/58925/1/697266613.pdf.

12. Gregory Lewis Bynum, "Kant's Conception of Respect and African American Education Rights," *Educational Theory* 61, no. 1 (2011): 17–40.

13. "Child Poverty in the United States 2009 and 2010: Selected Race Groups and Hispanic Origin," *U.S. Census Bureau* (2010), accessed August 6, 2013, http://www.census.gov/prod/2011pubs/acsbr10-05.pdf.

14. Aud, S., Hussar, W., Johnson, F., Kena, G., Roth, E., Manning, E., Wang, X., and Zhang, J., "The Condition of Education," *U.S. Department of Education, National Center for Education Statistics* (2012): NCES 2012-045, accessed August 3, 2013, http://nces.ed.gov/pubs2012/2012045.pdf.

15. Aud, S., Fox, M., and KewalRamani, A., "Status and Trends in the Education of Racial and Ethnic Groups," *U.S. Department of Education, National Center for Education Statistic* (2010): NCES 2010–2015, accessed August 3, 2013, http://www.air.org/files/AIR-NCESracial_stats__trends1.pdf.

16. "More Than 40% of Low-Income Schools Don't Get a Fair Share of State and Local Funds, Department of Education Research Finds," *United States Department of Education* (2010), accessed August 3, 2013, http://www.ed.gov/news/press-releases/more-40-low-income-schools-dont-get-fair-share-state-and-local-funds-department-.

17. "U.S. Education System is Failing Black Students," *YouTube*, accessed August 8, 2013, http://www.youtube.com/watch?v=i4dhGb3Q3hk.

18. Tara Béteille, Demetra Kalogrides, and Susanna Loeb, "Systematic Sorting: Teacher Characteristics and Class Assignments," *Sociology of Education* (2012), accessed August 6, 2013, http://cepa.stanford.edu/sites/default/files/Class%20Assignment%20Final%20Submitted%20Paper.pdf.

19. Sarah Almly and Christina Theokas, "Not Prepared for Class: High-Poverty Schools Continue to Have Fewer In-Field Teachers," *Education Trust* (2010), accessed August 5, 2010, http://www.edtrust.org/sites/edtrust.org/files/publications/files/Not%20Prepared%20for%20Class.pdf.

20. Aud, Fox, and KewalRamani.

21. Charles Payne, "Still Crazy after All These Years: Race in the Chicago

School System," presentation, University of Illinois at Chicago (UIC) College of Education, Chicago, Illinois, April 22, 2005.

22. Claude Steele, "A Threat in the Air: How Stereotypes Shape Intellectual Identity and Performance," *American Psychologist* 52, no. 6 (1997): 613–629.

23. Steele.

24. Ibid.

25. "Fast Facts," *National Center for Education Statistics* (2011), accessed August 7, 2013, http://nces.ed.gov/fastfacts/display.asp?id=28.

26. "Roses in the Concrete in the News—CBS 5 San Francisco," *YouTube*, accessed August 7, 2013, http://www.youtube.com/watch?v=R42ghux580U.

27. Gilberto Q. Conchas and James Diego Vigil, *Streetsmart Schoolsmart: Urban Poverty and the Education of Adolescent Boys* (New York: Teachers College Press, 2012), 79–80.

28. Marvin Lynn, Jennifer Nicole Bacon, Tommy L. Totten, Thurman L. Bridges, III, and Michael E. Jennings, "Examining Teachers' Beliefs about African American Male Students in a Low-Performing High School in an African American School District," *Teachers College Record* 112, no. 1 (2008): 289–330.

29. Michelle Rhee, "High Quality Education is the Best Tool to Fight Poverty," *YouTube*, accessed August 8, 2013, http://www.youtube.com/watch?v=PwzELBOC8nI.

30. Ibid.

31. Ibid.

32. "2013 Maryland Report Card: Baltimore City Assessment," *Maryland State Department of Education*, accessed August 9, 2013, http://www.msp.msde.state.md.us/Assessments.aspx?K=30AAAA.

33. Ibid.

34. "The New York State Report Card 2011-2012," *New York State Department of Education*, accessed August 9, 2013, https://reportcards.nysed.gov/statewide/2012statewideRC.pdf.

35. "2012 Population Estimates," *U.S. Census Bureau*, accessed August 9, 2013, http://factfinder2.census.gov/faces/tableservices/jsf/pages/productview.xhtml?src=bkmk; "The New York State Report Card 2011-2012."

36. Ibid.

37. "2012 Population Estimates"; "District Report Card: Philadelphia City 2011–2012," *Pennsylvania Department of Education*, accessed August 9, 2013, http://paayp.emetric.net/Content/reportcards/RC12D126515001.PDF.

38. "Massachusetts Comprehensive Assessment Systems Results of Spring 2012," *Boston Public Schools*, accessed August 10, 2013, http://www.bostonpublicschools.org/files/final_spring_2012_mcas_report_grades_3-8_and_10.pdf.

39. "2010-2011 LEA Report Card," *District of Columbia Public Schools*, accessed August 10, 2013, http://www.greatschools.org/catalog/pdf/dc-nclb/dc-nclb-lea-001.pdf.

40. Ibid.

41. "City of Chicago SD 299," *Illinois Interactive Report Card,* accessed August 16, 2013, http://iirc.niu.edu/District.aspx?source=Trends&source2=Achievement_Gap&districtID=15016299025&level=D.

42. Ibid.

43. "Achievement Level 4 Report: St. Louis School District," *Missouri Comprehensive Data System*, accessed August 16, 2013, http://mcds.dese.mo.gov/guidedinquiry/Achievement%20Level%20%204%20Levels/Achievement%20Level%204%20Report%20-%20Public.aspx?rp:DistrictCode=115115&rp:SchoolYear=2013&rp:SchoolYear=2012&rp:SchoolYear=2011&rp:SchoolYear=2010&rp:ContentArea=Mathematics.

44. "Ibid.

45. "Texas 2012 No Child Left Behind (NCLB) Report Card," *Texas Education Agency*, accessed Aug. 2, 2013, http://ritter.tea.state.tx.us/perfreport/nclb/2012/district.srch.html.

46. "2010-2011 Report Card," *Atlanta Public Schools*, accessed August 16, 2013, http://archives.gadoe.org/ReportingFW.aspx?PageReq=102&CountyId=761&T=1&FY=2011.

47. "Texas 2012 No Child Left Behind (NCLB) Report Card."

48. "2010–2011 Report Card."

49. "2013 California Standards Test Results," *California Department of Education Assessment and Accountability Division,* accessed August 16, 2013, http://star.cde.ca.gov/star2013/SearchPanel.aspx?lstTestYear=2013&lstTestType=C&lstCounty=01&lstDistrict=61259-000&lstSchool=&lstGroup=5&lstSubGroup=74.

50. "2013 California Standards Test Results," *California Department of Education Assessment and Accountability Division*, accessed August 16, 2013, http://star.cde.ca.gov/star2013/SearchPanel.aspx?lstTestYear=2013&lstTestType=C&lstCounty=19&lstDistrict=64733-000&lstSchool=&lstGroup=5&lstSubGroup=80.

51. "2013 California Standards Test Results," California Department of Education Assessment and Accountability Division, accessed August 16, 2013, http://star.cde.ca.gov/star2013/SearchPanel.aspx?lstTestYear=2013&lstTestType=C&lstCounty=01&lstDistrict=61259-000&lstSchool=&lstGroup=5&lstSubGroup=74.

52. Payne.

53. Lassiter.

54. Pedro Noguera, *The Trouble with Black Boys...And Other Reflections on Race, Equity, and the Future of Public Education* (San Francisco, CA: Jossey-Bass, 2008).

55. Esther Cepeda, "Lowering Bar for Minority Students the Wrong Approach," *Chicago Sun Times*, August 11, 2013.

56. Paul Kivel, "How White People Can Serve as Allies to People of Color

in the Struggle to End Racism," *White Privilege: Essential Readings on the Other Side of Racism,* 4th ed. (New York: Worth Publishers, 2012), 158.

57. C. W. Joiner, *Memorandum Opinion and Order,* 473 F. Supp. 1371E.D. Mich. 1979.

58. Geneva Smitherman, *Word from the Mother: Language and African Americans* (New York: Routledge, 2006), 12.

59. Molefi Asante, "Afrocentric Curriculum," accessed August 17, 2013, http://www.ascd.org/ASCD/pdf/journals/ed_lead/el_199112_asante.pdf.

Bibliography

"120 Years of Literacy." *National Assessment of Adult Literacy (NAAL), National Center for Education Statistics.* Accessed August 13, 2013. http://nces.ed.gov/naal/lit_history.asp#educational.

"2010–2011 LEA Report Card." *District of Columbia Public Schools.* Accessed August 10, 2013. http://www.greatschools.org/catalog/pdf/dc-nclb/dc-nclb-lea-001.pdf.

"2010–2011 Report Card." *Atlanta Public Schools.* Accessed August 16, 2013. http://archives.gadoe.org/ReportingFW.aspx?PageReq=102&CountyId=761&T=1&FY=2011.

"2012 Population Estimates." *U.S. Census Bureau.* Accessed August 9, 2013. http://factfinder2.census.gov/faces/tableservices/jsf/pages/productview.xhtml?src=bkmk.

"2013 California Standards Test Results." *California Department of Education Assessment and Accountability Division.* Accessed August 16, 2013. http://star.cde.ca.gov/star2013/SearchPanel.aspx?lstTestYear=2013&lstTestType=C&lstCounty=01&lstDistrict=61259-000&lstSchool=&lstGroup=5&lstSubGroup=74.

"2013 California Standards Test Results." *California Department of Education Assessment and Accountability Division.* Accessed August 16, 2013. http://star.cde.ca.gov/star2013/SearchPanel.aspx?lstTestYear=2013&lstTestType=C&lstCounty=19&lstDistrict=64733-000&lstSchool=&lstGroup=5&lstSubGroup=80.

"2013 Maryland Report Card: Baltimore City Assessment." *Maryland State Department of Education.* Accessed August 9, 2013. http://www.msp.msde.state.md.us/Assessments.aspx?K=30AAAA.

"Achievement Level 4 Report: St. Louis School District." *Missouri Comprehensive Data System.* Accessed August 16, 2013. http://mcds.dese.mo.gov/guidedinquiry/Achievement%20Level%20%204%20Levels/Achievement%20Level%204%20Report%20-%20Public.aspx?rp:DistrictCode=115115&rp:SchoolYear=2013&rp:SchoolYear=2012&rp:SchoolYear=2011&rp:SchoolYear=2010&rp:ContentArea=Mathematics.

Almly, Sarah, and Christina Theokas. "Not Prepared for Class: High-Poverty

Schools Continue to Have Fewer In-Field Teachers." *Education Trust* (2010). Accessed August 5, 2010, http://www.edtrust.org/sites/edtrust.org/files/publications/files/Not%20Prepared%20for%20Class.pdf.

Asante, Molefi. "Afrocentric Curriculum." Accessed August 17, 2013, http://www.ascd.org/ASCD/pdf/journals/ed_lead/el_199112_asante.pdf.

Aud, S., M. Fox, , and A. KewalRamani. "Status and Trends in the Education of Racial and Ethnic Groups." *U.S. Department of Education, National Center for Education Statistic* (2010): NCES 2010-015. Accessed August 3, 2013. http://www.air.org/files/AIR-NCESracial_stats__trends1.pdf.

Aud, S., W. Hussar, F. Johnson, G. Kena, E. Roth, E. Manning, X. Wang, and J. Zhang. "The Condition of Education." *U.S. Department of Education, National Center for Education Statistics* (2012): NCES 2012-045. Accessed August 3, 2013. http://nces.ed.gov/pubs2012/2012045.pdf.

Baldwin, Anderson J., J. Hamilton, T. Rahman, and A. Vanneman. "Achievement Gaps: How Black and White Students in Public Schools Perform in Mathematics and Reading on the National Assessment of Educational Progress." *National Center for Education Statistics, Institute of Education Sciences, U.S. Department of Education* (2009). Accessed August 7, 2013. http://nces.ed.gov/nationsreportcard/pdf/studies/2009455.pdf.

Bertocchi, Graziella, and Arcangelo Dimico. "The Evolution of the Racial Gap in Education and the Legacy of Slavery." *Institute for the Study of Labor* (2011). Accessed August 12, 2013. https://www.econstor.eu/dspace/bitstream/10419/58925/1/697266613.pdf.

Béteille, Tara, Demetra Kalogrides, and Susanna Loeb. "Systematic Sorting: Teacher Characteristics and Class Assignments." *Sociology of Education* (2013). Accessed August 6, 2013. http://cepa.stanford.edu/sites/default/files/Class%20Assignment%20Final%20Submitted%20Paper.pdf.

Bynum, Gregory Lewis. "Kant's Conception of Respect and African American Education Rights." *Educational Theory* 61, no. 1, (2011): 17–40.

Cepeda, Esther. "Lowering Bar for Minority Students the Wrong Approach." *Chicago Sun Times*. August 11, 2013.

"Child Poverty in the United States 2009 and 2010: Selected Race Groups and Hispanic Origin." *U.S. Census Bureau* (2010). Accessed August 6, 2013. http://www.census.gov/prod/2011pubs/acsbr10-05.pdf.

"City of Chicago SD 299." *Illinois Interactive Report Card*. Accessed August 16, 2013. http://iirc.niu.edu/District.aspx?source=Trends&source2=Achievement_Gap&districtID=15016299025&level=D.

Conchas, Gilberto Q., and James Diego Vigil. *Streetsmart Schoolsmart: Urban Poverty and the Education of Adolescent Boys*. New York: Teachers College Press, 2012.

Denton, Nancy A., and Douglas S. Massey. *American Apartheid: Segregation and the Making of the Underclass*. Cambridge: Harvard University Press, 1993.

"District Report Card: Philadelphia City 2011–2012." *Pennsylvania Department of Education*. Accessed August 9, 2013. http://paayp.emetric.net/Content/reportcards/RC12D126515001.PDF.

"Fast Facts." *National Center for Education Statistics* (2011). Accessed August 7, 2013. http://nces.ed.gov/fastfacts/display.asp?id=28.

Herrnstein, Richard J., and Charles Murray. *The Bell Curve: Intelligence and Class Structure in American Life*. New York: Free Press, 1994.

"Horace Mann on Education and National Welfare: 1848 (Twelfth Annual Report of Horace Mann as Secretary of Massachusetts State Board of Education)." Accessed August 13, 2013. http://www.tncrimlaw.com/civil_bible/horace_mann.htm.

Joiner, C. W. *Memorandum Opinion and Order* 473 F. Supp. 1371E.D. Mich. 1979.

Kivel, Paul. "How White People Can Serve as Allies to People of Color in the Struggle to End Racism." *White Privilege: Essential Readings on the Other Side of Racism*. New York: Worth Publishers, 2012.

Kozol, Jonathan. *Savage Inequalities: Children in America's Schools*. New York: Crown Publishers, 1991.

Lassiter, Mathew. *The Silent Majority: Suburban Politics in the Sunbelt South*. Princeton, NJ: Princeton University Press, 2007.

Lynn, Marvin, Jennifer Nicole Bacon, Tommy L. Totten, Thurman L. Bridges III, and Michael E. Jennings. "Examining Teachers' Beliefs about African American Male Students in a Low-Performing High School in an African American School District." *Teachers College Record* 112, no. 1, (2008): 289–330.

"Massachusetts Comprehensive Assessment Systems Results of Spring 2012." *Boston Public Schools*. Accessed August 10, 2013. http://www.bostonpublicschools.org/files/final_spring_2012_mcas_report_grades_3-8_and_10.pdf.

"More Than 40% of Low-Income Schools Don't Get a Fair Share of State and Local Funds, Department of Education Research Finds." *United States Department of Education* (2010). Accessed August 3, 2013. http://www.ed.gov/news/press-releases/more-40-low-income-schools-dont-get-fair-share-state-and-local-funds-department-.

"NAEP 2012 Trends in Academic Progress: Reading 1971–2012 and Mathematics 1973–2012." (2012). Accessed August 7, 2013. http://nces.ed.gov/nationsreportcard/subject/publications/main2012/pdf/2013456.pdf.

Noguera, Pedro. *The Trouble with Black Boys . . . And Other Reflections on Race, Equity, and the Future of Public Education*. San Francisco, CA: Jossey-Bass, 2008.

Payne, Charles. "Still Crazy after All These Years: Race in the Chicago School System." Presentation, University of Illinois at Chicago (UIC) College of Education. Chicago, Illinois. April 22, 2005.

Rhee, Michelle. "High Quality Education is the Best Tool to Fight Poverty."

YouTube. Accessed August 8, 2013. http://www.youtube.com/watch?v=PwzELBOC8nI.

"Roses in the Concrete in the News—CBS 5 San Francisco." *YouTube*. Accessed August 7, 2013. http://www.youtube.com/watch?v=R-42ghux580U.

Smitherman, Geneva. *Words from the Mother: Language and African Americans*. New York: Routledge, 2006.

Steele, Claude. "A Threat in the Air: How Stereotypes Shape Intellectual Identity and Performance." *American Psychologist* 52, No. 6 (1997): 613–629.

"Texas 2012 No Child Left Behind (NCLB) Report Card." *Texas Education Agency*. Accessed August 2, 2013. http://ritter.tea.state.tx.us/perfreport/nclb/2012/district.srch.html.

"The Black White Achievement Gap: When Progress Stopped." *Educational Testing Service*. Accessed August 13, 2013. http://www.ets.org/Media/Research/pdf/PICBWGAP.pdf.

"The New York State Report Card 2011–2012." *New York State Department of Education*. Accessed August 9, 2013. https://reportcards.nysed.gov/statewide/2012statewideRC.pdf.

"U.S. Education System Is Failing Black Students." *YouTube*. Accessed August 8, 2013. http://www.youtube.com/watch?v=i4dhGb3Q3hk.

9

"Nothing We Could Do or Say"

African American Young Men's Lived Police Experiences

Rod K. Brunson and Amanda D'Souza

> We understand that some of the violence that takes place in poor black neighborhoods around the country is born out of a very violent past in this country, and that the poverty and dysfunction that we see in those communities can be traced to a very difficult history. And so the fact that sometimes that's unacknowledged adds to the frustration. And the fact that a lot of African-American boys are painted with a broad brush and the excuse is given, well, there are these statistics out there that show that African-American boys are more violent—using that as an excuse to then see sons treated differently causes pain. . . .
>
> —President Barack Obama
> "Obama Trayvon Martin Speech Transcript: President Comments on George Zimmerman Verdict," July 19, 2013

Introduction

The tenuous relationship between African Americans and police has been well documented. In fact, troubling accounts of police misconduct are widespread in far too many African American neighborhoods, and a number of contemporary scholars have identified frequent, involuntary police contacts as serious threats to police legitimacy. Public discourse regarding racially biased policing, however, often is dormant until awakened by a revered Black person's well-publicized claim of mistreatment. In contrast, it usually requires immense tragedies involving poor Blacks and the police to elicit community action (e.g., Michael Brown, Eric Garner, Freddie Gray, and Walter Scott). Thus, adolescent Black males living in extremely difficult neighborhood contexts often receive indiscriminate police attention. Policy makers, however, have increasingly begun to make public statements touting aggressive policing tactics (e.g., increased stops, frisks, arrests) as effective crime-control strategies.[1] These rash proclamations fail to consider the diverse injuries borne by African Americans who disproportionately find themselves on the receiving end of heavy-handed policing strategies. For example, perceptions of, and experiences with, racially discriminatory policing efforts have the potential to reduce African American citizen confidence in the broader criminal justice system, increasing the odds that residents of highly disadvantaged neighborhoods will elect to settle disputes themselves, thereby increasing local crime and incarceration rates.[2]

Punitive crime-control strategies help to rid troubled communities of lawbreakers, allowing residents to live in a relatively safer environment.[3] The widespread use of proactive policing strategies toward this end, however, increases the likelihood that law-abiding community members will have involuntary police and criminal justice system contact.[4] And result in a disproportionate number of incarcerated, young, Black males.[5] In addition to the negative impact that imprisonment has on those individuals serving time, it also has dire consequences for the broader community. For example, studies have shown that high incarceration rates can trigger residential mobility (displacing children and/or entire families) and erode the effectiveness of local social institutions.[6] Moreover, research demonstrates that knowing someone who has been imprisoned negatively influences persons' assessments of both formal and informal control mechanisms.[7] For instance, these individuals express greater legal cynicism, appear more tolerant of deviance, and report less satisfaction with the police.[8] These factors collectively undermine the community's capacity for effective informal social control, resulting in greater reliance on formal systems of regulation (i.e., police intervention and suppression). Despite the obvious need for police presence within distressed communities, aggressive policing tactics lead to several secondary problems that ultimately thwart efforts to strengthen police-community relations.

Legitimacy, Procedural Justice, and Police–Minority Community Relations

Traditional police legitimacy frameworks were deeply rooted in rational choice theories, offering two primary explanations for why citizens by and large acquiesce to the police. First, it was argued that individuals obey the law because they fear being punished for wrongdoing.[9] Second, it was purported that citizens yield to police authority because they are forever mindful that officers possess state-sanctioned authority to use force.[10] Although these traditional rationales were insightful, improved understandings of the associated theoretical underpinnings demonstrate that police legitimacy is decidedly revocable. In fact, recent scholarship more fully illustrates the intricacies related to citizen compliance, underscoring that legitimacy is fluid and likely increases when officers consistently perform their duties fairly.[11]

Several scholars have identified procedural justice as an important mechanism for fostering increased police legitimacy. "Procedural justice is the process-based criterion by which individuals evaluate whether they were treated fairly and it can mean the difference between satisfied and disaffected citizens."[12] The contemporary procedural justice model focuses on approaches police utilize when interacting with the public, rather than the specific outcomes of such encounters.[13] In particular, police legitimacy frameworks posit that when the public believes that the police are professional, respectful, and impartial; they voluntarily comply.[14] Thus, the reliance on external incentives such as fear of punishment and/or use of force diminishes.[15] Finally, police researchers contend that gaining citizen compliance through cooperation rather than coercion represents a more evenhanded and effective neighborhood crime-control strategy.[16]

The public and police enjoy a mutually beneficial relationship. Undoubtedly, citizens depend on the police to maintain order and control neighborhood crime. On the other hand, the police rely on the public for assistance in reporting wrongdoing, providing credible court testimony, and obeying the law. Thus, the public's willingness to support the police in their crime-fighting efforts is largely dependent on the degree to which citizens consider the police legitimate.

The following sections underscore how aggressive policing tactics, routinely underway in disadvantaged neighborhoods, have the potential to seriously erode police legitimacy—especially among African American young men.[17] Hence, a number of factors that help to shape African American young men's police experiences are examined. Finally, this essay concludes with policy recommendations for improving police-minority community relations.

Factors Shaping Citizen Attitudes toward Police

An abundant body of literature reveals group differences regarding citizen attitudes toward the police. For example, studies have reliability shown that trust in, and satisfaction with, the police is highly influenced by race, age, and prior police contact.[18] In particular, whites report the highest level of police satisfaction, while African Americans typically express the lowest levels of trust; Hispanics generally fall in the middle of these two divergent views.[19] Moreover, research has consistently identified age as an important predictor for helping to shape citizen perceptions of the police.[20] That is, adolescents are more likely to have frequent, involuntary police contacts because they tend to socialize in public spaces and are disproportionately involved in criminal activities; both factors increase youths' visibility and risk of unwelcome police interactions.[21] Further, evidence suggests that police-initiated contacts with individuals are more likely to yield negative views of the police, compared to citizen-initiated encounters (e.g., emergency and nonemergency citizen calls for service) that typically result in positive opinions.[22] Finally, citizens' perceptions stemming from negative police interactions have been shown to be stronger and more enduring than those arising from favorable encounters.[23]

The vast majority of research on citizens' evaluations of the police has centered on person's direct encounters. Scholars have recently, however, begun to explore insights acquired through individual's knowledge regarding other group member's police contacts. Policing scholars have referred to these indirect police encounters as "vicarious" experiences. For example, Rosenbaum et al. demonstrate that vicarious interactions—hearing about instances of police misconduct from peers, for example—has a very strong, negative influence on an individual's perception of the police.[24] Rosenbaum and colleagues also report that African Americans and Hispanics are more likely to obtain vicarious information from friends and family, whereas whites are more apt to learn about police misconduct through media accounts.[25] Further, in a more recent study, Brunson and Weitzer find support for the widely held view that African American parents routinely counsel their children (and other African American youths) about the dangers of unwelcome police encounters, and seek "to equip youths with a set of conduct norms that would make them less visible to police."[26] For instance, Kurtis, one of their respondents, recounted a preemptive conversation that he had with his two sons. He noted:

> I tell them if you're driving and you're pulled over by the cops, make sure you're in an area with people; then you pull over and put your hands out the window, and don't make no move till they get there. I don't care if they're pulling you over for a driving violation. Put your hands out the window. Hold your hands up in the air. That's so

> there won't be no mistakes. . . . I talked to my sons about it. . . . Don't run, 'cause things can happen and it's their word against yours, and if you're young and you black, you're gonna lose that argument.[27]

Kurtis's sobering admonishment emphasizes that it is important to consider how African American young men's firsthand police encounters together with those shared by intimates (e.g., family members, peers, and neighbors), generate an accumulated body of negative police experiences.[28]

Both Race *and* Place Matter

Disadvantaged neighborhoods tend to have an abundance of discernible indicators of social and physical disorder.[29] Social disorder can involve a host of open-air public order crimes (e.g., aggressive panhandling, public intoxication, prostitution) and equally troubling signs of physical disorder (e.g., abandoned buildings, graffiti, and unsightly litter).[30] While social disorder is largely episodic, physical disorder involves an ongoing process of neighborhood decay.[31] Further, the most severely disadvantaged areas are distinguished by high rates of racial segregation, resident turnover, poverty, unemployment, and female-headed households.[32] The aforementioned social factors likely drastically weaken social bonds and produce low levels of collective efficacy among neighborhood residents.[33] Collective efficacy requires a social contract (informal agreement) among neighbors and is predicated on the belief that fellow residents will intervene after witnessing crime.[34] Thus, high levels of collective efficacy function to increase neighborhood surveillance, allowing for greater order maintenance. In the absence of informal social control, however, neighborhood residents must rely primarily on formal systems (i.e., the police) to regulate crime.[35]

Prior scholarship highlights that neighborhood conditions have the potential to impact police practices and behaviors.[36] This framework emerges from a fundamental realization that not all communities are policed the same. In fact, similar to how individual demographic factors (e.g., race, age, and gender) influence citizen views of the police, it stands to reason that a host of neighborhood characteristics also play key roles in helping to shape officers' perceptions of residents. This is an important consideration for inhabitants of communities plagued by unusually high rates of physical and social decay. Nonetheless, research has consistently shown that regardless of neighborhood context, young African American men report experiencing disproportionate police contacts.[37]

Overpolicing

Citizen evaluations of the police may also be influenced by the style of policing underway in their neighborhoods. For example, residents of disenfranchised, minority neighborhoods consistently express high levels of mistrust of, and dissatisfaction with, the police.[38] Interestingly, police administrators and city leaders routinely offer disproportionate crime rates as justification for officers' heavy reliance on aggressive policing tactics in poorer African American neighborhoods.[39] The overreliance on aggressive policing has resulted in crime-control strategies often likened to "urban warfare."[40] That is, the pervasive use of suppression tactics suggests that the police are engaged in an ongoing battle with *all* neighborhood residents, regardless of their law-abiding status.[41] The urban combat mind-set engenders tactical deployments like Los Angeles's former CRASH unit and Chicago Police Department's Mobile Strike Force.[42] These special operations typically alienate neighborhood residents, reducing their levels of trust in the police and willingness to partner in efforts to reduce crime. It is important to note, however, that residents of disadvantaged communities are not anti-police. In fact, the vast majority of urban residents understand that the police are essential for effective crime-control.[43] Nevertheless, what many people of color consider overpolicing, together with routine discourteous treatment from officers, contributes to African American young men's overall negative evaluations. For example, Will described an unsettling experience involving what he considered unwarranted police attention.

> A friend of mine and me were in the community, we were outside and it was a late night and I guess the officer that approached took us as gang bangers or whatever. He asked us what we were doing and we looked at each other and we said, "Nothing," and he [said] that we looked real suspicious. . . . He used the excuse that we had drugs in our mouth[s] and told us to take whatever we had in our mouths out. We had grills [decorative dental molds] in our mouth[s] and he made us take them out, we showed them to him in our hand[s] and [the officer] smacked 'em out and when they [hit] the ground, he stomped on them and laughed. But he was showing us that he had more power, authority over us at the time, so there was nothing we could do or say.[45]

In addition to being unnecessarily stopped, Will and his friend took particular exception to the officer's brazen destruction of their personal property. As Will's statement highlights, such encounters have the potential to leave citizens feeling belittled, dejected, and powerless.

Overpolicing refers to officers' intervening even when it would appear that the situation does not require any action. Overpolicing often occurs because the police perceive certain communities to be more dangerous, due to visible signs of disorder and perceptions that a disproportionate number of offenders reside therein.[45] Because the police regard particular areas as threatening, they generally approach otherwise routine situations with more suspicion and aggression than they would in more affluent areas.[46] Further, in highly disadvantaged neighborhoods, the police are likely to use greater levels of force when confronting suspects. Unnecessary use of force by officers, however, may also increase the likelihood of suspects taking on negative demeanors and refusing to cooperate voluntarily. There is a mutually reinforcing relationship between overpolicing and citizen evaluations of police legitimacy. Overpolicing increases the odds that citizens will behave disrespectfully (especially those who believe that the involuntary contact lacks merit), causing officers to use greater coercion and force to gain compliance. These events play out disproportionately in public spaces occupied by African Americans and potentially set the stage for future negative police-citizen interactions.

Brunson and Miller found that African American young men reported being regularly stopped and frisked by the police, despite doing nothing illegal.[47] As a result, an overwhelming majority of their respondents came to understand that no matter how they presented themselves, they remained tainted by both their race and neighborhood conditions, essentially making them perpetual targets for the police.[48] A number of scholars have sought to make clear how officers' predetermined views about race and neighborhood context lead them to paint inner-city African American males with a broad brush, labeling them both amoral and crime-prone.[49] As discussed previously, fairness and impartiality are extremely important components of police legitimacy. The heavy-handed policing tactics underway in some minority communities and an overarching presumption of African American young men's guilt seriously undermines efforts to improve police legitimacy, however.

Underpolicing

In addition to procedural justice concerns, African Americans often report considerable dissatisfaction regarding police effectiveness and responsiveness. In particular, African Americans consistently express frustration about slow response times, how calls for service are prioritized, and the overall perception that law enforcement is incapable of effectively solving crime.[50] The unfolding fiscal crisis in Detroit, Michigan provides an unfortunate but clear illustration regarding how resource scarcity proves especially harmful in locales were police-minority citizen relations are already fragile.[51] Specifically, there is grave concern that the City's recent economic struggles have adversely impacted police response times and crime solving effectiveness.[52] Interestingly, the ecological contexts associated with overpolicing also contribute to African American citizen claims of underpolicing. Brunson and Weitzer examined disadvantaged urban male's police experiences across three neighborhoods that varied by racial composition: one lower class and Black, one lower class and predominantly white, and one lower class and racially mixed.[53] They note that "perceived police under-protection or poor service in poor, minority neighborhoods has been complained about for generations, and some of [their] respondents made the same complaint: "Usually in a Black neighborhood there's always trouble and [the police] are not gonna care if somebody reports a [crime]," Shannon stated. "They might rush [the handling of the call] just to get it over with."[54] And according to James,

> [the police] react faster if somebody called from a White neighborhood, say somebody getting shot. They gonna get there faster and they gonna treat them with more respect. . . . They gonna be like, "Well, do you have any suspects? Do you know what happened or how it happened?" They gonna try to get to the point. But if they go through a Black [neighborhood] or if it's over here [in Hazelcrest] they say, "Well, they kill each other off anyway, so there ain't too much you can do about it."[55]

Brunson and Weitzer's multi-neighborhood study highlights the importance of citizen perceptions of racial discrimination regarding police service delivery across different kinds of place.[56]

Underpolicing occurs when the police seemingly fail to take certain citizens' calls for service seriously and/or refuse to make arrests in disadvantaged neighborhoods for behaviors that are not tolerated within more affluent communities.[57] Thus, it should come as no surprise that residents of seriously troubled neighborhoods generally report lower levels of police satisfaction, holding officers at least partially responsible for high crime rates.[58] In fact, residents of these communities routinely demand better police protection.[59] For example, in a survey administered in New York, 66 percent of Hispanics and 72 percent of African Americans supported the planned installation of 400 surveillance cameras throughout the city to enhance crime control.[60] Simply put, African American and Hispanic citizens recognize the need for improved police effectiveness, despite consistently reporting low rates of trust in, and satisfaction with, the police. Persistently high rates of crime and disorder ultimately leads urban residents to question whether they are receiving adequate protection, whereby reducing individual's confidence in the police.

Further, underpolicing is partially explained through the "overload hypothesis."[61] Specifically, the theory asserts that due to high levels of crime within disadvantaged areas, police resources are strained and reprioritized; hence, efforts are concentrated toward the most dangerous crimes; leaving "lesser" offences, unaddressed.[62] This phenomenon can be understood by examining police dispatch center operations. For instance, due to high levels of crime within certain neighborhoods, dispatchers assign the lowest priority to service related requests (e.g., caller locking his/her keys inside an automobile) and only send officers on calls involving very serious crimes.[63] Moreover, policing scholars observe that lesser crimes are often "normalized" or understood as a part of everyday life within distressed communities.[64] It makes sense then that officers might reach the erroneous conclusion that poor people of color are tolerant of crime.[65] On the other hand, minority residents of troubled neighborhoods might interpret slow police response times as further proof of their irrelevance. Finally, the cumulative impact of living within high-crime neighborhoods has the potential to impede citizens' notions of procedural justice.

Policy Recommendation

Commentators have recognized the long-standing, troubled relationship between African Americans and the police. And while economic, political, and social inequality persists in the U.S., conditions have improved. This is also the case concerning the relationship between officers and minority communities. Nonetheless, there are additional steps that can be taken. For example, there must first be a monumental shift in the police leadership culture. Specifically, mechanisms must be put in place to address repressive, inner-city policing tactics discussed earlier.[66] Further, a move toward a more procedural justice framework should involve all officers and be promoted by chiefs and police executives.[67] The inclusion of high-ranking officers will hopefully convey the seriousness and permanence of this viewpoint. Moreover, improved training and stricter discipline should be enforced for those officers who do not adhere to the procedural justice framework. Implementing a system of accountability would be beneficial since studies have shown that residents are unlikely to report incidents of abuse if they believe that officers will not be disciplined and/or investigations would not be properly conducted.[68]

Davis et al. documented the success of incorporating procedural justice goals within two New York precincts.[69] They found that during the implementation of broken windows policing in New York City, citizen complaints against officers increased at a substantial rate in most precincts, except two—the 42nd and 44th Precincts, where complaints actually declined at a significant rate.[70] Davis and his colleagues found that management within these units shifted focus and implemented programs which highlighted more respectful policing.[71] Moreover, they attached specific consequences to officers receiving citizen complaints. Most important, this strategy resulted in a significant reduction in complaints for officers who were known to have previously clashed with citizens.[72] This study is important because it showcases that procedural justice can be implemented in a way that does not hamper or decrease crime-prevention efforts.

There is no doubt that the lack of faith and trust in the police has a devastating impact on lower-socioeconomic minority communities. It is important to note that residents welcome and support increased police intervention, yet they vehemently oppose indiscriminate and aggressive policing.[73] As discussed earlier, heavy-handed policing tactics largely alienate and demoralize residents. Further, such strategies function in ways that hold *all* residents morally liable for the poor social and physical living conditions; thus facilitating an "us versus them" mentality. As noted earlier, the repressive and siege-like police mentality is counterintuitive to the procedural justice framework. Thus, it can be argued that police executives should adopt more effective and reliable procedures within inner-city neighborhoods, as efforts currently in use have proven to be ineffective and largely counterproductive to the general goals of policing—order maintenance and crime suppression.

Conclusion

The opening quote by President Barack Obama emphasizes that while advances have been made, large structural inequalities continue to hamper progress toward a truly postracial society. As we note, policing practices within many inner-city communities deny African Americans adequate police protection; leading residents to question whether police care about their well-being. Further, public support of the police influences the extent to which citizens' view police authority as legitimate. Thus, public willingness to support the police in their crime-fighting efforts is largely dependent on the degree to which citizens consider the police legitimate. Specifically, high levels of police legitimacy enhance cooperation and trust, whereby the alternative contributes to police officers' overreliance on violence and intimidation. The widespread use of heavy-handed tactics feeds the cycle of distrust and further hinders notions of police legitimacy.

Moreover, the aggressive policing efforts occurring in urban neighborhoods coupled with harsh mandatory minimum sentences have contributed to a dramatic increase in the prison population; whereas nearly one out of three Black men in their twenties are under some form of criminal justice supervision (i.e., imprisoned, or on probation/parole).[74] As evidenced previously, the removal of scores of African American young men results in large social and economic hardships for their communities (and families).[75] The recurring disruptions caused by individuals going in and out of prison hinders the stability of inner-city communities and results in their inability to progress socially and/or economically. Nevertheless, some officials attempt to justify racially discriminatory treatment of African Americans and their overrepresentation within the criminal justice system by arguing that these individuals are more likely to commit crime, hence, incarceration and repressive police tactics are necessary.[76] Blaming young Black men for their dire circumstances without reflecting on the historical and institutional inequalities that often inform their decisions, results in further frustration and alienation of the African American community.

Police strategies that hinge on establishing effective working relationships with important community liaisons have shown considerable promise for strengthening police-community relations. For instance, in 1995 Boston's Operation Ceasefire was implemented using interagency coordination among key criminal justice personnel and a group of activist Black clergy.[77] This focused deterrence strategy was largely heralded for significantly reducing shootings and youth gun assaults.[78] Further, police-community partnerships have also been found to be fairly successful at regulating open-air drug markets in a number of U.S. cities.[79] Specifically, effective police-community partnerships facilitate informal social control by increasing collective efficacy, an important crime-control feature absent from many disadvantaged, high-crime neighborhoods.[80] Further, positive police-community partnerships can increase police legitimacy. Despite their well-documented fragile relationship, community members depend on police assistance to address a wide range of neighborhood problems. The aforementioned innovative policing initiatives demonstrate that police-minority community relations can be improved.

Notes

1. Joseph Goldstein, "City Homicides Drop Sharply, Again; Police Cite New Antigang Strategy," *New York Times*, June 28, 2013.

2. Elijah Anderson, *Streetwise: Race, Class and Change in an Urban Community* (Chicago: University of Chicago Press, 1990).

3. Todd R. Clear, Dina R. Rose, and Judith A. Ryder, "Incarceration and the Community: The Problem of Removing and Returning Offenders," *Crime and Delinquency* 47, no. 3 (July 2001): 335–351.

4. Dina R. Rose and Todd R. Clear, "Who Doesn't Know Someone in Jail? The Impact of Exposure to Prison on Attitudes toward Formal and Informal Control," *Prison Journal* 84, no. 2 (2004): 228–247.

5. Ibid.

6. Becky Pettit, *Invisible Men Mass Incarceration and the Myth of Black Progress* (New York: Russell Sage Foundation, 2012).

7. Clear et al.

8. Rose and Clear.

9. Tom R. Tyler. *Why People Obey the Law* (New Haven: Yale University Press, 2006).

10. Egon Bittner. *The Functions of Police in Modern Society* (Rockville, MD: National Institute of Mental Health, 1970).

11. Tom R. Tyler, "Enhancing Police Legitimacy," *Annals of the American Academy of Political and Social Science*, 593 (2004): 84–99.

12. Jacinta M. Gau and Rod K. Brunson, "Procedural Justice and Order Maintenance Policing: A Study of Inner-City Young Men's Perceptions of Police Legitimacy," *Justice Quarter* 27, no. 2 (2010): 256. See also, Tom R. Tyler and Cheryl J. Wakslak, "Profiling and Police Legitimacy: Procedural Justice, Attributions of Motive and Acceptance of Police Authority," *Criminology* 42 no. 2 (2004): 253–282.

13. Tom Tyler "Enhancing Police Legitimacy."

14. Ibid.

15. Ibid.

16. Tom R. Tyler. *Why People Obey the Law.* See also Jacinta M. Gau and Rod K Brunson "Race, Place, and Policing the Inner-City," in *The Oxford Handbook on Police and Policing*, ed. Michael D. Reisig and Robert J. Kane (New York: Oxford University Press, 2014).

17. Gau and Brunson, "Procedural Justice and Order Maintenance Policing." See also Eric A. Stewart, "Either They Don't Know or They Don't Care: Black Males and Negative Police Experiences," *Criminology and Public Policy*, 6 (2007): 123–130.

18. Tyler. "Enhancing Police Legitimacy." See also Gau and Brunson, "Procedural Justice and Order Maintenance Policing."

19. Wesley G. Skogan, "Citizen Satisfaction with Police Encounters" *Police Quarterly* 8, no. 3 (2005): 298–321. See also Ronald Weitzer, "The Puzzling Neglect of Hispanic Americans in Research on Police–Citizen Relations," *Ethnic and Racial Studies* (2013).

20. Terrance Taylor, K. B. Turner, Finn-Aage Esbensen, L. Thomas Winfree Jr., "Coppin' an Attitude: Attitudinal Differences among Juveniles toward Police," *Journal of Criminal Justice* 29 (2001): 295–305.

21. Douglas Sharp and Susie Atherton, "To Serve and Protect? The Experiences of Policing in the Community of Young People from Black and Other Minority Groups," *British Journal of Criminology* 47 (2007): 746–763. See also Rod K. Brunson and Jody Miller "Young Black Men and Urban Policing in the United States," *British Journal of Criminology* 46, no. 4 (2006): 613–640.

22. Brenda L. Vogel, "Perceptions of the Police: The Influence of Individual and Contextual Factors in a Racially Diverse Urban Sample," *Journal of Ethnicity in Criminal Justice* 9, no. 4 (2012): 267–290.

23. Ibid.

24. Dennis P. Rosenbaum Amie M. Schuck, Sandra K. Costello, Darnell F. Hawkins, and Marianne K. Ring, "Attitudes toward the Police: The Effects of Direct and Vicarious Experience," *Police Quarterly* 8, no. 3 (2005): 354.

25. Ibid.

26. Rod K. Brunson and Ronald Weitzer, "Negotiating Unwelcome Police Encounters: The Intergenerational Transmission of Conduct Norms," *Journal of Contemporary Ethnography* 40, no. 4 (2011): 451.

27. Ibid.

28. Rod K. Brunson, "'Police Don't Like Black People': African-American Young Men's Accumulative Police Experiences" *Criminology and Public Policy*, 6 (2007): 81–101.

29. Robert M. Bohm, K. Michael Reynolds, and Stephen T. Holmses, "Perceptions of Neighborhood Problems and Their Solutions: Implications for Community Policing," *Policing: An International Journal of Police Strategies & Management* 23, no. 4 (2000): 439–465.

30. Wesley G. Skogan, *Disorder and Decline: Crime and the Spiral of Decay in American Neighborhoods* (New York: The Free Press, 1990).

31. Ibid.

32. Robert J. Kane, "The Social Ecology of Police Misconduct" *Criminology* 40, no. 4 (2002). See also Gau and Brunson, "Procedural Justice and Order Maintenance Policing."

33. Charis E. Kubrin and Eric A. Stewart, "Predicting who Reoffends: The Neglected Role of Neighborhood Context in Recidivism Studies," *Criminology* 44 (2006): 165–197.

34. Wesley Skogan. "The Promise of Community Policing" in *Police Innovation: Contrasting Perspectives*, ed. David L. Weisburd and Anthony A. Braga (New York: Cambridge University Press, 2006). See also Sampson,

Robert J., Stephen W. Raudenbush, and Felton Earls, "Neighborhoods and Violent Crime: A Multilevel Study of Collective Efficacy," *Science* 277 (1997): 918–924.

35. Kane.

36. David Klinger, "Negotiating Order in Police Work: An Ecological Theory of Police Response to Deviance," *Criminology* 35 (1997): 277–306.

37. Brunson and Weitzer. "Police Relations with Black and White Youths in Different Urban Neighborhoods." See also Eric A. Stewart Eric P. Baumer, Rod K. Brunson, and Ronald L. Simons, "Neighborhood Racial Context and Perceptions of Police-Based Racial Discrimination among Black Youth," *Criminology* 47, no. 3 (2009): 847–887; Andrea S. Boyles, "Meacham Park: How do Blacks Experience Policing in the Suburbs?" (Doctoral dissertation, Kansas State University, 2012).

38. Sandra Bass, "Policing Space, Policing Race: Social Control Imperatives and Police Discretionary Decisions." *Social Justice* 28, no. 1 (2001): 156–176. See also Neil Websdale, *Policing the Poor: From Slave Plantation to Public Housing* (Boston: Northeastern University Press, 2001).

39. Gau and Brunson, "Procedural Justice and Order Maintenance Policing."

40. Ibid.

41. Brunson and Weitzer, "Police Relations with Black and White Youths in Different Urban Neighborhoods."

42. Brunson and Gau, "Race, Place, and Policing the Inner-City."

43. Patrick Car, Laura Napolitano, and Jessica Keating, "We Never Call the Cops and Here Is Why: A Qualitative Examination of Legal Cynicism in Three Philadelphia Neighborhoods," *Criminology* 45, no. 2 (2007): 445–480.

44. Brunson and Weitzer, "Police Relations with Black and White Youths in Different Urban Neighborhoods," 866.

45. Klinger.

46. Ibid.

47. Rod K. Brunson and Jody Miller, "Young Black Men and Urban Policing in the United States," *British Journal of Criminology* 46, no. 4 (2006): 635.

48. Ibid.

49. William Terrill and Michael D. Reisig, "Neighborhood Context and Police Use of Force," *Journal of Research in Crime and Delinquency* 40, no. 3 (2003). See also Jerome H. Skolnick, *Justice without Trial: Law Enforcement in Democratic Societies* (New York: MacMillan, 1994); Elijah Anderson. *Streetwise: Race, Class, and Change in an Urban Community* (Chicago: University of Chicago Press, 1990).

50. Brunson, "'Police Don't Like Black People.'"

51. Monica Davey, "Financial Crisis Just a Symptom of Detroit's Woes," *New York Times* July 8, 2013.

52. Ibid.

53. Brunson and Weitzer, "Police Relations with Black and White Youths in Different Urban Neighborhoods," 861.

54. Ibid., 876.

55. Ibid., 876–877.

56. Ibid., 878.

57. Klinger.

58. Ronald Weitzer. "Race and Policing in Different Ecological Contexts" in *Race, Ethnicity and Policing New and Essential Readings*, ed. Stephen K. Rice and Michael D. White (New York: New York University Press, 2010), 118–139.

59. Ibid.

60. Ibid. See also Ronald Weitzer and Steven Tuch, *Race and Policing in America: Conflict and Reform* (New York: Cambridge University Press, 2006).

61. Klinger.

62. Ibid.

63. Ibid.

64. Kane.

65. Klinger.

66. Brunson and Gau, "Race, Place, and Policing the Inner-City."

67. Ibid.

68. Brunson and Weitze, "Police Relations with Black and White Youths in Different Urban Neighborhoods."

69. Robert C. Davis, Mateu-Gelabert, Pedro, Joel Miller, "Can Effective Policing Also Be Respectful? Two Examples in the South Bronx," *Criminology and Penology* 8, no. 2 (2005): 233.

70. Ibid.

71. Ibid.

72. Ibid.

73. Sharp and Atherton." See also Patrick Carr, Laura Napolitano and Jessica Keating, "We Never Call the Cops and Here Is Why: A Qualitative Examination of Legal Cynicism in Three Philadelphia Neighborhoods," *Criminology* 45, no. 2 (2007): 445–480.

74. Donna Coker, "Foreword: Addressing the Real World of Racial Injustice in the Criminal Justice System," *Journal of Criminal Law and Criminology* 93, no. 4 (2003): 827–879.

75. Ibid.

76. Ibid.

77. Edmund McGarrell, Steven Chermak, James Wilson, and Nicholas Corsaro, "Reducing Homicide through a 'Lever-Pulling' Strategy," *Justice Quarterly* 23 (2006): 214–229.

78. Ibid.

79. Anthony Braga and David M. Kennedy, "Linking Situation Crime Prevention and Focused Deterrence Strategies," in *The Reasoning Criminologist: Essays in Honour of Ronald V. Clarke*, ed. Graham Farrell and Nick Tilley (New York: Routledge, 2012). See also Nicholas Corsaro, Rod K. Brunson, and Edmund F. McGarrell, "Evaluating a Policing Strategy Intended to Disrupt an Illicit Street-Level Drug Market," *Evaluation Review* 36, no. 6 (2010); Nicholas Corsaro, Rod K. Brunson, and Edmund F. McGarrell, "Problem-Oriented

Policing and Open-Air Drug Markets: Examining the Rockford Pulling Levers Deterrence Strategy," *Crime and Delinquency* 59, no. 7 (October 2013): 1085–1107.

80. McGarrell, Chermak, Wilson, and Corsaro.

Bibliography

Anderson, Elijah. *Streetwise: Race, Class, and Change in an Urban Community.* Chicago: University of Chicago Press, 1990.

Bass, Sandra. "Policing Space, Policing Race: Social Control Imperatives and Police Discretionary Decisions." *Social Justice* 28, no. 1 (2001): 156–176.

Bittner, Egon. *The Functions of Police in Modern Society.* Rockville, MD: National Institute of Mental Health, 1970.

Bohm, Robert M., K. Michael Reynolds, and Stephen T. Holmses. "Perceptions of Neighborhood Problems and Their Solutions: Implications for Community Policing." *Policing: An International Journal of Police Strategies & Management* 23, no. 4 (2000): 439–465.

Boyles, Andrea S. "Meacham Park: How Do Blacks Experience Policing in the Suburbs?" Doctoral dissertation, Kansas State University, 2012.

Braga, Anthony, and David M. Kennedy. "Linking Situational Crime Prevention and Focused Deterrence Strategies." In *The Reasoning Criminologist: Essays in Honour of Ronald V. Clarke.* Edited by Graham Farrell and Nick Tilley. New York: Routledge, 2012.

Brunson, Rod K. "'Police Don't Like Black People': African-American Young Men's Accumulative Police Experiences." *Criminology and Public Policy,* 6 (2007): 71–101.

Brunson, Rod K., and Jacinta M. Gau. "Race, Place, and Policing the Inner-City." In *The Oxford Handbook on Police and Policing.* Edited by Michael D. Reisig and Robert J. Kane. New York: Oxford University Press, 2014.

Brunson, Rod K., and Jody Miller. "Young Black Men and Urban Policing in the United States." *British Journal of Criminology* 46, no. 4 (2006): 613–640.

Brunson, Rod K., and Ronald Weitzer. "Negotiating Unwelcome Police Encounters: The Intergenerational Transmission of Conduct Norms." *Journal of Contemporary Ethnography* 40, no. 4 (2011): 425–456.

———. "Police Relations with Black and White Youths in Different Urban Neighborhoods." *Urban Affairs Review* 44, no. 6 (2009): 858–885.

Carr, Patrick, Laura Napolitano, and Jessica Keating. "We Never Call the Cops and Here Is Why: A Qualitative Examination of Legal Cynicism in Three Philadelphia Neighborhoods." *Criminology* 45, no. 2 (2007): 445–480.

Clear, Todd R., Dina R. Rose, and Judith A. Ryder. "Incarceration and the Community: The Problem of Removing and Returning Offenders." *Crime and Delinquency* 47, no. 3 (2001): 335–351.

Coker, Donna. "Forward: Addressing the Real World of Racial Injustice in the Criminal Justice System." *Journal of Criminal Law and Criminology* 93, no. 4 (2003): 827–879.

Corsaro, Nicholas, Rod K. Brunson, and Edmund F. McGarrell. "Evaluating a Policing Strategy Intended to Disrupt an Illicit Street-Level Drug Market." *Evaluation Review* 36, no. 6 (2010): 513–548.

———. "Problem-Oriented Policing and Open-Air Drug Markets: Examining the Rockford Pulling Levers Deterrence Strategy." *Crime and Delinquency* 59, no. 7 (Oct. 2013): 1085–1107.

Davey, Monica. "Financial Crisis Just a Symptom of Detroit's Woes." *New York Times*, July 8, 2013.

Davis, Robert C., Pedro Mateu-Gelabert, and Joel Miller. "Can Effective Policing Also Be Respectful? Two Examples in the South Bronx." *Criminology and Penology* 8, no. 2 (2005): 229–247.

Gau, Jacinta M., and Brunson, Rod K. "Procedural Justice and Order Maintenance Policing: A Study of Inner-City Young Men's Perceptions of Police Legitimacy." *Justice Quarter* 27, no. 2 (2010): 256–279.

———-. "Why People Obey the Law." In *The Oxford Handbook on Police and Policing*. Edited by Michael D. Reisig and Robert J. Kane. New York: Oxford University Press, 2014.

Goldstein, Joseph. "City Homicides Drop Sharply, Again; Police Cite New Antigang Strategy." *New York Times*, June 28, 2013.

Kane, Robert J. "The Social Ecology of Police Misconduct." *Criminology* 40, no. 4 (2002): 867–896.

Klinger, David. "Negotiating Order in Police Work: An Ecological Theory of Police Response to Deviance." *Criminology* 35 (1997): 277–306.

Kubrin, Charis E., and Eric A. Stewart. "Predicting who Reoffends: The Neglected Role of Neighborhood Context in Recidivism Studies." *Criminology* 44 (2006): 165–197.

McGarrell, Edmund, Steven Chermak, James Wilson, and Nicholas Corsaro. "Reducing Homicide through a 'Lever-Pulling' Strategy." *Justice Quarterly* 23 (2006): 214–229.

"Obama Trayvon Martin Speech Transcript: President Comments on George Zimmerman Verdict." *Huffington Post*. Accessed February 14, 2014. http://www.huffingtonpost.com/2013/07/19/obama-trayvon-martin-speech-transcript_n_3624884.html.

Pettit, Becky. *Invisible Men Mass Incarceration and the Myth of Black Progress*. New York: Russell Sage Foundation, 2012.

Rose, Dina R., and Clear, Todd R. "Who Doesn't Know Someone in Jail? The Impact of Exposure to Prison on Attitudes toward Formal and Informal Control." *The Prison Journal* 84, no. 2 (2004): 228–247.

Rosenbaum, Dennis P., Amie M. Schuck, Sandra K. Costello, Darnell F. Hawkins, and Marianne K. Ring. "Attitudes toward the Police: The

Effects of Direct and Vicarious Experience." *Police Quarterly* 8, no. 3 (2005): 343–365.

Sampson, Robert, Stephen W. Raudenbush, and Felton Earls. "Neighborhoods and Violent Crime: A Multilevel Study of Collective Efficacy." *Science* 277 (1997): 918–924.

Sharp, Douglas, and Susie Atherton, "To Serve and Protect? The Experiences of Policing in the Community of Young People from Black and Other Minority Groups." *British Journal of Criminology* 47 (2007): 746–763.

Skogan, Wesley G. "Citizen Satisfaction with Police Encounters" *Police Quarterly* 8, no. 3 (2005): 298–321.

———. *Disorder and Decline: Crime and the Spiral of Decay in American Neighborhoods.* New York: The Free Press, 1990.

———. "The Promise of Community Policing" In *Police Innovation: Contrasting Perspectives.* Edited by David L. Weisburd and Anthony A. Braga. New York: Cambridge University Press, 2006.

Skolnick, Jerome H. *Justice without Trial: Law Enforcement in Democratic Societies.* New York: MacMillan, 1994.

Stewart, Eric. A. "Either They Don't Know or They Don't Care: Black Males and Negative Police Experiences." *Criminology & Public Policy* 6 (2007): 123–130.

Stewart, Eric A., Eric P. Baumer, Rod K. Brunson, and Ronald L. Simons. "Neighborhood Context and Perceptions of Police-Based Racial Discrimination among Black Youth" *Criminology* 47, no. 3 (2009): 847–887.

Taylor Terrance, K. B. Turner, Finn-Aage Esbensen, and L. Thomas Winfree Jr. "Coppin' an Attitude: Attitudinal Differences among Juveniles toward Police." *Journal of Criminal Justice* 29 (2001): 295–305.

Terrill, William, and Michael D. Reisig. "Neighborhood Context and Police Use of Force." *Journal of Research in Crime and Delinquency* 40, no. 3 (2003): 291–321.

Tyler, Tom. R. "Enhancing Police Legitimacy." *Annals of the American Academy of Political and Social Science* 593 (2004): 84–99.

———. *Why People Obey the Law.* New Haven, CT: Yale University Press, 2006.

Tyler, Tom R., and Cheryl J. Wakslak. "Profiling and Police Legitimacy: Procedural Justice, Attributions of Motive and Acceptance of Police Authority." *Criminology* 42, no. 2 (2004): 253–282.

Vogel, Brenda L. "Perceptions of the Police: The Influence of Individual and Contextual Factors in a Racially Diverse Urban Sample." *Journal of Ethnicity in Criminal Justice* 9, no. 4 (2012): 267–290.

Websdale, Neil. *Policing the Poor: From Slave Plantation to Public Housing.* Boston: Northeastern University Press, 2001.

Weitzer, Ronald. "Race and Policing in Different Ecological Contexts." In *Race, Ethnicity and Policing New and Essential Readings*, 118–139. Edited by Stephen K. Rice, and Michael D. White. New York: New York University Press, 2010.

———. "The Puzzling Neglect of Hispanic Americans in Research on Police–Citizen Relations." *Ethnic and Racial Studies* (2013).

Williams, Corey. "In Detroit, Nervous Residents Wonder If Bankruptcy Will Mean Less Crime, Higher Home Values." *Macleans* July 19, 2013.

Wilson, James Q., and George Kelling. "Broken Windows: The Police and Neighborhood Safety." *Atlantic Monthly* (March 1982).

10

African American Youth and the Postracial Societal Myth

Carl S. Taylor and Pamela R. Smith

Introduction

Historically, researchers have studied race, poverty, and other systems of oppression. In 1968, W. E. B. Du Bois stated in his autobiography that the future of the Negro race in America depended on a social uplift in regard to: education, housing, occupations, race relations, literature and art, history, science, and social progress as part of his critique of the National Association for the Advancement of Colored People's (NAACP) leadership.[1] In 1996, "The Culture of Poverty" article by Oscar Lewis was published and gave credence to the highly controversial Moynihan Report, *The Negro Family: The Case for National Action,* published in 1965. Moynihan argued that the treatment of Negroes, both past and present, eroded the Negro family. He examined fifteen years of the lives of Negroes and illuminated the situation of socio-economic deprivation and family disorganization from the data he collected.[2] The culture-of-poverty argument blames the poor for their circumstances. This theory suggests that poverty-stricken people remain in poverty because they adapt to their conditions in order to survive in a difficult economic environment.[3] Moynihan felt that Negro families were and would continuously be caught in a cycle of poverty, which he called the "tangle of pathology," if government did not intervene to strengthen the family.[4] Poverty is the key factor that sets the tone of inferiority by traditional interpretation, be it Black or white tradition.

Today, Michelle Alexander writes about the unfair treatment and social conditions of poor Black people in *The New Jim Crow: Mass Incarceration in the Age of Colorblindness.* Alexander professes that racial progress is not moving forward. She notes that "Thousands of Black men have disappeared into prisons and jails, locked away for drug crimes that are largely ignored when committed by whites."[5]

Matthew Hughey argues that racial inequality is well-entrenched in white supremacy, is not a natural or predestined occurrence and that the reality of race is a complex issue.[6] The images of African Americans have been a struggle since the beginning of their existence in the United States. While not all Africans began as slaves, most did, and historians are torn as to when their overall image, status, and identity began to differ. It is a unique position to consider, and more perplexing when you are always told to move on when inquiring about the beginning or status of Blacks early on. This point is being emphasized today, due to the realization that the present day is filled with past history. Dwell on the past? It seems important; even if one does not dwell on the past, the past is still present. As W. E. B. Du Bois, sagely warned the world, race was an issue that would need addressing since it was haunting America.[7]

The social ecology for Black urban youth in Detroit has been difficult. Over the last decades, our work in Detroit has kept track of the transitions from the civil rights era to the present. The parents, families, and communities of the poorest big city with the largest Black population in America have been the epicenter of racial polarization. A barometer has consistently revealed the tension and racial divide that has taken its toll on many. The groups of young men and women who are challenged by racial issues today, carry the burden of their families and ancestors. The following selected discussions are about the racial interactions, divide, and daily experiences from the perspectives of one hundred urban Black youth. The intent is solely to hear their viewpoints. It is their viewpoint that we seek; no other voices or views, especially not their parents or any other adults in the community. This factor is important, since our projects are based on unfiltered young people.

Postracial Youth Conversations

This essay consists of a series of group conversations—discussions with Detroit youth over a four-year period. The theme of this gathering was "Life of Detroit Young Folks." The particular set of questions was built around the discussion of race. Detroit is presently 80-plus percent Black. The election of the nation's first Black president was a lead in to how race impacts youth in Detroit. The mood of these meetings was not formal nor interview- like. We called these social informal gatherings, social conversations. Our one rule was that anyone could express their opinions and feelings, as long as they remained respectful of others. None of the names in this project are participants' names or nicknames; there are no identifying labels. True to this ethnographic composition, the originality of the dialogue exchanged in the focus groups is intact, along with the pseudonym coding that represents each participant's comments. The following discussion took place during the presidential campaign of Barack Obama. There are five young men and five young women; representing youth ages sixteen to nineteen.

We asked a simple question, "How does Senator Obama as a Black man impact you in his bidding for the presidency?" Our respondents answered in following ways.

Benny:
It shows me I can be anything I want. America doesn't care about race. He is qualified and so, he probably will win. I see dude, he is cool, he is smart. I like him, and he is young.

Marva:
Yeah, he is fine, he is a real Black man. Got a wife, kids, not an asshole like our mayor. I use to like our mayor, but he likes to strut. My mom said our mayor is a hoe. A big hoe, his wife is nasty acting. Every time you see her she acting like she better than everybody. I don't like her. So, it is good to see Obama wife is nice, she is smart, I think she went to Harvard?

Mary:
You believing everything the media say about Mayor Kilpatrick? They hate him because he is big, strong and a real Black man. I like him, he real. Lots of old people don't like hip-hop. They mess with him because he is the hip-hop mayor. (Laughing) His mother is a congresswoman. She is real good, she helps lots of people. Now, the Mayor should not have got his wife that red Navigator. He cool, it is how the press hates Black people. Mayor Kilpatrick likes women, so what? Black mayors always catching hell. The media likes Obama cuz his momma is white. Most times my grandmother said the media use to hate Coleman Young. Obama is not really Black, his wife is Black. He is half Black and half white. So what does that mean?

Billy:
Obama will get shot. America hates Blacks. Benny is silly, man, America had niggahs as slaves. White people hate Mexicans, Niggahs, A-rabbs, the Black man is doomed. My daddy lost his job in the plant because of white lies. Obama better sit his Zebra ass down.

Teresa:
If he becomes president it means we will have life good. If he is president he can help Detroit. Things are not fair, our schools are messed up. I hope he wins, I really like him. He can make Black good instead of everybody thinking Blacks are no good.

Benny:
Well, he is qualified and that is all you have to be today. He went to college. His wife went to college. When Blacks get good education they can make it. Education means a lot. Race? Well I know there is prejudice, but so what? Barak Obama is Black and he is gonna be the next president of the United States of America.

Mike:
You are stupid, he is Black and America will never let a Black man be shit. My daddy got killed by some racist-ass police and my granddaddy says the white man wants all Blacks dead. Shit, me and Billy got stopped by the police in Birmingham for nothing. Anytime a cop sees a young Black guy they on that ass. Go to the store, they follow you, why? The mother-fucking A-rabbs watch you in their stores. They don't follow white people. Detroit is where they talk about we ain't shit. If you Black you are fucked, that is a fact.

Tony:
Being Black is fucked up. I know if you Black the president can't do shit. I hate it, what you gonna do.

Wanda:
Life is always different for Blacks. Voting for Obama is a chance to change the world. We are just hit, young people are getting a chance to vote and that is good.

Joe:
The election means what? Can a Black president make a difference? Young Black men still going to catch hell, it means what?

Linda:
Election means what for people? I doubt if we are going to get treated any different. I don't think America will do it? Race matters, believe it. Trust me I know I am not like white people?

Postracial Black Youth

The discussions and serious conversations intertwined with various subtopics evolved from preracial to postracial topics; there is not a balance among the comments, but more so diverse enough to understand these young people are not one dimensional. As race is the center of our talks, it is evident that class, gender, and sexuality are some of the subtexts that drive racial perceptions. Perceptions play a significant role, as we allow the youth to define exactly what they feel is considered racial in the millennium. The subject matter of postracial society lends itself to how the mythology has clouded the actual understanding of race, Detroit, and the regional polarization. It is here that youth are explaining how the challenges of race matter, and for some does not mean the same view shared by others within the polarized region, nation.

Jamal speaks of how whites perceive young Black men. It is a discussion that openly draws the pain of Detroit past racial divide. He states,

> They always think we are criminals, white people in the suburbs. You know they watch us wherever we go. My grandfather says whites hate Detroit. Why? Everybody thinks Detroit is Black. White police just stop us no matter what. Hell, Black police in the city will mess with you. Being Black is just messed up. Me and my boys were hanging out with some friends from my school. See, I go to a private school because my grandfather pays for it. My father is all messed up since he went to the war. My mom is good, she teaches at an elementary school. She wants me not to hate white people. Hard not to do, whites never treat me like I am like anybody else.

During this discussion I asked the young man if he felt the entire nation believed that Blacks were bad. This group consisted of eight young men all of who were in high school or college. They represented ages sixteen to twenty-three, and none of them had criminal convictions. They all had been stopped more than once for what they feel is simply because they are Black. The group is adamant that race plays a major role every day in their individual experiences. The following conversation involved three of this group expressing their views about going to college. The question revolved around the question, "Does higher education help you understand the racial divide of this nation?" Three young men are agitated with three others who take a more moderate position. Robert, John, and William represent the belief that college was racially divisive.

> *Robert offered:*
> Race is in college just like everywhere else. I hate how they put us down without knowing shit. I do well in math, I am a math major. My grandfather has his own business. It is small, but he knows business. My dad works in business for a dry cleaning company that is big time. They do uniforms for all kinds of companies. My parents know math, my mom's works in a dentist office. So, math has been easy for me. 'Cause, I had people who went to college. My pops wanted me to go to Morehouse since my grandfather and father went there. I followed my girlfriend, and that was the worst mistake of my life. The whole damn school don't want Black people or China people. White universities and white college is race all day. Black means you gonna always be the suspect. White boys talked about Detroit like it was the worst shit on the planet. College? They like to get high with you. They like for their girls to dance like niggahs. White boys want to eat ribs, fried chicken, smoke dope, and drink out of the pimp cup. White people don't know that their white kids is buck wild. White girls acting like superhoes. College is full of silly-ass racist kind of people.

> *John supports the views of Robert:*
> College has racist-ass professors and the Black professors are not cool. Got this African bitch, she hates Blacks from Detroit. She said Detroit is filled with ignorant Blacks. Race in college just means they smarter. Most of my professors don't know shit. Worse they all act like you shouldn't be in college. My boy is Mexican, he is cool. His girlfriend is white, she is down. My boy loves him some Mexican food. Anyway we was all talking one day in the coffee house. Then a crew of white boys came in and one of them pointed at us. This white frat boy said loud, "Chilli-beans-and-cornbread-eating niggahs." That pissed us off, you get tired of that shit. Race is just life. It will always mean as a Black you are going to get the shit end of life.

> *William takes a militant stance on racial issues in college:*
> College means now we see lots of students think Detroit means crime. They think we are inferior. I think college could help change things. Guess what? College makes it worse. Me, I just say it will

always be racial. Blacks must stand up to all this racist society. I will never bow to someone saying I am less than them. Because I am Black, proud I ain't having it. Race means you know the game is fixed for white folks.

Postracial America and Youth: The Criminal and Juvenile System

This discussion within a group of seven young men and three young women, ages sixteen to twenty-six, is rapid fire with heated moments that erupted. The group is listening to music and watching videos when we commented on the theme of incarceration in Post Racial America.

Suzy:
Every young guy in our 'hood has been locked up. So it really means that Black guys are going to prison. They know it and we know it. Race doesn't matter? Right, we get locked up and white people don't. They shoot and kill and then they say, Oh, he was crazy, oh he didn't take his medicine. Oh, it ain't his fault.

Gail:
For real, race means Blacks, brown go to prison. Police are always on us, they get you if you Black. You know, Detroit got thugs, hoodlum, and gangsters. But my little cousin is a nerd kinda niggah. Boy likes school, always has. He is a momma boy, guess what? Gangs were beefing in our 'hood. Po-Po drove up and just arrested about twenty niggahs. My cousin was coming from school, boy is stiff, not cool, nerdy boy. They don't care he was with the white boys he goes to the charter school. Po-Po wasn't hearing shit.

Paul:
Race? Well, being Black means trouble. Lots of crazy niggahs out here. Fact, Black niggas are dangerous. Black motherfucka's kill. I just watch out for Black-ass G's. . . . now whites do shit, but most crime is us. Black niggahs be slanging out here. You know if you Black you got to survive. Do I have a gat? Sure, you got to have a gat. Who is going to protect me? Detroit Po-Po shoot anybody. My daddy says they gonna git you sooner or later.

Howard:
Being Black in Detroit is like no other place. I been other places but nobody has more Black people then Detroit. Guns, killing, no

jobs, gangsters, everybody is out here with their heat. It means Blacks are just some killing muthafucka's. Why? Cuz they know, it is either kill or get killed. If you Black or Mexican the Man is looking to snuff you.

Gwen:
Race? All I know is Black people. The police don't really come around here. If you Black you know. Race is what? If you want to get busy try fucking with some poor little niggahs. They will eat your ass, little young niggahs are smoking that shit. They drinking, they out here knocking them out. I got a crew, my girls are ready. Sometime you have to get with fellas, sometime you need your crew cuz it is dog eat dog. I'm young, know how to protect my shit.

Bart:
Look at what they did to Mike Tyson? They put Blacks away for anything. First they look at what color you are. Then they just say no if you are Black. I know what to do, be a thug. Racial talk is just that talk. White man own niggahs. I ain't getting no job if you Black. I know my peops, know they ain't white.

Rick:
The whole thing in college is about getting over for niggahs. I will do what I got to to make it. If you Black, you got to make it work. Black is shit.

Tim:
There ain't no jobs for the Black man no more. My grandfather use to work in the plants. Robots replaced them, he use to be a welder. School ain't teach you shit. Nobody wants us around so they like to send us to prison or kill the Black man.

David:
Well, I think race is okay, if you don't get caught up in that white, Black shit. I got a girl from Italy. She just see me as a human being. I go to college and some Blacks think it is about race. Race will always be in front of you. Racist are real, but Blacks think they the only ones. Shit, I hate the Arabs in Detroit. They always acting like Blacks steal. I see lots of Chinese at my school. Lots of people don't like Chinese. Is this racism? Blacks do get punk a lot, it is tough for Blacks.

Eddie:
The criminal justice system is fixed. We are what about 12 percent of population? Who is locked up the most? The criminal justice is fixed, nothing but Blacks, brown, and some Chaldeans. But Blacks are locked the fuck up. That is what America believes, lock Blacks up forever.

Postracial Crime from the Likes of Young Black Males

In another occasion, seven young Black males ranging from thirteen to nineteen years old discussed their experiences in Detroit during a session with Carl S. Taylor, Virgil A. Taylor, and Anthony Holt. The question was whether the election of President Barak Obama was an indicator that race was no longer an issue in their lives. I asked, "So is life better now? Are you experiencing a better sense of life since the election?" Here are the answers.

Cedric:
Detroit is the same, fellas out here doing what they do. President Obama? Well, I really don't think nothing has change or will change. Po-Po is still doing their shit. Now, my grandmother she loves the man. My grandfather voted before they opened up for voting place. Is life better, naw, not really. Naw, I think in the street we still just hanging. Nobody gives a damn. My life is still hard, po-po is on us. The damn gang squad messing with you every day around school. Life is the same and I can't see Obama doing shit about that. . . ."

Allen:
Life is hard, you out here like he said. Who really thinks about a president? President Obama cuz he blood don't mean he knows how it is out here. I hate school, me, I'm just wondering how to get money. Around here it is always the same. Boys out here gitting killed, getting shot. This is the same as always. Election? Man, that shit is for old people. We know what we know. Crime? Crime is your job. (Laughing) We smoke, hang around, go see shorties. Crime is what it is. Niggahs get smoked, you be gangster or you just get out of the way.

Steve:
Life is what you do, Right? I hustle and teach these here young boys how to live. Election? Crime? Y'all ask some silly shit. We

> just here like it always been. My female friend she says things are gonna be different. I say right, when? I am out here, I hustle. Obama bringing me a job? Obama is cool I guess, I think he is cool. But ain't no president gonna do shit for us. I liked Mayor Kilpatrick, he seemed cool. But the fellas say he is fake, it don't matter. My uncle says whites hate his ass. I really don't know? Here, what does shit mean? We out here and if you want to eat, get paid you got to do it for yourself. My friend is different. A female with parents, nice house. Her father got here back. She got things. Her best friend is a Mexican girl named Maria. She is cool, they both like Obama, I say its cuz Obama looks like them. . . . Look, some people is glad that we got a Black president. It don't matter to me, I think he is cool, like his daughters and his wife. Somebody say he white, nope, I mean half white. He look like Harold Jackson, and his mother is just light skinned. Crime, how do I feel about crime? I feel crime is something that just means big niggahs take shit from whoever they want. Crime is the gang squad, they be gangster out here. Muthafucka's got badges, so? Them police being talking shit. They the worse gangsters I know. Gang squad being taking your money, take yo trees, take whatever, cuz they being telling us. They the Law, that means they can do whatever they want. That shit ain't right. . . . so is this different? Especially the white police, including them scared as females, some of them Black females are hard, fat wearing weaves like they Mary J. (Laughing) White female police will talk shit like they hard. I hate them, I hate all the police. Nothing is different and no half-white president means shit down here. This is the same old shit. Trust me, this is where we live every day.

Postracial Society

Greg, now in his early twenties, is discussing his feelings about the question of postracial society now that he just got out of prison. His transgression was selling crack to an undercover agent when he was nineteen years old. While he did not have drugs on his person, he was with a group of young men who were found with drugs. The question is whether he felt that race played an issue in his conviction. He said,

> Being Black is what keeps a young niggah in trouble. You saying what? There is no race problem today? (Laughing) That is shit,

> Black niggahs catch it, always! No more race issues? Where did you hear that shit? I had not been in nothing serious and they send me off to prison. I didn't even have the shit on me. I got hit cuz I am a niggah, and was with some other niggahs. Lost my job, it wasn't much, but I just got that damn job. There was a crazy little white boy in the joint. That muthafucka talked shit, he knew all the laws. He was in prison for some silly shit. He knew it was silly, told us he be out in a few months. He helped me get out early, this boy hooked me up with a young white-girl lawyer. Babe looked too young to be a lawyer. Anyway it was good. I got treated good, she said my appeal was good. They got me out. Man, I hate it cuz I am a Black muthafucka and that is what it is. . . . no race, color means nothing cuz America doesn't treat race Black or white? Man, wacked-ass questions? Me, like my daddy said, you Black its get back. White is right, I know that shit. Black means you stay in the D. Go outside Detroit and get arrested for being Black. It is that way, always been that way.

We followed up by asking, "Do you believe race will change eventually? When?" Greg answered:

> Hell naw, never, white people like keeping niggahs down. I know since I was in prison lots of the guards is white and some Blacks act like they hate Blacks if they guards. Prison is sure to let you know. Prison is always racial. Black in prison is where white guards treat you bad. That will never change, never. I got called monkey, gorilla, sambo, crank-oil Black, Black dog, Black shit, Black bitch. When will it change? When the world blows up. (Laughing) The white man needs to feel good about his whiteness. Blacks, Nigga Ricans, Mexicans, hell even them A-rabbs, we all niggahs to the white people. My granddaddy said that the white man is just racist. He knows, he grew up in the south. Man, why y'all asking all that shit? Race? It don't matter to me cuz I rather be with all niggahs. White men get crazy if you look at that white woman. Now, check it out. The white girl, that white woman will make that white man crazy. Some of the crazy Black niggahs inside prison talk shit to those racist guards about fucking their women. Not me, no way, not smart. My granddaddy told me how that white man will chop a niggahs dick off for looking at their women.
>
> Y'all need to ask something else, race shit is stupid. Race means you Black and that means you gonna get messed over. Look at me,

sent to prison for being with some niggahs who were selling little bags of trees? I got sent away cuz the white man, that ugly-ass white bitch judge told my young ass I was no good. How that bitch know? Cuz she knows all niggahs is bad, we all like to do wrong. Well, that is what she told me before sentencing me. My mom was in court, fucked up cuz I didn't do shit. They send a niggah away for being Black. That is the law, you can't be Black (laughing), that really ain't funny.

Postracial Society

In this segment we revisit the introduction of postracial society with the changing of the political landscape in Detroit. There are some youth who are aware of how race is changing in the new inner city of Detroit. Here, race changes matter, because it shows a comeback, reconstruction that defines itself in a confusing way. Is it gentrification? Does the new prosperous, new Detroit with an Emerald City allure, have a racial intent or motivation? These are some of the questions posed to the youth. Is it racial for the business growth of sporting events professionally? Is there a difference of social and economic means of the old dysfunctional inner city versus the new downtown of sustainability? It is here that youth are addressing their viewpoint. There is an undercurrent of dismal poverty in the neighborhoods, while there is new growth of prosperity in Midtown, corporate advancements, and sport organizations like the Detroit Tigers, Detroit Red Wings, and Detroit Lions. Youth are speaking about how society has served postracial Detroit with a record of postindustrial poverty that is engulfed in social issues. What is the perception of race, equality, jobs, education? Is it filled with dreams or nightmares?

On this day, a group of five young girls, Patricia, Lauren, Darlene, Nancy, and Norma, and two boys, Byron and Mike, ages ranging from seventeen to twenty-four, talk about their future dreams in the City of Detroit. We asked them if Detroit was a good place to them.

Nancy:
I say yes, it is all we know. Detroit is Black, that is what we like. Whites don't come around much where we hang. Detroit is kind of rough. My mom worries about me, she is scared. Ever since they been killing girls, kidnapping them. Me? I don't worry, me and my girls we got a nice place. We all share a big house, it was my aunt and uncle, left it to me and moms. I like Detroit, I see white people when we are out at the mall. Me, I think the president is fine, wish

he was my daddy. (Big smile) I like his wife, they don't come to Detroit. That makes me sad, seems like everybody dogs Detroit.

Patricia and Norma:
Patricia: Nobody coming to Detroit, too many killings. Whites and some Blacks are scared of Detroit. We know it can be rough. Our next door neighbor is two Detroit cops. They cool, they just act like they not police when they home. One is a fat female, girlfriend need stop wearing tight clothes, she is thick, big fat ass.

Norma: They alright, sometimes in the summer they cookout. Some white cops be over there. It's cool, they know we ain't no ghetto hoes.

Patricia: Detroit is a good place. (Laughing) Well, if you got the police next door.

Lauren:
I don't like Detroit, too much shooting. Young niggahs be out here just acting like they all G's. Every young niggah I know got gats. We ain't looking for females to act like they do. Some females are just like niggah guys, want to get it on. Some white people treat me bad at work. Always looking at you like they better, you know? My future? Well, I might leave here. I think I want to go to Cali, maybe ATL, I don't know? Detroit is getting worse to me.

Byron:
Detroit in the future will be okay. Look at the downtown were I go see the Tigers. Now, that is where all the white people come. I work at Hockey Town, I work with white people, some okay, some are assholes? Dreams? Nope, I don't dream about nothing. Detroit is okay depending where you live. My grandparents got a real nice house. My grandfather will shoot anybody about his house or car. He is retired and he says Detroit is doomed. Me, will I got a good job, I am going to college part time. I think Detroit got some bad breaks. I was really surprised when Mayor Kilpatrick went gangster.

Mike:
My future is cool. I paint houses, got my own little hustle you know. I love Detroit, my folks live in Palmer Woods. Me and Byron been friends since elementary. I think Detroit future is good. The thug guys, you know the gang type is the only life they know. My folks help me start my paint company. I just don't go some places. I probably will move later because I think lots of places are dangerous now.

> Maybe, well, maybe it might get scary sometime. I just go to see the Pistons and Tigers. Avoid all the rough, dangerous places. Sometime it seems like everybody just say messed-up things about Detroit no matter what Detroit does. Anyway, I still think Detroit is going to make it. Race things are not cool. Race means some cops will assume that because you Black you gangster or something. I hate that, never been in any gang.

Postracial Society for Black Youth

The conversations about race are steeped in the social conditions of ruins of once well-organized neighborhoods. Is this caused by racial factors? The youth are questioning the role of race as the job loss takes its toll on the loss of commerce. Youth are involved in the role of race as political corruption is discussed. The role of Black families is discussed as poverty anchors declining decades of fleeing migrations. This is quite different from the external exodus within the abandoned communities filled with a racial population that is exclusively Black. Additionally, the ongoing conversation on so-called postracial Detroit never registered with the poor, Black, or uneducated lumpenproletariat. This segment of the discussion finds youth voices questioning the state of race in Detroit, comparing the postindustrial era with the postracial era ushered in by the election of Barack Obama.

This interview is with Chris who is in his late twenties and lives on the west side of the city. He discusses his feeling about the Detroit Police and police in the suburbs. His racial views collide with the subject of police. He said,

> The Detroit Police are always messing with me. The other police mess with me too. It is my rims on my car, maybe it's my car, got a Black Challenger with hyped rims. Detroit cops especially the white ones act like if you got rims, nice car, you into something thug like. See, I been in the war, went to Iraq, then the Army put me out because my eyesight is messed up. So, I work, pay my bills, and then the police mess with me everywhere I go. My older brother says police just hate Black people. My dad is handicapped, he got a van so he says it's our fault because police don't just stop you for nothing. My dad is probably the only Black man to ever to like cops.
>
> See Detroit Police are really messed up. When Mayor Kilpatrick was in office he let them do whatever. My father said that police

chief was foul, that woman. One time my parents was up at the store over in Harbor Town. That police chief was in the store with two police, my old man said they were her bodyguards. My mom was laughing, she said why she need bodyguards. My dad defended her, he just love police. In Detroit the police look fat, lazy, guess they don't have much money so they look like security guards. The worse is the female cops. This ugly, fat weave-wearing female sergeant made me move my car from front of the Coney Island downtown. Man, she had all this weaved hair and it was different colors. Loud colors, red, blue, blue hair? She dogged us, she had another female cop with her. I told her I was a veteran, you know so she could respect me. Later for that, the Black man got nothing. I wanted to kick her fat ass, she was swelling up, later for that fat bitch. I was in the war, I risked my life for America. So what is what she said when I told her that I was in the U.S. Army, infantry.

Tell you what I know about America. First, America hates Blacks, hates President Obama more. Second, in the military they got lots of people, white people who hate Blacks, hate A-rabbs, hate Mexicans, hate Orientals. My stay in Baghdad was wacked. Man, Army bosses were calling them sand niggers, like I know they call us niggers. White boys talk bad about Obama. Talked about his wife, shit, when I think about it makes me mad. My brother married a Mexican girl, she cool. Damn, my brother say, now they both catch it from the Detroit Police, especially around Mexican village. This white cop in Dearborn called me, my boys Moolies. Same shit we was out at the mall, you know Fairlaine Mall. Man, I got credit cards, I work full time. I go to school part time. So, guess what? This suburban cop tells me not to come out there? I told him this is America, he told me straight up again. Don't come out here with your fancy pimp car, playing that rap music. He was serious, him and another police car told us to keep our Black asses in Black Detroit. I can fight for this nation, and still I am a Black-ass nigger. Man, that is just wrong, it is messed up. My mother agrees it is wrong, my dad just shrugged his shoulders?

John and William Reason, brothers who are twenty-three and twenty-seven-year-old, respectively, give an interview about their life in Detroit. We asked them how they made a life in Detroit with a Black man being the president. John smiles looking at his brother as he begins to explain:

Make it in Detroit? Good question, don't really know? We are just barely making it out here. President Obama doesn't mean much to me. I think it is rough, fucked up for Black people. We been poor all our lives. Our mother put me and William out when were teenagers. I think it just something you got to accept. My old grandmother is in a home. She is cool, maybe the only person that cared about us. My mother is just about her. She kicked us out cuz she took up with this niggah who said he wasn't feeling no grown-ass men living off of him. So she told us we had to go. Fucked up when you own mother kick you out for nothing. Lots of young girls get kicked out. Lots of niggah kids got nobody. So, you Black, it is always been hard. My grandmother is in a fucked-up raggedy old folks home. I hate all the bullshit. I see all kinds of poor people, some Mexicans, some other white boys out here trying to survive.

Police watching you when you a young niggah. Me and Will get stopped all the time. Detroit Police like to fuck over niggahs. Even niggah cops they foul. You learn out in the street that life is hard for the Black man. We been homeless, first we had some relatives let us stay with them. That only can last for a minute cuz they got no funds for extra people. I got a job in a restaurant, you know, prepping food. Muthafucka paid me off the books. I didn't care, they let me get food at the end of the night. I bring home, at that time we stayed over on Victor street. William got into school, the community college. He was trying but he said it was hard. He got some funds for a bit. So, my money was all we had. The house had some of our boys living there. We had no water, electricity was a hook up. That place was so cold and we burn shit-old wood. It was the worse, now, we live in a motel over on Woodward. Place is fucked up, but it got water. This ugly old white man is the manager. He love to call me Willie, first I thought he had me and William mixed up. (Laughing) Guess what? He call every Black man Willie. We all named Willie. . . .

Neither of us been in trouble, never been arrested. Nope. Been stopped like one million times in my life. Stopped why? Cuz? Cuz I am a Black-ass nigga, I guess? William is trying to get into an art school now. The community college didn't work. Me? I am out here with three jobs. All of them under the table. I wash cars, prepped food, and sometime I do roofing with some fellas I know.

William, the older brother, nods as his brother talks. When asked if he had anything to say he muttered:

> No, he is right. We live hard. Life is hard. Our mother chose a man over us? Detroit is where we live. Police fuck with you. Me and John is just us, nobody gives a shit about us. The way I see it if I could get a chance I could become like people who live good. I got a chance if I just keep trying. Me and my brother is all we got. My father is dead or something, my mother never talked about him. One day she told us that we looked like our father. I guess that is why she hated us, cuz she really showed me that she hated us. Anyway, we just living in the street, you could say. The Black man is not needed no more. So, my grand says we gonna just kill each other, I guess that is it for us?

About two years later, we conducted another interview. We asked our interviewee, Nitra, how she saw herself in the United States as a citizen. Surrounded by six other youth, Nitra starts to respond:

> I see myself as a free Black woman who is bisexual. That means I got lots of trouble. My father put me out, and my mother is too damn scare to challenge his punk ass. He called me a lesbian, a pussy licker, he beats my mother. He used to beat me and my younger brother. My little brother joined me, and we said fuck that shit. We got out shit and we fought that punk-ass daddy back. I got some brass knuckles and I slammed my fist in his big-ass mouth. Damn, his teeth was broke, bleeding. My little brother got a bat, he hit that asshole in his back. My old daddy was all fucked up. Shit if you live in our America, that means you got to arm yourself. My life is good long as I make a bitch understand I ain't take shit off nobody.
>
> In our hood there are A-rabbs, Mexicans, Polish people, we got all kinds of people. I see myself in Detroit and in America as a person. I am going to make it despite all the shit they try to stop you with. Black women catch more hell than anybody. You a woman, you a Black woman, and then, me? I like girls, you know, you hear bitches trying to say shit like I like dick? Okay, I like both? A guy said I was confused? Why? 'Cause I like girls that means I have to quit boys? I can do what I want to do in America. . . . I see myself free, I am me, I am a bad-ass bitch. (Laughing)

In another interview, conducted on the Martin Luther King Day, Kelvar and Tookie, both in their early twenties, discussed what race meant to them. The group met in a neighborhood barbershop. The question is asked if it is disrespectful to use the face of Dr. King for a party invitation. The small poster party invitation and the Internet site of Dr. King depicts him wearing gold chains and hip-hop clothing, surrounded by young dancers with g-strings and bare breasts. The talk begins with criticism coming from an older barber who let it be known that he is furious with the depiction.

Kelvar:
We know that race means Blacks are nothing to America. Later for Rev. Sharpton and fuck Dr. King. We ain't down with shit, this here thing is about one thing. MONAY! It is just for a poster, letting muthafucka's know about the party. I get tired every time they start that Black history shit, I don't care about no King. Al Sharpton hollering all the time. I want my boys to make that loot. So what about Rev. King? They just selling their party, anyway, I heard Rev. King like hoes?

Tookie:
You are so ignorant. Why don't y'all respect Dr. King? I heard some shit, but so what? I don't think it means shit. Mr. Brown is all upset, I understand he is old. Old people love Dr. King. Kelvar, you don't respect nothing. He is a preacher, he is history for us. You niggahs love to be ignorant. Rev. Sharpton knows the president, he got a point. He fights against racism, but white people are foul. Race is always there; when white people think Black they think and see you ignorant-ass Kelvar. (Laughing) I agree with Kelvar, race means trouble. Black people go to jail. White people get off for crime all the time. Probably why these boys don't care, because they know. Race means Blacks get messed over. So? Dr. King is dead and he ain't coming back.

Kelvar:
Calling me ignorant don't mean shit. I never really believed in all that shit King said, but it don't matter if a muthafucka say something wrong, we just kick his ass. How you know Dr. King didn't have no gold chains? He loved him some hoes, right? All that civil rights shit happened long time ago. I am making out here. King and all that civil rights shit let muthafucka's beat their ass. Naw, ain't happening to me, my boys. You hit me, I will blast you. Anyway, King looks good in them posters. Rev. King looks like he likes the hoes and he is dressed down. (Laughing)

Reflection

The complexity of postracial feelings are found in the transition of the traditional older generation clashing with a younger generation that is questioning the reality of knowing or not knowing the legacy of Rev. Dr. Martin Luther King Jr. This conversation is powerful, disturbing for an older generation. Little open discussion hardly acknowledges or allows the class driven factors that are again about class, sexuality, economics, and education. Did the election of Obama change anything directly in the ghostlike communities outside of the new inner city? Young people talk about the future of themselves and what that means for Detroit. Does Detroit have a future that can be framed within a positive sense? Youths discuss the trials and tribulations of a dying industrial trained Black community. What does the future hold for these youths? Here we listen to the sentiments of feeling of discontent, disrespected and losing hope as they watch what their families had once felt was the Black American Dream dissipate, underscored by how Detroit was once the most powerful growing Black middle class. The youths understand the professional and working-class divide in Black America, especially in Detroit.

Race is tricky, divisive, and more problematic because most folks don't seem to understand what race means, did, or continues to do. As mentioned previously, Hughey points out that racial inequality is unnatural and a complex issue. The sociological definition of race informs us that *race* is a socially constructed category that divides groups of people according to certain characteristics, like phenotype and behavioral differences.[8] I, Carl Taylor, recall an interview with the late Max Roach. This great musician explained why he no longer subscribed to the notion of race being a means of judgment, evaluation, or anything significant in living life. Roach, a seriously intelligent man, shared impressive thoughts regarding race. I considered all the time, effort, and emphasis on race in society at large. How it feels when race seems to be critical in terms of how one is perceived in the world.

I had wondered a great deal about the candidacy of a Black junior senator from Illinois when it became painfully clear that it could really happen. I was listening to a group of older Black gentlemen who debated about the seemingly impossible electability of this tall, light-skinned Negro who was not all Black. I had not taken the discussion seriously. really. I watched the news, read the blogs, and even was impressed as he read more about Obama. I was trying to really look at this man who looked like a thousand other tall, cool Black men in my community. He was a mulatto? Wow, hadn't heard that word since my undergraduate history class. Max Roach was haunting me about race mattering. The world was getting deeper, stranger by the moment. Black folks were spinning, loving, hating, and more changes than I could understand about the street strive of this so-called candidate Negro. I even had a closer look in DC, at an event where my crew watched him walk slowly down the aisle at the Library of Congress to sit on the stage with the Black Caucus of the Congress. Not politically correct, but he did have that street thing on him. The candidate was pimp walking to the stage. Now for many in America, the whole notion of pimp walking will register as foreign, and for my spirit of Max Roach make it racial. His hair was cut in the same fashion of a 1964, nicely waved Quo Vadis. The style was supercool, he was tall, aloof, lanky, and I saw a fella, cool type of brother. The women were smiling proudly and whispering was buzzing. My brother Al was intently watching every step. Al was impressed as was Pamela Smith, researcher in charge of our female project. I don't know exactly but Pamela, the coauthor of this chapter, was listening as Al pointed to the lone figure heading toward the stage with an all-star cast of Black politicians.

The winds were blowing, and it was a packed auditorium of colored folks from all over the United States. Congressman John Conyers, Congressman Charles Rangel, and Congresswoman Maxine Waters all sat on the stage. It reminded me of my high school days, when the national honor society or something proudly achieved was on front and center. The golden voice of Professor Michael Eric Dyson was the master of ceremony. It was a memory that Al told me was historical, an event of a life for all of us who had traveled to support the leadership, image of one of the most important political families in Michigan—Detroit, to be specific. I had insisted that Pamela, who was constructing her dissertation around the images of African American female adolescence, travel to witness this day. The crowning of Detroit's own Congresswoman Carolyn Cheeks-Kilpatrick, who was being anointed as leader, head of the Black Caucus. It was our history. More importantly, it was rewarding the effort, hard work, and diligence of a career that was evolving over a period of political advancement, with Congresswoman Cheeks-Kilpatrick under the political wisdom of the political potentate Coleman A. Young. While the Congresswoman would later be hit by volumes of unfairness, character assassination, she nonetheless earned her way to this time of leadership.

Political winds blew cross the district that day. Congresswoman Nancy Pelosi opened the ceremony, and there was enough Black clergy that day to seem as if it was a Black capital and the second coming of a Black Messiah. Detroit folks were represented from city politicians, state politicians, and plenty of community groups, activists, and proud citizens. Al sensed something; Pamela scouted the event looking at all the people. More amazing for Pamela was the contrast of a former Black schoolteacher who had previously launched her political career as a state representative. Pam leaned over and wrote a short note that claimed, what about all the young girls interviewed in Detroit? What about them, at that moment Pamela wanted the young females to experience, see the new leader of the caucus. It was a Black woman who hailed from the same working-class city they now inherited in a much more troubled time. The images of a Black woman heading an important group of national representatives argued with me and that spirit of Max Roach. What was racial? Did race matter? Al was in heaven since he had served at the White House in the U.S. Navy. He appreciated every nook and cranny of the grounds of the White House, as it was quite apparent his dream come true was seeing the man who represented the potential of the junior senator becoming the leader of the free world.

The whole experience included the conflicted atmosphere of the supposed sure bet Hillary Clinton presidential candidacy. Sides were shaping and tension was high as many supporters of the chocolate flavor wrestled with their allegiances on that day. Who was down with the Clintons? Who was down with the new golden boy? Oh happy days? Cheeks-Kilpatrick was in her reign, in a moment of royalty it seemed her beloved son, the Mayor Kwame Kilpatrick, spoke to the packed auditorium. It was no secret the Cheeks-Kilpatrick clan had created an image of political dynasty in Detroit. Did race matter again? Aunt and sister to Congresswoman Kilpatrick, Marsha Cheeks held the same seat her nephew Kwame and sister Carolyn had held as state representative earlier. The popular congresswoman had a political network that went from Detroit to all over the nation. The undercurrent was strong as to who was for the newcomer or the sure bet of the former first Black president Bill Clinton and his wife Hillary. I was caught in other nets of confusion. Who was this new guy? What did Hillary mean to me? I knew nothing of this guy from Harvard? He looked cool and maybe, nah, a Black president? The whole idea of a Black president was not really processed? Racial issues? The greatest challenge is the racial divide and color blindness, where America is still entangled.

An Observation of Black Youth and Race

The question of race and Black youth in America finds Detroit in turmoil. In the past decades, youths have been an integral part of what Detroit is experiencing. This essay represents the years that were especially important, with the election of the first African American President Barack Obama. In the year 2014, it is apparent from our discussions, group talks, interviews, and individual conversations that race has not lost the challenge that famed sociologist W. E. B. Du Bois warned about in his insightful declaration that "race was the problem of the 20th Century facing America."

Among the hundred young people in our sample who we engaged in the discussions about postracial sentiments in America, three young people found that race was not an issue in their lives, while seventy-three young people felt that race was a problem with the American justice system, clearly feeling that race was the sole determinant for incarceration by the larger society. Seventy-seven young people in discussion did not feel that race would ever not be a determining factor in their lives as African Americans. Thirty-six youths felt that President Obama made no difference for their communities. Forty-one youths saw the betterment in racial matters after the election of President Obama. Eighty-four stated that America is not concerned about race equality. Ninety-one of the youths said that their racial status was always a concern when it came to getting a job. Finally, the key question was whether race matters in a significant way in their daily lives? Eighty-one youths said absolutely race mattered, and it was a negative for Blacks.

The research in Detroit has been going on for over forty years. There have been specific dissections of varied points with variables such as sexuality, class, religion, education, family, and the extremely sensitive issue of gender. While numerous points have been made, the underlining factor in this citywide focus is that race remains, as Du Bois claimed, the problem of the twentieth century, now the problem of the twenty-first century.

Notes

1. W. E. B. Du Bois, *The Autobiography of W. E. B. Dubois; a Soliloquy on Viewing My Life from the Last Decade of Its First Century* (New York: International Publishers, 1968), 338.

2. Daniel P. Moynihan, "The Negro Family: The Case for National Action"" in *The Moynihan Report and the Politics of Controversy*, ed. Lee Rainwater, William L. Yancey, and Daniel P. Moynihan (Cambridge: MIT Press, 1967), 85.

3. Lewis Oscar, "The Culture of Poverty," *Society* 35, no. 2 (1998).

4. Moynihan, "The Negro Family: The Case for National Action," 75.

5. Michelle Alexander, *The New Jim Crow: Mass Incarceration in the Age of Colorblindness* (New York: New Press, 2012), 180.

6. Matthew W. Hughey, "Measuring Racial Progress in America: The Tangled Path," in *The Obamas and a (Post) Racial America?* ed. Gregory S. Parks and Matthew W. Hughey (Oxford ; New York: Oxford University Press, 2011), 1–26.

7. W. E. B. Du Bois and Brent Hayes Edwards, *The Souls of Black Folk* (New York: Oxford University Press, 1903, 2007).

8. John Scott and Gordon Marshall, "Race," *A Dictionary of Sociology* (New York: Oxford University Press, 2012).

Bibliography

Alexander, Michelle. *The New Jim Crow: Mass Incarceration in the Age of Colorblindness*. New York: New Press, 2012.

Du Bois, W. E. B. *The Autobiography of W. E. B. Dubois; a Soliloquy on Viewing My Life from the Last Decade of Its First Century*. New York: International Publishers, 1968.

Du Bois, W. E. B., and Brent Hayes Edwards. *The Souls of Black Folk*. New York: Oxford University Press, 1903, 2007.

Hughey, Matthew W. "Measuring Racial Progress in America: The Tangled Path." In *The Obamas and a (Post) Racial America?* edited by Gregory S. Parks and Matthew W. Hughey, 1–26. New York: Oxford University Press, 2011.

Leonardo, Zeus. "Black Scholarship in the Interest of Black Folks." In *Reading African American Experiences in the Obama Era: Theory, Advocacy, Activism*, edited by Ebony Elizabeth Thomas and Shanesha R. F. Brooks-Tatum, 261–266. New York: Peter Lang, 2012.

Moynihan, Daniel P. "The Negro Family: The Case for National Action. "In *The Moynihan Report and the Politics of Controversy*, edited by Lee Rainwater, William L. Yancey, and Daniel P. Moynihan, 39–124. Cambridge: MIT Press, 1967.

Oscar, Lewis. "The Culture of Poverty." *Society* 35, no. 2 (1998): 7–9.

Oxford, Dictionaries. "Post-Racial." *Oxford Dictionaries.Com*: Oxford University Press.

Scott, John, and Gordon Marshall. "Race." In *A Dictionary of Sociology*. Oxford University Press, 2012.

part 4

Popular Culture

11

Leave the Prejudice, Take the Power

Crash, *Fruitvale Station*, and Race in Hollywood in the Twenty-First Century

Justin Gomer

> I don't know what most white people in this country feel, but I can only conclude what they feel from the state of their institutions.
>
> —James Baldwin, 1968

Introduction

On Sunday, March 5, 2006, as the 78th annual Academy Awards wound down, Jack Nicholson took the stage to hand out the night's final award—Best Picture. After breaking the seal on the evening's last envelope, Nicholson announced *Crash*—a film that explores racial tensions in Los Angeles through a diverse ensemble of the city's residents—as the winner of Hollywood's top prize. After reading the winner, a surprised Nicholson raised his eyebrows, looked off to his right and mouthed, "Whoa!" to some of his colleagues in the audience. The creators of *Crash* were equally stunned. As the broadcast cut away from Nicholson, the cameras captured the film's director Paul Haggis embracing his ecstatic wife saying, "Oh my God!" while the cast of the film maneuvered around their seats in a manner that combined the obvious excitement of winning an Oscar with real surprise at their coup.

Crash was one of the great underdogs to win best picture. It was released in May of 2005, long before the fall when studios release the majority of anticipated award contenders. And although the film garnered generally positive reviews and performed well at the box office, few thought the film would seriously contend for Best Picture award. The film did have its ardent supporters, however. Chief among them was the late Roger Ebert, who put the movie atop his "Best 10 Movies of 2005" list. "Much of the world's misery is caused by conflicts of race and religion," wrote Ebert,

> Paul Haggis' film. . . . uses interlocking stories to show we are in the same boat, that prejudice flows freely from one ethnic group to another. His stories are a series of contradictions in which the same people can be sinned against or sinning. There was once a simple morality formula in America in which white society was racist and blacks were victims, but that model is long obsolete. Now many more players have entered the game: Latinos, Asians, Muslims, and those defined by sexual orientation, income, education or appearance.[1]

Reviewers like Ebert applauded the film for its supposedly pull-no-punches depiction of racism in the twenty-first century. As the film's cowriter Bobby Moresco explains, he and Haggis were not interested in political correctness. Instead, they made a choice to deal with the issue of race "directly."[2]

This chapter explores the racial politics of *Crash* in order to better understand not only Hollywood's assessment of racism in the twenty-first century but also its contribution in framing racial discourse in the new millennium. The racial project of color blindness—the notion that race no longer matters and that our legal and political processes should not consider race—has become increasingly influential over the past three and a half decades, as the Supreme Court has gradually banned race-conscious college admission and hiring policies, most recently at the University of Texas.[3] Furthermore, in the mid-1990s, states began to ban race-conscious programs designed to promote racial inclusion and enhance diversity through ballot initiatives.[4] With *Crash*, Haggis, a self-professed liberal, takes the opposite view—that *everyone* harbors racial prejudices. Yet, however progressive Haggis's views of race, as represented in *Crash*, may appear, in actuality they are ones in which racism is depoliticized and relegated strictly to interpersonal interaction. In acknowledging that race still matters, *Crash* eschews the power relationships and the structural forces behind the manner in which racism operates in favor of individuals who harbor prejudiced attitudes. In this, the film replaces one racial fallacy—color blindness—with another, and leaves its audience at a dead-end without any perspective on the machinations of race in twenty-first-century America. Ultimately, *Crash* offers a neoliberal conception of racism in which, in Thatcheresque fashion, there are no groups in society, only individuals. David Harvey defines neoliberalism as a "theory of political economic practices proposing that human well-being can best be advanced by the maximization of entrepreneurial freedoms within an institutional framework characterized by private property rights, individual liberty, unencumbered markets, and free trade."[5] According to David Harvey, "The founding figures of neoliberal thought took political ideas of human dignity and *individual freedom* as fundamental, as 'the central values of civilization'" (emphasis added).[6]

While other scholars have noted the shortcomings of *Crash*'s racial politics, my aim here is twofold: exploring the ways in which *Crash*'s racial politics function not only at the level of narrative and dialogue, but in the movie's form and aesthetics; and situating the elision of power in the film's view of racism within the larger emergence of neoliberal hegemony.[7] This chapter begins with a close reading of the film to illustrate the manner in which the racial politics of *Crash* operate. It concludes with a brief discussion of the recently released *Fruitvale Station*, a movie that, like *Crash*, also concludes with the killing of a young Black man at the hands of a white police officer, yet ultimately offers a fundamentally different racial politics that challenges those of *Crash*. In the final analysis, when it comes to film, and Hollywood film especially, it is not merely whether or not the movie industry is willing to acknowledge that race still matters, but the role its movies allow race to play.

The Racial Politics of *Crash*

Crash takes viewers on a two-day journey ("Yesterday" and "Today") through the interconnected lives of a handful of racially diverse residents of Los Angeles, each of whom harbor and are subjected to racial prejudices. Characters include the white Los Angeles District Attorney (DA) and his wife, who are hijacked at the film's onset; the two young Black hijackers; the brother of one of the hijackers, a Black police detective; his Latina partner; a Latino man who changes the locks at the DA's house after the carjacking; a Persian store owner whose convenience store is destroyed after the same locksmith cannot repair his door; a white police officer who eventually kills one of the hijackers; another white police officer who molests and then saves a Black woman; that Black woman and her television director husband; and others. Over the course of forty-eight hours these characters' lives intersect and "crash" into each other in a number of often violent, traumatic, or damaging ways.

The film avoids the neat taxonomy of bigots and their victims. Instead, every character is both guilty of racial animosity and in some way the target of another's prejudice. Black Detective Graham Waters (Don Cheadle) assumes all Latinos are Mexican, asking if there is diversity among the wide array of people labeled Latino, "who taught them all how to park their cars on their lawns?" Similarly, Anthony, a young Black car-jacker (Ludacris) refers to all Asians as "Chinamen." After two carjackers steal the District Attorney's car at gunpoint, his wife, Jean Cabot (Sandra Bullock), demands her locks be changed twice because the original locksmith, a heavily tattooed Latino man, is, according to Bullock's character, surely a gang member who will sell their house keys to one of his "gang-banger friends." Rhea (Jennifer Esposito) mocks an Asian woman for her inability to pronounce certain English words. John Ryan (Matt Dillon), an angry racist LAPD officer berates his father's health insurance agent, a Black woman, saying that her hiring resulted solely because of affirmative action. And thieves vandalize a Persian family's liquor store with a series of anti-Arabic slurs—an act that combines the Islamophobia of the post-9/11 American society and the common American ignorance of the diversity of the Middle East. These are only a few of the many instances of bigotry that occur throughout the film. Paul Haggis, the film's writer and director, echoed Ebert's assessment of the extent of racism in American society that the film depicts, explaining in an interview,

> With *Crash*, I just wanted to fuck viewers up. I want to sit you down in your seat and make you feel really, really comfortable with everything you believe. All those secret little thoughts you have, I wanted to say, "Shh, shh, it's fine. We all think that way." And as soon as you get comfortable, I wanted to start twisting you around in your seat, until when you walk out, you didn't know what the hell to think.[8]

Haggis's comments reveal his intention to offer a radical antiracist politics that challenge the central tenet of color blindness—that racism no longer exists. As Eduardo Bonilla-Silva notes, within the logic of color blindness racial inequality is explained by supposedly nonracial factors that seek to "naturalize," "rationalize," or "minimize" racial disparities through tropes such as cultural deficiencies that in actuality insulate white privilege from critique. *Crash* avoids these tenets of what Bonilla-Silva calls "color-blind racism."[9] However, the film's challenge to color blindness also relegates racism strictly to interpersonal interaction. Never in the film do viewers see any discussion or interrogation of institutional racism. The privileging of interpersonal interactions occurs alongside the neglect of racism's systematic and institutional elements. Racial epithets are brought to the forefront at the expense of racial issues pertaining to education, wealth, income, housing, or the prison-industrial complex, to name a few.

Therein lies the central issue with *Crash*'s racial politics—the film fails to extend the scope of racism beyond individual feelings and emotions. Its neoliberal conception of race is entirely oblivious to the structural racism that produces the vast racial inequality in our society today. The film never provides insight into the social, political, legal, or geographic discrimination people of color face in Los Angeles. The entire structure of white privilege, and the disparities between whites and people of color in virtually every social, political, economic, and public health indicator is elided in favor of the hurt feelings we all are capable of feeling when someone hurls a slur our way. Racism is therefore little more than impolite. It is a zero-sum game in which white people say offensive things to Blacks, who say offensive things to Latinos, who make offensive comments toward Asians, and so forth. Ultimately, *Crash* envisions a society in which we are all equal—equally racist.

While *Crash* refutes the claim that we live in a color-blind society by arguing we live in an incredibly *prejudiced* society, the film does nothing to show the imbalance of power between races that results in a white supremacist one. Laws like Stop and Frisk, Stand Your Ground, and voter ID laws are incongruous in a neoliberal era in which notions of racism are limited to personal malice. If we limit our discussions of race to a debate over how many bigots there are—a debate in which on one side lie those who believe we've largely attained Martin Luther King Jr.'s color-blind dream, and on the other, those like Haggis, who argue that we are all prejudiced—we lose the capacity to perceive the active steps taken to disenfranchise and oppress people of color, that ultimately have little to do with an individual's attitudes about race. In fact, the privileging of personal feelings is itself the product of white privilege. Moreover, by limiting the scope of racism to individuals, racism becomes a disease in which no one benefits, everyone is both oppressed and the oppressor; there are no winners, only losers.

Yet, this is not the way in which racism operates. There are, in fact, "winners" and "losers" when it comes to racism. As George Lipsitz argues, "Whiteness has a cash value" that produces advantages and "profits" for white people in virtually all areas of society, including housing, education, employment, and intergenerational wealth.[10] Lipsitz continues, "white supremacy is usually less a matter of direct, referential, and snarling contempt than a system for protecting the privileges of whites by denying communities of color opportunities for asset accumulation and upward mobility."[11] A substantial amount of research demonstrates the manner in which whites have profited from discrimination, both past and present, and continue to do so today.[12]

Whites may, in other words, potentially have their feelings hurt by racial epithets, but those hurt feelings do not change the fact that their whiteness affords them an immense amount of privilege and a significant advantage over people of color in America. People of color, on the other hand, are not only subjected to hurt feelings but also the reality of significantly less income, less wealth, lower property-values, shorter life expectancy, and less access to health care than whites, and significantly larger prison sentences, incidents of police harassment and brutality than whites, to name only a few examples. This basic but indisputable reality of America's racial hierarchy is entirely absent from Haggis's film. *Crash* claims we are all equal; we most certainly are not. Haggis's film fails entirely to demonstrate the interconnectedness of economics and race. One cannot explain away the vast income and wealth inequality that exists between whites and people of color with economics alone. As Stuart Hall explains, "racial structures cannot be understood adequately outside the framework of quite specific sets of economic relations."[13] Yet *Crash*'s neoliberal racial politics disregard the entanglement of race and class in favor of a belief that discrimination exists exclusively between one individual and another, and all individuals can therefore discriminate or be discriminated against equally.

Moreover, *Crash*'s neoliberal conception of racism aligns it far more closely with the color-blind discourse it supposedly stands in direct opposition to. Despite the fact that *Crash* takes the opposite position of a color-blind America, that both sides of that argument limit the debate of the scope of racism to the number of racist individuals, attests to the hegemony of neoliberal thought on not only race, but society in general. For example, over the past several decades we have seen Black people's access to higher education and employment opportunities significantly curtailed by the rolling back and elimination of affirmative action programs. Those laws were, in many cases, thrown out or restricted by the Supreme Court in cases because of the perceived discriminatory effect of those programs on single white individuals. In an era where color-blind neoliberalism enables the rights of one white person—be it Abigail Fisher or Alan Bakke—to trump that of all Black people, *Crash* perpetuates the neoliberal foundation that we are an equal opportunity society of individuals in which race is insignificant.

There are two instances in which the film points, to some degree, to structural racism. In the first instance Officer Hansen, after witnessing his partner, John Ryan, molest a Black woman named Christine (Thandie Newton) during a traffic stop, requests a new partner. His

Black lieutenant (Keith Dixon), sarcastically asks Hansen how a racist police officer like Ryan could go undetected for seventeen years. He even characterizes the LAPD as a "racist organization." Yet, while this does to some degree expand the scope of racism to the police department as an organization, their discussion is nonetheless limited to the internal machinations of the department itself—how reporting such activity will affect each of their careers. The film offers nothing here about, say, the effects of this "racist organization" on the Black community of Los Angeles, or its contribution to the larger inequities of the criminal justice system more broadly.

The plight of Officer Ryan's father is most revealing regarding the film's limited attempt to engage structural discrimination. Unable to sleep because of a debilitating urinary tract infection, the audience learns that Ryan's father worked his entire life as a janitor, eventually starting his own company and hiring exclusively Blacks when, as Ryan claims, no one else was. However, years prior when the city implemented an affirmative action program prioritizing minority-owned companies for city contracts, Ryan's father lost everything—his business, his home, and his marriage. Yet, "not once," Ryan explains as he berates the Black woman handling his father's health insurance claim, "does he blame you people." In the case of Ryan's father, the film does address structural racism. However, people of color are not the victims; innocent white men are. Ryan's father, the nonracist man willing to hire Blacks when no one else would, is the victim of discrimination at the hands of the city of Los Angeles because of the color of his skin. His entire livelihood is destroyed for no other reason than the color of his skin. No person of color in this film suffers anywhere near as much as Ryan's father as a result of governmental policies. The experience of Ryan's father provides the only example where the film addresses the manner in which the legal system and governmental policy has historically discriminated against or disproportionately benefited certain groups. However, *Crash* inverts the victims and the beneficiaries of these policies; whites suffer and Blacks benefit. With this, *Crash* aligns itself with the white backlash to affirmative action beginning in the 1970s, that used the narrative and language of "reverse discrimination" to challenge civil rights programs.[14]

In another scene the film depicts the capability of the government to abuse its power and racially discriminate against a likely innocent man. The DA summons Detective Waters to his office to discuss the murder of an off-duty Black police detective by an off-duty white police officer, the third time the officer has shot Black men. Yet, Waters informs the

DA's deputy, Flanagan, that the Black detective had three-hundred thousand dollars in cash hidden in the spare tire of the car he was driving, complicating their assumption that the shooting was racially motivated. Yet Flanagan, determined to spin the incident as an open-and-shut case of racism in order to protect the DA from backlash from African Americans, insists on suppressing the information about the cash and instead blackmails Waters into playing along with the racial angle and framing a potentially innocent white man in Detective Conklin. Here the film suggests that incidents of racially motivated violence by the LAPD against Black Angelenos are inventions by politicians seeking votes. As with the previous example, the victim of this episode of state discrimination is white—in this case the reverse racism of assuming a white police officer would only shoot a Black man because of his race. In *Crash*, racism at any level beyond personal interaction, to the limited degree the film enables it, is limited exclusively to the "reverse discrimination" of white males through affirmative action policies and playing the race card where it does not apply for political gain.

Moreover, by restricting the scope of racism to personal interaction, the film is able to wrongfully equate the effects of racism on people of color to that of whites. As Ryan's father and detective Conklin illuminate, white characters suffer the as much if not more than the people of color in this film. Even the conversation between Hansen and his lieutenant goes so far as to depict Hansen, the progressively minded white male police officer who must endure Ryan's behavior, as the victim of his partner's bigotry. While one might point to the fact that two Black men are killed over the course of this film as evidence that Blacks ultimately suffer the most, as we shall see the racial motivation behind each shooting is at least ambiguous, if not nonexistent. The inability of the film to recognize the institutional aspects of racism entrenches it within the very racial discourse it seeks to transcend. In other words, the thought that everyone harbors racial prejudices may seem progressive in relation to the color-blind ideal, but its failure to complicate our understanding of the realities of racism undermines any of its progressive ambitions.

Furthermore, the racialized reality the film offers only confirms the most offensive stereotypes of people of color, Black men in particular. After her carjacking, an angry Jean explains to her husband that the incident was her fault "because she knew it was gonna happen. But if a white person sees two Black men walking towards her and she turns and walks in the other direction, she's a racist, right? Well I got scared and I didn't say anything and ten seconds letter I had a gun in my face."

Here, the film offers race consciousness not as an alternative to color blindness but as a necessary worldview of whites for their own safety. In fact, given that every Black character in this film commits a felony, the film implies that assuming all Black people are criminals is not only accurate, but is the best way to ensure white people's safety. Jean is the victim of a crime because of her racial progressivism—for not assuming Black men were criminals. Her color-blind attitude almost got her killed.

That every Black character commits a felony is not inconsequential. Instead, the film's plot relies on stereotypical portrayals of both Black criminology and white heroism. Perhaps the best example of this is the car-jacking incident near the film's beginning. The scene opens as an incensed young Black man named Anthony (Ludacris), and his friend Peter (Larenz Tate), also Black, leave a restaurant in a posh West LA neighborhood. As he pulls his jacket up over his shoulders, Anthony complains about their ninety-minute wait, far longer than any white person waited, and their waitress's refusal to offer them coffee in light of the fact that she poured "cup after cup" for every other person in the restaurant, all of whom were white. Anthony continues his rant about the discriminatory service he and his friend received before spotting an approaching white woman (Sandra Bullock), who, after noticing the two men, clutches the arm of her husband and shoots the men a nervous look. Anthony then rants about the woman's racist assumptions about the two of them despite the fact that they are not "dressed like gang-bangers"; he notes that if anyone has reason to fear, it is them—the only two Black men in an all-white neighborhood patrolled by the "trigger-happy LAPD." The two men then draw pistols from their belts and steal the white couple's luxury SUV at gunpoint.

Haggis insists that the point of this movie was to make viewers uncomfortable with their preconceived notions about race and ethnicity. Yet it is difficult to rationalize that idea in the context of the numerous scenes that only confirm stereotypes about Black criminality. Sandra Bullock's character, Jean, makes an assumption about Black masculinity—that because of the color of their skin these two men are to be feared. The subsequent actions only prove that her presumptions were correct. This becomes a major trope throughout the film. The stereotypes about African Americans, particularly about Black male criminality, are, in the world of *Crash*, accurate. In addition to the carjackers Anthony and Peter, Thandie Newton's fellating of Terrance Howard's in their SUV while he drives breaks a number of laws, including reckless endangerment and lewd conduct; and Don Cheadle's character obstructs justice with his complicity in keeping secret the money found in the trunk of the murdered Black police officer. Given this, it is hard to rationalize Haggis's intention to have viewers leave the theater "not knowing what to think." Instead, *Crash* begins with stereotypical assumptions about Blackness, and then fails to challenge those assumptions throughout the film. It invites white viewers to indulge in the discourse of Black inferiority and white heroism, and then does nothing more than confirm that indulgence.

If there is any discomfort on the part of the imagined white spectator, it is certainly does not arise from the uneasiness of having one's conceptions regarding race challenged. Instead, the discomfort in *Crash* derives from having their worst fears about Blackness validated on screen. Black criminality is not the only outmoded stereotype of Blackness the film reproduces. Detective Waters's mother is a drug-addicted woman who spends all day cooped up in her house, presumably not working and living off of welfare. At the end of the film, after her son is found murdered, she accuses her eldest son for her younger sons death because he was too busy working and being successful to check in on him. Graham's mother is, in other words, the pathological Black woman—lazy, drug-addicted, welfare reliant, and a bad mother. The discomfort experienced while watching *Crash* is, for the white spectator, one in which they are told some Black people are dangerous, the others are lazy; they will stick a gun in your face and use your tax dollars to feed their drug habit. During an NPR interview promoting the film shortly before its release, a caller asked Haggis about the manner in which the car-jacking scene seemed to corroborate rather than contest stereotypes about Black masculinity. The director responded by again referencing that he wanted to first make you comfortable, to know who were the "good guys" and the "bad guys," but then "start to mess with you." He continued, "We all embody great contradictions, and each of these characters embody those contradictions. And you never know which way a character is going to turn." While Haggis did not address the question directly, Brendan Fraser, one of the film's stars who was also part of the interview defended Haggis's choice, and, in referencing the "philosophical" conversations the two have about race relations in Los Angeles, called it a "wonderful conceit."[15] Yet, it is hard to make sense of Haggis and Fraser's assessment of Anthony and Peter, especially if analyzed from the point of view of Jean.

Moreover, while one might contend that the intellectual rant Anthony delivers about racism in the moments leading up to the carjacking and in other scenes throughout the film "complicates" his character—making him more than just a "thug"—the responses Peter gives Anthony's comments undercut any such work. After complaining that they were not offered coffee, Peter reminds Anthony that he does not drink coffee; after explaining that the waitress saw two Black men, assumed they would not tip well because they were Black, and therefore deliberately provided them bad service, Peter responds that the waitress was, like them, Black. He then asks Anthony how much he tipped her, to which Anthony responds that he left nothing. So in fact, Anthony and Peter are not only the Black criminals Jean fears, they also do not tip. Moreover, Peter's retorts work to undermine any validity behind Anthony's social commentary. Rather than read as legitimate assessments of the racial dynamics of west Los Angeles, *Crash* represents Anthony, in light of Peter's comments, as an angry Black man playing the race card whenever he is unhappy. Peter is the rational character in this scene, not Anthony. In Anthony, the film packs just about all of the worst stereotypes of Black men into a single character. He is an angry, bad-tipping, race-card playing, gun-wielding thug. In other words, he is everything Jean's initial look presumes and worse.

At the same time the film actively mobilizes the discourse of Black inferiority, it also represents a redemptive, heroic, and ultimately superior whiteness. Many of the white characters in this film who make bigoted comments ultimately do right by people of color. White racists in *Crash* are able to redeem their previous racist actions with equal, or even superior, acts of generosity. The best example of this occurs when Officer Ryan saves Christine's life the day after he molests her. As Christine lay trapped inside her rolled SUV with gasoline leaking out of the vehicle, it is Ryan who, risking his own life, rescues Newton from the enflamed vehicle a fraction of a second before it explodes.

The formal elements of the scene add melodrama to Ryan's heroic actions. As Ryan and his newly assigned Latino partner approach the multicar accident, Ryan races up a hill past a line of traffic, around another car involved in the crash that has caught fire to an overturned SUV leaking gasoline. As Ryan approaches the overturned vehicle, the camera cuts to a shot from inside the backseat of the vehicle. The shot looks out the afternoon Los Angeles sun, which makes the horizon appear a bright yellowish white intensified by the glare off two parked cars. In slow motion we see Ryan enter the frame, emerging angelically from the light. The diegesis is silent, and all the viewer hears is the melodic sound of a woman softly singing over a minimal score led by long-held chords on a synthesizer. As Ryan crouches down into the car a dazed Newton slowly recognized her savior as the man who sexually assaulted her the previous day. She begins to cry and screams "No! Not you!," before using what little strength she has to try and fight him off. Newton agrees to cooperate only after Ryan then assures her he will not harm her and will get her out of the car safely. However, before Ryan can remove Newton, the car catches fire and explodes. As the diegesis again goes silent, leaving only the sound of the score, Ryan's partner, along with a bystander, pull Ryan out of the engulfed SUV by his legs, as Newton thrashes to try and free herself. As Ryan's body clears the vehicle, he rolls onto his back, kicks the two men off of him, and dives back into the burning vehicle. As he grabs hold of Newton he yells "pull"—the first diegetic sound since the car caught fire—and Newton is rescued from the car seconds before it is engulfed by an even bigger explosion that surely would have killed both Ryan and Newton were they inside. Ryan then wraps a blanket around a sobbing Newton and cradles her in his arms.

So while Ryan commits one of the most heinous acts of this film, he is able to redeem himself the following day by saving the life of the woman he sexually assaulted. He risks his life in order to save his victim. The film's form only magnifies this. The use of the score, slow motion, and the silent diegesis add melodrama to Ryan's heroic act. The concluding slow-motion shot of the scene of Ryan on one knee alone in the frame enhances the emphasis on Ryan in this scene. It allows the audience to read the regret of his previous actions in his facial expression. The audience is left with the common Hollywood image of a hero alone in the frame. Instead of putting on his cowboy hat, mounting his horse, and riding off into the sunset, the audience can imagine Ryan getting back into his police cruiser and heading back to work patrolling the streets of Los Angeles.

Furthermore, the emphasis on Ryan in this sequence, who occupies the frame for the vast majority of the action, especially as the scene concludes, transforms Christine into nothing more than a tool to restore Ryan's heroism. The scene's form holds her experience of having to trust a man who molested her the previous evening to save her life at a distance. The audience does see a brief shot of her looking back at Ryan over her shoulder as she is led away by paramedics, but it is nowhere near as long as the shot looking directly at Ryan as the scene closes, and therefore does not allow the same intimacy with the viewer that the shot of Ryan does. The remainder of the film offers no further access to Christine's experience. The only time we see her again is briefly at the film's conclusion, where she and her husband exchange

"I love yous" on the phone. The experience of the sexually abused Black woman is not only secondary but is entirely occluded in order to restore the heroism of the white male. Christine is twice objectified—first sexually by Ryan and then second to mend his white male virtue. Moreover, this is not the only instance in which a white character is able to atone for his sins in the film. Officer Hansen, after idly standing by during Newton's molestation, convinces his fellow officers not to shoot Cameron and to let him go with only a warning after he leads police on a high-speed chase and resists arrest. He, like Ryan, saves a Black person's life. Together, these actions redeem white heroism. The prejudices of the white characters are secondary to their true intrepid character, which comes to the fore in moments of crisis.

Officer Hansen's actions after he saves Cameron's life appear to call into question the redemptive quality this film assigns whiteness. However, a close examination of his final scene reveal otherwise. Near the end of the film, Hansen (while off-duty) picks up a hitchhiking Peter. Once in the car Peter, after noting the country music Hansen listens to, remarks that he himself is beginning to like the genre, and in fact wrote a country song the day prior. After Hansen asks what Peter was doing so far out in San Fernando Valley, an unlikely destination for a young Black man in Los Angeles, Peter answers that he was ice-skating, has always loved to ice-skate, and aspired to compete as a hockey goalie as a child. Their conversation increasingly irritates Hansen, as he feels Peter is "having fun" with him, because Peter's comments depict a man who conflicts with Hansen's stereotypes of Black masculinity. Peter then notices a Saint Christopher statuette on Hansen's dashboard identical to the one he carries in his pocket, which causes Peter to laugh. Hansen then pulls over and asks Peter to get out of the car. As Peter reaches into his pocket, Hansen tells him to keep his hands where Hansen can see them. When Peter reaches into his pocket to show Hansen why he is laughing, Hansen, thinking Peter is armed, draws his gun and fires a single shot into Peter's chest before Peter can remove his hand from his pocket. As Peter takes his last breaths in Hansen's passenger seat, he opens his hand to reveal an identical Saint Christopher statuette.

This scene's escalation from a tense misunderstanding to Hansen drawing and discharging his weapon occurs in a matter of seconds. There is no time to think; only time to react. The complexity of the scene is therefore built on the conversation leading up to the shooting. Certainly, that Hansen was growing frustrated with Peter's comments, so much so that he had pulled his car to the shoulder and asked Peter to leave, plays some role in Hansen's subsequent reaction to Peter reaching for his pocket. In Hansen's view, a Black hitchhiker in San Fernando Valley who likes country music, ice skating, and hockey is not trustworthy. Hansen is therefore far more willing to react in a defensive manner when Peter reaches into his pocket as the two men argue. The important point here is that the reason for Hansen's suspicion is prejudice. Peter is honest with the police officer—he was ice-skating, he does like country music—yet because those activities and interests to not comport with those Hansen associates with Black men, Peter must be lying and is therefore suspicious. It is, in other words, Hansen's stereotypical views of African Americans that manufacture the tension that leads, to some degree, to Peter's slaying. Nonetheless, the manner in which the shooting plays out keeps the motive ambiguous. Peter does reach into his pocket after Hansen repeatedly tells him not to, calling the racial motive behind Hansen's reaction into question. The shooting is potentially justifiable as self-defense. In other words, both killings of Black men in this film—Peter and the off-duty officer—are potentially justifiable and nonracially motivated. There is therefore no need to redeem Hansen's final action in the film because it lacks the explicitly bigoted motivation of the other instances.

Fruitvale Station

In 2013, another movie about race—an independent picture based on real events—debuted titled *Fruitvale Station*. Like *Crash*, the film culminates with the killing of a young Black man by a white police officer. Specifically, the film depicts the final twenty-four hours of the life of Oscar Grant, a twenty-two-year-old Black man who was killed by a BART police officer, Johannes Mehserle in Oakland, California on January 1, 2009. Yet, while both *Crash* and *Fruitvale Station* dramatize the killing of young Black men by white police officers, the manner in which each film represents the shootings and the events leading up to them produce entirely different readings regarding the role of racism in each tragedy. *Fruitvale Station*, unlike *Crash*, reveals the structural elements of racism that sanction the murder of young Black men by white law enforcement officers. The different conclusions one draws from these two films are primarily the product of key differences in each film's form. Whereas the scene in *Crash* happens quickly, leaving only time to react impulsively, *Fruitvale Station* depicts its murder quite differently. In *Fruitvale Station*, the audience hardly sees the offending officer until he shoots Grant. Second, and more importantly, the action in *Fruitvale Station* does not require the split-second decision to fire a gun. Grant lies handcuffed face down on the pavement of the train stop, secured by another officer who has his knee firmly into Grant's back as Mehserle shoots him. This removes all doubt as to whether or not this incident was murder. Grant is clearly no threat to Mehserle, the officer restraining him, or anyone else on the platform at the time he is shot. Where *Crash* is ambiguous, *Fruitvale Station* is definitive—a white police officer murdered Oscar Grant.

Furthermore, *Fruitvale Station* is not an ensemble film. As film scholar Hsuan Hsu points out, *Crash* is just one of a long line of ensemble films set in Los Angeles that center around issues of race. A central theme of these films, Hsu argues, is the "vague sense that we are all in this together."[16] In other words, the ensemble film as a genre, in representing several perspectives and not privileging one character over another, has a democratizing effect on the film and its characters. An ensemble cast offers the ideal vehicle for Haggis and his everyone-is-racist-message. *Fruitvale Station*, on the other hand, is not an ensemble film. Instead, the perspective of the young Black victim of police brutality is the only viewpoint available to spectators. The choice to focus solely on the experience of Oscar Grant and elide the perspective of his killer reveals the fundamental differences in the ways in which these two films represent racism in American society. The ensemble of characters in *Crash* affords Haggis the opportunity to depict the omnipresence of racial prejudice in Los Angeles. However, such a conception of racism also authorizes the omission of power and, in the case of *Crash*, enables the privileging of white heroism capable of transcending racial intolerance. The decision of *Fruitvale Station*'s director Ryan Coogler to eschew alternative perspectives forces the audience to grapple with the fact that Oscar Grant alone is the victim of racism in this narrative. There is no racism democracy in Coogler's film in which we are all both guilty and victims of racial prejudice. One is instead either the victim or the beneficiary of white supremacy.

Perhaps the most important component of Coogler's message is his ability to depict both halves of the previous statement. At the film's conclusion, as the action fades to black the end titles indicate that Mehserle was found guilty only of involuntary manslaughter, sentenced to just two years in prison, of which he served a total of a year, including the time during his trial and while he awaited sentencing. The titles are then followed by a shot of Grant's daughter, visibly saddened and huddled against a loved one, at the four-year anniversary of her father's murder. In *Fruitvale Station*, the end credits and the final image of Grant's daughter transform the film from a story of one young Black man who was wrongfully killed by a police officer to an indictment on the entire criminal justice system that allows such a flagrant act of murder to result in a two-month jail sentence (Mehserle served ten of his twelve months during the trial). Moreover, the end credits cite the role massive uprisings and social unrest in the city of Oakland in the aftermath of Grant's murder played in Mehserle's conviction. The image of Grant's daughter then invites the viewer to weigh the cost paid by the Grant family, and the entire Black community of Oakland to the punishment given to Mehserle. As the screen goes Black for the last time viewers are left with questions not only about the racist attitudes of white police officers, but the structural racism that operates in the aftermath of such a crime and the pain inflicted on the family, friends, and community of the victim.

Furthermore, what *Fruitvale Station* offers in every frame is what eludes *Crash*, and Hollywood representations of Blackness more broadly—representations of multidimensional Black characters. *Fruitvale Station* begins with actual cell phone footage of Grant's murder. In other words, even if the audience is unaware of the story of Grant's slaying, they are told how his story ends mere seconds into the film. What Coogler wants to depict then is not a Hollywood drama that builds intrigue through the unknown destination of its plot. Instead, between the two depictions of Grant's murder—the documentary cell phone footage and the film's reenactment of it—the audience watches the story of an complex young Black man who, at the time of his death, was struggling to get his life on track and be the father his young daughter deserved. Unfortunately, Hollywood rarely affords people of color this level of complexity, humanity, and screen time.

Conclusion

In January 2014 the Academy released its latest Oscar Nominations. *Fruitvale Station* did not receive a single nomination, despite the fact that the Academy can nominate as many as ten films for Best Picture as opposed to five when *Crash* won. The inability of the motion picture industry's most prestigious awards to recognize *Fruitvale Station* illustrates Hollywood's investment in a neoliberal racial project that considers challenges to color blindness that elide structural inequality progressive, and views more complex representations of structural inequality unintelligible. *Crash* wholly fails to, as Cornel West puts it, "demystify power relations. . . ."[17] It does little to show the manner in which white supremacy operates at any meaningful level in America in the twenty-first century. *Crash*'s failures are more serious than merely "getting it wrong." Popular culture, and Hollywood especially, have played and continue to play a fundamental role in shaping the ways in which we understand the role of race in American society. Explaining this dynamic, Hall writes, "as popular culture has historically become the dominant form of global culture, so it is at the same time the scene, *par excellence*, of commodification, of the industries where culture enters directly into the circuits of a dominant technology—the circuits of power and capital."[18] *Crash* is not the contrarian masterpiece many critics insist, but instead the latest entry on a long list of Hollywood failures that attempt to tackle the issue of race. *Fruitvale Station*, on the other hand, offers a far more complicated picture of racism that reveals the manner in which white supremacy operates structurally to privilege some at the expense of others in many different but interconnected ways. Unfortunately, the creators of one film left the Oscars Ceremony with Hollywood's top prize; those of the other will not even be invited to the event this year.

Notes

1. Roger Ebert, "Ebert's Best 10 Movies of 2005," accessed August 7, 2013, http://www.rogerebert.com/rogers-journal/eberts-best-10-movies-of-2005.

2. "Behind the Scenes," *Crash*, directed by Paul Haggis (Lionsgate, 2005), DVD.

3. The Supreme Court first struck down a university's affirmative action admission policy in *Regents of the University of California v. Bakke* (1978), which deemed UC Davis's medical school admission policy illegal. Since then, a series of other rulings, including *Hopwood v. Texas* (1996), *Johnson v. University of Georgia* (2001), *Gratz v. Bollinger* (2003), and most recently *Fisher v. University of Texas at Austin* (2013) have restricted, if not outlawed, universities' ability to consider race in their admissions policies.

4. In 1996 California passed Proposition 209, which banned considerations of race in public employment, public education, and public contracting. In the wake of Proposition 209 several other states, including Washington, Nebraska, Connecticut, and Michigan passed similar measures.

5. David Harvey, "Neoliberalism as Creative Destruction," *Annals of the American Academy of Political and Social Science* 610, no. 1 (March 2007): 22.

6. David Harvey, *A Brief History of Neoliberalism* (Oxford: Oxford University Press, 2005), 5.

7. See Hsuan L. Hsu, "Racial Privacy, the L.A. Ensemble Film, and Paul Haggis' *Crash*," *Film Criticism* 31, no. 1/2 (Fall 2006): 132–156; David G. Holmes, "The Civil Rights Movement According to 'Crash': Complicating the Pedagogy of Integration," *College English* 69, no. 4 (March 2007): 314–320.

8. Vince Beiser, "An Interview with Paul Haggis," *The Progressive*, accessed August 7, 2013. http://www.progressive.org/mag_haggis0108

9. Eduardo Bonilla-Silva, *Racism without Racists: Color-Blind Racism and the Persistence of Racial Inequality in the United States* (Oxford: Rowman and Littlefield Publishers, 2006).

10. George Lipsitz, *The Possessive Investment in Whiteness: How White People Profit from Identity Politics* (Philadelphia: Temple University Press, 1998), vii.

11. Ibid., viii

12. For a brief overview of this data see, for example, the introduction of George Lipsitz, *How Racism Takes Place* (Philadelphia: Temple University Press, 2011); George Lipsitz, "The Possessive Investment in Whiteness," *The Possessive Investment in Whiteness: How White People Profit from Identity Politics*; and Bonilla-Silva, *Racism without Racists.*

13. Stuart Hall, "Race, Articulation, and Societies Structured in Dominance," in *Black British Cultural Studies: A Reader,* edited by Houston A. Baker, Manthia Diawara, and Ruth H. Lindeborg (Chicago, IL: University of Chicago Press, 1996), 19.

14. For more on white backlash, see Thomas Edsall, and Mary Edsall, *Chain Reaction: The Impact of Race, Rights, and Taxes on American Politics* (New York: W. W. Norton, 1992); Matthew Lassiter, *The Silent Majority: Suburban Politics in the Sunbelt South* (Princeton: Princeton University Press, 2006); Kevin Kruse, *White Flight: Atlanta and the Making of Modern Conservatism* (Princeton: Princeton University Press, 2005); Robert O. Self. *American Babylon: Race and the Struggle for Postwar Oakland* (Princeton, NJ: Princeton University Press, 2003); Lisa McGirr. *Suburban Warriors: The Origins of the New American Right* (Princeton: Princeton University Press, 2001); and Ronald Formisano, *Boston against Busing: Race, Class, and Ethnicity in the 1960s and 1970s* (Chapel Hill, NC: University of North Carolina Press, 2003).

15. Paul Haggis, and Brendan Fraser, interview by Neal Conan, *Talk of the Nation*, National Public Radio, April 18, 2005.

16. Hsu, 135.

17. Cornel West. "The New Cultural Politics of Difference," in *The Cornel West Reader* (New York: Basic Books, 1999), 131.

18. Stuart Hall, "What Is This 'Black' in Black Popular Culture," in *Stuart Hall: Critical Dialogues in Cultural Studies*, edited by David Morley and Kuan-Hsing Chen (London: Routledge, 1996), 469–470.

Bibliography

Beiser, Vince. "An Interview with Paul Haggis." *The Progressive*. Accessed August 7, 2013. http://www.progressive.org/mag_haggis0108.

Bonilla-Silva, Eduardo. *Racism without Racists: Color-Blind Racism and the Persistence of Racial Inequality in the United States*. Oxford: Rowman and Littlefield Publishers, 2006.

Crash. Directed by Paul Haggis. Lionsgate, 2005. DVD.

Ebert, Roger. "Ebert's Best 10 Movies of 2005." Accessed on August 7, 2013. http://www.rogerebert.com/rogers-journal/eberts-best-10-movies-of-2005.

Edsall, Thomas, and Mary Edsall. *Chain Reaction: The Impact of Race, Rights, and Taxes on American Politics*. New York: W. W. Norton & Company, 1992.

Formisano, Ronald. *Boston against Busing: Race, Class, and Ethnicity in the 1960s and 1970s*. Chapel Hill, NC: University of North Carolina Press, 2003.

Fruitvale Station. Directed by Ryan Coogler. The Weinstein Company, 2013. Film.

Haggis, Paul, and Brendan Fraser. Interview by Neal Conan. *Talk of the Nation*. National Public Radio. April 18, 2005.

Hall, Stuart. "Race, Articulation, and Societies Structured in Dominance." In *Black British Cultural Studies: A Reader*. Eds. Houston A. Baker, Manthia Diawara, and Ruth H. Lindeborg. Chicago, IL: University of Chicago Press, 1996.

———. "What Is This 'Black' in Black Popular Culture." In David Morley and Kuan-Hsing Chen, eds. *Stuart Hall: Critical Dialogues in Cultural Studies*. London: Routledge, 1996.

Harvey, David. "Neoliberalism as Creative Destruction," *Annals of the American Academy of Political and Social Science* 610 (March 2007): 22–44.

———. *A Brief History of Neoliberalism*. Oxford: Oxford University Press, 2005.

Hsu, Hsuan L. "Racial Privacy, the L.A. Ensemble Film, and Paul Haggis' *Crash*." *Film Criticism* 31, no. 1/2 (Fall 2006): 132–156.

Holmes, David G. "The Civil Rights Movement According to 'Crash': Complicating the Pedagogy of Integration." *College English* 69, no. 4 (March 2007): 314–320.

Kruse, Kevin. *White Flight: Atlanta and the Making of Modern Conservatism*. Princeton, NJ: Princeton University Press, 2005.

Lassiter, Matthew. *The Silent Majority: Suburban Politics in the Sunbelt South*. Princeton, NJ: Princeton University Press, 2006.

Lipsitz, George. *The Possessive Investment in Whiteness: How White People Profit from Identity Politics*. Philadelphia: Temple University Press, 1998.

———. *How Racism Takes Place*. Philadelphia: Temple University Press, 2011.

McGirr, Lisa. *Suburban Warriors: The Origins of the New American Right*. Princeton, NJ: Princeton University Press, 2001.

Self, Robert O. *American Babylon: Race and the Struggle for Postwar Oakland*. Princeton, NJ: Princeton University Press, 2003.

West, Cornel. "The New Cultural Politics of Difference." In Cornel West, *The Cornel West Reader*. New York: Basic Books, 1999.

12

African American Female Athletic Image

What We Should Take Away from the London 2012 Olympic Games

Rachel L. Myers

Introduction

For citizens of the United States, the London 2012 Olympic Games were captivating for a number of reasons. Swimmers Michael Phelps, Ryan Lochte, and Missy Franklin had Americans holding their breath with each stroke, as they set world records and won multiple medals for the United States. Young Americans tuning into the archery competition watched the accuracy of Khatuna Lorig, the woman who taught actress Jennifer Lawrence how to impress with a bow and arrow for her admired role as Katniss Everdeen in *The Hunger Games*. It is also certain that U.S. feminists and young female athletes alike were proud to see that, for the first time in history, the number of females on the Olympic team outnumbered the males. The performances of the United States' Black female athletes also captured the interest of many Americans.

Gymnastics and track and field were two Olympic events in which U.S. Black female athletes shined exceptionally brightly. Gymnast Gabby Douglas became the first African American to win the Olympic all-around competition gold medal. Long jumper Brittney Reese; sprinters Carmelita Jeter, Tianna Madison, Allyson Felix, and Dee Trotter; as well as hurdlers Dawn Harper and Kellie Wells dominated the track and field competitions in London. While it is expected for the media and society to keep focus on the successes of these athletes, the opposite happened for a few of these Olympic medalists—Gabby Douglas, Dawn Harper, and Kellie Wells.

After her historic accomplishment of winning both Olympic all-around and team gold medals, controversy *within* the African American community arose over Gabby Douglas's hair texture and style. Meanwhile, shortly after winning a bronze and silver medal, respectively, in the hundred-meter hurdle finals, Dawn Harper and

Kellie Wells spoke out against the media "hype" over fellow compatriot hurdler, Lolo Jones (she finished in fourth place). These two incidents are very important, not because all Americans should be celebrating the athletic successes of our Olympians instead of looking for areas of criticism (that is common sense), but because of what these two incidents reveal, generally, about the pervasiveness of structural and internalized racism in twenty-first-century U.S. society.

What follows here should not serve as a comprehensive historiography, but rather a sliver toward the proper contextualization of some of the history and experiences of U.S. Black female athletes. The limited aim of this chapter is to show how structural racism and internalized racism are still persistent in U.S. society through the lens of sport. After all, "sport is influenced by the state of the general society, and reflects [and for the most part, reinforces] that society."[1] Why is Gabby Douglas's hair a contentious matter for African Americans? Why would the media choose to focus on Lolo Jones, rather than Harper and Wells? And how do these athletes, as well as other Black female athletes, feel about the way they are portrayed in society? In a broader sense, why are some differences (and people) held with such importance over others, and how do individuals in society use these differences to uphold a general system of beliefs and attitudes—in this case, internalized racism and structural racism? Society must acknowledge the remaining obstacles and hopes these female athletes have in order to attain a better African American community, mainstream society, and future for women's athletics.

Gabrielle Douglas and Internalized Racism

The controversy over Gabby Douglas's hair is a convincing example of the pervasiveness of internalized racism within African Americans. *Internalized racism* should be understood as the "acceptance by members of stigmatized races of negative messages about their own abilities and intrinsic worth."[2] The results of internalized racism are devastating. These members of society tend to view themselves and others who look like them as having limited humanity; limited self-determination, dreams, and self-expression. Camara Jones states that "it manifests as an embracing of 'whiteness' (use of hair straighteners and bleaching creams, stratification by skin tone within communities of color, and 'white man's ice is colder' syndrome); self-devaluation (racial slurs as nicknames, rejection of ancestral culture and fratricide); and resignation, helplessness, and hopelessness (dropping out of school, failing to vote, and engaging in risky health practices)."[3] The manifested internalized racism at play with regards to Gabby Douglas and those Black Americans who commented negatively about her hair, however, is not as clear-cut as Jones's explanation. As I noted elsewhere,[4] it is safe to state that sport in the United States is racially categorized by its own athletes—and therefore by general society. Gymnastics is viewed as a "white" sport in the United States, and throughout the world within the context of Olympic history. Being a racial "outsider" in one's preferred sport can be very hard, especially if the athlete achieves success in that sport. In her autobiography, *Grace, Gold, and Glory: My Leap of Faith*, Gabby Douglas shares some of the racialized experiences she has had as a gymnast and their effect on her.

Much like the autobiographies of tennis star Serena Williams and former standout Zina Garrison, Douglas's autobiography reveals that blatant experiences of racism began once her skill level improved and she began surpassing some of her white teammates in competitions. In chapter 8 of her book, Douglas explains that part of a gymnast's day requires one to participate in the maintenance of the equipment, with her and her teammates taking turns in these tasks. On a particular day, it was a white teammate's turn to scrape all the excess chalk off the uneven bars:

> That's when the girl said, "Why doesn't Gabby do it? She's our slave." I looked over to see the girl standing there with this smirk on her face. I could feel my stomach muscles tighten and my heart sink. I wanted to cry—but I didn't. Instead, I just stared at her. "That's not cool," another gymnast said to the girl. "Well, you make jokes all the time too," the girl shot back. "I do," the other gymnast said, "but not that kind of joke. You should never joke about something like that."[5]

One would think an immediate response would be to retaliate verbally, tell a coach, or a parent. Gabby does none of these things. Instead, she breaks down in the privacy of her bedroom and tells her mother that everything is "fine" when she returns home from work. This incident shows that some of Gabby's teammates at Excalibur gymnastics club view her with a white supremacist attitude; even though she is exceeding them in gymnastics, she is still automatically "less than" because of her race.

Douglas's rationale for keeping this experience to herself is most revealing. Anyone who watched coverage of gymnastics during the London Olympics knows that Douglas's mother (a single mom) and siblings had to sacrifice a lot financially for Gabby to pursue her gymnastics career, but another reason Gabby cites for her silence is:

> I also didn't want to start a big drama with the other girls by bringing it up to my coaches. I knew that would make the other gymnasts dislike me even more . . . So because I loved my sport so much—and because I didn't want to seem like a tattletale—I just dealt with my feelings of isolation.[6]

This rationalization shows evidence that Gabby is already struggling with internalized racism at twelve years old. In feeling that making a case for the respect of her own humanity would cause a "big drama" with the other girls, she is effectively *supporting* the belief that her full humanity is limited through her silence. Douglas also makes clear that she cares about whether these racist gymnasts will "dislike [her] even more." Valuing the opinions of a handful of white girls who do not value her as a person gives the impression that Gabby is embracing "whiteness"—that their acceptance of her is more important than how she feels about herself around them.

A second, more impactful racist incident occurred during Douglas's time at Excalibur, but this time it involved a white, male coach. One day, Douglas heard this coach say to another coach that she needs a nose job. Once again, Douglas fails to act in response to the incident, expressing, "That night and for a long time afterward, I didn't tell my mother what happened—for all the same reasons I hadn't told her about the growing isolation I'd been feeling at the gym."[7] Gabby's silence did not make things better for her because the offensive comments about her nose—and the overt racism of her coach and teammates—intensified. A few weeks later, the same coach tells Gabby directly that she needs a nose job, in front of a few of her teammates. While she stood stunned, a couple of teammates broke the silence with laughter. A few days after that, those same teammates began to joke about her nose, calling it "flat" and asking "how do you even breathe out of it?" Gabby responds with a sarcastic "Thanks, guys" and walks away. Inside, Gabby was hurting and clearly grappling with internalized racism, beginning to doubt her external beauty and self-assurance in her sport:

> "Am I pretty, mom?" I asked my mother one evening about a month after that party. "Of course, Brie," she said. "You've always been beautiful." But I was starting to have my doubts . . . Even as I pushed to lift my skill level, my self-assurance sank—and not just because of the

> cruel comments. My coach and I were butting heads over which skills I should be learning . . . Over time, I began to question my capabilities.

Much like the first experience, Gabby did not open up about her true feelings from this experience until years later. Keep this in mind as this essay examines the scrutiny over Gabby Douglas's hair.

Hair Matters

Historically, hair is of importance to all members of the Black community, but more so to Black women. Understanding the importance of Black hair means looking to the continent of Africa. In their 2001 publication, *Hair Story: Untangling the Roots of Black Hair in America*, authors Ayana Byrd and Lori Tharps inform readers that "this frizzy, kinky hair insulates the head from the brutal intensity of the sun's rays."[8] Of course, hair serves as much more than a form of protection. In the early fifteenth century, hair had a number of practical societal functions in most West African societies. Ever since African civilizations bloomed, hairstyles have been used to indicate a person's marital status, age, religion, ethnic identity, wealth, and rank within the community.[9] It was also significant for one's hair to be aesthetically pleasing. Byrd and Tharps reveal that, "to the Mende [of Nigeria], unkempt, 'neglected,' or 'messy' hair implied that a woman either had loose morals or was insane."[10] And for the Wolof of Senegal, "an unkempt or disheveled hairdo was often interpreted as a sign of dementia."[11] In other words, it is literally a sign of lunacy to neglect hair care in many West African societies.

These same members of West African societies are the black bodies that filled slave ships bound for the "New World"; the same individuals that gave birth to the first generation of American-born Blacks. While unfamiliar territory and the oppressive system of slavery may have suppressed the expression of some indigenous African hairstyles, the personal and societal pride in well-coiffed hair remains strong. In the United States, aside from skin color and eye color, hair is one of the most identifiable differentiations between Blacks and whites; a guaranteed way to "other" Blacks further in society. Rather than trying to understand the science and culture of Black hair, most whites choose to remain ignorant about the texture of hair belonging to those they believe to be inherently lesser than they are. Unfortunately for Blacks, the "twin legacies of slavery and racism have traditionally defined 'good hair' as hair more like white people's."[12] If a Black person is told over and over again that white hair is "good," chances are high that this person is going to start internalizing this view as fact, rather than as popular racist societal opinion.

While the straightening comb and the chemical makeup of the relaxer—both products that help straighten Black hair—had emerged and been popularized among Blacks in the first half of the twentieth century, natural hair took precedence in conjunction with the Black Power Movement of the late 1960s and 1970s. Since the 1990s, young African Americans have rocked dreadlocks and braids, which are particularly popular among artists.[13] The popularity of sporting natural hair has fluctuated for African Americans, but straightening ones hair has never gone out of style. Black hair is sparking everything from small hair salon debates to national news coverage.

However, the controversy over Gabby's hair is just one of the *most recent* athletic notable moments to go down in Black hair history. For instance, in the 1999 Australian Open, Venus Williams suffered a point penalty in the semifinal match because some of the beads on the ends of her braids fell off and onto the court. And in 2007, white radio announcer, Don Imus, referred to the predominately Black Rutgers women's basketball team as "nappy-headed hoes." What differs between these two previous incidents and Gabby Douglas's is that her critics were other African Americans.

The comments on popular networking site, Twitter, began after the team competition—where the U.S. women's team clinched the gold for the first time since the 1996 Olympics. Some of the negative Twitter comments were:

- *Why hasn't anyone tried to fix Gabby Douglas's hair?*
- *Gabby Douglas gotta do something with this hair! These clips and this brown gel residue ain't it!*
- *She needs some gel and a brush.*
- *Someone needs to give her a hair intervention.*
- *She has to "represent."*

In both the immediate days following the "tweets" and in *Grace, Gold, and Glory*, Gabby informs her hair critics that she does not understand what is wrong with her hair and they are focused on the wrong thing. In *Grace, Gold and Glory*, she shares:

> When I heard about the tweets, I thought, *I'm competing for the top prize in an elite sport, and you're talking about my hairstyle?* Though it

> did sting at first, I made a choice: I couldn't let that distract me . . . I refused to waste even a second on negativity . . . This moment wasn't about the hair on my head. It was about the courage in my heart.[14]

Gabby's response at first glance reads mature and noble, but if one takes into consideration how Gabby responded to the two other racially charged incidents she had with former teammates and coaches at Excalibur—as well as other comments she makes throughout her book—assumptions and predictions can be made about her true emotional reality.

It has been over two years since the London Olympic Games. While Gabby did a great job focusing on the individual all-around competition, she has since had ample time to let the feel of the "sting" of the hair comments back into her personal focus. Less than twenty pages before she shares her reaction to the hair controversy, Gabby discusses her experience adjusting to training in the cold of Iowa—she is originally from Virginia Beach, Virginia—and her personal style:

> Whatever the season, I enjoyed being stylish, and I loved experimenting with my hair. Though I had to wear it up and out of the way during training, I usually let it fall loosely over my shoulders on the weekends.[15]

Gabby continues on, closing out the chapter with a discussion of painting her nails and designing her own leotards for the GK gymnastics sportswear company. The comments she includes about her hair seem thrown in purposefully, perhaps to convince any doubtful readers that she *really, really* does care about how her hair looks. In addition, one can assume that Gabby was affected more deeply by the hair comments than she will publicly admit yet, based on how she handled her previous racial incidents. Internalized racism has already affected her emotionally before and it may affect her again with hair comments. With all of the lucrative sponsorships Gabby has earned from her historic Olympic success, she may decide to hire (or already have) a personal hairstylist. Maybe in a few years from now, Gabby will pen another autobiography and reveal how emotionally affected those comments left her. After all, she was only sixteen years old when the national media and fellow African Americans decided to focus on her hair care; it would be hard not to internalize that.

Internalized racism could be an explanation as to why her fellow African Americans criticized her in the first place. Viewing photos of

Gabby's hair from the 2012 Olympics reveals that she did not have any chemical straightening products in her hair. Some Black women straighten their hair simply to mimic the texture of white women's hair. For many Black women, straight, perfectly styled hair is a shield against a society that does not appreciate Afrocentric features.[16] No matter how much it should not matter how Black women wear their hair, it does. In a country where commercials, magazines, and TV shows mainly cover white beauty products, topics, and characters, many Black American girls are growing up *wishing* they had hair like white people and scrambling for weaves and relaxers. Some of the negative Twitter posts about Gabby could have easily come from Black Americans who are self-hating.

Jones, Harper, Wells, and Structural Racism

The key factor in understanding internalized racism is acknowledging that it does not persist without the persistence of structural racism. The media attention lauded over Lolo Jones and denied to Kelli Wells and Dawn Harper in the months and days leading up to the London Olympics, is tied to the perpetuation of structurally racist and sexist hegemonies existent within athletics and society. Structural racism, also known as institutional racism, is the "differential access to the goods, services, and opportunities of society by race."[17] The majority of female Olympic track and field athletes cannot afford to live off of running alone. Therefore, national media attention to a female runner's life story and Olympic medal aspirations can lead to change in socio-economic status—access to a better life in society. For Lolo Jones, the road to the 2012 Olympics was very lucrative; endorsement deals from brands like Asics, Degree, Oakley, Red Bull, McDonald's, and others abounded. Unless Olympic fans checked online for the hurdles roster or tuned in for the Olympic trials, chances are slim that they had even heard of Dawn Harper or Kellie Wells. The disparity in coverage should be easy to explain; Jones is a former Olympic (2008 Beijing) medalist already, right? Wrong.

While Lolo Jones was the 2008 Olympics American favorite for the hundred meter hurdles, she fell in the final heat and failed to medal. Dawn Harper, however, won the 2008 Olympic gold medal for the hundred meter hurdles (Kellie Wells failed to make the 2008 Olympic team due to a hamstring tear suffered in the Olympic trials, but was the 2011 U.S. Outdoor hundred meter hurdle champion). Rather than shine a bright light on Dawn Harper after the 2008 games and leading up to the games in London, media kept focus on Lolo, because she is the perfect female athlete to perpetuate the racist, sexist agenda of the predominantly white controlled American media.

The racism at play may be confusing to some, considering that Lolo Jones, Kellie Wells and Dawn Harper are "Black" by American standards. Lolo Jones has a white mother and a Black father, but in the United States:

> Black and White racial classification appears to be quite simple. Operating by the "one-drop" rule, anyone who has a drop of African-American blood in them is technically considered Black by White racist standards. A White person is technically anyone who is of European lineage. The word *technically* is used because since enslavement, Whites and Blacks have been procreating with one another, both forcibly and by choice. The majority of the "mixed" population—meaning those Americans with one Black parent and one White parent—are usually identified as Black, unless they can "pass" for White. Put simply, United States racial classification is based upon individually recognized racial difference.[18]

Jones's "mixed" lineage has given her obvious physical differences in comparison to Dawn Harper and Kellie Wells. Jones boasts a different skin tone, bone structure, and eye color than Wells and Harper.

While all three women have the spectacular well-toned bodies of Olympic-level sprinters, Harper and Wells are darker in complexion than Jones. Moreover, Wells and Harper have the typical dark brown eyes and wider noses of most African Americans, but Lolo Jones's nose is narrow and her eyes seem to shift between the colors hazel and green. Simply phrased, Lolo Jones looks "closer to white," than Harper or Wells. The way in which television covers, or fails to cover, women engaged in athletics affects the way in which female athletes are perceived, and also tells us something about the status of women in our society.[19] Factor in race and the intended message is clear: emphasize Lolo Jones because she is the next best thing to having an attractive white female hurdler to cheer for.

From a televised media perspective, the only thing that would make a push for the support of Lolo Jones's Olympic dreams, aside from her physical beauty, is if she had a compelling story of struggle. Televised sport is an event that is mediated by the "framing" of the contest by commentators and technical people.[20] As a result, viewers form opinions and even emotional connections about athletes based solely on the limited picture presented by commentators. Based on televised coverage of U.S. female hurdlers, Lolo Jones was the only important American to watch and the only story that deserved to be shared with the world. Luckily for the racist and sexist white patriarchal media power structure, Jones's story is rife with struggle, making her the perfect fresh Black athletic "tragedy-to-triumph" story.

While tragedy-to-triumph stories are certainly inspirational, it is an issue when the media presents these stories as always belonging to African Americans. Not all successful Black female athletes come from poverty and limited role models. For example, there is former U.S. tennis player, Zina Garrison, who discusses her dislike of the media's presentation of her life as a tragedy-to-triumph story in her 2001 autobiography:

> Some people, especially those in the media, want to believe that I am a typical poor little black girl from Texas who made good. That's not the way I see myself. I lived in a decent neighborhood, had plenty of food, and never went to school without lunch money. I was spoiled and had everything I wanted. How can I say I was poor?[21]

By framing Black athletic success as tragedy-to-triumph, media helps structural racism persist because the message to the American public is that Blacks do not have access to power in society, such as the access to information, wealth, organizational infrastructure, and so on. There is statistical socioeconomic difference between Blacks and whites—with whites having a higher socioeconomic status—but that is not to say there are *no* poor whites or poor white athletes with their own tragedy-to-triumph stories.

Perhaps the most thorough glimpse into the tragedy to triumph story of Lolo Jones is the 2012 pre-Olympic documentary film, *SEC Storied: Lolo Jones*. This forty-nine-minute documentary is moving. Her story is compelling and inspirational. Lolo grew up in Des Moines, Iowa, with four siblings, a white mother, and a Black father who was in and out of jail. For a time period during her childhood, the family was homeless and allowed to sleep in the bottom of a church basement. She began running with her dad because the old cars he drove used to constantly break down; he said the running would keep them warm in the cold weather. She was hooked after that, sharing with viewers that "running was the friend that never left . . . only constant thing in my life."[22]

After working incredibly hard (even staying behind at her current high school, while her family moved away during her senior year) toward a track and field scholarship, Lolo attended Louisiana State University (LSU). The transition from Iowa to Louisiana gave her culture shock and being there resulted in her becoming much better at her craft and the inspiration toward Olympic-level achievements. She traveled all over the world to compete, improve, and support herself economically. Lolo's work paid off again, and her making it to the Olympics comes true, but she hopes to finally medal in the London games. *The End.*

It is the subtext within the documentary that is not so good. Rory Karpf, a white male who is lauded for documentaries on white male athletes, directs this feature. There are a few distinct racist and sexual agendas at play. These agendas have to deal with sexual objectification, socioeconomics, and white male dominance. Whether Karpf is himself consciously or unconsciously racist and sexist, or if he is merely editing to please the agenda of the *SEC Storied* powers-that-be, is anyone's guess.

Within the first two minutes of the documentary, the audience is given an overt cue to gaze on Lolo Jones as a sex object. The first words spoken are in the form of a question that comes from an unseen interviewer (perhaps Karpf):

> [unknown interviewer]: Are you comfortable being like a . . . like a sex symbol?
>
> [Lolo]: (Laughter) I never consider myself to be a sex symbol. I think that's hilarious because there's been so many ups and downs in my life. I just learned the quality to fight.[23]

Even though Lolo laughs off the idea of being a sex symbol, it has been established that she *is* an American sex symbol, regardless of whether she thinks it is amusing. Before she can establish herself—in her own words—as a "fighter," viewers have etched in their minds that special attention should be paid to her outward appearance.

Once Lolo begins to discuss her childhood, there are subtle references to socioeconomics and a promotion for the "pull yourself up by the bootstraps" (aka improve your situation by your own efforts) mentality among the impoverished. For example, in recalling those times when her family was homeless, Lolo says that she "was a professional shoplifter by the sixth grade . . . but *only* of food."[24] And some minutes later, Lolo states that the "drive wouldn't have been there had I not grown up in poverty."[25] This supports the notion of some citizens in this country that (Black) people living in poverty are abusing government assistance programs, and these programs should be ended and the impoverished should just help themselves. Lolo Jones is the ideal model for the success of this notion. Sure, she stole some food to survive, but that is better than what the nation sees in the televised news almost daily about robberies involving Blacks. She is the best role model every anti–affirmative action supporter could hope for to inspire poor Blacks.

Finally, a subtext for the entrance of a "great white (male) hope" into Jones's story comes in her acceptance to LSU and its national championship track and field team. The only positive relationship with a male that is highlighted in this documentary is the one Lolo had with former LSU Assistant Coach Dennis Shaver. Shaver begins with an interesting recollection of his first impression of Lolo:

> In the recruitment process, Lolo wasn't even on our radar. I found out about Lolo Jones through Kim (Carson), and we brought Lolo in for an official visit . . . and I have to admit somewhat reluctantly because she wasn't one of the top performers at the high school level at that time. But during the interview process here, she seemed highly organized, very motivated, and she seemed very goal oriented.[26]

The statements Shaver makes are interesting because there is an immediate establishment of power; he does not need Lolo, rather it is Lolo who needs him. There is also an underlying tone of negative racist perception about Black athlete character traits. Shaver was clearly impressed with Lolo's organization, motivation, and goal orientation. This creates the impression that the Black female athletes he does recruit are lacking these characteristics.

The power position Coach Shaver is in is further emphasized when Lolo discusses almost leaving LSU after her freshman year. Lolo shares that:

> Coach told me, "well, you can leave," but he wanted to talk to me and he was like, "you can be the best here at LSU; you just have to learn how to kind of control your emotions."[27]

Here, it is directly established that Lolo's leaving would not hurt Coach Shaver; it would be Lolo who would be missing out on something if she left him and his program. So, viewers then learn that Lolo decided to stay at LSU, and coach Shaver became the father figure she always wished she had grown up with, stating, "you know, I've had my dad in-and-out, but you know, coach Shaver has just been *rock solid*."[28] No real positive experiences with her biological father are mentioned in the documentary, which leaves viewers to believe there probably were none.

This documentary is just one of the structurally racist media's platforms in which society's racist patriarchal ideals are dispensed and perpetuated to the masses. In addition to this documentary, Lolo was featured in numerous commercials, on billboards, appeared on talk shows, and was lauded for her physique in the highly coveted annual *ESPN: The Body Issue* magazine in 2009. Beijing Olympic *champion*, Dawn Harper, never got any of this attention and it hurt her. In an interview with the *New York Times* days before the London Olympics, Harper said she reconciled her hurt feelings by praying, but was also shocked at how much Jones was revealing for publicity. Harper told the *New York Times*, "I've had family issues as well, but I'm not willing to say all of them just so it can be in the papers."[29]

It would appear that Harper's reconciliation with Jones's media attention was never reconciled, just dormant. After Harper's silver medal performance in the 2012 hundred-meter hurdle race, she and Kellie Wells sat down with *NBC* journalist Michelle Beadle and spoke candidly. Harper said:

> I feel as if I had a pretty good story. Knee surgery two months before Olympic trials in 2008 to make the Olympic team by .007, not have a contract . . . working three jobs, living in a frat house trying to make it work. Umm, coming off running in someone else's shoes getting the gold medal [in 2008]. Uhhh, sounds pretty interesting! Coming from East St. Louis, I just felt as if I worked really hard to, you know, represent my country in the best way possible and to come away with a gold medal. And to honestly seem as if their [the media's] favorite didn't win, all of a sudden it was just like, "well we're kinda gonna push your story aside and we're still gonna push this one." That hurt . . . but you know, I feel as if I showed I can deal with the pressure. I came back and I think you gotta respect it a little bit now.[30]

Wells and Harper are admittedly close friends with one another, and when Beadle inquired about whether there was fighting among them and Lolo or if they have all moved on now that the race is over, Wells calmly shared her opinion:

> Well I think, on the podium tonight, the three girls that earned their spots and that got their medals and that worked hard and did what they needed to do, prevailed. And that's all that really needs to be said.[31]

Many people took the words of Harper and Wells to be nothing but jealousy and bitterness, but this researcher is not one of those people. The issue is not about Lolo's media—and thus financial—success. It is about the fact that she did not really *earn* any of it. At some point, Lolo had to understand that the media has an agenda for her; a devious plan to use her body and story to increase ratings, profits, and keep Black people "in their place." Sorry Dawn and Kellie. Winning just is not enough if one is a Black female athlete that the media does not deem as physically attractive and poor enough to market to the nation and the world; if it were, how would the rest of the country know with certainty that successful Black athletes—and all Blacks in general—are still lesser than whites?

What is sadder is that Lolo has publicly placed blame on Kellie and Dawn for their lack of media attention and marketability. In an interview with *ESPNW* journalist, Kate Fagan, in late August 2012, Lolo had this to say:

> I'll say this of Dawn and Kellie, I know they didn't have marketing agents. So if they want to blame me for getting the deals because I'm pretty, or other various things, I think when it comes down to it, I was the only one who had a marketing person.

Jones's rationale just does not make sense; at least not in the case of Dawn Harper. Sure, Kellie Wells was not on the 2008 Olympic team, but Harper won *gold*. When it comes to the Olympics, the media and sponsors go after whom they feel is most marketable. As scholar Lois Bryson states in his article, "Sport and the Maintenance of Masculine Hegemony," "this ignoring of women's achievements is by no means confined to situations in which they fail to win, it extends to situations in which they do win."[32]

Dawn Harper and Kellie Wells deserve praise for "standing up" to the media and calling Lolo out for her complicity in their not-so-hidden agenda. Mass media and advertising see to it that we consume visible difference daily.[33] It is alarming to think that the media is telling society that light-skinned (aka closer to white) and what *they* consider sexy is whom everyone should be cheering for and encouraging young Americans to aspire to be and look like. It truly makes an impact. For example, one Internet commenter of the Glenn Davis article that covered Harper and Wells's interview with Michelle Beadle, referred to the silver and bronze medalists as "Darkie Harper" and "Blackie Wells." This means one of two things; either this person ignores the fact that Lolo Jones is half Black or the only acceptable version of Black for this person is someone who has white physical features. With structural racism, not all whites are racist—unlike that commenter—but they "can still benefit from a system that is organized to benefit some at the expense of others."[34] The media and marketing support of Lolo Jones over Wells and Harper keeps the U.S. system of white privilege alive.

Conclusion

Ultimately, the Olympics are the perfect site to showcase how nations around the world handle the topics of race and gender within their respective societies. In the London 2012 Olympic Games, it became evident that the United States still has work to do when it comes to reaching racial and gender equality in both sport and society. Gabby Douglas certainly inspired many young African American girls who had never seen a Black gymnast before, but will these new Black gymnasts go into competitions comparing their hair to their white teammates and competition? Dawn Harper and Kellie Wells were unafraid to openly challenge the media in its neglect of coverage of their own stories—or in other words, unafraid to ask, "hey . . . what's your *real* agenda in covering Lolo and not us?" It is never an issue of race or gender for Black women; it is race *and* gender.

This work the United States needs to do, ideally, would tackle the issues of structural racism and internalized racism at the same time. After all, these incidents over hair and the media are not isolated to the realm of the athlete. In late June, 2013, the Lorain Horizon Science Academy in Ohio issued a letter to parents about a change in the schools dress code and personal appearance policy. Two different lines from the letter state:

- *Hair must look natural, clean, well-groomed and should not cover the face*
- *Afro-puffs and small twisted braids, with or without rubber bands are NOT permitted*[35]

With public outcry over the line about Afro-puffs and braids, the school quickly apologized and deleted it from their final version of the dress code and personal appearance policy. However, if one looks at these two lines side by side, the structural racism is clear and so is the obvious potential to develop internalized racism within the school's African American student body. Black hair in its natural state—that is, without chemicals or flat irons—is an Afro. Therefore, the administration of this school believes that natural, clean, and well-groomed hair is *not* natural Black hair. Please believe that if this policy had not been challenged and overturned, a lot more young Black girls would be going to get chemical relaxers to "fix" their natural hair; perhaps even growing up hating the hair they were born with because a structure in society has told them it is essentially ugly and unnatural. Hair may seem like an insignificant thing in the grand scheme of American society, but when it is used by racist structures to oppress, those structures must be challenged.

Another controversial incident surrounding Black hair came in the form of a live exhibit that was organized by African American women in New York City's Union Square in early June 2013. It was all part of a two-day "interactive public art exhibit," titled "You Can Touch My Hair," during which people were encouraged to get up close and personal with various forms of Black hair on live models.[36] Organizers of the event were seeking to eradicate ignorance about Black hair. The event was not embraced by all members of the Black community, however; other women joined the exhibit's models in the park to protest against the touching of Black hair. In an interview with *theGrio.com*, a young woman named Jenifer explained why she was out protesting:

> I wanted to strike a balance . . . I feel very vehemently against putting yourself on display like you're some kind of zoo animal. Black people have a history of being property in this country and countries all over the world. To me, this hearkens back to those days. We're doing it this time. We're making ourselves objects to be prodded, touched, examined and ogled.[37]

This exhibit and the protestation of it, serves as a great example of why change must come at the structural level *and* internalized/emotional level of racism. It is admirable and brave of the exhibit organizers and models to try and educate non-Blacks about the realities of Black hair. At the same time, it is understandable that protesters like Jenifer feel strongly against it. The protesters would rather see a change within racist structures like the media to familiarize non-Blacks about Black hair, such as more advertisements and commercials for Black hair products, television shows featuring Black women with natural hairstyles, and so forth. If the power structures showed more initiative in moving toward antiracist practices, perhaps the "You Can Touch My Hair" exhibit would have been embraced by some of the protesters. Progress in eradicating structural racism will lead to progression in eradicating internalized racism and a focus on a better future, rather than a continued focus on racism of the past.

Undoubtedly, this progress will come slowly, but it must be celebrated when it does come. A recent commercial released for the popular children's cereal, Cheerios, became a hot topic among U.S. citizens because it featured a multiracial family. The commercial centers around a mixed little girl, with a white mother and a Black father. She pours Cheerios on top of her Black father's heart while he is sleeping because her mother confirmed to her that Cheerios are good for the heart. The commercial ends with dad awaking to a chest covered in the cereal and a look of confusion; it's adorable! The number of Americans identifying as "mixed race" is on the rise. People who reported a background of mixed race grew by 32 percent to 9 million between 2000 and 2010.[38] The Cheerios Facebook page received a number of supportive and praising comments, but it also got some nasty responses to the commercial. One negative comment read, "More like single parent in the making. Black dad will dip out soon."[39] The idea that all Black fathers leave was supported in the Lolo Jones documentary and obviously reappears in other forms of media output. Why else would this commenter post something like that? And the race of the commenter does not make it any better or worse; if the commenter is Black, they are suffering from internalized racism, and if they are white, they are another racist, supporting the maintenance of structural racism.

The incidents that took place in the London Olympics should serve only as a lens into the massive issues of structural and internalized racism. No matter what the reason for posting negative comments about Gabby Douglas's hair, the root of the problem—pun intended—is that internalized racism is still pervasive in the United States. With the 2016 Olympics in Rio not too far away, attention should be paid to the athletes in the spotlight. Who are Americans supposed to admire and aspire to be in 2016; another poor Black girl with a tragedy-to-triumph story? Let us hope not. If society can look to positive changes and opportunities for destroying racism and achieving gender equality in and outside the realm of sports for inspiration, race in the next century will *finally* matter a whole lot less.

Notes

1. Paul Willis, "Women in Sport in Ideology," in *Women, Sport, and Culture*, ed. Susan Birrell and Cheryl Cole (Champaign: Human Kinetics, 1994), 33.

2. Camara Phyllis Jones, "Levels of Racism: A Theoretic Framework and a Gardener's Tale," *American Journal of Public Health* 90, no. 8 (2000): 1213.

3. Ibid., 1213.

4. Rachel Gayle Laws, "South African and U.S. Black Female Athletes Compared: A Critical Ethnography Focused on Image, Perceptions, and Narratives" (PhD dissertation, Michigan State University, 2012), 104.

5. Gabrielle Douglas, *Grace, Gold and Glory: My Leap of Faith*, ed. Michelle Burford (Grand Rapids: Zondervan, 2012), 59.

6. Ibid., 59.

7. Ibid., 66.

8. Ayana Byrd and Lori Tharps, *Hair Story: Untangling the Roots of Black Hair in America* (New York: St. Martin's Press, 2001), 1.

9. Ibid., 2.

10. Ibid., 4.

11. Ibid., 4.

12. Maria Puente, "Chris Rock's 'Good Hair' Gets Tangled up in Controversy," *USA Today*, last modified October 25, 2009, http://usatoday30.usatoday.com/life/movies/news/2009-10-22-good-hair-main_N.htm.

13. Vanessa Williams, "Gabby Douglas's Hair Sets off Twitter Debate, but Some Ask: 'What's the Fuss?'" *Washington Post*, last modified August 3, 2012, http://articles.washingtonpost.com/2012-08-03/lifestyle/35490477_1_natural-hair-gabby-douglas-black-women.

14. Douglas, 150.

15. Douglas, 133.

16. Williams.

17. Jones, 1212.

18. Laws, 12.

19. Margaret Duncan, Michael Messner, Linda Williams, Kerry Jensen, and Wayne Wilson, "Gender Stereotyping in Televised Sports," in *Women, Sport, and Culture*, ed. Susan Birrell and Cheryl Cole (Champaign: Human Kinetics, 1994), 249.

20. Ibid., 266. Also see Alan Clarke, and John Clarke, "Highlights and Action Replays: Ideology, Sport, and the Media," in *Sport, Culture, and Ideology*, ed. Jennifer Hargreaves (London: Routledge & Kegan Paul, 1982), 62–87; Margaret Carlisle Duncan, and Barry Brummett, "The Mediation of Spectator Sport," *Research Quarterly for Exercise and Sport* 58, no. 2 (1987): 168–177; Todd Gitlin, "Prime Time Ideology: The Hegemonic Process in Television Entertainment," in *Television: The Critical View*, ed. H. Newcomb (New York: Oxford University Press, 1982), 426–454; M. Morse, "Sport on Television: Replay and Display," in *Regarding Television*, ed. E. A. Kaplan (Los Angeles: American Film Institute/University Publications of America, 1983), 44–66; Lawrence Wenner, *Media, Sports, & Society* (Newbury Park: SAGE Publications, 1989).

21. Zina Garrison, *Zina: My Life in Women's Tennis* (Berkeley: North Atlantic Books, 2001), 180.

22. Rory Karpf, *SEC Storied: Lolo Jones,* 49-minute documentary, from

Netflix, *ESPN Films*, 2012, http://movies.netflix.com/WiMovie/SEC_Storied_Lolo_Jones/70262419.

23. Ibid.

24. Ibid

25. Ibid

26. Ibid

27. Ibid

28. Ibid

29. Jeré Longman, "For Lolo Jones, Everything Is Image," *New York Times*, last modified August 4, 2012, http://www.nytimes.com/2012/08/05/sports/olympics/olympian-lolo-jones-draws-attention-to-beauty-not-achievement.html?_r=0.

30. Glenn Davis, "Medal-Winning American Hurdlers Aren't Too Happy About all the Lolo Jones Hype," *SportsGrid*, last modified August 8, 2012, www.sportsgrid.com/media/dawn-harper-kellie-wells-interview/.

31. Ibid.

32. Lois Bryson, "Sport and the Maintenance of Masculine Hegemony," in *Women, Sport, and Culture*, ed. Susan Birrell and Cheryl Cole (Champaign: Human Kinetics, 1994), 55.

33. Christine Anne Holmlund, "Visible Difference and Flex Appeal: The Body, Sex, Sexuality, and Race in the *Pumping Iron* Films," in *Women, Sport, and Culture*, ed. Susan Birrell and Cheryl Cole (Champaign: Human Kinetics, 1994), 300.

34. Margaret L. Andersen and Patricia Hill Collins, "Conceptualizing Race, Class, and

Gender," in *Race, Class, and Gender: An Anthology*, ed. Margaret Andersen and Patricia Hill Collins (Belmont: Wadsworth/Thomson Learning, 2004), 81.

35. "Ohio School Bans Afro Puffs and Braids," *BlackGirlLongHair.com*, last modified June 20, 2013, http://blackgirllonghair.com/2013/06/ohio-school-bans-afro-puffs-and-braids/.

36. Ramsey, Donovan, "'You Can Touch My Hair': NYC Black Hair Exhibit Draws Controversy, as Many Protest Spectacle," *theGrio.com,* last modified June 10, 2013, http://thegrio.com/2013/06/10/you-can-touch-my-hair-nyc-black-hair-exhibit-draws-controversy-as-many-protest-hair-feeling-spectacle/#s:touchmyhair_dxr_001.

37. Ibid.

38. Moni Basu, "Census: More People Identify as Mixed Race," *CNN.com*, last modified September 27, 2012, http://inamerica.blogs.cnn.com/2012/09/27/census-more-people-identify-as-mixed-race/.

39. "Why Is Ad Featuring Multiracial Family Causing a Stir?" *CNN.com,* last modified May 31, 2013, http://inamerica.blogs.cnn.com/2013/05/31/why-is-ad-featuring-multiracial-family-causing-stir/.

Bibliography

Andersen, Margaret L., and Patricia Hill Collins. "Conceptualizing Race, Class, and Gender." In *Race, Class, and Gender: An Anthology*, edited by Margaret Andersen and Patricia Hill Collins, 75–98. Belmont: Wadsworth/Thomson Learning, 2004.

Basu, Moni. "Census: More People Identify as Mixed Race." *CNN.com*. Last modified September 27, 2012. http://inamerica.blogs.cnn.com/2012/09/27/census-more-people-identify-as-mixed-race/.

Bryson, Lois. "Sport and the Maintenance of Masculine Hegemony." In *Women, Sport, and Culture*, edited by Susan Birrell and Cheryl Cole, 47–64. Champaign: Human Kinetics, 1994.

Byrd, Ayana, and Lori Tharps. *Hair Story: Untangling the Roots of Black Hair in America*. New York: St. Martin's Press, 2001.

Clarke, Alan, and John Clarke. "Highlights and Action Replays: Ideology, Sport, and the Media." In *Sport, Culture, and Ideology*, 62–87. Edited by Jennifer Hargreaves. London: Routledge & Kegan Paul, 1982.

Davis, Glenn. "Medal-Winning American Hurdlers Aren't Too Happy about all the Lolo Jones Hype." *SportsGrid*. Last modified August 8, 2012. www.sportsgrid.com/media/dawn-harper-kellie-wells-interview/.

Douglas, Gabrielle. *Grace, Gold & Glory: My Leap of* Faith. Edited by Michelle Burford. Grand Rapids: Zondervan, 2012.

Duncan, Margaret Carlisle, and Barry Brummett. "The Mediation of Spectator Sport." *Research Quarterly for Exercise and Sport* 58, no. 2 (1987): 168–177.

Duncan, Margaret, Michael Messner, Linda Williams, Kerry Jensen, and Wayne Wilson. "Gender Stereotyping in Televised Sports." In *Women, Sport, and Culture,* edited by Susan Birrell and Cheryl Cole, 249–272. Champaign, IL: Human Kinetics, 1994.

Garrison, Zina. *Zina: My Life in Women's Tennis*. Berkeley: North Atlantic Books, 2001.

Gitlin, Todd. "Prime Time Ideology: The Hegemonic Process in Television Entertainment." In *Television: The Critical View*, 426–454. Edited by H. Newcomb. New York: Oxford University Press, 1982.

Holmlund, Christine Anne. "Visible Difference and Flex Appeal: The Body, Sex, Sexuality, and Race in the *Pumping Iron* Films." In *Women, Sport, and Culture*, edited by Susan Birrell and Cheryl Cole, 299–313. Champaign, IL: Human Kinetics, 1994.

Jones, Camara Phyllis. "Levels of Racism: A Theoretic Framework and a Gardener's Tale." *American Journal of Public Health* 90, no. 8 (2000): 1212–,1215.

Laws, Rachel Gayle. "South African and U.S. Black Female Athletes Compared: A Critical Ethnography Focused on Image, Perceptions, and Narratives," PhD dissertation, Michigan State University, 2012.

Longman, Jeré. "For Lolo Jones, Everything Is Image." *New York Times*. Last modified August 4, 2012. http://www.nytimes.com/2012/08/05/sports/olympics/olympian-lolo-jones-draws-attention-to-beauty-not-achievement.html?_r=0.

Morse, M. "Sport on Television: Replay and Display." In *Regarding Television*, 44–46. Edited by E. A. Kaplan. Los Angeles: American Film Institute/University Publications of America, 1983.

"Ohio School Bans Afro Puffs and Braids." *BlackGirlLongHair.com*. Last modified June 20, 2013. http://blackgirllonghair.com/2013/06/ohio-school-bans-afro-puffs-and-braids/.

Puente, Maria. "Chris Rock's 'Good Hair' Gets Tangled up in Controversy." *USA Today*. Last modified October 25, 2009. http://usatoday30.usatoday.com/life/movies/news/2009-10-22-good-hair-main_N.htm.

Ramsey, Donovan. "'You Can Touch My Hair:' NYC Black Hair Exhibit Draws Controversy, as Many Protest Spectacle." *theGrio.com*. Last modified June 10, 2013. http://thegrio.com/2013/06/10/you-can-touch-my-hair-nyc-black-hair-exhibit-draws-controversy-as-many-protest-hair-feeling-spectacle/#s:touchmyhair_dxr_001.

"SEC Storied: Lolo Jones," available through Netflix, 49 minutes, *ESPN Films*, 2012, http://movies.netflix.com/WiMovie/SEC_Storied_Lolo_Jones/70262419.

Werner, Lawrence. *Media, Sports, and Society*. Newbury Park: SAGE Publications, 1989.

"Why Is Ad Featuring Multiracial Family Causing a Stir?" CNN.com. Last modified May 31, 2013. http://inamerica.blogs.cnn.com/2013/05/31/why-is-ad-featuring-multiracial-family-causing-stir/.

Williams, Vanessa. "Gabby Douglas's Hair Sets off Twitter Debate, but Some Ask: 'What's the Fuss?'" *Washington Post*. Last modified August 3, 2012. http://articles.washingtonpost.com/2012-08-03/lifestyle/35490477_1_natural-hair-gabby-douglas-black-women.

Willis, Paul. "Women in Sport in Ideology." In *Women, Sport, and Culture*, edited by Susan Birrell and Cheryl L. Cole, 31–45. Champaign, IL: Human Kinetics, 1994.

13

An Obama Effect?

African American Voting Behavior and the Political Symbolism of a Black President

David C. Wilson, Samantha S. Kelley,
Emmanuel Balogun, Christian Soler, and Sahar Salehi

Introduction

In a political period during which the United States has witnessed its first self-described African American president—Barack Obama—questions abound about how such a phenomenon might affect political participation among African Americans. Given that African Americans have undertaken a near universal quest for equality in social, economic, and political areas, one might expect that President Obama's ascent to political prominence would have a substantive and positive effect on African American's political engagement. Newspaper coverage of the first three months of the Obama candidacy made these aspirations known, as race and leadership were prominently featured in media accounts about Obama.[1] Yet, there are limited scholarly empirical studies documenting, theorizing, or analyzing a so-called Obama effect on reported turnout among African Americans.

This chapter explores the question of whether President Obama's presence as a political candidate, national leader, and influential cultural figure has progressed, hindered, or had no effect on Blacks' political participation. In theory, Obama's presence should have a positive symbolic meaning to African Americans, promoting positive affect (e.g., hope, excitement, and pride), and thereby enhancing their group identity and subsequent engagement in the political process.[2] This increased engagement should be associated with a rise in political behaviors such as casting a ballot (i.e., voting).[3]

Few will doubt that Obama's presence in American politics has anecdotal and historical significance; however, claims of his importance in this research will rely on empirical effects from individual-level survey data. This chapter analyzes data collected, from 2000 to 2012, by the U.S. Census Bureau in November of presidential and midterm election years, to help to assess the potential effects of Obama's presence on African American's self-reported voting behaviors, as well as reasons for not voting. The multiple years of analysis, the examination of voting as well as nonvoting, and the specific focus on African Americans make for an unprecedented examination of African Americans' voting behavior.

This study argues that Obama's candidacy in the 2008 presidential election has created a positive affective response, and increased political engagement among African Americans because of the symbolic meaning attributed to him. Using a theoretical approach that explores political behavior in terms of symbolic politics and political empowerment, as well as empirical research, the results support the hypothesis of an Obama effect. Significantly higher African American voter turnout is associated with Obama's presence, and the concluding analysis will investigate the implications of these findings, particularly related to African American political participation in a larger social context.

Voting as Political Participation

While political participation includes activities such as "engaging in political discussions with friends" or "giving money to candidates," this study operationalizes participation as behaviors directly tied to the act of voting.[4] Federal elections involve voting for the president, vice president, and members of Congress. With more high-profile candidates and available offices, presidential elections tend to have higher voter turnout than midterm elections.[5]

When it comes to presidential campaigns, candidates who seek the highest elective office often rely on the predispositions of the electorate to attract support. Predispositions generally include any psychological factors that form the basis for political decision-making.[6] Candidates go to great lengths to appeal to the identities and values of voters, including their group identities related to race-ethnicity, gender, age, military veteran status, business acumen, and ideology as liberal or conservative. The more candidates can promote shared values and identities, the greater the likelihood that they will connect with the public and receive support. Examples of this from the 2008 election include Barack Obama politically posturing to identify with the African American community or John McCain appealing to low-income voters by championing drilling to offset the energy crisis.[7] It follows then, that a candidate must symbolize one or more meaningful and positive attributes (e.g., trust, hope, change, courage) to members of the electorate so they not only feel affinity for the candidate, but will vote for the candidate as well.

The question for this research is to gauge the extent to which Obama was able to produce such a symbolic effect, if any, generating increased political engagement among African Americans, and potentially contributing to increases in African American voter turnout. The research will demonstrate that race is still a significant factor affecting African American political engagement, but only to the extent that a candidate's presence has a positive symbolic meaning that enhances group identity.

Obama as a Political Symbol for African Americans

The most prevalent symbolic information associated with Obama's political rise has been his racial identification as an African American, as well as the strong affective response attributed to him as the first viable African American presidential candidate.[8] Obama's race was symbolic in that it signaled a sense of shared fate, and promoted group consciousness among African Americans; in essence, Obama's success symbolizes descriptive progress for all African Americans who share his race even if not all of his political values.[9]

Political symbols are loosely defined as affectively charged political phenomena, where the symbolic meaning is felt by the individual perceiver due to congruence with strongly held predispositions.[10] *Political predispositions* are preferences developed early in life through socialization, leading us to judge an object in a particularly symbolic way.[11] These preferences serve as filters for incorporating new information into existing political beliefs. As mentioned earlier, predispositions include group identities (e.g., race, gender, social class), attitudes (e.g., explicit likes and dislikes), and values and core beliefs (e.g., responsibility, equality, fairness, and freedom).

Having an African American in office or in a leadership position is likely symbolic for African Americans in general. Research examining African American political participation has focused on in-group leadership cues that signal a motivation for increased engagement. Obama's race might have served as a cue to African Americans that they were now empowered to promote and affect political change. Research supports this position. For example, the Black empowerment hypothesis proposes that descriptive (i.e., same race) representation contributes to increases in African American political participation by impacting "levels of political trust, efficacy, and knowledge about politics."[12] Essentially, more descriptive representation signals higher empowerment, and an increased ability to affect political outcomes. Lawrence Bobo and Franklin Gilliam found that Blacks in high-empowerment areas are more politically active than Blacks in low-empowerment areas, particularly at the local (e.g., city or county) level.[13] Bobo and Gilliam conclude that Black representation is a "contextual cue of likely policy responsiveness," giving African Americans a feeling that participation has an intrinsic value.[14]

Not all research supports a strict interpretation of the Black empowerment hypothesis. Claudine Gay's study found only occasional increases in political participation rather than consistent and systematic increases.[15] Similar to Gay, Katherine Tate examined Jessie Jackson's presidential bids in 1984 and 1988, and found that although he received widespread African American support in 1984, this support was largely lacking in 1988.[16] The studies by Gay and Tate suggest that simply having an African American candidate is not reason enough to motivate political engagement. This is further confirmed by the many African American Republican candidates, and even some Democrats, who fail to garner strong African American support.[17]

In spite of the inconsistency of the Black empowerment hypothesis in explaining African American voter turnout, it does suggest that shared in-group membership, or racial identity, between leaders and the electorate is an important part of the civic engagement process. In this respect, group identity serves to heighten group consciousness or linked fate, where African American individuals may feel that their own individual life outcomes are inseparable to the circumstances of African Americans as a whole.[18] Importantly, Charlton McIlwain's research found that while the media's focus on Obama's lack of experience could have been detrimental to his candidacy, his race served as the most visible characteristic that distinguished him from the other candidates, and signaled his political transcendence.[19] While race alone cannot generate the mobilization needed to increase substantial African American voter turnout, it can have substantial symbolic meaning.

For many people, particularly African Americans, Obama may have specifically been viewed as a type of "condensation" symbol.[20] Condensation symbols activate value-laden predispositions, which help individuals to reduce (condense) inexact information about objects to which they have minimal experience, into meaningful categories, thereby making it easier to evaluate and pass judgments about political ideas and individuals. Condensation symbols include political groups, contentious policy issues, and political figures like the pope, the president of the United States, and popular military leaders, whose role or social position help to inform their importance and potential influence. Condensation symbols are potentially the most powerful tools that can be used to sway the mass public, because they innately tie affect to images.[21] When individuals see the pope, they feel a certain way, as they do when they see their nation's flag. Similarly, when people, especially African Americans, *saw* Obama, they *felt* something, arguably pride, hope, and enthusiasm. Supporting this, in a study conducted by Finn and Glaser, they found that the emotions of hope and pride played a contributing role in explaining presidential voters' choice in 2008.[22] The data in this research aims to further elaborate such findings and should reveal an Obama effect even after controlling for other important individual-level factors related to voting, such as education, income, and age; as well as aggregate factors related to the generally increasing turnout levels among Blacks over the past decade.

Overall, the strengths of the present study reside in its multilayered approach. While other studies have discussed the importance of African American candidates, they have not focused on one which has won the nomination of a major party. Additionally, many studies that have sought to disprove an Obama effect have investigated cross-race voting trends rather than focus on the behavior of a single racial-ethnic group. Studies have also typically focused on one or two election years in isolation, while this study has explored multiple-year voting patterns for both presidential and midterm elections since the early 1990s. Finally, conventional studies have typically failed to control for other factors that could have intervened in the relationship between the Obama effect and increased African American voter turnout. Consequently, this study takes a more holistic approach to investigating a probable Obama effect, with all signs pointing to its likely existence.

The perspectives on descriptive representation as empowerment, and the symbolic importance of race through shared identity, lead this group of researchers to expect that Obama's presence has significantly increased turnout among African Americans. Obama, as the first viable African American presidential candidate, should have cued symbolic group attachment (i.e., group identity) and positive affect to such a degree that African American voter turnout would increase for the years that he ran for and served in office.

African American Turnout over Time

Over time, there have been various attempts at correcting the plight of African Americans through inclusion in the political process. The first notable instance was the Fifteenth Amendment in the U.S. Constitution, which stipulates that the right to vote cannot be denied based on race, color, or previous servitude. States remained the ultimate determinant on the process of voting. States used mechanisms to limit African American participation such as the "Jim Crow" laws, poll taxes, literacy tests, and statutes such as the Grandfather clause.[23] The residual effects of these mechanisms induced economic and education inequalities between whites and African Americans.[24] African American leaders and organizations led a persistent effort in the early 1900s through the 1960s battling for supplemental legislation from Congress to enforce the Fifteenth Amendment.

The Voting Rights Act of 1965 passed one year after the landmark Civil Rights Act of 1964. The Voting Rights Act served as the supplemental legislation that would provide Congressional oversight to ensure that the Fifteenth Amendment was implemented in the way it was intended to, and effectively terminate practices of "prerequisite" voting. Given the political energy of the African American Civil Rights movement, and the legal elimination of racial barriers to voting, African American political participation overall was still limited.[25] The literature on African American political engagement cites that low levels of participation have been a result of a lack of direct mobilization and/or the result of a sentiment of low levels of political opportunity.[26] Given this context, we remain interested in the trajectory of African American political participation.

Much of the literature charting the voting behavior of African Americans argues that the economic and social realities of African Americans serve as indicators of party identification, with African Americans tending to support Democrats, and are on the far-liberal end of the political spectrum. Some literature has gone as far as to state that African Americans have developed an interrelated cognitive schema that manifests itself through the different political and social heritage of white and African American citizens.[27] This literature argues that Black autonomy, closeness to Black elites, closeness to Black masses, and a propensity to positive or negative stereotypes about Blacks serve as a cognitive schema for African Americans. This coheres with symbolic politics literature indicating that the conditions for creating collective memories and salient political events enable the acquisition of crystallized, collective predispositions.[28] Following this logic, the civil rights movement was not just a legislative move to solidify African American participation. Rather, it served as a basis toward the development of an autonomous and politically unique voting bloc that has been type-casted to emit particular behaviors based on their historical experiences in the United States, and the residual socioeconomic effects derived from these experiences.

The standard SES model of participation argues that socioeconomic factors and individual resources will lead to higher or lower levels of sociopolitical engagement.[29] According to SES, African Americans are "resource poor" and tend to have lower levels of political skills, access to relevant information, and formal education.[30] This reinforces the idea that measures of African American participation are rooted in the historic suppression of African American engagement, enabled by the U.S. political system.

Another paradox that substantiates the idea that African American plight remains is in the continuity of disproportionate representation in government institutions. African Americans represent 7.8 percent of the 113th Congress. There are currently forty House of Representative members who are African American, and only two senators. These senators, Tim Scott and William Cowans, were appointed to fill the seats of Jim Demint (retired) and John Kerry (secretary of state). Historically, there have only been eight African American senators. On the state level, African American representation is rare, as there have only been four African American governors in U.S. history. Two of those governors have emerged within the last ten years (Gov. David Patterson in New York and Gov. Deval Patrick in Massachusetts).

Given the historical trajectory of African American political participation, and the lack of African American representation in government institutions, it becomes even more important to gauge the attitudes and behaviors of African Americans in the age of Obama. We aim to discover whether apathy turned to activism and if Obama, by virtue of the symbolism of being an African American, had an added effect in his ascension to the presidency.

We look into the prospect of increased African American participation in the age of Obama for a number of reasons. Polling research during the 2008 election year showed that public opinion was high on the prospect of electing an African American president.[31] Some literature argues that there are considerable same-race voting preferences, and the effect of same-race preferences increase as the office gets more important.[32] There is also research that argues that the same-race preference has a marginal or nonexistent effect.[33] We also look into the prospective increase in participation following the assumptions that associate emotions and personality effects on African Americans.

If symbolism is attached to Obama, it is necessary to pinpoint where the symbolism comes from. The symbolism is in part historical, as he was a high-profile candidate in the Democratic Party, which is typically representative of African American interests. The symbolism is in part opportunistic, as Obama represented a minority candidate who seemed to have a chance at winning the party nomination and subsequent general election. African Americans also might have held an emotional bond with Obama, as they might have seen linkages with his charisma, and that of other prominent African American civic leaders.[34]

Data

Data from the Current Population Survey (CPS) is effective for analyzing voting-related behavior. The CPS is a nationally representative monthly survey of U.S. households. Data are collected by the U.S. Bureau of the Census for the Bureau of Labor Statistics (BLS). Every two years in November, after the presidential and midterm elections, the CPS includes a political participation supplement of questions, which cover self-reported voting, and nonvoting behaviors.[35] The voting and registration supplemental questions were asked of all respondents who were U.S. citizens and eighteen years or older, but the analysis will focus only on those respondents who self-identified as Black/African American. All statistical estimates from the CPS are weighted to reflect demographic proportions in the larger U.S. adult citizen population.

This study examines two main variables from the CPS Voting and Registration supplement: (1) voting behavior (PES1), and (2) reasons for not voting (PES4). PES1 asked, "In any election, some people are not able to vote because they are sick or busy or have some other reason, and others do not want to vote. Did (you/name) vote in the election held on Tuesday, November [DAY], [YEAR]?" If respondents indicated that they did not vote, PES4 asked, "What was the main reason (you/name) did not vote?[36]

The analysis considers several other factors including demographic variables measuring age, sex, education level, household income, and geographic region; and survey variables related to year and mode (in person or phone) of data collection.

African American Turnout over Time

An analysis of Census trend data from 1990 to 2012 shows a consistent upward trend in the turnout for presidential elections, but a nearly flat trend in mid-term elections. This trend is presented in fig. 1.[37]

Fig. 1 shows trend lines for presidential and midterm election years from 1990 to 2012. Over this period, the average change in African American turnout for presidential election years is +1.3 percentage points, while in midterm years it is only +.3 points. If Obama had no effect on African American turnout, one might expect the same respective percentage point changes between 2004 and 2008. In fact, the percentage point change between 2004 and 2008 is about 4, while the change from 2008 to 2012 resembles the average, as it is close to 1. In addition, the midterm election change in African American turnout between 2006 and 2010 is 2 percentage points. Both increases in turnout for elections between 2008 and 2012 point to an Obama effect, but more analysis is required to see if the effect is due to Obama or some other factor related to individuals, the general trend over time, or an additional determinant. To assess the Obama effect controlling for these other factors, the attention turns toward an analysis of individual-level data which served as the basis for the aggregate results presented in fig. 1.

Factors Affecting African American Voter Turnout

Logistic regression analysis was used to predict whether individuals voted (= 1) or not (= 0) in each of the election years. The independent variables in the model include demographic variables—sex, age, household income, educational levels, and respondents living in the South—along with control variables for election year, election type (i.e., presidential or midterm), mode of interview (phone or some other method), and a dummy indicator for Obama's presence (2008, 2010, 2012 = 1, 2000 through 2006 = 0). This last variable, capturing the presence or absence of Obama as presidential candidate or officeholder, is important because it illustrates the statistical Obama effect. Controlling for all other variables, the Obama effect will demonstrate the impact, or lack thereof, of Obama's candidacy and/or presidency on African American voter turnout. The Obama effect serves to test the hypothesis that an African American candidate and president is positively correlated with Black voter turnout. The analysis included two models; both are shown in table 1.

The first model (Model 1) included only the main effects of the predictor variables, while the second model (Model 2) included the interaction effects: each variable interacted with the Obama presence variable. The columns contain logistic regression coefficients (b), which represent the magnitude and direction of the relationships, as well as the standard errors (SE) in estimation, between the row variable and the odds of voting. Main effects, the most meaningful of which are symbolized by one or more asterisks ("*"), would show the effect of a variable while controlling for others in the model. An interaction effect would suggest a variable has a stronger or weaker effect in years (i.e., 2008–2012) when Obama was present.

The results from Model 1 show that age, educational attainment, and income are each positively correlated with voting; increases in each of these variables are associated with greater odds of voting. The year variable is also significant, suggesting a generally upward trend in self-reported voting since 2000. Also, the results find that African American males are less likely to vote than females, which is consistent with findings that show that females, regardless of race, have accounted for a greater share of the Democratic presidential vote than males in the latter part of the twentieth century, an observation studies attribute to a host of reasons ranging from women's dependence on Democrats'

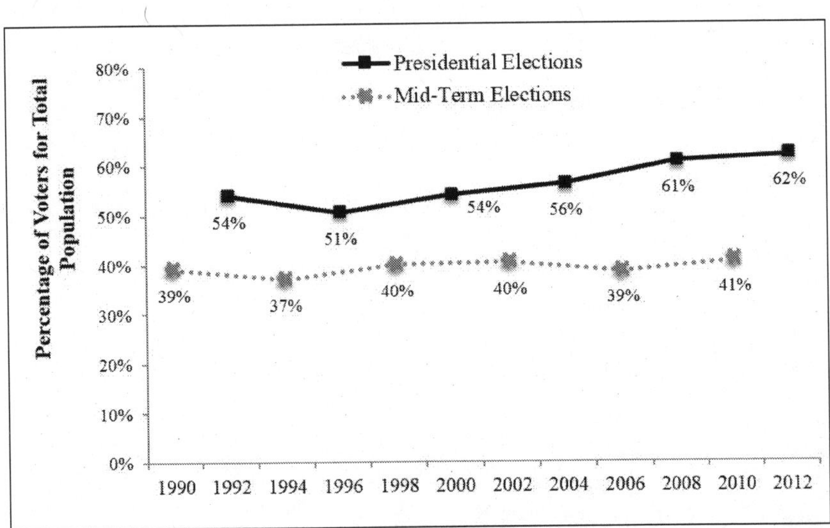

Figure 1. African American Turnout for Presidential and Mid-Term Elections, 1990–2012

Source: U.S. Census Bureau, Population Characteristic Reports.

Table 1. Regression Coefficient and Standard Errors for Voting and Registration, 2000–2012

	Voting (Yes = 1)	
Variables	Model 1 b(SE)	Model 2 b(SE)
Main Effects		
Constant	–44.42 (12.19)**	–18.25 (12.74)
Age	.03 (.00)**	.03 (.00)**
Education Level	.46 (.01)**	.47 (.02)**
Household Income	.08 (.00)**	.09 (.00)**
Sex (Male = 1)	–.39 (.02)**	–.34 (.03)**
Region (South = 1)	.00 (.02)	.02 (.03)
Year of Election	.02 (.01)**	.01 (.01)
Election Type (Presidential = 1)	1.07 (.02)**	.92 (.03)**
Obama Effect (= 2008, 2010, 2012)	.13 (.05)**	.55 (.12)**
Mode of Interview (Phone = 1)	-.15 (.02)**	-.16 (.03)**
Interaction Effects		
Age * Obama Effect	–	–.01 (.00)**
Education Level * Obama Effect	–	-.01 (.03)
Household Income * Obama Effect	–	–.02 (.01)**
Sex (Male = 1) * Obama Effect	–	–.12 (.05)**
Region (South = 1) * Obama Effect	–	–.04 (.05)
Election Type * Obama Effect	–	.33 (.05)**
Mode of Interview * Obama Effect	–	.01 (.05)
Model Fit		
-2LL	45439.72**	45348.17**
R^2	.234	.237
Percent correctly predicted	71.9%	71.9%
N	41,110	41,110

Notes: $^{*}p \leqslant .05$; $^{**}p \leqslant .01$

Source: U.S. Census Bureau, Current Population Survey Voting and Registration Supplement Public Use File (2000–2012).

welfare policies to their aversion to the use of force, one of the defining traits of Obama's predecessor.[38] There is a nonsignificant effect for living in the South; Southern African Americans are no more likely to vote than those from other regions of the United States. Also, the mode of data collection variable is statistically significant, indicating that African Americans are more likely to say they have voted when participating in the CPS using the phone. Unsurprisingly, African Americans are more likely to cast their ballots during presidential than midterm elections. Yet, the most substantive finding is that even when controlling for the type and year of the election, African Americans were more likely to vote in 2008 through 2012 than during the 2000 to 2006 election years, when Obama was not a candidate or presidential officeholder. The Obama effect is represented by a coefficient of .13, which can be interpreted to mean that in the years when Obama was present, the odds of voting increased by 1.14 when controlling for other factors in the model. Model 1 also estimated the predicted probability of voting in 2008 or beyond to be .68, compared to .57 before 2008. These main effects are important because they show the value of each individual factor in the model, however, interaction effects are necessary to help tease out some important nuances of the found Obama effect.

Model 2 runs the same logistic regression predicting voting, but now includes interaction terms. If significant, the interactions show the effect of each factor since Obama has been a candidate for president or held the office. The interactions of region *x* Obama effect and mode *x* Obama effect are nonsignificant, meaning that southern residing African Americans are no more likely to vote since 2008, and the mode of data collection is not associated with a willingness to say one voted. Among the statistically significant interaction effects, the negative age *x* Obama effect and household income *x* Obama effect coefficients show that older persons and higher-income households have been less likely to vote, respectively, since Obama's candidacy in 2008. These statistics can also be interpreted to indicate that younger persons and those with lower-household incomes are more likely to vote since 2008. These are very important indicators for an Obama effect because lower-income and less-educated voters are typically less likely to partake in politics.[39] The results from Model 2 also reveal a negative gender *x* Obama effect coefficient, which can be interpreted to mean males have been less likely to vote (or females have been more likely to vote) since the 2008 election.

The final statistically significant interaction is election-type *x* Obama effect, which shows that most of the increases in voting have come in presidential elections when Obama is explicitly on the ballot. Fig. 2

provides a bar chart with the predicted probability of voting since 2000 for midterm and presidential election years, and overall voting based on Model 2. The different color bars indicate average probability of voting in years prior to Obama's presence versus years where he is present. The Obama effect is clear across the types of elections and overall, but it is most evident when Obama is explicitly on the ballot (i.e., 2008 and 2012). In 2010, when Obama was not on the ballot, but was in office, the average voting levels were higher, but were roughly consistent with the average voting increases over time.

In summary, the findings show that Obama's presence had a positive effect on African American political participation, especially in presidential election years. The analyses also show that since 2008, lower-educated, lower-income, and lower-aged voters are more likely to turnout than prior to 2008. These are important and substantial findings that speak directly to an empirical Obama effect.

Why Are African Americans Not Voting?

An often-ignored aspect of voting behavior is nonaction. The CPS data asked respondents who did not vote whether they were registered to vote, and if they said yes, they were further asked why they did not

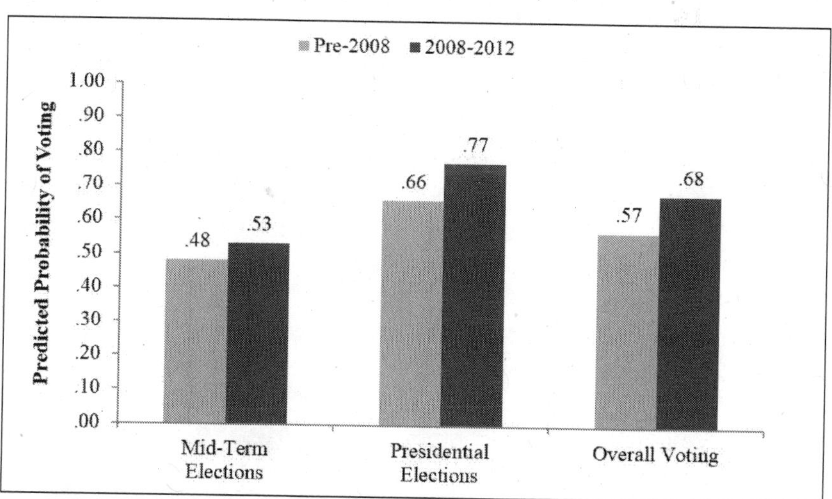

Figure 2. Average Predicted Probability of Voting for African Americans in Elections from 2000–2012

Note: Predicted probabilities are based on estimates from logistic regression controlling for selected demographics, time (year), and mode of data collection. *Source:* U.S. Census Bureau, Current Population Survey (CPS).

participate. If Obama had a significant effect on African American voting behavior then one might expect lower reports of engagement-related pretexts such as nonregistration, forgetting to vote, feeling that one's vote would not make a difference, or not liking the candidate or campaign issues. On the surface, these justifications are linked to political interest and engagement, and if Obama had a positive effect their prevalence should be lower in 2008 and potentially beyond. African Americans faced difficulties when trying to vote in 2008, as efforts had been made to decrease early voting periods and restrict voter registration drives. Ansolabehere reports that in 2008 among the Super Tuesday primary states, only 53 percent of white voters were asked to show photo identification compared to 73 percent of African Americans.[40] Thus, in many instances, there were increased costs to voting for African Americans that would have had to been overcome by their increased interest in political participation.

The analysis is presented in table 2, which is separated by presidential (left side of the table) and midterm elections (right side of the table) columns, and higher-engagement (upper rows) and lower-engagement (lower rows) justification categories. The percentages in table 2 indicate the proportions of African Americans who gave the reasons for not voting listed on the left; these data are only collected for those who did not vote. Nonvoters were first asked if they were registered, and if they said no, they were not asked any additional reasons for not voting.

Results from the analysis of nonvoting in presidential elections reveal mixed results in terms of a consistent Obama effect. African Americans were initially moved to reduce many of the higher-engagement-related reasons for not voting, but those reductions were short-lived. For example, fewer respondents in 2008 than in 2004 reported forgetting to vote, feeling that their vote did not make a difference, that they were too busy, or did not like the candidates or campaign issues. These shifts, while small, were still statistically significant and likely indicate the presence of an Obama effect. Interestingly, responses that would not likely change as a measure of political engagement—such as reporting being out of town, transportation problems, or inconvenient hours at the polling center—did not considerably change between 2004 and 2008. By the 2012 presidential election year, almost all of the reasons returned to their 2004 levels or slightly higher, including forgetting to vote and interest levels. Still, the "didn't like candidates or campaign issues" reason for not voting has continued to decline, suggesting that affect or feelings about Obama are not an influential factor for African Americans who do not vote. In general, lower turnout is still mostly attributed

Table 2. Reasons for Not Voting in Presidential and Midterm Elections among African Americans

	Presidential Elections				Midterm Elections		
Reasons for Not Voting	**2000**	**2004**	**2008**	**2012**	**2002**	**2006**	**2010**
Higher Engagement Related Reasons							
Not registered	66.3%	65.5%	72.9%	65.8%	56.2%	51.8%	48.5%
Didn't like candidates or campaign issues	1.4%	2.4%	1.2%	1.0%	2.5%	3.0%	2.6%
Forgot to vote (or send in absentee ballot)	2.3%	1.5%	1.0%	2.2%	3.3%	4.1%	4.6%
Not interested, felt my vote wouldn't make a difference	4.8%	4.0%	2.6%	4.3%	5.2%	5.9%	8.6%
Lower Engagement Related Reasons							
Too busy, conflicting work or school schedule	7.1%	8.0%	5.3%	8.2%	11.7%	13.1%	13.1%
Out of town or away from home	2.7%	2.1%	2.0%	2.0%	3.3%	4.0%	3.9%
Transportation problems	2.1%	1.7%	1.6%	2.5%	1.9%	2.2%	2.8%
Illness or disability (own or family's)	5.6%	6.7%	6.4%	5.9%	8.3%	7.0%	7.6%
Registration problems (i.e., didn't receive absentee ballot, not registered in current location)	2.4%	2.9%	1.6%	2.5%	2.3%	1.9%	1.8%
Bad weather conditions	.2%	.1%	.4%	.1%	.5%	.4%	.2%
Inconvenient hours, polling place or hours, or lines too long	.7%	1.0%	1.0%	1.3%	.9%	1.4%	1.7%
Other Reasons	4.5%	3.9%	3.9%	4.1%	4.1%	5.0%	4.5%
Total	100% (2,244)	100% (1,959)	100% (1,349)	100% (1,503)	100% (3,632)	100% (3,187)	100% (2,995)

Notes: Percentages are weighted.

Source: U.S. Census Bureau, Current Population Survey Voting and Registration Supplement Public Use File.

to nonregistration, opportunity costs of voting related to other activities, and illness or disability. While the costs of voting represent a significant element affecting voter turnout among all races, as previously discussed, costs in the form of voting restrictions disproportionately affect racial minorities over whites.[41]

The results from the midterm election analysis also illustrate mixed results for a possible Obama effect. On the one hand, between 2006 and 2010, fewer African American respondents reported that they were not registered, suggesting the likelihood of higher engagement in the political process following Obama's 2008 election. Additionally, there was a decrease in respondents reporting that they did not like the candidates or campaign issues. On the other hand, however, between 2006 and 2010, there was an increase in respondents reporting that they forgot to vote or had a lack of interest in the midterm elections, suggesting that higher-level political engagement was not consistent across categories. Similar to the conclusions drawn from the analysis of presidential, these findings suggest that affect toward Obama cannot be attributed to changes in midterm election political participation. Aside from not registering, the majority of African Americans have reported that their choice not to vote was associated with opportunity costs and illness, largely reasons unrelated to the possible influence of Obama.

Implications for African American Voting

This study has sought to explore whether Obama's historic presence as the first viable African American presidential candidate influenced Black political participation. While few studies have offered empirical evidence of an Obama effect, this study analyzed African American voting trends over the past two decades and finds, when controlling for other factors, there was statistically significant evidence to support the hypothesis of an Obama effect. The analysis also found that lower age, education, and income were factors associated with increases in African American voting in 2008 and beyond.

While the most frequent answer overall was a failure to register, between 2004 and 2008, there were statistically significant decreases in African Americans reporting that they forgot to vote, felt that their vote would not make a difference, were too busy, or did not like the candidate or campaign issues. This suggests the likelihood of increased levels of engagement among African Americans in the 2008 presidential election, which can be attributed to an Obama effect. However, despite the increase in the proportion of African Americans who voted in

2012, there were also more African Americans reporting decreased engagement in the election, as measured by the aforementioned indicators. These findings suggest that Obama likely served as a political symbol in the 2008 election, yet in 2012, African Americans may no longer have been as symbolically attached to Obama because they were able to actually judge his performance in office. However, this had little effect on turnout as the trend did not decline from the 2008 to 2012 elections.

It is clear that Obama's presence, particularly when he was on the ballot, has helped increase African American participation in the voting process. It is unclear what participation will look like in the next presidential election since Obama is limited by two terms, but if African American voter turnout continues to rise there are several important implications to consider. First, increased turnout among African Americans could bring a different set of values and opportunities to the American electorate as a whole. This could be seen in areas such as the rise of civil engagement or advocacy for high-quality public education. The increased political participation of African Americans symbolizes progression on the front of minority inclusion in the American political process. It could also lead to a ripple effect, providing opportunities for other marginalized racial groups such as Hispanics and Asians, who have historically exhibited lower levels of electoral participation than Blacks, to participate politically.[42] Increased minority turnout and participation would significantly alter the interactions between the citizenry and the political system, which would likely require changes in political strategies, and how candidates shape their political communications and culture. In order for an increase in minority turnout to increase further, voting costs as previously discussed would have to be offset by heightened engagement in the political process. This research has argued that the positive affective response triggered by the symbolic presence of Obama has begun to pave a way for overall increases in African American political participation.

The findings herein also raise questions about attempts to limit voting going forward. In 2011, thirty-four states introduced or attempted to revise voter identification requirements, largely sponsored by Republican legislators. While outwardly these actions were said to decrease the prevalence of voter fraud, they were implicitly interpreted as attempts to disenfranchise minority voters who typically vote for the Democratic ticket. These findings suggest that African Americans are emerging as an influential voting bloc, which could affect the extent to which voter identification laws are introduced going forward, since these have targeted poorer and less-educated Black voters who are less likely to have driver's licenses or the means to obtain other forms of photo identification.[43]

This research also has implications as it pertains to party politics. The emergence of African Americans as an influential voting bloc may lead to political parties assuring that their party organization and party platforms account for issues salient to African Americans. While it is true that African Americans overwhelmingly identify as Democrats, our analysis suggests that race is not enough, and that the more important factor in channeling the preferences of African American voters is likely the selection of the right candidate, who evokes positive symbolic predispositions.[44] Political parties may engage in new strategic thinking around candidate selection in an effort to keep African Americans engaged—learning from and building on those particular predispositions Obama attracted when running future presidential candidates. Additionally, if African American voter turnout progresses on its current trajectory, it will continue to surpass regularly that of whites, making it more necessary to debunk the stereotypical logic of the low-information, and insular, African American voter.

Conclusion

The authors of this research believe these findings to be important; they suggest that Obama has potentially changed the political landscape of American politics in terms of both substance and sheer numbers. According to the empirical findings discussed in this study, African Americans are more engaged in the political process during the Obama administration. In a larger social context, increased rates of political participation by African Americans signal a new era that is witnessing political representation as less exclusionary and more pluralistic. The collective action literature may help to contextualize a possible continued increase in momentum regarding African American political participation going forward. Currently, Blacks are likely responding to increased political opportunity and decreased threat, perceiving both material and ideological incentives to political participation that had formerly been absent, with Obama's presence being a catalyst in this transformation.[45] This perception of increased access to the political sphere for African Americans may not only lower the costs of participation in the form of voting, but also lower the costs for Blacks seeking to become political leaders at the local, state, and national level. As a result, should the momentum continue, we are likely to see more diversity in the form of increased African American representation, as well.

The attention to a leader's symbolism also provides a perspective into how voters internalize particular characteristics of candidates. For example, race may be a heuristic, generating an evoked set for African American voters.[46] Assuming any element of the same-race voting preference is true, by focusing on the African American's attention to the candidate's race, we assume that the African American's voter apathy will diminish. The logic behind an evoked set for African Americans is that race stipulates a perception that the African American candidate is or would be susceptible to the immediate concerns of African Americans. Race as a heuristic invokes the idea that race serves as a substitute for substantive or greater political knowledge.[47]

Conversely, the implications of this study suggest that the emotive and affective responses to Obama's symbolism also represent a belief in progress held by African Americans in civic and political participation. As we have highlighted, the substantial barriers to voting for African Americans have decreased. By virtue of President Obama's political success, African Americans can now believe that they will have a role in shaping their preferences for candidates, and thus engage more in the political process. With the increase of African American political engagement, there is a significant possibility that civic organizations and political parties will channel their resources into cultivating the voting preferences of African Americans.

Additionally, while not addressed explicitly, this research also speaks to possibilities for increased political participation for other racial minorities, particularly Hispanics. The Hispanic population continues to rise in the United States, which makes winning the Hispanic vote increasingly important with each presidential election. President Obama was successful at this endeavor, capturing about 70 percent of the Hispanic vote in both the 2008 and 2012 presidential elections. Although this study has focused on the symbolism of Obama and its effect on African American voting, a similar parallel can be drawn for a prospective Hispanic presidential candidate. As such, a viable Hispanic presidential candidate who could trigger a positive affective response among Hispanic voters through symbolism would likely be a force to contend with in 2016. Hispanic voter turnout has been comparatively low, remaining at 32 percent for the last two presidential elections. However, with the right candidate who could mobilize emotions into action, this percentage could rise significantly, and potentially lead to the first Hispanic president of the United States.

The findings from this study suggest that candidates and identity matter. President Obama was probably able to tap into the symbolic predispositions of African American voters, leading to a significant increase in African American voter turnout, which contributed to his win in 2008. Future research into not only African American political participation, but also political participation as a whole, should continue to take up the relationship between voting and the symbolism behind candidates, especially with regard to race.

Notes

1. Charlton D. McIlwain, "Perceptions of Leadership and the Challenge of Obama's Blackness," *Journal of Black Studies* 38, no. 1 (September 2007): 64–74.

2. David O. Sears, "The Role of Affect in Symbolic Politics," in *Citizens and Politics: Perspectives from Political Psychology*, ed. James H. Kuklinski (New York: Cambridge University Press, 2001), 14–40; R. Michael Alvarez and John Brehm. *Hard Choices, Easy Answers: Values, Information, and American Public Opinion* (Princeton, NJ: Princeton University Press, 2002).

3. Although nearly every public opinion poll shows African American support for Obama to reside in the 90 percentage, we do not examine voting "for" Obama, rather we are simply concerned with the act of voting.

4. John Zaller, *The Nature and Origins of Mass Opinion* (New York, NY: Cambridge University Press, 1992).

5. Nelson W. Polsby, Aaron B. Wildavsky, and David A. Hopkins, *Presidential Elections: Strategies and Structures of American Politics* (Lanham, MD: Rowman and Littlefield Publishers, 2008), 7.

6. Alvarez and Brehm, *Hard Choices.*

7. Ron Walters, "Barack Obama and the Politics of Blackness," *Journal of Black Studies* 38, no. 1 (September 2007): 7–29; Kate Kenski, Bruce W. Hardy, Kathleen Hall Jamieson, *The Obama Victory: How Media, Money, and Message Shaped the 2008 Election* (Oxford, UK: Oxford University Press, 2010), 109–110.

8. Michael Tesler, and David O. Sears, *Obama's Race: The 2008 Election and the Dream of a Post-Racial America* (Chicago, IL: University of Chicago Press, 2010).

9. Michael C. Dawson, *Behind the Mule: Race and Class in African American Politics* (Princeton, NJ: Princeton University Press, 2010); Katherine Tate "Black Political Participation in the 1984 and 1988 Presidential Election." *American Political Science Review* 85 (1991): 1159–1176.

10. Sears.

11. Roger W. Cobb and Charles D. Elder, *Participation in American Politics: The Dynamics of Agenda-Building* (Boston, MA: Allyn & Bacon, 1983).

12. Lawrence L. Bobo and Franklin D. Gilliam, "Race, Sociopolitical

Participation, and Black Empowerment," *American Political Science Review* 84, no. 2 (June 1990): 377–393.

13. Ibid., 382.

14. Ibid., 387.

15. Claudine Gay, "The Effect of Black Congressional Representation on Political Participation," American *Political Science Review* 95, no. 3 (September 2001): 589–602.

16. Tate.

17. The names that come to mind include Michael Steele who ran for a Maryland U.S. Senate seat, and Ken Blackwell who ran for an Ohio U.S. Senate seat. Other Republican names include Allan Keyes (president and IL Senate), Lynn Swann (PA governor), Virginia Fuller (CA Congress), and Jackie Robinson III (MA Senate). Also, Artur Davis, a Democratic congressman from Alabama, lost his 2010 Democratic primary to Alabama's Agriculture commission, Ron Sparks. Davis was a lifelong Democrat, had legislative experience, was Harvard educated, and chaired Obama's campaign in the state. Yet, analysts say he lost his election because he did not vote for the controversial Democratic health-care bill (i.e., the Affordable Care Act of 2010)—an attempt to be less liberal—and openly rejected support from African American political organizations. Davis changed his party affiliation to Republican in 2012.

18. Paula D. McClain, Jessica D. Johnson Carew, Eugene Walton Jr., and Candis S. Watts, "Group Membership, Group Identity, and Group Consciousness: Measures of Racial Identity in American Politics?" *Annual Review of Political Science* 12 (2009): 471–485.

19. McIlwain, 73.

20. Doris A. Graber, *Verbal Behavior and Politics* (Urbana, IL: University of Illinois Press, 1976).

21. Ibid.

22. Christopher Finn and Jack Glaser, "Voter Affect and the 2008 U.S. Presidential Election: Hope and Race Mattered," *Analyses of Social Issues and Public Policy* 10, no. 1 (December 2010): 262–275.

23. These mechanisms, as they are termed, were barriers instituted by individual states to prohibit African Americans from voting and registering. The logic behind installing these barriers was to highlight the blatant poverty African Americans lived in, the lower levels of education they were exposed to, and (in the case of the Grandfather clause) punish African Americans because of their ancestral servitude.

24. Rebecca E. Zietlow, *Enforcing Equality: Congress, the Constitution, and the Protection of Individual Rights* (New York: New York University Press, 2006).

25. Literature on African American participation during the 1960s, and the subsequent passage of the Civil Rights Act of 1964 and Voting Rights Act of 1965 conflicts on this point: Beyerlein and Andrews argue that despite

political literature stipulating that participation was low in the 1960s, African Americans had increased social capital, which theoretically constitutes civic engagement. See Kraig Beyerlein and Kenneth T. Andrews, "Black Voting During the Civil Rights Movement: A Micro-Level Analysis," *Social Forces* 87, no. 1 (September 2008): 65–93.

26. On direct and indirect mobilization, see Brian McKenzie, "Religious Social Networks, Indirect Mobilization, and African-American Political Participation," *Political Research Quarterly* 54, no. 4 (December 2004): 621–632. For literature on Movements and Political Opportunity, see David Meyer, and Susan Staggenborg, "Movements, Countermovements, and the Structure of Political Opportunity," *American Journal of Sociology* 101, no. 6 (1996): 1628–1660.

27. Richard L. Allen, Michel C. Dawson, and Ronald E. Brown, "A Schema-Based Approach to Modeling an African American Racial Belief System," *American Political Science Review* 83, no. 2 (June 1989): 421–441.

28. See Sears.

29. See Sidney Verba, Kay Lehman Schlozman, and Henry E. Brady, *Voice and Equality* (Cambridge, MA: Harvard University, 1995), 228–240.

30. M. J. Marschall, "Does the Shoe Fit? Testing Models of Participation for African-American and Latino Involvement in Local Politics," *Urban Affairs Review* 37, no. 2 (November 2001): 227–248.

31. Robert Bohm, Friedrich Funke, Nicole S. Harth, "Same-Race and Same-Gender Voting Preferences and the Role of Perceived Realistic Threat in the Democratic Primaries and Caucuses 2008," *Analyses of Social Issues and Public Policy* 10, no. 1 (December 2010): 248–261.

32. Ibid.

33. Ibid., 251.

34. G. E. Marcus, "Emotions in Politics," *Annual Review of Political Science* 3 (2000): 221–250.

35. The Voting and Registration Supplement of the CPS measures the total voting age citizen population, excluding noncitizens from the statistical measurement.

36. PES4 was name PES3 prior to the 2004 Current Population Survey.

37. U.S. Department of Commerce, U.S. Census Bureau, Population Characteristic Reports, 1990–2012, table 4.

38. Carole Kennedy Chaney, R. Michael Alvarez, and Jonathan Nagler, "Explaining the Gender Gap in U.S. Presidential Elections, 1980–1992," *Political Research Quarterly* 51, no. 2 (June 1998): 311–339.

39. Christine Barbour and Gerald C. Wright, *Keeping the Republic: Power and Citizenship in American Politics, 5th brief ed.* (Thousand Oaks, CA: CQ Press, 2013), 386–387.

40. Stephen Ansolabehere, "Effects of Identification Requirements on Voting: Evidence from the Experiences of Voters on Election Day," *Ps-Political Science & Politics* 42, no. 1 (January 2009): 127–130.

41. Raymon E. Wolfinger, Benjamin Highton, and Megan Mullin, "How Postregistration Laws Affect the Turnout of Citizens Registered to Vote," *State Politics & Policy Quarterly* 5, no. 1 (Spring 2005): 1–23.

42. Verba, Schlozman, and Brady; Pei-te Lien, "Asian Americans and Voting Participation: Comparing Racial and Ethnic Differences in Recent U.S. Elections," *International Migration Review* 38 (2004): 493–517.

43. Richard Sobel and Robert Ellis Smith, "Voter-ID Laws Discourage Participation, Particularly among Minorities, and Trigger a Constitutional Remedy in Lost Representation," *PS: Political Science and Politics* 42 (2009): 107.

44. According to Pew Research Center's exit polls, 88 percent of African Americans voted the Democratic ticket in 2004 compared to 95 percent in 2012. See http://www.pewresearch.org/2008/11/05/inside-obamas-sweeping-victory/.

45. Sidney Tarrow, *Power in Movement: Social Movements and Contentious Politics* (Cambridge, UK; New York: Cambridge University Press, 2011), 16–33.

46. Evoked set refers to the usage in cognitive psychology, marketing and international relations as it refers to the way individuals look for details in a present situation that is similar to information of past situations.

47. For literature on the effects of political knowledge, see Sidney Verba, and Normal Nie, *Participation in America: Political Democracy and Social Equality* (Chicago, IL: University of Chicago Press, 1972); Zaller.

Bibliography

Allen, Richard L., Michel C. Dawson, and Ronald E. Brown. "A Schema-Based Approach to Modeling an African American Racial Belief System." *American Political Science Review* 83, no. 2 (June 1989): 421–441.

Alvarez, R. Michael, and John Brehm. *Hard Choices, Easy Answers: Values, Information, and American Public Opinion*. Princeton, NJ: Princeton University Press, 2002.

Ansolabehere, Stephen. "Effects of Identification Requirements on Voting: Evidence from the Experiences of Voters on Election Day." *Ps-Political Science & Politics* 42, no. 1 (January 2009): 127–130.

Barbour, Christine, and Gerald C. Wright, *Keeping the Republic: Power and Citizenship in American Politics, 5th brief ed.* Thousand Oaks, CA: CQ Press, 2013

Beyerlein, Kraig, and Kenneth T. Andrews. "Black Voting during the Civil Rights Movement: A Micro-Level Analysis." *Social Forces* 87, no. 1 (September 2008): 65–93.

Bohm, Robert, Friedrich Funke, and Nicole S. Harth. "Same-Race and Same-Gender Voting Preferences and the Role of Perceived Realistic Threat in the Democratic Primaries and Caucuses 2008." *Analyses of Social Issues and Public Policy* 10, no. 1 (December 2010): 248–261.

Chaney, Carole Kennedy, R. Michael Alvarez, and Jonathan Nagler. "Explaining the Gender Gap in U.S. Presidential Elections, 1980–1992." *Political Research Quarterly* 51, no. 2 (June 1998): 311–339.

Cobb, Roger W., and Charles D. Elder. *Participation in American Politics: The Dynamics of Agenda-Building*. Boston, MA: Allyn & Bacon, 1983.

Dawson, Michael C. *Behind the Mule: Race and Class in African American Politics*. Princeton, NJ: Princeton University Press, 1994.

Finn, Christopher, and Jack Glaser. "Voter Affect and the 2008 U.S. Presidential Election: Hope and Race Mattered." *Analyses of Social Issues and Public Policy* 10, no. 1 (December 2010): 262–275.

Gay, Claudine. "The Effect of Black Congressional Representation on Political Participation." *American Political Science Review* 95, no. 3 (September 2001): 589–602.

Graber, Doris A. *Verbal Behavior and Politics*. Urbana: University of Illinois Press, 1976.

Kenski, Kate, Bruce W. Hardy, and Kathleen Hall Jamieson. *The Obama Victory: How Media, Money, and Message Shaped the 2008 Election*. Oxford, U.K.: Oxford University Press, 2010.

Lawrence Bobo, and Franklin D. Gilliam. "Race, Sociopolitical Participation, and Black Empowerment." *American Political Science Review* 84, no. 2 (June 1990): 377–393.

Lien, Pei-te, "Asian Americans and Voting Participation: Comparing Racial and Ethnic Differences in Recent U.S. Elections," *International Migration Review* 38 (2004): 493–517.

Marcus, G. E. "Emotions in Politics." *Annual Review of Political Science* 3 (2000): 221–250.

Marschall, M. J. "Does the Shoe Fit? Testing Models of Participation for African-American and Latino Involvement in Local Politics." *Urban Affairs Review* 37, no. 2 (November 2001): 227–248.

McClain, Paula D., Jessica D. Johnson Carew, Eugene Walton Jr., and Candis S. Watts. "Group Membership, Group Identity, and Group Consciousness: Measures of Racial Identity in American Politics?" *Annual Review of Political Science* 12 (2009): 471–485.

McIlwain, Charlton D. "Perceptions of Leadership and the Challenge of Obama's Blackness," *Journal of Black Studies* 38, no. 1 (September 2007): 64–74.

McKenzie, Brian. "Religious Social Networks, Indirect Mobilization, and African-American Political Participation." *Political Research Quarterly* 54, no. 4 (December 2004): 612–632.

Meyer, David, and Susan Staggenborg. "Movements, Contermovements, and the Structure of Political Opportunity." *American Journal of Sociology* 101, no. 6 (1996): 1628–1660.

Polsby, Nelson W., Aaron B. Wildavsky, and David A. Hopkins. *Presidential Elections: Strategies and Structures of American Politics*. Lanham: Rowman and Littlefield Publishers, 2008.

Sears, David O. "The Role of Affect in Symbolic Politics." In *Citizens and Politics: Perspectives from Political Psychology*, edited by James H. Kuklinski, 14–40. New York: Cambridge University Press, 2001.

Sidney Verba, Kay Lehman Schlozman, and Henry E. Brady, *Voice and Equality*. Cambridge, MA: Harvard University, 1995.

Sobel, Richard, and Robert Ellis Smith. "Voter-ID Laws Discourage Participation, Particularly among Minorities, and Trigger a Constitutional Remedy in Lost Representation." *PS: Political Science and Politics* 42 (2009): 107–110.

Tarrow, Sidney. *Power in Movement: Social Movements and Contentious Politics*. Cambridge, U.K.: Cambridge University Press, 1988..

Tate, Katherine. "Black Political Participation in the 1984 and 1988 Presidential Election." *American Political Science Review* 85 (1991): 1159–1176.

Tesler, Michael, and David O. Sears. *Obama's Race: The 2008 Election and the Dream of a Post-Racial America*. Chicago, IL: The University of Chicago Press, 2010.

U.S. Department of Commerce. U.S. Census Bureau. Population Characteristic Reports, 1990–2012, table 4.

Verba, Sidney, and Norman H. Nie. *Participation in America: Political Democracy and Social Equality*. Chicago, IL: University of Chicago Press, 1972.

Verba, Sidney, Kay Lehman Schlozman, and Henry E. Brady. *Voice and Equality*. Cambridge, MA: Harvard University Press, 1995.

Walters, Ron. "Barack Obama and the Politics of Blackness." *Journal of Black Studies* 38 (2007): 7–29.

Wolfinger, Raymon E., Benjamin Highton, and Megan Mullin. "How Post-registration Laws Affect the Turnout of Citizens Registered to Vote." *State Politics & Policy Quarterly* 5, no. 1 (Spring 2005): 1–23.

Zaller, John. *The Nature and Origins of Mass Opinion*. Cambridge, U.K.; New York: Cambridge University Press, 1992.

Zietlow, Rebecca E. *Enforcing Equality: Congress, the Constitution, and the Protection of Individual Rights*. New York: New York University Press, 2006.

Contributors

Editor

Yuya Kiuchi is an assistant professor in the Department of Human Development and Family Studies at Michigan State University. His research interests include African American studies and history, popular culture studies, and youth development. He is the author of *Struggles for Equal Voice: The History of African American Media Democracy* (SUNY Press, 2012), and a coauthor of *Packaging Baseball: How Marketing Embellishes the Cultural Experience* (McFarland, 2012) and *The Music of Counterculture Cinema: A Critical Study of 1960s and 1970s Soundtracks* (McFarland, 2015). He has also edited *Soccer Culture in America: Essays on the World's Sport in Red, White and Blue* (McFarland, 2013). He has translated over seven books from English to Japanese, including Barack Obama's *Dreams from My Father: A Story of Race and Inheritance*. Dr. Kiuchi is a sports area cochair for the Popular Culture Association and American Culture Association, and also serves on the Editorial Advisory Board for the *Journal of Popular Culture*.

Authors

Emmanuel Balogun is a PhD student in the Department of Political Science and International Relations at the University of Delaware. His research interests are political psychology, foreign policy decision-making, and African politics, with a regional focus in West Africa. He holds an MA in political science from Western Illinois University.

LaToya T. Brackett is currently adjunct faculty at Whitworth University on a semester basis in the History Department. She is also a quarterly faculty member at Eastern Washington University in the Race and

Culture Studies program. Dr. Brackett received her doctorate degree in African American and African studies from Michigan State University in 2011. For a short time in 2012, Dr. Brackett worked on a campaign to inform all people, especially young people, about Social Security and it was at this time that she gained interest in the economic situations of African Americans. Dr. Brackett works in the community to bring discussions about micro-aggression to all groups on all levels, in hopes of assisting in creating active and forward-moving discussions. Her focus expands beyond the realm of race; it broadens to encompass gender, sexual orientation, disability, economic status, and religion. Dr. Brackett continues to strive to make a difference in the Black community, and all communities, using her learned knowledge and knowledge from experience.

Rod K. Brunson is a professor in the School of Criminal Justice at Rutgers, the State University of New Jersey. His research examines individuals' experiences in neighborhood contexts, with a specific focus on the interactions of race, class, and gender, and their relationship to criminal justice practices.

Daniel R. Davis received his PhD from Michigan State University in African American and African studies. He is currently serving as an instructor for the African American Studies program at Kennedy-King College, one of the City Colleges of Chicago. Dr. Davis specializes in twentieth-century African American urban history, and he is also interested in education and the slavery era in the United States.

Amanda D'Souza earned a master's degree in criminal justice from Rutgers University, the State University of New Jersey in 2013, and is currently pursuing a PhD in criminal justice at Rutgers. Her research interests examine perceptions of procedural justice and legitimacy of the police within various communities and socioeconomic groups.

Justin Gomer is a lecturer in the American Studies Program at the University of California, Berkeley. His current book project is titled, *Colorblindness, A Life: The Political and Cultural Biography of An Ideology*. He earned his PhD in African American studies from the University of California, Berkeley in 2014.

Travis L. Gosa is an assistant professor of social science at Cornell University's Africana Studies and Research Center. He holds faculty appointments in Education and American Studies, and is affiliated with the Cornell Center for the Study of Inequality. Since 2008, he has served on the advisory board of Cornell's Hip Hop Collection, the largest archive on early hip-hop culture in the United States. He teaches courses on hip-hop culture, educational inequality, and African American families. His most recent work has been published in the peer-reviewed journals *Poetics, Journal of Popular Music Studies, Teacher's College Record, Popular Music and Society*, and the *Journal of American Culture*. He also writes regularly for popular outlets, including the *Root, FoxNews, Ebony*, and the *Chronicle of Higher Education*. He is currently at work on his manuscript, *School of Hard Knocks: Hip Hop and the Fight for Equal Education*, for University of Illinois Press.

Samantha S. Kelley is a PhD student in the Department of Political Science and International Relations at the University of Delaware. She holds an MA in International Policy Studies with a specialization in International Development from the Monterey Institute of International Studies. Her current research interests investigate the intersection of migration, security, and gender.

Rachel L. Myers is currently an English Faculty member at the Hotchkiss School, a coeducational 9–12 boarding school in Connecticut. In addition to teaching, Dr. Myers serves as the assistant coach of the Varsity Girls Basketball team and Track and Field team at Hotchkiss. She earned a BA in Africana studies with a minor in sociology from Binghamton University, then went on to earn her PhD in African American and African studies with a concentration in English from Michigan State University. Her dissertation, titled "South African and U.S. Black Female Athletes Compared: A Critical Ethnography Focused on Image, Perceptions and Narratives," was inspired by her experiences as a former Division I basketball player and time spent in South Africa in 2008 and 2009. Myers's current research interests include: the experiences of NCAA Division I– and II–bound student-athletes of color while in boarding schools; Black participation in predominately "white" sports; the negotiations of the Black-white athlete friendship; and the emerging public voice of the LGBTQ collegiate and professional athlete. Dr. Myers resides in Lakeville with her husband and their son.

Herb Ruffin II is associate professor of African American Studies at Syracuse University. He holds a PhD in American history from Claremont Graduate University, California. His research examines the African American experiences in Silicon Valley (California), San Antonio (Texas), and in particular, the process of Black suburbanization in the American West from 1945 to 2010. Professor Ruffin's book, *Uninvited Neighbors: African Americans in Silicon Valley, 1769–1990*, was published by the Oklahoma University Press in 2014. In addition, he has authored numerous articles, book reviews, and online academic publications that focus on African diaspora history and culture, the Black West, urban studies, and social movements. Moreover, Ruffin serves as an appointed committee member on the Organization of American Historians Committees on Committees, and on Blackpast.Org's academic advisory board. He has also been an active consultant in regard to organizing curriculum, public exhibits, and historical presentations on Africa and African diaspora history and culture, including work with the Smithsonian Institution, Africa Initiative, and serving as U.S. Historian Delegate to South Africa.

Sahar Salehi graduated from the Department of Political Science and International Relations at the University of Delaware with an MA. She also received an MA from Salisbury University in 2011 in Conflict Analysis and Dispute Resolution. Her research interests are women and politics, elections, and political movements in the Middle East.

Danielle Porter Sanchez is an assistant professor of history at Muhlenberg College. She holds a PhD in history from the University of Texas at Austin, a master's degree in Africana studies from Cornell University, and a bachelor's in history from the University of Texas at Austin. Danielle Sanchez's research focuses on daily life in Brazzaville during the Second World War. Her previous publications include *African Culture and Global Politics* and multiple book chapters.

Pamela R. Smith is a visiting assistant professor and research associate in the Department of Sociology at Michigan State University. Currently, Dr. Smith is directing the Detroit Urban Research Project on Urban Families. She has emphasized the growing issues linked to poverty in urban America for single parents, public education, social work, and the criminal justice system. She has coauthored *Growing Up Urban* with Dr. Carl Taylor, and has also published journal articles and book chapters in various areas, all directly in the urban experiences of America.

Christian Soler is a PhD student in the Department of Political Science and International Relations at the University of Delaware. He received his MA in Population Studies at the University of the Philippines in 2010. His areas of research interest include political and urban geography, world-systems theory, capital accumulation, and labor migration.

Christopher Strain is professor of American Studies at the Harriet L. Wilkes Honors College of Florida Atlantic University (FAU). A historian whose research interests include civil rights, hate crime, and violence, he is the author of three books: *Pure Fire: Self-Defense as Activism in the Civil Rights Era* (Athens: University of Georgia Press, 2005), *Burning Faith: Church Arson in the American South* (Gainesville: University Press of Florida, 2008), and *Reload: Rethinking Violence in American Life* (Nashville: Vanderbilt University Press, 2010). He has published work in several edited volumes and journals, including the *Journal of African American History*, the *Journal of Hate Studies*, and the *Journal of Florida Studies*. He was named Researcher of the Year at FAU in 2011; and in 2006, he was Researcher of the Year when he participated in the NEH Summer Institute, "African American Civil Rights Struggles in the Twentieth Century," at the W. E. B. Du Bois Institute for African and African American Research at Harvard University.

Tad Suiter is a PhD candidate in American History at George Mason University. His major research areas include the history of communications and media, as well as public history. He received his MA in American studies from the University of Massachusetts, Boston. He has worked at the Smithsonian National Postal Museum and at the Center for Local History at Arlington Public Library, in Arlington, Virginia.

Costellia H. Talley is an assistant professor in the College of Nursing at Michigan State University. Dr. Talley has over thirty years of nursing experience. She received her BSN from the University of Alabama at Birmingham, and an MSN and PhD from the University of Tennessee Health Science Center–Memphis, Tennessee. Dr. Talley's research focuses on the translation of evidence-based science on cancer into community-based interventions designed to eliminate racial and ethnic disparities in health and health care. More specifically, her research has focused on understanding issues that shape attitudes and behaviors of underserved populations toward health promotion and prevention.

Henry C. Talley is an associate professor in the College of Nursing at Michigan State University and director of the nurse anesthesia program. He is a retired officer in the U.S. Army Medical Corps, and has over thirty-five years of experience as a Certified Registered Nurse Anesthetist. He received his BA from Ottawa University, Kansas City, an MS from Mount Marty College, Yankton, South Dakota, an MSN and PhD from the University of Tennessee Health Sciences Center, Memphis, Tennessee. His research interests include neurocognition and anesthesia in older adults and the efficacy of complex simulations in the education of Certified Registered Nurse Anesthetists.

Carl S. Taylor is a professor in the Departments of Sociology and African American and African Studies, an MSU Extension Specialist, and a Senior Fellow in University Outreach and Engagement at Michigan State University. Dr. Taylor has extensive experience in field research aimed at the reduction of violence involving American youths. He has worked with communities, foundations, and government agencies in understanding gangs, youth culture, and violence. Some of the organizations include the Guggenheim Foundation, the C. S. Mott Foundation, the FBI Academy, and the Children's Defense Fund. Additionally, he serves as the principal investigator for the Michigan Gang Research Project.

Karlin J. Tichenor is a PhD student in the Couple and Family Therapy Program at Michigan State University. He received his MA in Marriage and Family Therapy in 2011, and is currently a licensed marriage and family therapist. He is a graduate of Denison University in Communication and Psychology. It is there where he developed a strong passion and belief in social justice programs that aid in the successful development and advancement of underserved populations. He worked as the program manager and director of a research-based mentoring program and developed several other programs for underserved communities. Tichenor's research and clinical interests include African American couples and families and the adaptation of current treatment modalities to the context of African American couples and families. Tichenor currently works in the Lansing School District (Lansing, Michigan) as the director of the Student Assistance Provider–Behavior Intervention Monitor program, and as the project director of the Project Prevention/PEACE federally funded grant through the Department of Education. He is also a two-term Minority Fellow through the Minority Fellowship Program of the American Association for Marriage and Family Therapy (AAMFT) and a member of the Michigan Association for Marriage and Family Therapy (MAMFT). Tichenor is also a King-Chavez-Parks Future Faculty Fellow through the State of Michigan and Michigan State University.

David C. Wilson is an associate professor of political science and international relations, holding joint appointments in the Departments of Psychology and Black American Studies at the University of Delaware. He is currently the associate dean for Social Sciences in the College of Arts and Sciences at the university. His research interests are political psychology, political behavior, racial attitudes, and survey research methodology. He holds a PhD in political science from Michigan State University.

Index